P9-DOF-303

NO MAN ALONE

Other Books by Wilder Penfield

No Other Gods
The Torch
Speech and Brain-Mechanisms
The Second Career
The Difficult Art of Giving: The Epic of Alan Gregg
The Mystery of the Mind

NO MAN ALONE

ALONE

A Neurosurgeon's Life

by Wilder Penfield

with a foreword by Lord Adrian

Little, Brown and Company   Boston/Toronto

FIRST EDITION

T 09/77

Grateful acknowledgment is made to Norma Millay Ellis for permission to quote from "Goose Girl" from *Collected Poems* by Edna St. Vincent Millay, published by Harper & Row. Copyright 1932, 1951 by Edna St. Vincent Millay and Norma Millay Ellis.

An excerpt from "The Explorer" from *Rudyard Kipling's Verse: Definitive Edition* is reprinted by permission of The Executors of the Estate of Mrs. George Bambridge and Doubleday & Company, Inc.

Library of Congress Cataloging in Publication Data

Penfield, Wilder, 1891–1976
  No man alone.

  1. Penfield, Wilder, 1891–1976 2. Neurosurgeons—Québec (Province) — Biography. 3. McGill University, Montreal. Montreal Neurological Institute — History.
I. Title.
RC339.52.P46A34   616.8'092'4 [B]   77-22350
ISBN 0-316-69839-3

DESIGNED BY JANIS CAPONE

PRINTED IN THE UNITED STATES OF AMERICA

Dedicated with affection and gratitude to the memory of my mother

Jean Jefferson Penfield

She preserved, edited, and typed out my weekly letter from 1909 to 1935 and thus made contemporary accuracy possible in the telling of this story

Publisher's Note

No Man Alone was completed in final draft just three weeks before Wilder Penfield's death at the age of eighty-five on April 5, 1976. We are deeply grateful to Dr. Penfield's family and to his associates on the staff of the Montreal Neurological Institute — especially Miss Anne Dawson, Miss Suzy Gordon, and Dr. William Feindel — for their generous assistance as we prepared *No Man Alone* for the press.

Foreword

by Lord Adrian

The human brain is the organ which has raised mankind to the summit of the animal world: it gives us the skill of our hands and the words and the pictures we use in our thoughts; it stores our memories and makes our plans for the future. It is an assembly of many millions of nerve cells and fibers: we know something about the signals which enter and leave it to make us act as intelligent beings, but we know little, as yet, about all that goes on within the brain to make us behave as we do. The brain, moreover, is a delicate structure. Although it is enclosed in a rigid skull, it can be damaged by a blow on the head, compressed by a tumor within the skull, or deprived of oxygen by a leak or a clot in one of the cerebral arteries.

This is the story of a neurosurgeon, Wilder Penfield, who has been concerned with the functions and dysfunctions of the brain almost from the time of his qualification in medicine. It is also the story of a landmark in medical progress: the foundation, in 1934, of the Montreal Neurological Institute — l'Institut Neurologique de Montreal — which did much to enlarge the field of study and treatment of the brain by drawing together the disciplines of neurosurgery, neuropathology and related basic sciences, with traditional neurology.

For most of the nineteenth century, disorders of the brain, whatever their nature, had remained in the hands of the physician, who was sometimes a competent neurologist but never a neurosurgeon. The general surgeons could deal with a fractured skull but in spite of the new anesthetics there were few who were bold enough to operate on the brain or the spinal cord. Toward the end of the century the prospects for neurosurgery were better. X rays had been discovered, some cerebral tumors had been successfully removed, and there were a few pioneers in neurosurgery on both sides of the Atlantic. In the fighting of 1914 to 1918, though there were many wounds of the brain and the spinal cord, the major problem for surgery was that of wound infection — and this had remained unsolved. After the war there were young neurosurgeons with time to be more enterprising, and one of the most enterprising was Wilder Penfield.

He was in charge of the neurosurgical work at the Presbyterian Hospital in New York until 1928, but had always dreamed of an "Institute for Disorders of the Nervous System," where neurology, neurosurgery and neuropathology would meet on an equal footing, with equipment and time for research as well as for treatment. In 1927 he had been invited to move to Montreal and had suggested a plan for such an institute.

To test his plans for research, he traveled to Europe again in the spring of 1928. This time he went to the clinic for neurosurgery which Otfrid Foerster had established at Breslau, and worked with Foerster on the surgical treatment of epilepsy caused by head wounds. He was then familiar with most of the neurosurgery in Europe as well as in the United States. He was thirty-six, already well known as a skilled neurosurgeon, a distinguished scientist and a clear and engaging writer, and above all, as having the qualities of leadership which attract devoted colleagues. He decided to leave New York for Montreal in the hope that his dream would come true. In Montreal, he and his able associate, Dr. Cone, were soon on good terms with their medical and surgical hosts in the French-Canadian as well as the English-Canadian hospitals, and as far as possible, the plans for an institute took shape.

In atomic physics the great advance had started as soon as the 1914–1918 war was over, but in medicine, the pace was slower. In the decade 1920–1930, biochemistry won its independence; there was considerable progress in the other supporting sciences and in medical practice, there were two major successes, insulin for diabetes in 1921, and the cure of pernicious anemia in 1926, but it was not until 1930–1940 that the spectacular advance in medicine really began. That was the decade of chemotherapy, beginning with the sulfonamides (when lobar pneumonia became a mild disorder instead of a killer) and ending with penicillin, which changed the whole weight of infectious disease. There were also the new anesthetics, hypnotics and drugs to influence the brain as well as new instruments for diagnosis and treatment.

With so much that was new and important, it was natural that the traditional distinctions within the art of healing should cease to be rigidly applied. It was agreed that in Penfield's new institute, the divisions of neurology, neurosurgery, and neuropathology should meet on equal terms, and in fact, within a few years of its founding, another division was added, when Herbert Jasper joined the staff, that of electroencephalography, to study the electrical activity generated by the brain, as an aid to the diagnosis and treatment of cerebral disorders. This was accompanied by clinical neurophysiology and soon followed by neurochemistry with the coming of K.A.C. Elliott to Montreal.

The institute at McGill has now been in action for nearly forty years. Its plan has been followed in other countries and it has trained neurologists and neurosurgeons from all parts of the world. The technique of brain operations has been much improved and we have far more understanding of what can and what ought to be done to help the patient whose brain is diseased or damaged.

Much of the most interesting research that Penfield himself has done was concerned with a form of epilepsy where the attack begins with the emergence of a particular memory in the mind of the patient. Research in such areas brings us nearer to one of the ultimate problems which face the scientist and the philosopher — the link between brain and mind. But Penfield can be content with his chosen calling. He is intrigued with the problems of thought and of memory in their relation to brain activity, but his first concern is and has always been the patient who needs his surgical skill.

Lord Adrian
Trinity College, Cambridge

Author's Preface

This is the story of an idea. One might say that it is the *biography of an idea* from its conception to its birth and onward through its growth and change to independence. But it is, of necessity, also the biography of a man, or rather enough of it to explain the origins and purposes of the idea.

Many helped to establish this project and there were two, at least, who should be looked upon as founders. They believed in the idea and, becoming its advocates, raised the money required to build and endow the project here in Montreal. The first was an American, Dr. Alan Gregg, a wise medical philanthropist. The second was a Canadian, Dr. Charles Martin, dean of medicine in McGill University, a brilliant medical educator.

Perhaps I should explain how I came to undertake this book: I was the first director of the Montreal Neurological Institute, from 1934 to 1960. Not long after my retirement, Professor Theodore Rasmussen, who had succeeded me as director, asked me to write the story of what had happened before the institute opened its doors to the sick in 1934. I refused at first. I had already begun another task, that of writing the biography of Alan Gregg. Also, I had no desire to undertake any writing that remotely resembled autobiography.

But Ted Rasmussen was persistent, and after the Gregg biography was finished I had come to realize how exciting and challenging authorship can be, outside the field of scientific reports. Then, too, I realized that I had already in my hands a most remarkable *aide-mémoire*, the body of letters I had written to my mother. From the time when I left home in 1909 and went away to college, I had written to her almost every week. At the end of fifteen years she gathered those letters together, edited them, and, typing out this record with great care, sent it to me in loose-leaf notebooks from her home in far-off California. She continued to preserve this contemporary record after we had moved from New York to Montreal, until her death in 1935.

So, at last, I said yes to the director. And now that this story is completed at last and is to be published by Little, Brown and Company, from whom I have had much wise counsel when I needed it most in the past, I am content.

More than that, I am delighted that an old friend, Professor Edgar Douglas Adrian, has written the Foreword. In 1932, when he was a surprisingly young man, he brought the Nobel Prize to Cambridge University, because of his research in neurology. No one, today, could have a clearer vision of this field in which man may yet learn to understand himself, by study of the mind as well as the brain.

Wilder Penfield

February, 1976
The Montreal Neurological Institute
3801 University Street
Montreal, Canada

Contents

Illustrations

NO MAN ALONE

I

The Origins of Purpose

Spokane, Wisconsin, Princeton

There are moments in a man's life when purpose comes to him suddenly. As I grope back through memory's haze, I come to a time of earliest decision in my life. When I was a boy, my mother, brother and sister and I lived with our grandparents, Amos and Elizabeth Jefferson, in Hudson, Wisconsin. One evening Mother returned to the house in great excitement. She wanted to tell me what she had learned at a lecture about Rhodes Scholarships at Oxford. The scholarship plan had been recently founded by the will of an Englishman living in South Africa, Cecil Rhodes. The first scholars had arrived at Oxford in 1903 and this was the end of their first year there, the summer of 1904. She had heard a scholar, just returned from Oxford during his first vacation, describe it.

"This scholarship is just the thing for you, Wide," she said, and smiled at me as if I had already won it. I was thirteen years old that summer.

Mother had the gift of making her son feel that she relied on his strength, believed in him, and trusted him. In order to win this three-year scholarship, all I had to do, during the next eight years, was to make myself into an "all-round" scholar and athlete and leader of other boys. The fact that my mind was really that of a plodder, and that my gangling body was slow and awkward, would be, it seemed, no obstacle whatever. She would never have admitted these obvious facts to be defects in her son. She *knew* I could do it.

To my mind, Hudson was not a small, faraway town at all. It was the happy place. From it, roads led out to all the world. Oxford was only just over the hill. Or so it seemed on that summer evening in 1904 as we sat together, my mother and I, and talked on the front porch while the streetlights came on, and the breeze caused the branches of the elms to sway back and forth. Those elms were a source of pride to us. We were the lucky ones, who lived on Third Street in Hudson.

I can see it now, as I saw it then, and I can see, too, the picture Mother conjured up — the towers of Oxford and the college quadrangles where scholar-athletes studied and were "served breakfast and lunch, each in his own sitting room." In my fancy, I followed them to their classes, bicycling down the ancient streets, and, later in the day, watched with delight as they ran across the college lawns on their way to the playing field and the river, all dressed in white.

It is such youthful daydreams that set the stage for the purposes and the ambitions of maturing years. Yes, I would prepare myself to compete for the scholarship. If I should win it, it would bring me three years in Oxford, England, all expenses paid, after I graduated from an American university. That was quite enough for a boy's ambition. What he would study and what he would do with his life were obviously decisions he would make later.

I was born in the United States, in Spokane, Washington. My father and my grandfather Penfield were physicians and practiced medicine there. I gather that the only certain virtue that came into the world with me was tenacity of purpose. Some would say this is no more than stubbornness, which, at least when it appears in others, is more of a nuisance than a virtue.

The Penfields had emigrated from Cornwall, where stubbornness is a very common characteristic. In England there is a saying: "By Tre-, Pol-, and Pen-, you can tell all Cornish men." The Penfields came across the sea to Connecticut and on to Ohio. My father moved on out to Spokane, followed by his father.

My mother was a Jefferson. They came of stubborn American stock, drawn from England and Scotland through the farming country of northern New York State and on out to Wisconsin where she was born, in Hudson.

I grew to the age of eight in Spokane. Then it was that my father and mother parted company. It was to have been only a temporary arrangement due to his financial embarrassment. Something, as I understood it, had gone wrong with his practice of medicine, a situation he would soon correct. Meantime Grandfather Jefferson would take care of us. My father came to the train, I remember, and gave us games to while away the time on the long train journey eastward to Wisconsin. He would send for us very soon, he said. In Hudson I used to dream of returning to Spokane. I suspect that Mother may have done the same. But his call to return never came, and we made the Jefferson house our home for six years.

My mother filled her life with various interests during those years. She had an excellent mind and was keen to discuss almost anything, from history to current affairs and politics, with any thoughtful or well-informed person. She loved to read aloud and she did so to me, her youngest child, whenever I could spare the time from study and sports and chores.

Presently my brother, Herbert, ten years my senior, was married and left the family circle. In 1905 my sister, Ruth, was married, to John Inglis, her former high-school teacher. It was then that Mother left the Jefferson household and helped to found a private school for boys, which was named Galahad, two miles outside Hudson on the high bank of the Saint Croix River. The school became her home and mine. She acted as "School Mother." Jack Inglis was one of the teachers. Jack and Ruth lived in one of the school cottages, and the following year he shared the headmastership with another splendid teacher, William MacQuarrie.

My mother's intimate friends used to say, with a laugh, that she had set this project going just to provide her younger son with an excellent education. That was nonsense, of course, but it was true that the school and the teachers were excellent. I was delighted with the life and participated with enthusiasm in every sport and competition possible, indoors and out.

Four years later I graduated there and Grandfather Jefferson made it possible for me to go to Princeton. In those days a Rhodes Scholarship was awarded in each state two years out of three. Since

New Jersey, where Princeton is located, is small, I argued that I would meet less competition for the scholarship there than at Yale or Harvard.

Princeton, with its rural setting, classical buildings, and pleasant campus, challenged and delighted me. Little by little I made friends who would be mine for a lifetime, and when, at last, I heard strangers call me a "Princeton man," I felt a surge of (carefully concealed) pride, a small vanity that has never left me. We who were to graduate in 1913 accepted the traditions of the generations of students who preceded us, the childish ones with a sense of amused superiority and certain others in deadly earnest.

The ideals of the undergraduates' Philadelphian Society and the university chapel at Princeton were what I had learned to accept in the Presbyterian environment of Hudson during my childhood. What was important to me was that since my mother had adjusted her own religious belief to the facts of science and evolution, university teaching brought me no period of disillusionment.

I plunged with abandon into college life and even made friends, that first year, with certain interesting faculty daughters, a pleasant relief in an otherwise all-male environment. I was ready for everything but was also incredibly naïve and easily hurt.

I had been captain of the football team at the Galahad School, where there were never more than fifty boys. But when I answered the call for candidates for the Princeton freshman team, I was astonished and awed by the towering regiment of young men who reported to the field house, most of them heavier and speedier than I. They had played at large eastern schools, such as Exeter and Hill and Mercersburg and Lawrenceville.

One day, entering the university commons where we took our meals, I heard one of the football candidates laugh in derision at the mention of the Galahad School and felt a hot flush of shame and anger sweep over me when he made a joke that I could not quite hear — something about "Sir Galahad." It was obvious that he meant me.

My effort to become a member of the freshman football team was a serious one, and certainly my achievement in the classroom, at first, was no better than average. I had to "make the football team." If I did not make it as a freshman then I must make the varsity later on. This was part of the plan I had made, as a first step toward the Rhodes Scholarship.

At the end of the first football season, I had been taken along to all the games played away from Princeton by the freshman team but only as a first substitute, not as a regular player. So, at the close of the season, I became a candidate for the wrestling team immediately. I had been advised by Heff Herring, an enormous young hero who was an English instructor in the university as well as a football and wrestling coach, that it would add to my muscle and weight.

His advice worked. My shirts were soon too small for me because of the enlargement of my neck muscles. Heff had been famous as an undergraduate football player at Princeton, and later as an Oxford Rhodes scholar and rugby "blue."

When I won the interclass freshman-sophomore wrestling match, the resulting brief acclaim that came to me was reassuring for a time.

In preparation for football season of the second college year, I came back two weeks before the opening of term to be on hand for early varsity football practice. During this second season, my mother subscribed to the *New York Times*. The sports page, where she expected to see my name appear, followed the detail of daily football practice at Princeton in those days. My brother Herbert took the *New York Herald* that autumn for the same reason.

The coaches offered a cup for punting and drop-kicking. I won it. Again, this was to my great surprise. It was the result of some extra practice at kicking that I had carried out during the summer while I was working as a carpenter for my brother. Herbert lived outside Hudson and I built a small barn and a well-house for him while he went into town each day to work in Grandfather Jefferson's bank. This had not been a difficult task since Mr. MacQuarrie's class in "manual training" had been excellent and I found carpentry intriguing.

Each evening through the summer I had kicked my own football down the country road that passed Herbert's door and had tried to increase my starting speed by sprinting down the road after it. Oddly enough, however, this kicking success was actually an embarrassment to me since it caused the coaches to try to make me into a first-rate running back. But I continued to be a little too slow for real excellence at quarterback and fullback, in spite of every effort. At last I stepped out of the backfield and into the line and found my proper place on the regular team as a tackle.

As soon as this success came to me on the football field, I realized how unimportant sports were in terms of the future. Consequently I turned my thoughts toward the somewhat neglected academic front. I was interested in getting a broad, well-balanced education and in all the extracurricular activities that came along. I thought I would decide what to specialize in after graduation when (and if) I should reach Oxford.

Toward the end of my second year, however, word came from the dean of the college that those undergraduates who had not chosen a life career would be well advised now to make up their minds. There were prerequisite courses to be selected. I was one of those who had never successfully faced that choice. When I was asked about it, I had said only, "I don't know. I'm certainly not going into medicine."

I was not ready to decide, I thought. But decide I must. So, reluctantly, on the afternoon before the day on which the choice of courses was to be made, I took a long blank sheet of paper with me and hid myself away at a table in the gallery of the university library. A blank sheet of paper has often helped me to crystallize my thoughts and to force a reluctant spirit into action. I had developed an aversion to medicine and had put it out of my mind, but I had not thought of anything else. I decided I would still list it, but put medicine at the bottom, just to make the list complete.

I meant to excel, of course. Rhodes Scholarships were not to be won in any other way. But where, and to what purpose? Should I take prerequisite courses now that would lead to a life of engineering, or architecture, or science, or medicine? For all I knew, there might be prerequisite courses for the ministry, teaching, law, politics, philosophy, journalism, authorship. I jotted down some twenty possibilities.

At the top of the page, I wrote: "Objective — To support myself and my family, and somehow to make the world a better place in which to live."

I listed arguments doggedly for and against each of these careers, all afternoon. Some men in my class had long known what they wanted to do in life. Not I. Others had fathers to advise them and to give an example. Some had a family business or responsibilities that would be theirs later in life. There was none of this for me. My mother, I suppose wisely, had given me no specific advice. She would, no doubt, have approved of the vague objective that I had written at the top of the sheet of paper. I had no other clue to her thinking.

At thirteen I had made a plan of preparation. Now at nineteen, another moment of decision had come, as it must to anyone who would carry out creative work in the world. In the end we must make use of the gifts of body and brain that have come to us from who knows what ancestors. Those ancestors, I fancy, stand in the wings as if to enter the action again. But the plot of the new play is never the same as the plays that have gone before. My most congenial classmates, who had formed with me a small discussion group, had each a totally different perspective and would have another stage setting.*

No. There was no help to be had from others. The decision was mine to make. I had a broad hand and short, strong fingers, typically the hands of a carpenter, one who might have enjoyed his trade well enough to become a professional cabinetmaker. It was like the hand of many a surgeon, and the hand of my father. But those things I did not know, not then.

My early prejudice, which was so strong against medicine as a profession, can be explained by the fact that as a boy I was puzzled by what I could not understand in the career of my father, who was a doctor.

As a little boy, I had admired my father. Later I realized that he was a failure in medicine and could not support his family. My grandfather took us in. I was ashamed of the man I had loved and I did not speak of him. That was the "skeleton" in my small closet. I had been told that I was very much like him and had been advised, although not by my mother, not to become a doctor. I suppose that explains my early decision, which I had thought was firm, not to go into medicine. By telling my father's strange story, I hope I may come to understand what I did not, as a young man, under-

* See note 1.

stand. In a sense, this is, for me, a project in real research analysis. The story belongs here. Perhaps it may help others to put together the missing pieces in their own past.

My grandfather, Ephraim P. Penfield, was a physician who began his professional career in Bucyrus, Ohio. The first child born to him and his wife, Delia Smith, was my father, Charles Samuel. That was in 1858. In his teens, Charles attended Oberlin College, Ohio, where his intimate companion was Wilder Metcalfe, for whom I was to be named. Charles graduated from Oberlin and moved on to Chicago, to the Hahnemann Homeopathic Medical College. After receiving his medical degree he entered into partnership with an older physician in Chicago.

Jennie Jefferson, my mother, was born in Hudson, Wisconsin, March 9, 1858. She was educated at Milwaukee Ladies Seminary (afterward called Milwaukee Downer College). Later, she accompanied her brother Thomas when he became an undergraduate at Oberlin, and they came to know young Charles Penfield and Wilder Metcalfe. According to my mother, those two were always seen together and were popular and much admired by other undergraduates. Thus, it is easily understandable that, after he had become a doctor, Charles found his way to Hudson, Wisconsin, where he courted Jennie (somewhere along the line she changed her name to Jean), and married her in 1880. They set up housekeeping in Chicago, a happy and very handsome young couple.

But alas, almost at once, Charles was struck down by the first of a series of attacks of a mysterious illness. It is clear now that this was acute appendicitis. But this was before the first appendectomy operation, and very little was understood about such an attack. It was called "inflammation of the bowels." It was recognized all too well that any such attack might result in rapid death.

The cause was thought by some, however, to be tuberculosis. So, for treatment, the young couple was first advised to choose another climate. They chose Kansas City, Kansas. But there the strangely terrifying disease struck again, and for a time Jean despaired of his life. But somehow he did recover and a further consultation was called in Chicago. The doctors then decreed in their wisdom (or was it in the desperation of their perplexity?) that he should be banished to the most distant frontier of the American wilderness, there to live "under canvas." Perhaps they thought

Jean Jefferson Penfield in middle age

that Mother Nature had healing powers and secrets not yet shared with the medical profession. In any case, death, if it came in the next attack, would under these circumstances come quickly without the bother of another useless and baffling consultation.

The nature of the illness that drove my father into the wilderness continued to be a mystery until about 1886, when Dr. Reginald Fitz in Boston published the autopsies of a series of such patients who had died from this ailment. An infection of the vermiform appendix (which, as everyone knows now, is a useless little appendage on the large bowel) had produced a hidden abscess that caused peritonitis and resulted in death in each of the cases he reported. Fitz recommended that surgeons should learn to remove the appendix in its early stages of inflammation. But it was not until 1889 that Dr. J. B. Murphy, a surgeon in Chicago, made the diagnosis before death and carried out the operative removal successfully, a story told in easily readable form by Dr. Loyal Davis.*

Evidently in my father's case, after repeated attacks, nature did the job herself. She did finally manage to wall off the abscess and to drain it into the canal of the large intestine. Perhaps, after all, the rugged outdoor life he lived did give him the resistance that saved his life.

Given the dangers of such surgery until well into the twentieth century, perhaps it was just as well that Charles Penfield developed appendicitis when he did. In any event, in 1882, he gave up medical practice. He took his young wife, who was by now pregnant, back east to Bucyrus to live with his own father and mother while he himself journeyed west to Porcupine Creek, Montana, with a gun and a dog for his companions. He pitched his tent there, on the very border of trackless "Indian Country," and became, what he had never been before, a woodsman and a hunter. But, in spite of this regime (or was it because of it?), he was to have no further attacks of appendicitis for some years.

Then in 1883, only a year later, a self-reliant young hunter, with a luxuriant growth of hair and beard, rode into the pioneer settlement of Spokane Falls in Washington Territory. He had ridden through some six-hundred miles of Indian country straight

* *J. B. Murphy — Stormy Petrel of Surgery* (New York, 1938).

to the West, followed by his dog and a lead pony piled high with precious furs. Unprepared as he was for all this, he had endured the loneliness, learned to survive, and defied the illness that might strike again and kill, at any time.

He was magnificent in his newly discovered physical strength and in his defiance. Instead of returning to the East, he had set out to explore the West himself "all the way to the Pacific." He had mastered the wilderness, and at the same time had learned to love it more profoundly than he himself would have guessed.

Entering the settlement of road-builders and miners that he discovered clustering about the high beauty of Spokane Falls, Charles decided to stay here awhile. So he left his dog and his belongings with the settlement's storekeeper, and went in search of a bath and a barber and a suit of "store clothes." On his return, the storekeeper shook his head. He thought this well-dressed doctor with the carefully trimmed Vandyke beard might have made away with the shaggy woodsman whom he had watched as he came riding into town. And so in a sense he had. Or, was it the other way around? When the storekeeper opened the stable, however, the Penfield dog that bounded out in joyful greeting left no question as to his owner's identity.

In the evening Charles sat at dinner with a stalwart pioneer by the name of Cannon.

"This," he told my father, "is our promised land. This is the gateway to the wealth and the beauty of Washington Territory. Don't go any farther. We have no doctor here yet. As a matter of fact I need your help right now. A friend of mine died, and we had to bury him out in the new burying ground. But I'm suspicious. I've got to know, in the name of justice, how he came to die."

Spokane Falls, destined to become Spokane, the "Capital of Washington's Inland Empire," acquired one more settler. He was her first physician, and his first medical service to the community was to carry out an autopsy that very day before sundown. I have no doubt that Cannon and Penfield found all the evidence that was needed in those days of rough-and-ready justice.

My father had fallen in love with the wilderness. Here if anywhere he thought he would be safe from the malady that had struck him down. Since he was well here, he would stay here, and when the time came, he would die here. He would send for his wife with their infant son to join him.

The Northern Pacific Railroad Company was, at that time, building its transcontinental line through the passes of the Rocky Mountains in Montana and on through the "Bitter Roots," the mountains of Idaho. Six months later, on the first passenger train to enter Spokane Falls, came my mother with Herbert, her first-born baby, in her arms. Reunited at last, the young couple lived together happily. The freshly cut pine boards of the first little house on Riverside Street shrank promptly and let the cold and the snow of the first winter blow in through the widening cracks. But my mother was never daunted.

Many years later I wrote to ask her about it and she answered at once, "Oh! Spokane was a gorgeous place in which to live during those early days when we were all so young and sure of ourselves."

Four years after Herbert's birth in Bucyrus, my sister, Ruth, made her lovely blue-eyed appearance in Spokane, and I followed her six years later in 1891. Dr. Penfield seems to have been a good physician and a highly successful surgeon in the early days. Before long, he and Mother built a new house and stable on the corner of Washington Street at Seventh Avenue. It was considered an early showplace.

Presently my grandfather, Dr. Ephraim Penfield, came from Bucyrus to settle in Spokane and to live in the house across Washington Street, facing that of his son. There he practiced medicine until he died in 1902, an old-fashioned doctor with a very long white beard, much loved by his patients.

As I recall my father, he was of moderate height but straight and very strong, a handsomely bearded man, immaculate and jovial at home. He sang in a deep bass voice and played the French horn. He was said to have sung in the church choir with Mother in the early days. I used to hear the clicking of the billiard balls and his laughter that floated down with the cigar smoke from the billiard room at the top of our house. I boasted to my playmates of how he used to win the billiard competitions at his club.

I watched him, too, as he made preparations for his next big-game hunting expedition far away from us in the mountains. Sometimes he pointed to the well-mounted heads of wild animals that jutted out from the walls of his consulting room at home — elk and moose and mountain goat, and peccary from Mexico. Sometimes, I remember, he told me various exploits related to one head or another.

He had patented a cleverly devised camp stove that folded up miraculously, and stormproof lanterns and numerous other things to make hunting and camping more efficient and enjoyable, but no surgical instruments as far as I know. When he went on his prolonged hunting expeditions, it was often with a half-breed Indian guide whom we called "Mr. Wright." I remember him well — a tall, handsome figure of a man with the quiet dignity of an Indian.

Even I was aware that my father's prolonged absences caused his medical practice to suffer. But, to me, it always seemed that we were "well enough off." For two months each summer, my father established us in a model camp in the deep woods with tents for every purpose and a Chinese cook in charge of the cook tent and the large dining tent. At first, I remember, it was Spirit Lake, Idaho, and later Coeur d'Alene. Once the camp was established, he would go back to Spokane and return at what seemed to me to be long intervals. Mother organized things and ran the camp. There were many visitors, including my dearest friends, Dorothy, Warren and Margaret Bean. I suppose in time they paid their way. But it was all delightful and great fun for me, from the age of four to eight.

After the departure of my mother with her three children for Wisconsin in 1899, I saw my father only for a few days during one summer five years later. It was in 1904 when I was thirteen, the year in which my mother and I discovered the existence of the Rhodes Scholarship. I left Hudson for Spokane to go on a six-week camping trip with my cousin, Roy Smith, and two other boys of fourteen in the Forest Reservation of Priest Lake, Idaho. My father gave me a beautiful Marlin rifle but he did not accompany us. Instead he arranged that we pitch our tents near Mr. Wright, who was building a log cabin for a wealthy hunter on the lake that summer.

Mr. Wright, the professional guide, was completely at home in the woods. He showed us how to find a white pine tree that was dry and sound, having been killed a year or two earlier by high water. After we had felled the tree he showed us how to hollow it out with an adze and how to weather it with linseed oil and how to make of it a dugout canoe and how to fashion paddles of clear cedar. In the end, ponderous though it was, the pine canoe slipped swiftly through the water and carried the four of us and all our plunder on many a formidable expedition across that magnificent lake.

On our return, I remained for a few days in Spokane with my grandmother Penfield, who had stayed on in their house after my grandfather's death. Our house across the street had been sold. My father's consulting room was now in the Rookery Building downtown. One afternoon, I came there at his suggestion. He did not arrive and I waited for him all afternoon long. Patients came and waited too. They asked me when the doctor would be in. I blushed and could not answer. Finally I watched them shake their heads and go away.

When they had all gone he did arrive, obviously excited. He took me for an unforgettable drive in his buggy behind a magnificent but half-broken horse. The horse ran away galloping through Spokane traffic and I was quite terrified. But he conquered it and calmed the animal in the end. I admired his courage and strength and skill. He was superb. We talked and he smiled at me as he mentioned the fact that Mr. Wright had said I was a good shot with the rifle, and laughed when we talked of the woods. I wanted so much to be proud of my father and to love him.

But there were so many questions I could not ask. Why did he neglect the patients in his consulting room? Didn't he care for them as people whom he could help? Didn't he care for the consultation fees they might have paid when he was so obviously short of funds? Had he been trying to tame the horse that afternoon? Or was he engaged in winning a billiard tournament at his club? I realized that behind his pride my father was profoundly lonely. Was this strong man, this hunter, himself caught in a trap?

As I grew older, I continued to wonder about this matter. Eventually I had the opportunity to question my uncle Tom — Thomas Jefferson, my mother's brother. Uncle Tom was a fascinating individual — an adventurer, a promoter of mines, and a remarkable storyteller, who was said to have made and lost several fortunes in an exciting, up-and-down lifetime. Every year after we moved east, when he passed through on his way from some mine in Alaska to meet his shareholders in New York, he would stop in Hudson to see my mother and they would sit up all night talking of many things. They shared a common gift for intelligent and amusing conversation.

I must have been seventeen or eighteen years old when I asked him privately about my parents. I shall set down here what he said, as if in his own words.

"After your father and mother were married," Uncle Tom began, "he had that very serious illness. To cure it, as you know, he lived completely alone for more than a year in a tent he pitched in the deep woods. When they were reunited in Spokane Falls, they were very happy, and continued so during those early pioneer years. Charles did well in his medical practice at first. He was a very good surgeon. Then something happened to him. I say it was the 'call of the wild.' He began to go off on those hunting trips into the mountains, looking for the most difficult game, you know — mountain lions and grizzly bear and mountain sheep. The trips he took were longer and longer. His medical practice dried up. Although people liked him and called for him, he wasn't there, and his practice simply would no longer support the house and family.

"The basic trouble was something he could not resist. The wilderness seemed to have its hold on him."

Then Uncle Tom added seriously to me: "Whatever you do, my boy, don't you try to succeed at any indoor profession. You like sport much more than study, I see."

"No," I replied, remembering my secret dream of winning a Rhodes Scholarship. "I like both."

"Well," he said, "I know the stock you come from. Your ancestors were farmers way back on both sides. No one but your grandfather Jefferson was ever much of a success indoors. He gave up the farm to be a trader and then a banker, and did very well in a small town. But the rest have all been like me and like your father when they tried to live indoors. I meant to have a career as a lawyer and I ended up in the mines. I went as far north as I could go. I've done very well as long as I live in the open."

Such were the things to which my mind could turn back. But it was time for decision. Sitting there alone in the gallery of the Princeton library where I could look down on students and professors and no one noticed me, I considered again the arguments for, and against, the careers I had struck out, and struck them out again one by one. I was happy as it was. They did not tempt me. But this student life, I reflected, would not last forever.

In spite of Uncle Tom, one career had not been crossed out, and only one — MEDICINE. I realized that I could not strike it out because of something that had been happening to me during the current year in E. G. Conklin's biology course. But my prejudices were still strong against it, and I was afraid I too would be a failure as a physician. Would not the "call of the wild" and my love of violent sport defeat me when I tried to live the life of a medical man?

I thought I *had* to make a choice. It did not cross my mind that I could drift and not decide. I believed strongly that there was work in the world for everyone to do as part of an overall plan. Where, and at what, was I to work?

For a time I was confused. Should I consider medicine? No. I would be a failure, I was sure. Too bad! I liked the woods and football. But I also liked English poetry and, of course, physics, and then there was biology. My mind kept going in a circle.

Then I began to think seriously about Professor E. G. Conklin, who lectured to us in biology. I did not know it at the time, but I learned in later years that Conklin was a truly distinguished scientist and investigator. As he had been telling us the story of his own research so quietly — how tiny cells within the living, growing body bud and multiply — I had been fascinated. I had begun to wonder more and more about the mysteries of living things.

Would the "call of the wild" ruin my career? Wasn't it that which was already making football and wrestling so much fun? But there was more to life than play and fun. Biology laboratory was fun too. I stopped. This was *my life,* not my father's, not my uncle's. I would live it as I liked. Then, as I laid the pencil down, I saw, with a lift of the spirit, what has been so evident to me ever since — how directly one would be helping human beings in medical research and how satisfying it would be to treat the sick yourself. How better could I fulfill the purpose I had written at the top of this page on which there were now so many crossings-out?

I read it again: "Objective — To support myself and my family, and somehow to make the world a better place in which to live." I brought my fist down on the table with a bang.

"Why not medicine? It's a long road. But that's what I'll do." Suddenly my vision seemed to clear. The fog of indecision seemed to lift. The sun came out and I could see the way ahead toward a career in medicine. Suddenly, fear was gone. I was no longer afraid of being a failure.

After that session in the Princeton library I never looked back or had a doubt. I had opened the door toward medicine. If I did my best now to prepare for my work in the world, the paths to follow and the doors to approach would be evident when the time arrived. This was, I think, my mother's faith and it was mine. It seems to me something quite different from "predestination," although it is derived from a belief in the vast purpose and plan for our universe.

My immediate proposal was to finish at Princeton according to plan, spending only the least time on premedical science so as to leave opportunity for a broadening education: the German and French that I might need in foreign study; the philosophy and psychology that I had to have to meet the requirements of my so-called major that would get me a degree of bachelor of literature; the English literature that I wanted for enjoyment.

On graduation from Princeton, I would knock on the door of the Rhodes Scholarship. If that did not open, I would have to make plans to finance the seven to ten years that I foresaw of medical preparation after Princeton.

But now I saw, clearly and urgently, another very difficult problem. It had to do with my discovery of a very special young woman. Princeton, for me, had been an ideal place for freedom of growth and evolution. I couldn't afford the long journeys home at the times of Christmas and Easter vacations, and so I spent the time at college earning much-needed pocket money, or with friends in the East. I found girls charming.

But it was not at Princeton that I fell in love. It was in Wisconsin. She had something mysterious and wistful in her lovely blue eyes. She had not looked for me, nor I for her. But, there she was, the daughter of Dr. Edward Plews Kermott, a practicing physician in Hudson, and his wife Mary Cordelia McCorkle. And there we were, near each other, with our friends, in houseboat and canoe and singing in friendly circles about the campfires, along the shore of the Saint Croix River during a few grand summer days and weeks. It was after the close of my second year at Princeton. It was a time of unforgettable discovery.

Though I knew that at least seven years of study after graduation from Princeton would be required before I could hope to become a physician like Professor Conklin and a man capable of supporting a wife and family, I had found the girl I would like to marry. But I had found her too soon!

With all of this indefinite time of preparation ahead of me, I could not marry her or ask her to wait for me. And yet she must know my mind. So, I told her simply, I would propose marriage to her someday if she should wait. That was all I could do, unless I retreated from the plan of my approach to my work in the world. It was all I could do without asking too much of her.

There were no other words of promise, at least none that lips expressed. She only smiled, as if in disbelief. There was no kiss. But her eyes did speak. No one else knew what I had said and no one knew what she had thought or would be thinking. Perhaps not even she.

It would be logical for me to describe Helen Kermott as she was then. I have done this for other less important characters in this story. But, curious as it may seem, I find it almost impossible to do. I am well aware and remember distinctly what her eyes seemed to say to me from time to time. Did she really mean it? That was the question.

I remember that she was tall, graceful and blond. She was quick to understand. She laughed at the things that made me laugh. Whenever we were together in any company, she was more aware of me than she was of others, or so I thought. And yet she had a shy reserve and withdrew into herself in a way that made her altogether unpredictable and therefore doubly delightful and desirable as a companion.

As I look back, I realize that this was a true love story in which I was an actor. I realize how much of the current talk of undiscriminating "sex appeal" is false, unless a man and a woman are seeking mere sensation. To fall in love is, I suspect, an affair that has to do with two minds, two persons, two spirits. Beauty in a woman and strength in a man may serve as introductions. Sexual desire is an eventual and an inevitable addition, or it should be. It may become — and ought to — an important reinforcement. But, for a man — to fall in love is to find the companion he cannot bear to live without. Thus, primarily, it is not a thing of the body. It is, rather, a thing of the mind. Perhaps it seems otherwise to some, but not to the one for whom I had laid my plans of capture, or for me, who hoped against hope that she could care for me and no one else.

During the week that followed my declaration, we took a canoe trip up the Saint Croix to the famous falls. My married sister, Ruth Inglis, accompanied us in the big canoe, as did my Princeton classmate Bill Chester, who had come for a week's visit from his home in Milwaukee. The sky was blue each day all through. By night, at last, we slept on fragrant beds of pine boughs. The moon was full and, added to its mystery, Nature seemed to have undertaken to show what she too could say to Helen without the use of words. The northern lights marched and flickered across the heavens as none of us had ever seen them before.

I had promised to propose marriage someday and I had told Helen she need give no answer. But I was content. I would work on toward my own purpose, hoping that her happiness might become bound up with mine. Was this selfish? Yes, in the eyes of one who does not take a whole view of life. I was planning a career and would have gone on. Ultimate happiness for me would be possible only when I had done the best I could. The same would be true for her, I thought. She would never have been happy to live with me if I were to become a quitter and if I were not a wise planner. I would have put her first before career, had there ever been an issue. I did not dream then how much she herself could help me.

My academic performance at Princeton had not been spectacular. I had found Latin difficult and dull, English literature always delightful, French and German heavy going, physics and biology continuously intriguing, and philosophy intriguing in a different way.

But in my senior year, the situation changed. I had played on a good football team and had been elected manager of the baseball team and president of my class. My name appeared on the class balloting as the "best all-round man" as if my classmates had read the wording of the Rhodes Scholarship brochure! I had known the joys of successful competition, such as they are in undergraduate life. Most important of all, I had learned the ways of teamwork in athletics. I had grown up fast and now suddenly some things seemed childish. I realized that the four years of college life would be over soon. Social and athletic success would leave nothing behind but the ashes of a fierce little fire.

Curiously enough I remember still a moment of suddenly altered understanding: It was a cool sunny day in late autumn. I had taken some reading and a notebook with me and climbed out of the dormitory room that Bill Chester shared with me, onto the fire escape of old Edwards Hall and up to the highest iron platform. It was just below the eaves of that towering building. From there I could look out over the trees on the college campus to the town of Princeton and beyond. I felt myself aloof and alone.

I fancied I was seeing the towers of the Arts and the Sciences in a dreamlike city of the intellect. There was so much to learn there and, beyond the learning, there was truth unguessed and yet to be discovered. There was work for me to carry out, and that work could only be on this same higher level somewhere in the world. I wondered whether it was too late for me to change, to do better work and to move from the commonplace toward true excellence along some highway of the mind.

I had given all this so little thought. Now I would give it the drive I had used up in so many directions. Athletics would still be part of life, but in second place. I was still mindful of my uncle's warning that there would be danger for me if I were to give up vigorous living in the out-of-doors. Perhaps it would always be prudent to keep in physical training and thus close my ears to the "call of the wild," if indeed there was such a thing? I still wondered about that, undecided.

This sudden concentration on scholarship may sound like a fantasy. I might think so myself if it were not that those who kept the academic score observed a change. In the final year my course standings rose suddenly to the honors level. Perhaps it was only that I had grown up at last.

But my primary objective in life did change fundamentally. Perhaps it was only what may be hoped of every college graduate who has a sense of humor. I discovered a world and purposes far, far beyond myself.

In June 1913, my mother made the long-anticipated journey, her first to the East Coast. She attended my graduation and all the exercises that preceded it. The dean of the university and Mrs. McLenahan welcomed her as a houseguest, and President and Mrs. Hibben invited her to dinner before the Senior Promenade, where she sat beside the German ambassador, who had come to receive an honorary degree. I wish I'd been privy to their conversation. Count von Bernstorff was ambassador from Germany to the United States from 1908 to 1917. He tried to conciliate American public opinion. During the First World War he warned his government repeatedly that unrestricted submarine warfare would bring the United States into the conflict against them. Later on, he went into exile in Geneva when Hitler took over control in Germany.

My mother knew my college friends and their names already, remembering my letters. And her enthusiasm and quick perceptions made her son proud of her during the week in Princeton.

Leaving Princeton, Mother and I set out on an exciting excursion up the Hudson River, across Lake George and Lake Champlain to Montreal, and down the Saint Lawrence River to Quebec. There, in a room high in the tower of the Château Frontenac, she read aloud in installments *Le Chien d'Or,* a novel of early Quebec.* Leaving the hotel from time to time, we wandered through the old streets.

My mother laughed and told me tales of the Spokane days. I believe that she continued to hope my father would reestablish his practice even to the end, and send for her to return to Spokane. Meanwhile, however, without his help, she had given her three children a double portion of all those things of the spirit that a son or daughter needs in life.

This journey was, on my part, a gesture of thanks for her wise and loving single-parenthood. I bought her a handsome, but not

---

* *The Golden Dog: A Novel of Old Quebec,* by William Kirby, Canadian novelist and editor, 1896.

too expensive, maple-leaf pin, which in the years that followed she wore from time to time, with a reminiscent glance in my direction.

In Quebec, I put my mother on the train for the West. She returned to the Galahad School while I turned my face to "the East." As a boy in Wisconsin, we had called any place "the East" if it was somewhat nearer the eastern seaboard. I was, it seems, destined to spend the rest of my life in "the East" or "abroad."

Events had not worked out for me quite according to the boyhood plan. At Christmas of the final year at Princeton, I had applied to the Rhodes Selection Committee in the state of New Jersey, for a scholarship. But it was given to a candidate from Rutgers University, an excellent fellow whom I met in a second elimination confrontation before the committee. I liked him very much, in spite of what he, Valentine Havens, did to me.

Well, although I had planned for eight years to get that scholarship at that time, I had also planned what I would do if it should not come to me. Consequently I was now prepared to devote the year of 1913–1914 to earning enough money to finance the beginning, at least, of my medical education. The study of medicine, I knew, must always be a full-time occupation. To abandon my career in medicine did not occur to me.

My first employment was to be a two-month "summer job" in Canada, at Chester, Nova Scotia. Not long after my arrival there, came the news that my grandfather, Amos Jefferson, had died in Hudson, Wisconsin. Alas, that he should go, this kindly old man! I had loved him. I had felt secure in my boyhood because of him, the strong, self-made man of few words who helped others all through his life.

That summer too, while I was at Chester, word came to me of another death. My father had died in Spokane, of a heart attack, at the age of fifty — the man I had not understood, the man whose failure in the practice of medicine had prejudiced me so strongly against becoming a doctor myself.

As I write this story today, I understand my father at last. After all, I am his son. My surgeon's hands are his hands, and who knows what else of him may be in my genes? During my initial college course in biology, it had been the mystery of life as presented by the budding of living cells that intrigued me. In the end this had made it quite impossible for me to plan to enter any other profession. It may well have been so with him when he chose medicine as a student in Oberlin College.

My father had faced death with courage, alone in the silence. He had explored the wilderness, defiant no doubt, then intrigued and curious. He had hunted and killed and skinned the wild animals about him. He had learned to understand this wilderness and he seemed to have conquered it. In the end, it conquered him.

The urge to explore the unknown world about one is born in every normal child, like the urge to eat and the urge to love and be loved. It is thus that the child learns. Urges are normally developed into balanced strengths. The urge to explore subsides in most individuals. But like other urges, exploration can be built up into something irresistible, like the appetite for food or drink.

My father became an explorer without intending to be one. Returning to civilization and practice, all went well. So it seemed. But something was calling within him, making him dream and long for life in the wilderness again. Through the years the call had a more and more compelling effect. I suppose he did not understand it.

But at last, he gave the call a name: "I'm going hunting for a grizzly," he said. And he went. The trap was sprung. He was caught for life. He left his home and medical practice. He returned to Spokane and took up life there as before, struggling to reestablish practice, only to slip away again and again. "To get a grizzly bear," he said on each occasion.

That was the most dangerous animal in the Rockies, the most difficult to surprise, living as it did in the most inaccessible silent canyons, hidden deep at the bases of the Bitterroot peaks. He did go on practicing on his return to Spokane each time. As far as I know, he never brought back the trophy he seemed to go after.

My mother's brother, uncle Tom Jefferson, said simply, "Charlie was caught by the 'call of the wild.' " Uncle Tom thought of it as a strange malady of the mind to which our family was prone. It is not for me to judge my father, whom, it seems, I resemble very much. Later on in this book when I have, myself, become an explorer, although of a different sort, perhaps I will be in a better position to quote from Rudyard Kipling his own analysis of what may and does happen to explorers.

2

Toward Medicine

Boston, Oxford, Baltimore, Boston, Oxford, London

After graduation from Princeton, I spent a year earning and saving all the money I could toward the cost of the study of medicine — using such skills as I had, as tutor, football coach, and schoolteacher.

My first employers were Dr. and Mrs. John M. T. Finney. Dr. Finney was a famous Baltimore surgeon, who paid me quite generously to come as a tutor to his Canadian summer home at Chester, Nova Scotia. There I spent two months sailing, fishing, and living an outdoor life with his three sons and one daughter.

My meeting with the Finneys had come about while I was still an undergraduate at Princeton. The doctor was well known by reputation to us who were undergraduates at Princeton. When I was a freshman, Woodrow Wilson resigned as president of the university to become governor of New Jersey. Finney was chosen then by his fellow members of the Princeton Board of Trustees to succeed Wilson as president. He refused. After all, he was a very active general surgeon in Baltimore at Johns Hopkins — clinical professor of surgery and close associate of the head of the university department, William Halsted. But the invitation was a very great honor — an obvious indication of his stature within the Princeton community.

My acquaintance with him came about in a curious way. Professor Conklin, lecturing in the regular Princeton biology course, described children who failed to grow and became dwarfs due to gland deficiency. I realized that the lad from the town of Princeton who had appeared on the baseball field and had been made mascot to the university baseball team might be such a dwarf, a "cretin." Dressed in a tiny baseball uniform, mascot "Hughie" Golden went everywhere with us. I wrote to Lewellys Barker, the famous professor of medicine at Johns Hopkins, but he did not trouble to reply. Finally, since I was manager of the baseball team and we would soon be passing through Baltimore on our way south to Washington and to the University of Virginia for the spring vacation baseball trip, I decided to act. We would take Hughie along as usual and I would get off the train in Baltimore and take him to the hospital with me. But how was I to gain entrance to the hospital? In my perplexity, I phoned Baltimore and asked for Dr. Finney. I knew he had himself been famous as a football player at Princeton, before he went on to the Harvard Medical School, and I thought he would want to help.

"Of course," he exclaimed over the telephone. "I've noticed the little fellow at baseball games. Bring him to the Johns Hopkins Hospital on your way through Baltimore. I will ask them to study the boy for a week." After I had taken Hughie to the hospital, I had lunch in the Finney home before taking the train on south to Washington, where the team would play its first game. Thus I became acquainted with the Finney family and had my first exposure to the heartwarming hospitality of a gentle Baltimore household.

When the team returned through Baltimore on our way back to Princeton, I stopped off for Hughie. The tiny fellow had, in his own right, become a great favorite with the doctors and nurses in the hospital but, alas! the verdict was that it was too late for the growth hormone to help him. Hughie and I spent the night in the Finney home and Hughie himself was *so* proud of his vast double bed and a room of his own. We returned to Princeton next day and he continued, as before, to bring "good luck" to the ball team. I wondered about Hughie. If he had been given the hormone ten years earlier, when he began his career as a dwarf-mascot, he might well have grown to be just an ordinary big man and never known the distinction of being a mascot. Medical and human successes are not always the same.

Officially, during my stay with the Finney family at Chester, I was tutor to George Finney, the youngest son. In reality, the work was all play. The Finneys lived for two summer months on an absurd-looking little island, called by local residents "Mrs. Finney's Hat." I liked and admired Dr. Finney greatly and he was to play an unexpected role in my life before my medical study had come to an end.*

From Finney Island, I returned to Princeton at the end of the summer. There for the two autumn months of 1913, I was paid to coach the freshman football team. That team, with which I was given a completely free hand, did well. In fact we beat the Yale freshmen 35 to 0. Late in October, I hurried west and spent the rest of the academic year in Wisconsin, where I became a teacher of German and of English in the Galahad School. I had come to consider the school my home. Mother was, of course, still there.

Here, at the New Year, wonderful news came. A Rhodes Scholarship had been awarded to me, after all, without my being present at the competition. My mother and I called to mind how she had said to me on the porch in Hudson that summer evening of 1904, "This is just the thing for you, Wide." Now, at New Year's 1914, our wish had come true. And now I could see my way to pay for most of my medical education with that and what I was to earn this year.

I quickly applied to Merton College, Oxford, and was accepted for admission in the autumn of 1914, but with one condition: I must pass the Oxford entrance examination in Greek, called "responsions." This had been demanded for centuries. They would send me the paper in the spring. It would call for a sight translation of a passage from Xenophon's *Anabasis*. I should have had two years of school Greek to do that. But I hadn't. I asked Mr. Weston, a teacher at the school who had had Greek at Princeton. A queer genius, he was, with a photographic memory. It's easy, he said, and told me to buy a two-volume Greek dictionary and a copy of the *Anabasis* in Greek; also an English translation and a grammar.

So I started grinding away all alone. I had my teaching to do,

---

* J.M.T. Finney was an expert surgeon, a humanitarian and distinguished citizen. He had a delightful sense of humor, and his own autobiography, *A Surgeon's Life* (New York: G. P. Putnam's Sons, 1940) is excellent reading.

the athletic coaching and the Greek that winter. That was all. I had expected to see something of Helen Kermott in Hudson. But she had gone away to be a teacher herself in Houston, Texas, although she knew I was to be at Galahad that year. I wondered if she was avoiding me, but we wrote occasionally and she did send a snapshot of herself picking an orange. I kept it on the bureau.

In the spring I took the responsions examination — and failed. Weston shook his head and looked at me in sorrow. But I had better news as well. Because of my good luck with the freshman football team against Yale, I had been invited to become head field coach of Princeton's varsity football team for the autumn of 1914. I was thrilled. I liked coaching and the money they offered would help greatly in medical school. But I could not bear to postpone the start of medicine, and I therefore arranged to spend the summer of 1914 at Harvard doing a medical course in human anatomy. Then I obtained permission to be admitted late to Oxford, after football season was over. All this was on the doubtful supposition that I would be able to translate what seemed to me the hateful Greek of Xenophon at the next examination in the autumn.

I arrived in Boston a little early on the day the summer course in anatomy began and was shown to the dissecting room. I stood alone there for a time waiting and trying to adjust to the smell of the place. I looked with suspicious horror at the strange forms that I could see under heavy canvas sheets on the tables, row on row. It was very quiet. Was this the way the art of the practice of medicine had to be learned?

At nine o'clock, the other student in the course came in. He was followed by the teacher. The course was to be conducted every morning by this teacher, Dr. Robert Green, an erect little man with a luxuriantly bristling blond mustache and bright blue eyes. He seemed to be excited about what lay before us.

"I hope you understand Latin and Greek," he began. "It makes it so much more interesting." He turned to me. "Latin, yes," I replied, wondering if this difficult subject was to be some good to me after all, "but Greek, no. I am just now trying to learn it. But I don't seem to make much progress." He looked at me in surprise. So I explained that during the past year, while I was a schoolteacher, I had tried to learn it on the side. I felt a hot flush as I admitted that I had taken the Oxford entrance examination in Greek and failed. I added that I was studying it now and would try the examination again in September.

Dr. Green astonished me then by his delighted expression.

"How wonderful! Could you arrive here at eight o'clock each morning instead of nine?" he asked.

"Yes."

"There is nothing I would enjoy more than to read with you for an hour each morning. What are you reading?"

"Xenophon," I explained apologetically. "I must be able to translate any part of Xenophon's *Anabasis* at sight."

"Splendid!" Green said. "I'll bring along my copy."

And so next morning, promptly at eight o'clock, we were sitting at a vacant table in that sepulchral classroom. All about us, almost cheek by jowl, were the cadavers, in awful unchanging attitudes. To make it worse, if anything could be worse, there was the disgusting smell of strong preservative.

This was part of my baptismal experience. It comes in some form to every medical student, that initial shock of the dissecting room. And though medical students quickly adapt to the experience, I doubt anyone entirely forgets that first dreadful moment.

Dr. Green was a young obstetrician in active practice. But nonetheless, every morning throughout the summer, excepting two or three, when he simply could not leave a confinement case, he met me smiling in anticipation with his copy of Xenophon in his hand. Thus there was always an hour of Greek before the anatomy. He listened to the labored translation I had prepared before dropping asleep the night before. He would even exclaim, from time to time, at the beauty of the language — comparing the text to similar passages stored away in his amazing memory.

Green was a bachelor at that time. Once he invited me to dinner and I discovered that, only a few years earlier, he had himself been a disappointed candidate for the Rhodes Scholarship from the Commonwealth of Massachusetts. As we talked, I came to realize that he was dreaming, a little wistfully, of what he thought would have lain before him, had he gone to Oxford himself.

From a practical point of view, I who had detested Greek soon looked forward to his tutorial with pleasure. Eventually I had quite a different feeling for Xenophon. In September, I passed the examination.

Then, a few days later, word came to me from Oxford University that the Greek entrance requirement, demanded of all students entering Merton College, as far as I know, ever since the college was established almost seven hundred years earlier, *had been abolished.* I thought of my months of distasteful toil. Suddenly, the beauty of Greek scholarship was forgotten. The newly converted leopard had not changed his spots. I looked about; the only Greek book within my reach was the big English-Greek dictionary. I seized it and hurled it out of the open window and never did recover it, although later in life I have often wished I had it. My conversion from football to scholarship was not very convincing at that moment, for I still recall the exhilaration that came to me in that delightfully blind act of throwing the tome through the window.

And yet, from a more reasonable point of view, what an extraordinary piece of good fortune it was for me that here at the very beginning of my medical studies I should fall into the hands of a great teacher of anatomy and of the classics. Great teachers do not merely teach, they excite the student's curiosity. Green taught the meaning and the sound of Greek words and he showed me the shape of that most difficult of all bones, the sphenoid at the base of the skull. I remember how he began his lecture on that bone. Holding up a dried specimen, he said: "This, gentlemen, is the sphenoid bone, and to quote from Dr. Oliver Wendell Holmes, 'Damn the sphenoid bone!'"

What Robert Green aroused within me was curiosity, interest, thirst for understanding. He showed me the delight that can come with discovery. What a great teacher does that is most important is to make it possible for a student to share with him his own enthusiasm and happiness in the pursuit of knowledge. Learning can hardly be prevented after that.*

No man goes alone on his eventful journey through medical school. He makes his own little images of those whom he chooses

* See note 2.

to be his heroes, setting them up in his personal shrine as he progresses. The student who has an open mind is inevitably accompanied by an ever-enlarging company of such heroes.

Thus, at the beginning of my course in medicine, I had already three: E. G. Conklin, Princeton, cell biologist; J.M.T. Finney, Johns Hopkins, surgeon, humanitarian and good citizen; and now Robert Green, a great Harvard teacher.

During the summer of 1914 I had other important business in mind beyond my plans for medicine and football. Two years earlier I had told a young lady I loved her, and would propose marriage when I could lay plans more clearly. During those two years I had seen little of her, but realized she had been socially very popular, perhaps too popular. So in June 1914, a year after my own graduation from Princeton, I asked her to join me at the commencement dance. I wanted us to renew our acquaintance against a background that was something other than that of Wisconsin — or, perish the thought, Houston, Texas. She accepted, coming in a cruise ship from Texas to New York with her friend Rebecca von Kaas. After a happy weekend together at Princeton, Helen Kermott visited her ancestral home in Southampton, Long Island, where her mother, Mary Cordelia McCorkle, had been born, while I hurried back to my anatomical studies in Boston.

But in the autumn, after the anatomy course was over, I made a quick trip to Wisconsin. I began now to see the future more clearly. Could she care for me even if our life together would have to wait for the evolution of my work in the world? Could she love that kind of man? And was she willing to plan her own work-in-the-world parallel to his?

Helen said yes, and so we were engaged to be married. She wore the ring for all the world to see, and our letters had new and exciting meanings. Now that we were engaged, it was a reassurance to realize that each of us was preparing for married life. It gave us a sense of security. She chose to spend a year at home and then go back to Milwaukee Downer College for two more years of organized college life including foreign languages and the degree of bachelor of arts.

This was our plan, our choice: to work toward the contentment and happiness that we knew we would find in life together.

To retreat from my plan or shorten it, or to turn aside and to work for nothing more than a livelihood, without a concern for the balanced purposes of our lives together, need not now be considered.

And then, that autumn, came a change in life's background — the beginning of the First World War. When the news broke that Great Britain had declared war, I was standing on the football field surrounded by players and coaches. It was a moment of incredulity and wonder for all of us: war in Europe that could mean world war and tragedy for millions. For me it meant, as I thought, a personal loss of the money for three years of medical training, and the loss of so much more that I had dreamed of and worked for. I gave up all hope of going to Oxford.

But I had saved enough to start, at least, on the long trek of medical training. I wondered if any major American medical school would accept me so late after football season, and, indeed, Johns Hopkins refused. But the College of Physicians and Surgeons in New York agreed to admit me in view of the fact that I had taken the two months of anatomy at Harvard during the previous summer. So, in mid-November, a day or two after the Princeton-Yale game, which Yale had won 19 to 14, I matriculated at the College of P. and S., Columbia, New York City.

I liked it there. But again my plans were changed. After six weeks of studying in New York, the Christmas mail brought me news from Oxford. "Medical teaching here," an undergraduate wrote, "is better than ever." English students, it seemed, had gone away to war. But the small classes were still being taught and senior professors were doing it. The news came on a postcard from Wilburt Davison, a former classmate of mine at Princeton. He had won a Rhodes Scholarship from New York State and entered Oxford as a medical student the year before. "Americans are welcome," he added.

So I cabled my second application to Oxford and, being accepted, said good-bye to the new-made friends at P. and S. and sailed for England to spend the remainder of my first two years of medicine in Oxford.

I had the scholarship I had dreamed would open doors to the future. I had the purpose. It was vague but real. It was to make the world a better place in which to live. But first it was necessary for me to qualify in medicine, select a specialty, and find a place to work.

One does not see into the future. As one moves through life, memories fade except for a few sharply etched recordings. This may make autobiography unreliable and even wrong. Fortunately for me, the letters that my mother kept and typed created a bridge from youth to manhood that has made it easy to pass back and forth across the decades, and to see things as they were. Mother was capable of understanding my reactions at every stage in life. And, since she never criticized and I knew she was sad when I missed a week, and since this was small payment on my debt to her, I kept it up.

I was an independent-minded American, fiercely resentful of contempt. Contempt was not unknown in those days on the part of some Englishmen. They felt it even for their own countrymen if not "to the manner born." And they felt it for the untutored-from-America in particular. At the same time I was deeply grateful for help and understanding and I think I came to understand English men and women quickly. I certainly came to admire and to love some of them, especially during the tragic years of world war conflict.

When I arrived at Merton College, Oxford, I was given rooms in Mob Quadrangle, which, with the chapel beside it, dates back to the thirteenth century. Wilburt Davison had his rooms there across the quad, as did another American, a Harvard graduate, T. S. Eliot, who was to remain in England and to receive the Nobel Prize for his poetry.

So it was that the dream of my boyhood in Hudson, Wisconsin, came true. I took delight in rugby, as a game, and I took up boxing and tennis. My rooms with their enormously thick stone walls were colder than anything I have ever tried to live in. There was no running water except the baths in a quadrangle a hundred yards away from Mob Quad. There was no indoor toilet. But, to offset that, my scout had built a beautiful coal fire in the fireplace of my sitting room on that first evening, and he did bring me a pitcher of hot water every morning as well as producing breakfast and lunch from the central kitchen.

I unpacked my seven-volume set of *The System of Medicine* by

William Osler and his associate John McCrae and placed it on an empty shelf: Osler was a hero to me before I met the man. In the next few days I was given interviews by various members of faculty. No, I was told, the work I wanted to cover before returning to the United States could not be done in two years at Oxford. It called for three years. I was depressed and defiant. My only hope was to see Sir William Osler himself, the Regius Professor of Medicine. So I produced my letter of introduction from Dr. Finney. Lady Osler promptly invited me to tea.

On January 27, 1915, I wrote my mother a hurried card: "Osler says: 'Certainly you can do it in two years here. You have twenty-one months left, and I can fix up any additional courses you may need to take at Edinburgh or some other university during your vacations. . . .' Then he added, 'You are an old man,' and laughed." I was just turned twenty-four, and that did seem old then.

The English students, who should have been our companions at Oxford, had gone away to war, many of them, alas, to die. Medical students were few indeed. Except for two Englishwomen, they were all Rhodes scholars and of course all men — one from Tasmania, three from South Africa and three from the United States. It was two and a half long, long years before the entrance of America into that war.

But Oxford was carrying on. That was the phrase one heard on the lips of men and women throughout the land: "Carry on" — in spite of the fear, indeed the expectation, that the enemy would invade their island. This explains how I came at once into such close contact with the great neurophysiologist Professor Charles Sherrington, a quiet man of many talents who had come to Oxford from Liverpool. (He was to be knighted in 1922, to receive the Order of Merit in 1926 and the Nobel Prize in 1932.)

I could watch him work in the animal laboratory. He was always a kindly experimentalist. No animal, whether cat or monkey, ever suffered needless pain there. In his lectures, he described to us the unsolved mysteries of neurology that were beckoning to him, as well as retelling us the story of the acquisition of current knowledge and of theories of brain function. In those lectures, he treated us as equals, admitting us to his confidence as if we were indeed intellectual adults.

Outside the laboratory, Sherrington was secretly a poet and, as he was later to show, a philosopher. But his major preoccupation, in the laboratory, was to describe the mechanisms of the reflex action within the brain and spinal cord, and to discover by what circuits such mechanisms are integrated.

I looked through his eyes and came to realize that here in the nervous system was the great unexplored field — the undiscovered country in which the mystery of the mind of man might someday be explained. It was because of this that I was to return to Oxford for a second period.

But let me return to Osler for a moment, since I was destined not to see him again on my second visit. During those first two years as a medical student Sir William Osler had befriended me almost from the day of arrival. He was, as I have said, the Regius Professor of Medicine. This is an appointment made by the king, after formal invitation from the prime minister. It carried much influence and, in those days, made few demands upon the incumbent. Osler was a Canadian, a doctor who contributed more than anyone, in his time, to the art of the practice of medicine. He was the great humanitarian in our profession. Physicians and students admired him and strove to imitate him. Patients loved him.*

During the spring vacation of 1915, I served for several weeks in a Red Cross hospital in France. In the 1916 spring vacation, I again set out to cross the English Channel, for the same purpose. Being an American citizen, I could do this freely. But the ship, S.S. *Sussex,* was blown up by a German torpedo. I was returned, with a badly shattered leg, to a hospital in Dover. An acquaintance on shipboard sent a cable for me to Helen Kermott at Milwaukee Downer College and she forwarded the news to my mother that I was alive. I had been reported in press dispatches among the dead. Indeed, the *St. Paul Pioneer Press* had printed my obituary.

After a month in hospital, I spent a fortnight of convalescence at the Osler home in Oxford, called by grateful guests "The Open Arms." In retrospect, these days of convalescence make it possible for me to throw even now new light on Osler and on the source of his strength. There was a moment too in the course

* See note 3.

of this adventure that throws a light, which is clearer than an "analysis," on the thinking of this Oxford student.

Here is the moment: When the torpedo exploded under the forward deck on which I stood, I was thrown high in the air. By curious chance, I remained fully conscious and realized what had happened. I could see the wreckage of the broken ship turning with me, slowly as it seemed, while I rose in the air and fell again. I could hear the continuing roar of sound and I thought to myself, "This is the end. I'm falling into the sea." Then conviction came to me like a flash: "This cannot be the end. My work in the world has only just begun. This cannot be the end." I fell on the wreckage of the bow and lay there, watching the debris drift down out of the air. I looked about me.

Then I crawled back toward the stern. The left leg had become a flail bending in all directions. Shortly after I reached the unbroken part of the ship, the wreckage of the bow end broke off and sank. But then the rest of the ship continued to float, miraculously.

You, reader, may laugh at the reasoning that went on in the air. Call it naïveté or colossal egotism. I *was* naïve and, surely, egotistical. Nevertheless, it happened that way, and it demonstrated my deep conviction that there was work in the world for me to do. This was, in fact, a central concept in my own personal religion. Purpose and a plan in life seemed to me, then, things to cling to. They still do, after these many years.

When Lady Osler admitted me to the Osler household, it was more than my leg that had been shattered. Those were days when many were being driven here and there by the fortunes of war. The Osler home at 13 Norham Gardens was a defiantly cheerful citadel devoted to hospitality. From within that family circle I saw that greatness in the Regius Professor of Medicine was matched by the unpretentious distinction of his charming American wife, Grace Revere Osler.

It was she who welcomed me to the Open Arms, spoiled me, kept people away at first, and planned my days. It was the time when their much-loved only child, Revere, was home on leave from the fighting in France, and I was, for the moment, made a member of a never-to-be-forgotten family.

Lady Osler organized family affairs, which included the butler (called "William" without the "Sir") and the maids. It was a happy, smooth-running household. She spent some time each day at her desk as executive, letter writer, and social organizer.

None of the suggestions for entertainment that came from Sir William was refused. Hospitality was the business of that family and it was she, not he, who carried the load of detail. She it was who took charge in all gatherings with a somewhat frightening authority made lovable by humorous flashes of wit and understanding. She made it possible for him to play the lead and then to run away from home, with his mind on other matters.

They were much in love, if I am any judge, although never ostentatious about it. He relied on her appraisal of his addresses. He teased her and she treated him, at times, as the unpredictable rascal he was, especially when he knew he could shock her and then appease her and hear her delightful contralto laughter.

She was often genuinely provoked with him, but always appreciative of the greatness of this seemingly simple man, this bad boy, this brilliant talker and host, this physician, teacher, speaker and writer and friend of the young. She made it possible for him to do so many things so well, and with such a happy impact on the thousands who turned to him for counsel or example.

Thus I came to the halfway mark in medical school, passed the Oxford examinations, and learned to admire two great men, Sherrington and Osler, whose writings I would study through the years ahead and whose example I would follow as best I could, the one in science and the other in medical practice and personal life.

By the autumn of 1916, I had discarded my crutches for a cane and had entered Johns Hopkins Medical School for the third year of the medical course. That was an important year of uninterrupted work, and, at the end of it, came important examinations.

On June 6, 1917, I was married to Helen Katherine Kermott in Hudson, Wisconsin. By then, we had been engaged for three long years and had expected to wait longer. But now, the United States had entered the war and no one of our age knew what the future would hold for him or her. So, Helen decided to cast in her lot with that of her wandering medical student. I had one more year at medical school before me.

We sailed for France immediately after the wedding, to work in a French Red Cross military hospital in Paris. L'Hôpital V.R. 76 had been located at Ris Orangis, France, when I served there for a six-week holiday from Oxford in the spring of 1915, but it had moved to rue Picini, Paris, by 1917. The chief surgeon was Dr. Joseph Blake, formerly professor of surgery at Columbia and chief surgeon at the Presbyterian Hospital in New York. There Helen became a volunteer in the surgical supplies room, and I a "dresser." I had been on my way to work in this same hospital when intercepted by the German torpedo fifteen months earlier.

As the summer wore on, American troops and medical personnel came pouring into Paris. Volunteer aid such as we were giving would not be needed much longer. What should we do? Finally, I decided to enlist as an orderly in the American Army Medical Corps and Helen planned to undertake volunteer Red Cross work in France. But, just in time, Dr. J.M.T. Finney arrived in Paris. He had been named Chief Surgical Consultant to the American Expeditionary Force with the rank of general. He laughed when he heard of our plans.

"Your country needs well-trained doctors much more than it does orderlies in the Army Medical Corps. Go back to Hopkins. Get your degree and take an internship. No one knows how long this war will last."

Johns Hopkins did take me back, although late, for the final year of medical training. In the spring, June 1918, I was given the degree of doctor of medicine at the Johns Hopkins University. Almost simultaneously — it was our first wedding anniversary — on June 6, our son Wilder Junior was born. How happy we were that this event had not taken place in France! And how lucky we were that Dr. Finney could have spoken with authority to stop me from the foolish step of enlistment as an orderly.

Meanwhile the Galahad School had closed its doors. My sister, after her husband, Jack Inglis, enlisted in the army, took her growing family to Los Angeles. My mother with my brother and his family decided to go with them, feeling the lure of the West. So it was that, suddenly, there were no Jeffersons and no Penfields left in Wisconsin. Only my wife's parents remained, the Kermotts. And in a few years, they were to follow in the trek to California.

But certain facts had now to be faced: I had become a father and a doctor. There was still so much to learn and I had now no financial backing. My brother suggested that I borrow on what would be mine someday from my grandfather's modest estate to supplement what I might receive in scholarships.

Helen and I remained in Baltimore through a hot July while she regained her strength, and I finished up my first research project — a study of the value of blood replacement, by substances other than blood, to combat conditions of shock. The study was carried out in the physiology laboratory of Professor William Howell at the Johns Hopkins and was obviously an appropriate wartime problem.

During the year of 1918–1919, I was surgical intern in the Peter Bent Brigham Hospital, Boston. About the time of my arrival in Boston, Harvey Cushing returned from his war service and resumed his post as the hospital's chief surgeon. Cushing had proven, or rather he was in the process of proving, to the world that although brain surgery had become the most dramatic and dangerous of specialties, it could be carried out with a reasonably low death rate. In a sense, he had succeeded in making the specialty respectable in the eyes of the public and, at the same time, had given it dramatic luster.

But Cushing's patients were largely sufferers from brain tumor or from painful neuralgia. These conditions interested me little at that time. On the other hand, the memory of the "undiscovered country" I had glimpsed through Sherrington's student lectures did intrigue me greatly. It was something I could not forget. Cushing was showing the world *how* to be a brain surgeon. Perhaps, I thought, if I could return to Oxford for graduate study, and learn what was known about the neurophysiology of animals, I might gain a broader view of man, find more constructive approaches to human neurosurgery. I wanted to know all that was known about the human brain, neuropathology, neuroanatomy, neurocytology. Then, I argued, I would learn clinical neurology and finally go on to the operative technique of neurosurgery.

How could we afford the luxury of the all-embracing approach that intrigued me now? A partial answer presented itself. The third and final year of my Rhodes Scholarship was still available to me. Postwar regulations entitled me to take it up, even though

I was married. We decided to go to Europe for two years of graduate study, however impractical that might seem, borrowing the additional money we might require if need be. And so we sailed from Boston for Liverpool on the S.S. *Winifredian,* a ship that was slow and steady and cheap.

During twelve days of rest and relaxation at sea, my purpose in life took clearer shape. Life had changed for me. I had someone with whom to share the planning now. Indeed, my wife had brought me certainty and an unexpected kind of security. Even if my professional career did not work out as planned, there could never be a better life than this! And indeed so it seems to us today.

My mother had come East once more and she sailed with us, to remain with us for a year of the two we spent abroad. She was delighted with all she saw in Oxford and (thank heavens) she and Helen were excellent companions and friends from their first acquaintance until the end.

Wilder Junior was an interesting sixteen months and Ruth Mary, born on July 16, 1919, an intriguing few weeks old. With our Boston friend who was going to Oxford to study, Abigail Adams Eliot, we entered that ancient citadel of learning on a brilliant, cold October day by train. A covered wagon might have served our purposes better.

Oxford in peacetime was not the same as it had been on my arrival five years earlier. The man who had been my first friend there, Sir William Osler, was ill. When I called at 13 Norham Gardens, sounds were strangely hushed. Some weeks before, while driving across England to see a patient in consultation — it was during the great railway strike — he had caught cold and come down with pneumonia. Complications had followed. He was in bed at home now, dying.

And other things had happened to change the life in that home. Revere, their only son, had been killed at the front. That had been while Helen and I were at the Red Cross hospital in 1917 in Paris. Lady Osler had sent us word then and we had published the news for her in the Paris edition of the *New York Tribune.* Sir William's nephew, Dr. William Francis, was there at Norham Gardens. During the next few years, life in that household was to revolve about Sir William's plan that his library of medical books should go to McGill University and that Dr. Francis should go with them in charge of the Osler Library.*

We found lodgings in town, for I was allowed to live outside Merton College now that I was a graduate student.

Next, I called on Professor Sherrington. I told him my all-embracing plan. He nodded when I said I hoped to master all of the basic approaches to the nervous system! He might well have laughed aloud, but he only smiled. Then he added quietly, "You could perhaps begin by helping me to study a problem that puzzles me in regard to the reflex action of a cat's hind leg."

The idea of being a partner with him in his research, now that the war was over and life was routine once more, thrilled me at first. But, alas for me (and for him too in a certain sense), after our first few experiments, he was elected the president of the Royal Society of London and he could not, for the present, find time to work on at his research in Oxford.

So I turned to his two assistants, joining Cuthbert Bazett in an experimental study of decerebrate rigidity. With Harry M. Carleton, the other assistant, I embarked on research studies of the microscopical structure of the nervous system. These studies will be referred to in later chapters.

Curiously enough, Sherrington's temporary withdrawal from active experimentation did serve my eventual purposes remarkably well. Collaboration with Bazett led to later study of the function of the human brain-mechanisms related to consciousness. Carleton's studies with the microscope launched me in neurocytology, which was to become my first serious approach to the human brain in health and disease.

During the first year of graduate study while we were living

---

* Nine years later, in 1928, when I arrived in Montreal with my family, I discovered that an "Osler Library" had been built in McGill Medical School, and Osler's books were being installed reverently, with Francis as librarian. The catalog of that library on which Sir William was working at the time of his death had been completed slowly and well in Oxford by Francis with the help of the other two editors, R. H. Hill, Bodleian Library, and Archibald Malloch, New York Academy of Medicine Library. This remarkable catalog is called *Bibliotheca Osleriana*. The housing for the books provides a gemlike setting for the best in the medical literature of the past. More than that, it is a shrine for the art of the practice of medicine and medical humanism, from the time of Hippocrates to William Osler.

in Oxford, I did learn something about how to carry out research. Needless to say, I did *not* "cover the whole field of neurophysiology," but I completed two very different types of investigation.

When my Rhodes Scholarship ran out at the end of the year of graduate study in Oxford, Sherrington applied for a Beit Memorial Fellowship for me. It was granted, and it opened the way to London and its hospitals, as well as the Royal College of Surgeons, the Royal College of Physicians and the Royal Society of Medicine, all of which gave graduate medical students much needed assistance in the way of libraries and current directories of meetings. It opened the way also for occasional strategic visits to Paris, where the great Salpêtrière beckoned, an ancient almshouse that rivaled London's center for neurological diseases, the National Hospital at Queen Square.

For some months I worked in London but returned to Oxford at each weekend, leaving the family there. This continued my official academic residence there a little longer for the purposes of a research degree. After that the family moved to London so we could be together.

At that time (1920), medical schools in general seemed to look on clinical neurology as a baffling, discouraging and somewhat mysterious specialty. Psychiatry was just emerging from the asylums, but it was not looked upon as a separate scientific division of medicine, except in such rare clinics as that of Adolf Meyer at Johns Hopkins. Sigmund Freud and Alfred Adler had only recently begun their approach to psychiatric therapy. Psychoanalysis was in its infancy.

Neurology is that branch of medical practice and medical science that deals with the nervous system. The specialties of *clinical neurology* and *psychiatry* and *neurosurgery* should always be considered parts of a functional whole, at least for the purposes of medical education and medical therapy.

Neurosciences of various types appeared in the capitals of the world: pathological, anatomical, cytological, chemical and physical. When I came to London in 1920, I had decided to be a neurosurgeon. That neurosurgery should be practiced as a specialty had been recognized ever since Victor Horsley had begun to be the full-time neurosurgeon at Queen Square in 1886. But elsewhere, during the remaining years of the nineteenth century and in the first decade or two of the twentieth, it had been more often carried out occasionally, as a sideline, by some general surgeon.

But Horsley, the most distinguished pioneer neurosurgeon, had died in 1916 without having established a Horsley school of neurosurgery. It was clear, then, that London was not the place to learn neurosurgical technique. I had seen it done better elsewhere. But I would learn all I could about the man who, with the help of neurologists, had founded the specialty. Beyond that, I would spend my precious year learning all that I could about what was basic in the specialty of neurology.

Thus, my two years of graduate study were devoted to neurophysiology in Oxford and to neurology, basic and applied, as far as I could encompass it, in London. I began coming up to London in the summer of 1920. By that time the London neurologists who, with the neurologists of Paris (Jean-Martin Charcot, J. J. Déjerine, Pierre Marie *et al.*), had established the specialty of clinical neurology and neuropathology were stepping offstage or had already done so. Hughlings Jackson died in 1911, William Richard Gowers in 1915 and Victor Horsley, as I have said, in 1916. Sir David Ferrier, neurophysiologist and clinician, had retired.

But an excellent new generation of clinical teachers had appeared. And I dare say that nowhere in the world was there a group of clinical teachers in neurology to be compared with those that I found at Queen Square in 1920. The honorary physicians saw their own outpatient consultations on certain days in the week without remuneration and they cared for them in the great hospital wards. Each physician was advanced to increasing stages of authority in the National Hospital on the basis of years of seniority, while he made his living from private patients seen in his Harley Street office. General practitioners from all over Great Britain sent their most puzzling patients to the neurologists of their choice at Queen Square. At the same time graduate students who hoped to learn the art of quick, presumptive neurological diagnosis came to Queen Square to see these specialists examine and diagnose.

This was a time in the evolution of modern medicine when

practitioners were apt to deal as best they could with other diseases, but would shake their heads when presented with problems
of the brain and mind. It was a time when advance in knowledge
of anatomy and physiology of the brain was rapid, and neurologists were beginning to apply the new understanding to brain
disease.

The most outstanding of the new generation of neurologists
in London was Gordon Morgan Holmes (later to be Sir Gordon).
He brought to Queen Square what it needed most in order to
compete with the Salpêtrière in Paris. In 1904 a new post was
created for him in the National Hospital, and Holmes became
Pathologist and Director of Research.

Holmes was an Irishman. As a young, broad-shouldered, athletic graduate of Trinity College, Dublin, he won a Stewart
Scholarship in Nervous and Mental Diseases and, with it, set out
to spend two years in Germany, where he studied neuropathology
with Karl Weigert and neuroanatomy with the famous Ludwig
Edinger. In 1901, although Edinger urged him to remain on his
teaching staff, Holmes returned to London and was taken on
staff, as house physician, in the National Hospital, Queen Square.
In 1912 Holmes gave up direction of Queen Square neuropathology in order to devote himself to neurological practice and
teaching and research. He handed on a well-established hospital
laboratory to a younger neurologist, a brilliant Scot, S. A. Kinnier
Wilson. But Wilson retired from that position after two years,
leaving it to J. Godwin Greenfield, who became the first permanent full-time pathologist-in-charge at Queen Square, and so
carried the load for years. Henry Head at the London Hospital
impressed me, too, and other younger neurologists became my
friends, among them George Riddoch, Charles Symonds, Russell
Brain, and F.M.R. Walshe.

There were many excellent older teachers at Queen Square but
I wish to describe Holmes, who came close to me and influenced
me profoundly.

The teaching clinic that Gordon Holmes conducted in the
dispensary of the National Hospital showed me what neurological
teaching could be, at its best. The waiting room of the Outpatient
Clinic seemed to be always crowded with patients of all descriptions. Some were paralyzed, some making movements they could

not stop, some talking too much and laughing, some silent and sad — each waiting for the specialist to whom he was referred.

Once a week a notice appeared on the door of the large teaching room: "Dr. Gordon Holmes will examine patients at two o'clock."

Before the hour, graduate physicians from many nations crowded into the room in advance of his appearance, filling all the chairs, and leaving only a small space free in front of the blackboard. One chair was left empty in the front row. They had come, as if to the Mecca of Neurology, from all over the world, to learn the art of presumptive diagnosis — how to take a history and examine a patient when something had gone wrong within the nervous system.

These graduate students were well aware that the key to diagnosis was knowledge of the complicated functional pathways of the brain and spinal cord. Diagnosis would make it possible to label, and then, at least, to comfort and guide these patients — even if no physician anywhere had, as yet, learned to cure the ailment. Holmes was famous as a neuroanatomist. He would, the students knew, give these patients simple tests and turn to penetrating discussion of the mysteries of the structure of brain and spinal cord, instead of repeating the descriptions called "syndromes" in the textbooks of older neurologists.

On one such afternoon we sat waiting while last arrivals filtered in, to stand at the back. On the tick of two, the door burst open and Gordon Holmes entered. He stood for a moment while he inspected his audience, tall and erect with black eyes and dark curly hair. When the resident physician wheeled the patient into the room, Holmes sat down abruptly in the single seat reserved for him in the front row.

The patient, in a dressing gown, sat upright before him. Thus, Holmes faced her squarely, as everyone else did, while the light from the high windows over his shoulder fell upon her.

She was an appealing young Cockney woman. As she entered, she looked up, frightened to see the audience. But Holmes spoke, and she looked back at him, and continued to keep her eyes on him throughout the interview as if she had forgotten the others. She needed help and this man gave the impression that he would give her help if there was help to give.

We realized that Gordon Holmes was seeing this young woman

for the first time. There was no time to lose since another patient must be seen before the end of the period. When Holmes examined, there was always a sense of urgency. There must be no mistakes, no misunderstanding. A life could hang in the balance.

He questioned and we heard the patient make a simple statement of her complaints. It was simple, perhaps in spite of herself, guided as she was by this compelling interrogator.

"Notice the smile," Holmes remarked in a clearly audible undertone. "Notice, too, that the angle of the mouth moves less actively on the left than on the right when she laughs. You remember that she told me she has lost consciousness on several occasions. She told me too that each time she did so, it was preceded by difficulty in finding her words. She was aphasic."

Then to the woman, he said, "Are you left-handed?"

"Yes," she replied.

Holmes drew the dressing gown aside and asked her to lean back against the chair. He broke a thin wooden spatula and used the tapering end as a wand to stroke the abdomen.

"When I stroke the skin," he said to us, "here on the right side of the abdomen, the umbilicus moves to the right quite briskly. Not so on the left. There is only a flicker there in the upper quadrant. In the left lower quadrant, the abdominal reflex is absent."

He scratched the soles of her feet with the spatula; glanced back at us, then turned and stroked them, once more, with great attention.

"I think Babinski's sign is positive on the left," he said. "The great toe makes a small abnormal movement upward there, but not on the right."

He talked to the woman then with brief kindness, and asked the clinical clerk to prescribe phenobarbital to protect her from more of the attacks. As she left the room he turned to us.

"So much to live for, with a husband and two little children! The attacks are epileptic. The cause is a lesion in the cerebral cortex of the right cerebral hemisphere. Like most left-handed people, the speech area is in the cortex of the right instead of in the left hemisphere."

He made a drawing on the board to show what he believed to be the limits of the speech area and the pathway of the motor tracts. Even slight interference with these tracts by any sort of lesion would cause the reflex abnormality he had demonstrated by scratching the abdomen and the sole of the foot on the left, and the underaction of the smile on the left. Then he drew the location of the lesion where it was causing the epileptic attacks.

"What is the lesion?" he asked. "It can be an abnormality of a blood vessel or it could be a scar. But I'm afraid this is a tumor. It is located too near to tne speech and the motor area for me to call in the surgeons safely." Although he did not say it in so many words, it was clear he felt he must protect the patient from the blundering of a surgeon.

I would never be content, I thought, to be such a neurological surgeon. I must learn what was known about two subjects: pathological lesions, and neuroanatomy. Finally, someday, I would study two other things: the mystery of epilepsy, and how the human brain does what it does.

Neuropathology was well taught at Queen Square by J. Godwin Greenfield to the clinical clerks and residents who found their way into his laboratory. I felt that he treated us a little too much like schoolboys. But he allowed me to do autopsies for him from time to time. The microscope work was easy for me to take up at Queen Square because of my experience in Oxford.

But I found no teaching of neuroanatomy. So I went to Dr. Greenfield. "I want to learn the anatomy of the central nervous system," I said. "I don't usually remember things of that sort, unless I see them and make drawings of them and can look back at the drawings. Have you a complete series of transverse sections of the spinal cord upward through the brain?"

He shrugged and shook his head. "You may use this microscope but the only person who has a complete series of stained sections that run through the human spinal cord and upward, as far as the midbrain even, is Gordon Holmes. He prepared his set when he was a graduate student in Germany."

Then he added: "To study the brain stem above that, I suggest that you speak to Kinnier Wilson. He prepared a series of transverse sections when he was studying the thalamus and making observations on what has come to be called 'Wilson's disease.' You will have to make your own arrangements with them."

I did so. And each senior neurologist smiled, I thought with pride, as he lent me his early handiwork. My plan was to make my own series of drawings, working through the summer months and labeling the cell groups after they were drawn and the tracts of nerve fibers as best I could with the help of the laboratory's anatomical atlases.

I did not see Dr. Wilson again until I brought his sections back to him in the autumn. But Holmes, to my delighted surprise, came to the laboratory to see my drawings as they progressed and to criticize them, and to argue about the labeling of nuclei and tracts. Like Robert Green, he acted as if it were important, and as if it were his hobby, not my task.

Mrs. Holmes had taken their two infant girls to Ireland that summer while he remained in London. Each Wednesday he asked me to bring the sections and drawings with me to their home in Wimpole Street, where we dined alone and discussed the drawings on into the night.

During the summer of 1920 when I was making that set of drawings of man's central nervous system, I was still of the opinion that, because of the special peculiarity of my own in-herited makeup, I must have exhausting outdoor exercise to balance hard indoor work. Perhaps that was so. Who can say? In any case, since my family was still living in Oxford at that time, I bicycled the fifty-odd miles from London back to Oxford at the end of each week, returning the other way by train. Pedaling up the long slopes of the Chiltern Hills gave me the fatigue that I fancied I needed, as well as much time for the idle dreaming that some call reflection, or reconsideration or contemplation.

It was the old coach road to Oxford that I traveled. When I described the Stratford Arms as a charming spot for tea some twenty miles short of Oxford, my wife rose to the challenge. She "took the fly," so to speak, and found a way of leaving the house-hold in Oxford. After that she often bicycled out the twenty miles to meet me there for the thrill of a five o'clock rendezvous for two, and the companionship of pedaling home together.

I suspect now that calling upon the body to take the lead for a time is a very good way of allowing the mind to look out dreamily on the world. Dreaming is the pastime of creative minds. Thus an answer to an unsolved problem may flash into the dreaming mind of an investigator. Thus a poet may range to other fields. Thus inspiration came to Robbie Burns, a poet-plowman, staring down into his freshly turned furrow. So he saw the world as if through the eyes of a mouse: "Wee, sleekit, cow'rin', tim'rous beastie, / O what a panic's in they breastie!"

In the two years of my graduate work in England, with occasional trips to France in 1919–1921, I spent my time on neurophysiology, medical neurology, neuroanatomy and neuropathology. I hoped to earn my living as a neurosurgeon but these things it seemed to me must be studied, if not mastered, first.

It may be said that neurosurgery as a specialty began in 1886 when Victor Horsley was appointed as the specializing neurological surgeon at the National Hospital, Queen Square. Horsley (later to be Sir Victor) had prepared himself for the role of founder of neurosurgery by operating on animals at the Brown Institution in London. At this institution for the care and treatment of domestic animals, he had preceded young Charles Sherrington as professor-superintendent. On leaving the Brown Institution Horsley worked in experimental laboratories at London's University College.

He was a neurophysiologist first. But unfortunately, as neurosurgeon in the National Hospital, he operated only by invitation. He had no beds of his own, he had no surgical service, no laboratories. Had it been possible to give him these things, he might well, in my opinion, have created a Horsley school of modern neurosurgery. But this he did not do.

He and William Macewen, professor of surgery in Glasgow, stood out as pioneers in the early period of neurosurgery. This specialty, in which the operator must cross the frontier that separates body from brain, called for basic study and a greater refinement of surgical technique. The speedy, but rough-and-ready, nineteenth-century surgeon might often succeed with his operations in the abdominal cavity and in operations on the extremities. But in neurosurgery, infection and paralysis resulted all too often from his bold action.

Horsley must have seen what was needed in order to lower the death rate. Macewen, too, must have seen it. But it called for hospital support. Perhaps if Macewen had accepted the post of chief surgeon at Johns Hopkins Hospital when it was offered to him in 1889, he might have done it there, in Baltimore. Who can say? When Macewen refused to come to Baltimore, however, the post was given to William Halsted, who had taken his graduate training in Germany and had developed into a brilliant young surgeon in New York. In accepting the Baltimore appointment, Halsted had the guiding inspiration of association with William Welch, the great pathologist and medical educator, and of William Osler. He had, too, the academic and financial support that was available to those who took part in the launching of the Johns Hopkins Hospital and Medical School.

As a medical student, I had already seen George Heuer and Walter Dandy, who were Halsted's residents, operating on the brain in the Johns Hopkins Hospital. As an intern, I had watched Harvey Cushing in Boston and had made my own detailed notes and drawings of his techniques and instruments. All three of them had been trained in fastidious surgical technique and the use of silk sutures by Professor Halsted.

As I look back to the two years in England spent in what was basic work for a neurosurgeon, I recall many pleasant adventures. Gordon Holmes had remained a bachelor until the age of forty-two. But in 1918, immediately after the First World War, he married a perfectly charming physician, Rosalie Jobson. They invited Helen and me to their home when we moved to London and in June 1921, just before the close of our two years of graduate study, Dr. Holmes asked us to be his guests on an expedition during which we were to row with him and his wife down the River Thames from Oxford to London, spending the nights at inns along the way.

By that time my funds were very low. So we left our children in London and took our bicycles back to Oxford, where we had bought them secondhand, and sold them to a thirdhand purchaser for exactly the same price. Then we joined the Holmeses for three enchanting days, taking turns at the oars, he and Helen alternating as oarsmen with Rosalie and me.

Among other things we discovered the little island in the Thames where the Holmeses had moored their boat when he proposed marriage to her. We learned, too, that it was the great Sir Victor Horsley who had first introduced Holmes to the pleasures of boating along the Thames.

And so, our term in England came to an end. These two years of graduate study were all we had hoped they would be. The education and the previous preparation for which each of us had taken time before we sailed from Boston had made our life together fuller and deeper and more effective. And we were ready now with the moderate knowledge of foreign languages that would make possible and enjoyable sudden expeditions to foreign countries that were yet to come on sudden impulse.

3

1921: The Presbyterian Hospital, New York

We sailed back across the sea and docked in New York, May 31, 1921. The wander years of graduate study were over and I was acutely aware of the need to face our economic problems. How was I to make a living for my family? How to acquire the practical skills of neurosurgery? And how to continue the basic approach to neurology? All the money I had saved and borrowed for education was gone. I was still receiving the Beit Memorial Fellowship stipend that had come to me when the Rhodes Scholarship ran out. But this could not continue forever and it was time to earn my own living.*

During the time I had been away, I had relied on a tentative promise of full-time employment in Detroit at the newly built Henry Ford Hospital. The full-time salary that would go with the Detroit job spelled what seemed to me security. In any case, there was no alternative in sight. So, although the offer was subject to approval after an on-the-spot interview, I sent off our trunks and books to Detroit and put Helen and the children on the train for a visit to Helen's parents in Wisconsin.

I remained behind in the East in hopes of making contact

---

* The Beit Fellowship, which Sherrington had secured for me, was, like the Rhodes Scholarship, founded for graduate study primarily in Great Britain. One who was a young American must pay grateful tribute to the memory of these farseeing British subjects whose generosity helped him so materially toward his goal in life.

again with the medical profession in the United States. Dr. Foster Kennedy was a famous neurologist, professor of neurology at Cornell Medical School (located in New York City). So I remained in New York a few days, presenting the letter of introduction to him that Sir Gordon Holmes had given me. I followed Kennedy on his daily rounds. Most of our time was spent going about from bed to bed of that vast hospital of last resort, Bellevue. Most of the patients were poor, many of them helpless, and so many, alas, were hopeless.

But at Bellevue, loyal young medical disciples followed Kennedy each day on his rounds. He was an excellent teacher, an intuitive clinician, and he had an inquiring mind on a superficial level. He was an Irishman who, like Holmes, had gone to London for his training in neurology at the National Hospital, Queen Square. After his residency there, he had come to live in New York, where, to many, this eloquent Irishman was a figure of romance.

But I was disappointed. In spite of his brilliance and the fact that this was clinical neurology at its best, it seemed to me to have no promise. It was the same old game handed down through medical generations, with all too little basic investigation of cause, and little hopeful search for a cure. It was just a good copy of neurology in London and Paris.

We had timed our return to the United States to coincide with the annual meeting of the American Medical Association. That year it was to be in Boston. So I left New York and went on to Boston, hoping to learn what was new at home. I stayed there with my friend and former Princeton classmate, Dr. Francis Hall.

Here, a letter caught up with me. It came from Philadelphia. The Englishman who had been Sherrington's assistant in Oxford, Cuthbert Bazett, had just come out from Oxford to become the new professor of physiology at the University of Pennsylvania. He wrote: "I have a job for you as my assistant. You and I can finish up our work on decerebrate rigidity and eventually," he added, knowing the direction of my ambition, "you might work into the private practice of brain surgery." It was reassuring, at least, not to be quite forgotten.

I could have been happy as an animal physiologist, teaching

and doing research perhaps. But that would have been falling short of my plan to approach the human brain with all the insights of science. Also it was obvious that the thirty-five hundred dollars a year Bazett offered would present difficulties, to say the least, for a family of four in Philadelphia.

I visited the Peter Bent Brigham Hospital in Boston where I had had my surgical internship, and sought out Dr. William Quinby. He was the urologist in chief of that hospital. I admired him greatly, and I felt closer to him than to the chief surgeon, Harvey Cushing. In my spare time as an intern, I had done a small piece of research on the rabbit's ureter under his direction, carrying out the work in the adjacent Harvard laboratory.

When Quinby saw me entering his office, he called out, "Wilder! I thought you would come. We didn't know how to reach you."

The greeting thrilled me. It was good for the lonely, unwanted feeling that had been mine since I landed in New York. "Allen Whipple," Quinby continued, "came here from New York to inquire about you. Great opportunity there — wonderful man, Whipple — just what you want. I'll let him know you've come back."

But nevertheless, in spite of Quinby's reassuring talk, I traveled on from Boston to Detroit since I had promised to do so. There I met the chief surgeon of the Henry Ford Hospital. Dr. R. D. McClure was a former surgical resident at Johns Hopkins and a general surgeon of undoubted ability. He showed me their splendid new modern hospital. But he was not free to choose his staff by himself. There would be no place for me unless the superintendent, a Mr. Liebold, decided to offer it. Mr. Liebold had been secretary to Henry Ford. The chief surgeon and I entered the hospital superintendent's imposing office and the interview was on.

As the talk neared its close, he mentioned that he would pay me five thousand dollars a year. This would have been enough to live on. But I confessed to him then that I wanted something more: the opportunity to carry on research. I was interested, I told him, in decerebrate rigidity. I knew the words meant nothing to him, so I added quickly, "I suppose there is a laboratory where

I may carry out some experiments that might be of importance in neurology?" He looked surprised. So I added, "I would only work at that when I am not needed on service, of course."

"No," he said, and brought his hand down on his desk. "Our policy is this: You finish your day's work." He mentioned the number of hours per day. "After that we don't want you around the hospital. If you have a problem, turn it over to the man in the laboratory. We have a very smart fellow in the laboratory." The chief surgeon interposed then, supporting my request and arguing for freedom to investigate. (I learned later that he had done this before.) But the superintendent stood firm. He had closed the door of that hospital as far as I was concerned.

"I'm sorry, Mr. Liebold," I said with a sudden sense of relief. "I would rather not stay." He was silent for a moment. He looked at me then as if for the first time, as if perhaps he thought I was bargaining. "All right," he said, "I'll give you five hundred dollars more."

If I had countered with a thousand, would we have settled at seven hundred and fifty? I have described this interview because it throws some light on the risk that comes to medical advance and hospital care when our institutions are controlled by men of business or politics, even though they have the best of intentions. It is a danger that does at times threaten the successful evolution of socialized medicine. (I hasten to add, however, that this super- intendent was replaced a few years later and the staff, under the leadership of R. D. McClure, surgeon, and Dr. Frank Joseph Sladen, physician, were given a free hand and did, in fact, create a first-rate modern institution in Detroit, the Henry Ford Hos- pital.)

Before leaving Detroit, I wired Helen. She was at Devil's Lake, Wisconsin, where she and the children were having a well- deserved holiday with her parents: "Detroit impossible, are you game for Philadelphia or New York?" Her reply was contained in a telegram waiting for me on my return to New York: "Timbuktu if you like." That was all it said.

Next morning, I left the New York hotel and walked up Fifth Avenue. I was thirty. I had played hard and worked hard. I had finished one stage in life and was ready for the next. Was a door about to open? Or, was my appointment here to be another blind lead?

It was one of those beautiful days that come to New York in June when the wind is out of the west and the north. The sun sparkled on buildings and passing cars; the sky was blue and the cool air made me long to run. Dr. Whipple had received word from Quinby and had sent me an invitation, before I left Boston, to come to see him at the Presbyterian Hospital. I had to take a job somewhere — would it be as a neurosurgeon, or as a neurophysiologist? Or could it be as both?

Across the avenue, little children were running along the paths of Central Park and uniformed nurses followed them, gossiping and pushing their baby carriages. I was in fashionable uptown Manhattan, very different from the district about Bellevue Hospital. I turned away from Fifth Avenue at Seventieth Street and, crossing Madison, I stood in front of the old Presbyterian. It was a red-brick pile, a group of partly separated buildings in assorted styles of architecture. I entered under a Victorian porte cochere and climbed a short flight of steps, marveling that I should arrive here at the very time of transition in its history.

The College of Physicians and Surgeons (P. and S.), which is Columbia's medical school, had formed an alliance with the Presbyterian in preference to the other hospitals of New York. Dean William Darrach had planned this alliance with financial backing from the Carnegie Corporation, the Rockefeller Foundation, the General Education Board, and from Mrs. Stephen Harkness, who was the mother of Edward Harkness, a close friend of Darrach.

This hospital to which I had come in New York had been built and endowed by substantial citizens and opened in 1872 "without regard for race, creed or color." It was located in what were then the outskirts of the city, a stone's throw from the New York Central railroad tracks that entered the city from the north along what is now Park Avenue. In those days, the trains must have come puffing and clanging past. Sometimes a train stopped, it is said, to discharge a patient.

But in 1921 the tracks were covered and sleek automobiles came and went along Park Avenue's pavement that hid the tracks. In the spring of 1921, the Presbyterian Hospital signed an agreement with Columbia University and became the primary teaching hospital. To this end, the services of medicine and surgery were reorganized on a "full-time" basis.

In view of this plan, the Rockefeller Foundation and its ally, the General Education Board, made a large initiating contribution. By agreement, a medical center was to be built at 168th Street and Broadway, where the American League baseball park had been purchased high above the Hudson River. Columbia's College of Physicians and Surgeons planned to join forces with the Presbyterian for all the purposes of modern medical treatment, teaching and research.

On July 1, 1921, the Presbyterian Hospital took the initial plunge and set out on this adventure. The doctors, previously on the attending staff, resigned by arrangement. All of them had been earning their living by private practice.*

Walter W. Palmer, the young, newly elected physician in chief and professor of medicine, returned from the Johns Hopkins Hospital, bringing with him a brilliant group of assistants. They had had two years of experience with the full-time scheme in Baltimore and were accustomed to it. Palmer was a good physician, investigator and administrator. He had, that spring, been offered the chairs of medicine at Yale, Michigan, Johns Hopkins and Columbia.

Allen O. Whipple, the chief surgeon and professor of surgery, a product of P. and S., was young too. Unlike Palmer, he was relatively unknown in 1921. But, as one looks back across the years, he stands out now, a splendid leader in American surgery — unassuming, skillful, scholarly, humane. He was elected to take over the surgical service at the time of this change with only two attending surgeons and two associates. By a strange turn in the wheel of fortune, I was one of the associates. The others were making a financial sacrifice to do it on "full-time." Not I! Almost any salary would have been an improvement for me at that stage. The Allen O. Whipple Surgical Society is, today, an active group of American surgeons, made up of his disciples and admirers.

It was promised that we would be moving uptown to the new

---

* Albert Lamb, who was a member of the new staff, has written an excellent history of the medical center, *The Presbyterian Hospital and the Columbia-Presbyterian Medical Center* (New York: Columbia University Press, 1955).

medical center in four years' time. But, as it turned out, there were many delays and complications before the center was finally built and ready for occupancy in 1928. In 1925, the Babies' Hospital, the Sloane Hospital for Women, the old Vanderbilt Clinic and the New York Neurological Institute were all affiliated with the Presbyterian and began to lay their own plans for an eventual move uptown.

In 1925, according to rumor, the whole plan almost miscarried. Abraham Flexner, secretary of the General Education Board, discovered that what might be called the Flexnerian full-time scheme, which was in force during the first year of the new regime at the Presbyterian Hospital, had been modified. He threatened (whether or not with the backing of the related boards) that the two million dollar contribution of the General Education Board and the Rockefeller Foundation would be withdrawn. He even came to a crucial conference with papers all prepared that would have broken off the Rockefeller part of the contract. But Bill Palmer rose to the occasion.

He explained that the private patients, who had paid their fees to us for consultation or operation in the hospital, had taken no more of our time than patients in the public ward. They had proved to be no less helpful when we taught the students. The private patients, themselves, had thus had expert treatment equal to that of the public patients, which was sometimes not the case in private hospitals. He pointed out finally that the teaching doctor who had the correct humanitarian as well as academic spirit could be trusted to work within the hospital for the common good. The explanation was accepted.

During this period there was, within the Rockefeller Foundation, a growing opposition to the dictatorial leadership of Abraham Flexner. This opposition was to lead to his resignation in 1928.*

At 10:30 A.M., June 11, 1921, I entered the office of Allen Whipple. He was the newly appointed surgical chief and professor of surgery, an unassuming, thoughtful man with high forehead and strong, delicate, classical features. Born in Persia of missionary parents, he had graduated from Princeton nine years ahead

* See note 4.

of me. I asked him how he had come to send for me, an unknown postgraduate student, when I had been working so far away from New York. He laughed.

"Harry Murray told me you were working at Oxford and in London and that you intended to become a neurosurgeon. Harry is an intern here now. He met you when you were both attending a physiology congress in Paris last year."

I remembered Murray well, a tall, young New Yorker who had been educated at Harvard. He had a grand sense of humor. We met by chance at the congress and went for a walk through the streets of Paris.*

"I remembered," Dr. Whipple continued, "that you were coach of the football team at Princeton. But after Harry told me of your meeting in Paris, I checked up on you.

"Now," he continued, "I'd like to have you join my staff to do the neurological surgery." I felt giddy for a moment but he went right on: "You would have to take your turn with the other surgeons in general surgery during the first few years. If you join us, we will pay you forty-five hundred dollars a year as a full-time salary to begin with. I would expect you to help with the teaching of the medical students at P. and S. and I would want you to carry on with your research." I said nothing. So he added, "You will be on hospital service nine months, have one month for vacation, one for travel perhaps to other clinics, and one to concentrate on some scientific project."

As he talked, my heart had leapt. Then it fell (if hearts can fall) to a new low. I realized suddenly how ill-prepared I was to be an attending surgeon in this, the foremost teaching hospital in New York. "I'm not much of a surgeon," I blurted out, "not yet, anyway."

"I know that." He laughed in the quiet way he had. "We want you because of your training and your interest in physiology and pathology. We can teach you surgery. When you do need help, as a surgeon, one of us will always be free to come to your aid at the bedside or in the operating room."

I took a long breath. "One thing I can promise you now," I said. "I will never bluff when I do not know what to do for a patient or how to do it. But, well, I'm ready now to start work."

* See note 5.

There are times when understatement helps a man to hold back tears of joy. This proposal was what I would have conjured up, if I had been the possessor of Aladdin's wonderful lamp. I accepted, of course, and discovered that I was "junior attending surgeon," on the Second Surgical Division, one of five surgeons — two seniors, two juniors, and the director, Dr. Whipple. The others lived near the hospital. When Helen arrived in New York, we considered what to do and heard much ready advice. The salary was less than that offered in Detroit.

We consulted the Presbyterian minister Maitland Bartlett, who, four years earlier, had come out to Wisconsin to marry us. Bartlett was small in stature, but wise and urbane, a diminutive bachelor who knew New York and its ways. He was a minister of the gospel of a most unusual type. He lived in lower Manhattan, where his friends were editors and writers of national repute, and commuted daily out to a suburban church. I had met him through my Princeton friends, particularly Susan Cleveland and her mother, Mrs. Grover Cleveland. Bartlett had, earlier in his career, been pastor of the Presbyterian church on the campus at Princeton. I knew that he made it an invariable habit to visit his mother each spring in Wisconsin. She was a friend of my mother, and lived not far away in the town of New Richmond. Thus, when Helen and I decided suddenly to be married in June 1917, I had wired him and he came from New York to carry out the wedding ceremony for us in the Kermott home in Hudson.

"You *can* live on forty-five hundred dollars a year in New York," he said, "although it is not easy. You'd better find an apartment in a suburb near the site on which they are going to build the new Presbyterian Hospital. The other full-time surgeons," he added, "must have some private means to be able to live downtown near the present hospital."

We followed Mr. Bartlett's advice and found an apartment just north of New York, in Yonkers. We lived there through that first year. It was not too far from the proposed medical center, but a long way from the old Seventieth Street hospital. My clever wife made the salary do. She found Yonkers far better than Timbuktu and we were happy there, all four of us.

During the year that followed, the full-time scheme was modified, and the income was increased. We moved a little closer then, into the delightful Riverdale community with its agreeable social life and its rural setting high above the Hudson River.

I was considered to be the hospital's neurosurgeon from the beginning, but during the first two of the seven years in New York, I took my turn in the work of general surgery at the Presbyterian. Since I had had only a surgical internship my surgical colleagues, Allen Whipple, Hugh Auchincloss, Fordyce B. St. John and Barclay Parsons, whom I consulted frequently at first, taught me the essentials of the art of surgery and became my life-long friends. There were two surgical divisions and I was the junior on the second service. Parsons, the junior surgeon who corresponded to me on the first division, was debonair, handsome, skillful and all the things that I was not.

It fell to me at certain times to conduct "rounds" on the Second Surgical Service with the junior members of the staff. I prepared myself each time in advance as well as I could, and I remembered my promise never to bluff when I did not know. Some who followed me from bed to bed and who were below me in the hospital hierarchy had had more actual experience in general surgery than I. But only one, an assistant resident, showed the contempt he apparently felt for me, the young attending surgeon who had been set over him. From time to time, I detected a pitying smile — or found myself embarrassed by an unnecessarily awkward question.

At last, I could take it no longer. There are limits to the control of anger. At least there are to mine. After making rounds in the surgical ward one day, I led him to a place where there were no observers. We faced each other there alone.

"I need your help to make our service run as it should," I said. "From now on you're going to play this game and play it fair. You know very well what I mean." I had meant to keep cool. But a wave of anger blew off the lid. "If you don't, I'm going to knock your (blank blank) block off and I'd be delighted to do it right now." It was not an idle threat. I had boxed, and I was strong and fast. He stood for a moment in silence. Then he declared himself a loyal member of the team.

From that moment onward, he put on the garb of admiring respect and we worked together as friends do. I wondered, as years passed and he became a successful surgeon, what thinking went on at the back of his mind. There are, I know, many kinds of respect and differing forms of friendship. Medicine in a large hospital is, after all, something like football. Teamwork and loyalty are essential to success. I am not now excusing myself or suggesting that violence or the threat of violence is always the best approach to harmony. But it did work this time.

One of the academic duties I at once undertook led me across Central Park to the College of Physicians and Surgeons. There I was to act as an instructor in a remarkable course conducted by William C. Clarke, professor of surgical pathology.

Bill Clarke was, in appearance and in turn of mind, a modern version of the Greek philosopher Socrates. He taught, as Socrates did, by asking questions. I remember our initial interview well.

"It is," he said, "the healing process that every surgeon must learn to understand because he is a surgeon. And he should be able to teach it. It differs in certain respects when one must handle each of the tissues of the body, from the glandular wall of the stomach to the skin and the muscles and the nervous system. Here is where you come in, Dr. Penfield." The shadow of a smile passed across his face. He was a rough man who dressed more like a farmer than a professor, a man whose aim in life seemed to be to expose pretense and call for basic understanding. "What goes on in the brain?" he asked. "How does it heal? I don't understand it. Will you teach it? They say you know the best methods of staining and preparing microscopical sections of the nervous system. Is that so?"

I felt my face grow hot. "I've never made a study of the healing of brain wounds," I said. "But I do know the staining methods used in the laboratories of London."

He looked at me quizzically for a moment. "Are you planning to devote your life to neurosurgery?"

"Yes."

"Wouldn't you like to see how the nerve cells, and all the other cells that surround them and nourish them, behave when the blood supply is shut off by a stroke? Or when the brain is injured in other ways or when you make an incision in the brain to remove something?"

Here I interrupted him. "Yes, of course." And, trying to justify myself, I added: "I have studied the cytology of normal cells at Oxford, and the pathology of the cells one sees under the abnormal conditions of disease and injury at Queen Square. But I know very well that the methods we use show only half of the picture."

Bill Clarke smiled. He extended a hand toward the microscope that stood on the table before him. The forefinger on his right hand was crooked, suggesting the sort of bony fracture so common among baseball catchers. The hand was not very clean either. He lived on a small farm across the Hudson River from New York in Tenafly, New Jersey. The farm was a very popular place, I learned later. Medical students and young doctors, among them Harry Murray, gathered there on the weekends. For them, Bill Clarke was a fascinating figure, an impractical prophet but a prophet nonetheless. They did everything for him, from planting his trees to repairing his roofs and subscribing to a Clarke Farm Development Fund. And when they gathered there, they had their reward — long, delightful discussions with him. I came to realize, when I knew them better, that all the surgeons on the staff of the Presbyterian Hospital had been taught and, to some extent, molded by this sagacious and lovable genius. And now the direction of my personal interest and plan was to be redirected by him.

"But," he continued, "wouldn't you like to see it all as clearly as you can through the microscope? — the structures of the normal brain and the changes that occur when the brain heals and the scars that follow?" He seemed to be talking to himself now. Suddenly he stopped and was silent for a moment before he asked: "What is the cause of epilepsy?"

"There are different causes," I replied. "Wounds of the brain will certainly produce epileptic attacks. They occur after at least thirty percent of all reported penetrating brain injuries. Statistics of the 1914–1918 war show that."

He grinned at me as if he had not heard what I said because of an inspiration of his own. "A series of experimental wounds in laboratory animals," he said, "examined after different intervals of time, would make a wonderful addition to our teaching collection here. My technicians will do the work if you will carry out the operations and teach them the techniques. The students could study the sections. And you, yourself, might learn something in the process."

He didn't wait for my reply. He was on his feet now, walking toward the animal quarters. "You will have to keep a case record for each animal, using this standard form." He had picked up a form and was handing it to me. "You will have to leave it here in this file, so we can all turn to it in caring for the animal when you are not here. You will get the case number by entering the name of each animal and its experimental number in this book." He had preceded me into the animal quarters now and dogs were jumping up on him, barking and wagging their tails. He stooped to pet and to talk to them, calling each by name.

This was something I had not considered. Yet of course he was quite right. A brain surgeon was not different from those who operated on other parts of the body. He too should study the healing process of the organ he treats. But no one had done it, as far as I was aware. I would do it. Clarke's laboratory gave me every facility. His staff would help me. Here was an opportunity.

Yes, I would accept Clarke's practical proposals. After I finished writing up the reports of my past studies for publication, I would, I decided, shift my research approaches to the practical problems of my own patients in my own immediate field. At least, I would do this for the next few years.*

The first patient who was admitted to my care suffering from a brain tumor was F. S., a handsome little Italian boy with curly black hair. The only hope of saving Frederico's eyesight and indeed his life was an operation to remove the tumor. I asked for a consultation from the Department of Neurology. To my surprise, the professor of neurology himself, Frederick Tilney, came to see him. He came without notifying me and left a note on the patient's chart. No operation was to be carried out. The statement was categorical. The outlook was hopeless. Tilney took an attitude like the one adopted at London's Queen Square hospital — that a neurologist knows best and may dictate his opinion to a neurosurgeon and expect him to accept it as a final decision.

I examined the boy neurologically. He was certainly going

* See note 6.

blind, due to a growing pressure within the skull. I called up Dr. Tilney, hoping to discuss the location of the probable tumor, and to question whether it was not just possible that I could remove the cause of trouble before it was too late. I reached him by telephone late in the evening after reading his note. He gave his advice to me abruptly. Indeed, I thought he was rude. I would have liked to see the boy with him. But he had no time for that.

My own reaction was this: Frederico was my patient. I would welcome advice. I would not accept dictation. Dr. Whipple, my chief, looked grave when I told him what had happened. He agreed in principle. Next day he talked to Tilney at a meeting of the medical faculty and came to see me afterward. "The whole issue of the disposition of the neurological department," he said, "is to be decided in a few days when the dean of medicine, William Darrach, returns from Europe. Unless there is a real chance to cure the boy or to save his life, please don't push the issue too quickly."

Tilney wanted to gain control of all neurological and neuro-surgical cases in any of the university hospitals. He wanted neuro-surgical operations to be carried out in the New York Neurological Institute by their own neurosurgeons. This was contrary to Whipple's plan. It was a time of major organization.

In the letter to my mother at the close of that week I summed up the situation. "Finally we decided, Allen Whipple and I, that I was free to carry out an operation on this boy if I thought best." Then I added this: "I fear there will be friction with the Department of Neurology, which is what I most desire not to happen."

I had hoped to find friendship and cooperation among the neurologists of New York. I would need their consultation and I hoped they would accept mine. We in the full-time departments of medicine and surgery at the Presbyterian Hospital were in a strong and independent position as part of Columbia University's effort to create, within the city of New York, a center of medical practice that was scientific as well as humane.

But now I faced a grave responsibility. This boy's life and eye-sight must be saved soon if they were going to be saved at all. That was more important than any question of departmental rivalry. I must be wise. I must decide whether Tilney was right or not, decide where the tumor was located and if I was really capable of taking it out.

A new procedure, called ventriculography, had been published by Walter Dandy of Johns Hopkins while I was in Europe. This, it was said, would show the position of a brain tumor, if present, with great accuracy. But Harvey Cushing in Boston and Charles Elsberg, chief surgeon at the New York Neurological Institute, looked upon the procedure, at that time, as too dangerous to use, and as unnecessary. Dandy was contemptuous of this adverse opinion.

I had watched Dandy while I was a student at Baltimore and respected his ability. I decided I would see him carry out the procedure and judge for myself.

Walter Dandy was at loggerheads with other neurosurgeons. He had refused membership in the newly formed Society of Neurological Surgeons. But his assistant resident in neurosurgery at that time was William Rienhoff, a friend and former classmate of mine in medical school. I telephoned to Rienhoff and in a day or two he sent me word to come. I made a quick trip to Baltimore and watched Dandy, whom I found to be both hospitable and helpful, carry out a "ventriculogram."

I watched while the ventricular fluid was drawn off and air injected by a long, hollow needle inserted through a hole in the skull, deep into the ventricular cavity within the brain. The air, which replaced the fluid, did not seem to disturb the patient at all. It cast a clearly outlined shadow when X rays were made of the head. The shadow showed the exact shape and position of the ventricular cavities within the brain.

It was clear to me now that this was an important step forward, a surgical method of locating tumors and, even more important in my view, of studying the brain. It could be dangerous on occasion, yes, but only, I thought, when unwisely employed. Indeed, ventriculography was the first of a whole series of technical procedures that were to make the neurosurgeon master of exact diagnosis in his own field. Instead of accepting the humiliating role of being a passive technician, as Horsley had been forced to do at Queen Square, surgeons who learned the art of neurological diagnosis for themselves and added to that such technical procedures as ventriculography could make their own diagnosis, and bring a new accuracy into operative handling.

On returning from Baltimore, I carried out a ventriculogram on Frederico. It did not disturb him and there was no bad result. But I was forced to agree with Tilney. I could not be sure of saving the boy, and it seemed kinder and wiser not to try.

Alas! He was such an appealing youngster! But, at least, I had made up my own mind in regard to the patient. I would continue to do so with future cases. I sent for the parents to come to the hospital so I could talk with them as I had when the boy was admitted. They were recent immigrants from Italy and spoke no English, but the boy's uncle, a tall, handsome Italian, interpreted for me. I explained that the tumor was too deep for operation and we feared the growth was malignant.

"I am afraid your little boy is going to die," I said. "But I may be wrong. Doctors *are* wrong sometimes, you know."

No physician, it seems to me, should ever presume to close the door to hope completely, or use the dreadful phrase "hopeless prognosis." To be honest, he never does know enough for that. Men and women in a darkened room will look at the light however tiny. Stubbornly they may even live by it and rejoice in it — provided the door is not quite shut.

One morning, two or three weeks later, the uncle telephoned me. The boy had seemed to do quite well when he first returned home, but had died suddenly the day before and the funeral was scheduled for that same afternoon. Here was a dilemma! I felt I must know the answers that only an autopsy would give me, but the boy was at home, and the funeral to take place in a few hours. So many questions. Could I perhaps have saved this lad of ten? I remembered how he had looked at me with his appealing dark eyes when I realized that vision in them was a light about to fail. Some pictures one never forgets.

In the autopsy room at Oxford, Sir William Osler had taught me how to remove the brain. At the same time, he had made me realize that a postmortem examination is admirable, a splendid thing in which the physician takes pride. It brings always the hope that this patient did not die in vain. Fortunately, too, I had carried out autopsies later, from time to time, for the pathologist Godwin Greenfield, in London.

I made a quick decision and asked my intern to come with me.

I remember that young man quite well, a fine fellow. I can see him now, and hear his voice, for this adventure is still vivid in my mind. But his name escapes me. We took the subway downtown and emerged in the poorest Italian district. As we climbed the stairs of a gloomy tenement, I explained to him that there might be danger here, due to misunderstanding. I gave him the empty satchel, which was empty except for the instruments — and we agreed that, if we should succeed, he was to vanish with the precious specimen in the satchel, leaving me to talk with the parents.

The front room was crowded with people. They were obviously dressed in their best. The mother, in black, was weeping. I tried to explain. There was a shocked silence in the room and then a hubbub. All the talk was in Italian. Some were shouting, "No, no." At last, the uncle took me out into the hall. "I know you done your best," he said. "Now you wanna save — maybe another Italian boy? Maybe this might come to Frederico's little brother? Yes? All right, I guard the door. You sure you make him look the same when you're finished? Sure? Okay."

I remember my feeling of reassurance in the presence of this ally. He was intelligent, gentle, intuitive; he had understood everything. That feeling was reinforced when I realized what a big fellow he was, a northern Italian who towered above all the others.

In the back room, the child lay on a table, beautiful in death. He was dressed in white silk! Doctors are like other people. Nothing could have been more distasteful to the intern and to me. But this had to be done. We worked feverishly, with sidelong glances at the flimsy double doors that separated us from the front room.

The uproar that interrupted the quiet talk from time to time in that front room might have been used for the sound effects in some operatic mob scene. But, at last, the job was done, the boy dressed as before. All was the same that met the outward view. I opened the door and entered the front room, while my stalwart intern slipped away and down the stairs with the satchel.

I told them the boy could not have been saved. But perhaps we would learn enough to save other Italian boys, someday. The uncle helped me out of the front room and I, too, slipped away and down the stairs, with a sense of vast relief, to the welcome anonymity of the New York subway.

What I had told them was the truth, and I had done my first

autopsy on a patient of my own. There would be many others. I would know many failures like this. But, in time, I would learn to save some, God willing, who were condemned to death without me. I had begun to play the game in which we, as physicians, were pledged, to put it simply, to learn the whole truth and to do our best.

It was a rule established by Professor Whipple that the surgeon in charge of any patient who died while in hospital should present a "death analysis" to the staff. I asked to present F. S. In my death analysis, I admitted that Tilney's advice against operation had been justified by the evidence of autopsy. The tumor had grown from within the third ventricle and was too deep to be removed by me without loss of life. But the ventriculogram had shown its location just as clearly as the autopsy did. The procedure had done the patient no harm. I decided then to continue to use Dandy's method of ventriculography, regardless of the disapproval of elder clinicians.

There was a principle involved here too: A neurosurgeon should be responsible for his patient like any other physician. He might ask for consultation but he should not be expected to accept dictation. It was his duty to learn, as best he could, the clinical neurology related to his patients and the anatomy and the pathology as well. I realized then that to make the best use of neurologists and pathologists and others as consultants, I must, myself, be a neurologist and a pathologist and other things.

For example, sections of the Italian boy's tumor were made for me in the hospital's pathology laboratory. They puzzled Dr. William von Glahn, the pathologist. I took them to Columbia's professor of pathology at the medical school, James Jobling. He looked at the sections with me and shook his head. "We don't know how to classify these tumors," he said. "I wish you would make a study of them yourself. You must discover better staining techniques for us."

About a month after my visit to Dandy to watch him do a ventriculogram, I returned to Baltimore for a second visit, this time to learn how he was treating hydrocephalus, or "water on the brain," since several babies had been brought to me with enormous heads due to this condition, and no one had yet devised a cure. This visit was important to me, not because I learned anything more from Dandy, but because of meeting the professor of anatomy who was also dean of medicine, Lewis Weed, and because of the chain of events that this meeting set in motion.

"That was a great day," I wrote my mother on the following Sunday. "I realized that Dandy was getting nowhere with his various new operations for 'water on the brain' so I went over to see [the professor of anatomy] . . . Lewis Weed. He has been doing research on the problem of hydrocephalus experimentally. . . . I had lunch with him and his assistants — about ten men who teach anatomy in the morning and do research in the afternoon. . . . Each man washed his dishes and went off to his own room. Weed was very nice and we had a long talk that was very stimulating to me. He told me too of the projected Department of Neurology.

"In the past," the letter went on to explain, "neurology at Johns Hopkins has been a specialty within the Department of Medicine as neurosurgery is part of surgery. . . . Weed wondered if I would care to come down when the new arrangement was made and take charge of the service [neurology] and do some research, or was I bound to go into surgery. I said I thought that such a neurological department should include neurological surgery as well. The subject was dropped then. . . ."

It was at about this time that I carried out my first major brain operation at last. It was followed by a second before the week was out. The first was for brain abscess. The second was for brain tumor. Both patients were comatose before they reached the hospital. Both would surely die within hours if nothing was done. I undertook each with high hopes, determined to win, for by this time I was completely prepared as far as instruments and team of assistants and courage were concerned. But, although each operation was long and agonizing, each was followed by death.

That week of depressing deaths was described simply in the letter to my mother: "November 20, 1921. . . . This has been a curious week in some ways. At the beginning . . . I was called down to the hospital to see a man at midnight. He was unconscious and just about to breathe his last. I thought he had an abscess deep in the brain and so we operated, finishing at six o'clock in the morning. I had to stop then, without quite reaching the abscess, because his condition grew suddenly worse.

"But he was much improved after that," the letter continued. "My hopes rose. Then he started down the long road again in two days. So I took him back to the operating room and opened up the wound again. This time I found the abscess at once. It was like a great lemon filled with pus. Again I thought I had saved him. But, alas, he died a few hours later. So, you see, I was pulled head-first into this, my first major brain operation."

The second operation was for brain tumor. "It came," the letter went on, "the day before yesterday: A woman was admitted who, like the man I've just described, was in coma. We figured out the location of trouble and I turned down my first 'bone-flap.' That means making a trapdoor in the skull that may be closed when you are through. This time it proved to be the malignant kind of tumor that cannot be removed completely. So I took a piece out for microscopic study and quit. Last night she died." Then I added, "Brain surgery is a terrible profession. If I did not feel it will become very different in my lifetime, I should hate it."

Depressing these operations were, but I did not despair, not quite. I talked to Hugh Auchincloss, my surgical division chief. He was a lovable man, a splendid surgeon, fastidious in his technique and a perfectionist in all that had to do with patient care, and above all a kindly doctor. Much of what would prove to be good in the training of my assistants, when I came to have them, would be derived from Hugh Auchincloss. I have other fond memories of him, too. Before Christmas, it was his custom to invite us to his home for a splendid dinner after which he read the whole of Charles Dickens's *Christmas Carol* from beginning to end! After seven such "Scrooge parties," in seven successive years, we carried that custom with us to Montreal and continued it with modifications. It became a yearly event in our home for our professional group and family.

As I have said, I talked to Hugh Auchincloss. Possibly I looked tired. In any case he said, "Pen, take off a week. Stay out in Yonkers. I'll look after your cases. You want to write up your research studies, don't you?"

So, I turned with a sort of fierce enjoyment and relief to the task of scientific writing after a week of clinical failure.

"What Ho!" I wrote to my mother on November 27. "A whole week ahead . . . and a chance to be with the family! . . ."

During that winter, in our little apartment on Valentine Lane, we made it a habit, Helen and I, to read aloud, of an evening, over our after-dinner coffee. That week of November 27, we were reading *Hamlet*. I hoped it would improve the writing of the report on decerebrate rigidity.

Did I hope that Shakespeare would teach me to describe the reflexes and the seeming behavior of a brainless cat in musical phrase and with pleasing metaphor? No. Not really. But the careless and untutored writer may so easily use words that blur and distort the meaning. That was the essential skill that seemed to come so naturally to Shakespeare — to choose the word that fitted the meaning. That it fitted the rhythm and the music of his context is something more. The scientist may have little concern for rhythm and music, yet this too should condition him for writing. And beyond this, Shakespeare can teach him to discard professional lingo and choose those words from his own vocabulary, however poverty-stricken that may be, to fit his meaning exactly.

And there is a final advantage — verbal expression leads the student to creative thought. I discovered that the effort to express conclusions in language that was altogether clear and simple helped me to criticize, and to reconsider, my own understanding. It helped me to see the relationships of cause and effect in sharpest perspective. I discovered that setting it all down on paper could become a fascinating end in itself.

4

Neurosurgery

My failure to save the patients in my first two major operations on the brain was hard to take. But all patients admitted to my care in those early months were about to die as they entered the hospital. There were successes too. I liked working with my hands as in carpentry. That is what had drawn me toward surgery in the first place. Perhaps it was the strong, broad hands, inherited from my father, that made it possible to do well what I had in mind to do in surgery, although I never became as speedy or as dextrous in certain procedures as some of my friends in the art.

On March 9, 1922, the weekly letter home referred to a "formal offer from Johns Hopkins." It was an offer of the position of "Associate in Neurology at a salary of $5,000 a year." Weed had not let the matter drop as I thought he would.

The invitation to come to Baltimore as a neurologist caused me to pause and to reconsider. Lewis Weed, who issued the invitation, had himself worked with Sherrington and with Harvey Cushing before coming to the Johns Hopkins, where he had inaugurated promising basic researches on the brain and spinal fluid of animals. He wanted to see similar work begun as applied to man. It was the very thing I had dreamed of, during my years in England.

At the same time, the professor of pathology, W. G. MacCallum, wanted to turn over the pathology of the nervous system to me if I would undertake direction of a projected subdepartment of neuropathology. He had pathological material at that time that could, I realized, be converted into a gold mine of research.

Allen Whipple agreed that I must visit Baltimore and talk to the promoters of the plan. It was a great adventure, that visit, particularly because of the high caliber of the teachers involved and the excellence of the academic atmosphere. The professor of medicine welcomed me and went over the plans for separate beds in a full-time Department of Neurology to be established in the new hospital building. The current professor of neurology, H. M. Thomas, who was a popular clinician well advanced in years, welcomed the project.

Perhaps the most exciting event of the visit was my discussion of neurology and psychiatry with Adolf Meyer, professor of psychiatry. He was, I suppose, the leading American psychiatrist. His opinion at that time is interesting. There should be, he said, "a neuropsychiatric clinic with neurology and psychiatry on an equal footing. Psychiatry could relieve neurology of the neurasthenics and suchlike."

I had been his student and had discovered that his own approach to psychiatry had included studies of the anatomy and pathology of the brain. I, myself, had yet to complete that approach. Would I ever meet a psychiatrist like him when I was able to do my part? I wondered.*

To work with these three men at the Hopkins — Weed, MacCallum and Meyer — was challenging. It stirs my imagination today. But in 1922 I had enough to do to become a neurosurgeon, and enough to learn in the broad field of neurology. If the neurosurgeon Walter Dandy had wanted to welcome me I suppose I might have moved to Baltimore. But no. He was not interested in the dean's plan to cut across departmental lines and thus create a new enlarged department. This made my decision to remain in New York inevitable.

During this period, while I balanced a career in neurology against one in neurosurgery, there was no word of welcome or

---

* Charles Symonds refers to the address of Adolf Meyer given in the same year, 1922 (A. Meyer, *Archives of Neurology and Psychiatry*, 8:111, 1922), in his (Symonds's) excellent Cairns Lecture on the relationship of psychiatry, neurology and neurosurgery, September 1970.

cooperation from surgery or the neurosurgeon at Hopkins. But this is easily understandable when considered in longer perspective. More than three decades had followed the opening of Johns Hopkins Hospital and the appointment of Halsted and Osler there (1889). In 1921, William Halsted, still professor of surgery, was ill. In 1922, he died.

William Halsted established an American school of surgery characterized by his scholarly approach to surgical problems and by a new elegance of operative technique. He created a residency training system. Many men, so trained by him, became teachers and established their own resident-training programs. After being a Halsted resident, Harvey Cushing began to specialize in the surgery related to the nervous system. That had been about 1901.* It was through the career of Halsted more than that of any other individual that leadership in certain aspects of surgery came to the United States.

In 1886, when Victor Horsley went to Queen Square, Halsted was a dashing young surgeon in New York. Trained in Germany, he was doing the preliminary experimental work that was to make possible the use of regional, or local, anesthesia. This was to be very important to many of us. It fell to others to publish the method since he, alas, had experimented upon himself, injecting cocaine with a view to using it for anesthesia. He was "hooked" before he knew it, and the dreadful hunger of drug addiction caught him. But after many months of struggle, he regained control and accompanied his friend, the pathologist William H. Welch, to Baltimore, where he embarked on a new career, a more scholarly one, as described by Whipple.†

In 1913, Cushing went to Boston while Walter Dandy, another resident, took up the responsibility for neurosurgery at the Hopkins. Dandy had been Cushing's assistant. But he was a lone worker and, no doubt, was wise not to go along but rather to remain behind in Baltimore. Dandy was an able surgeon and a thoughtful investigator of surgical problems. He came from the Middle West, as I did. He is said to have given up the possibility of a Rhodes

---

* See J. F. Fulton, *Harvey Cushing — A Biography* (Springfield, Ill.: Thomas, 1946).
† A. O. Whipple, in *Surgery*, 32:524–550, 1952.

Scholarship to Oxford in 1907 when he received his doctorate of medicine and decided to become a surgeon.

Dandy's brilliant contribution to neurosurgery, after Cushing's departure, lay especially in the field of surgical and diagnostic technique. By 1922 he felt no need for assistance from a beginner like me. He felt no interest in the development of Weed's plan for neurology. Samuel Crowe, also a distinguished pupil of Halsted who specialized in the surgery of nose and throat and who became, eventually, the biographer of Halsted,* concluded that "Walter Dandy to an even greater extent than Cushing had the kind of creative imagination, intuition and persistence which we are accustomed to regard as the highest form of genius."

Dandy and Cushing made their own contributions to surgery of the nervous system and to physiology of the brain. What Lewis Weed and W. G. MacCallum and Adolf Meyer hoped to see done in neurology was exactly what I wanted to do — but I wanted to do neurosurgery as well, and I hoped to do it as skillfully as the leaders of the specialty at that time — Cushing and Dandy and Charles Frazier and the rest.

In my first months of practice as a neurosurgeon, I had seen Fred Tilney struggling to fit a newly created New York Neurological Institute into a workable academic relationship with medicine and surgery, and I had been asked to do something similar at the Johns Hopkins. Three options lay before me: first, to go to Baltimore; second, to join Tilney and accept his leadership in New York; or, third, to continue with Whipple as a neurosurgeon with freedom to make my own approach to further neurological study and treatment.

The balance of my own decision might have tipped in either direction, it seems — toward Baltimore or New York — for on April 17, 1922, Helen wrote an addition to the weekly letter to my mother: "After we had ordered our seeds for the garden, we talked and talked over the Baltimore problem. At present it seems one is almost as good as the other."

But at last the die was cast. On April 30, 1922, I wrote: "We are going to remain in New York. I have sent a letter to the Johns

* S. J. Crowe, *Halsted of Johns Hopkins — The Man and His Men* (Springfield, Ill.: Thomas, 1957).

Hopkins dean." Then I added, "Had I gone, I would have expected to spend three or four years hard at work learning the fundamentals of medical neurology and laying the groundwork for experimental investigation. At the end of that time," the letter predicted, "if I failed, I would have been condemned to spend my days in futile medical neurology with only the solace of animal experimentation.*

"In case I made good [in Baltimore]," the letter concluded, "I would become Professor of Neurology. It is possible, then, I might get a neurological institute including neurosurgery (even in Baltimore). It is along that line that the real future of neurology lies, I believe."

This letter makes it clear that less than ten months after our arrival in New York I was firmly of the opinion that "the real future of neurology" called for a neurological institute in which neurology and neurosurgery were not to be divided. Whether I was to be called a neurologist and go to Johns Hopkins or whether I was to be called a neurosurgeon and remain at Columbia-Presbyterian, I faced a similar personal challenge. I must first make some sort of effective basic approach to the neurology of man. That I had yet to do.

There were fifty-one days of indecision in regard to the invitation from Johns Hopkins. Two months, at that time, January and February of 1922, I spent in bed due to a febrile illness. It was called "flu," for want of a more exact diagnosis. This interrupted my clinical work but not the scientific writing, and I had much time for reflection. During this period, Professor Whipple made the prospect of life in New York more attractive to us. My full-time salary from the medical school was increased to half as much again. We were happy enough in our New York life.

It was a life of hard work, but seasoned with happy family living, and we were content with the decision we had made. That summer, we rented a house on the grounds of the Riverdale Country School and a sparkling Model T Ford car came to stay in our small tin garage, and in the autumn a Swedish kitchen maid, Alice,

---

* For me, without neurosurgical opportunity, neurology might seem "futile." But for the man who could approach it through the basic sciences of internal medicine and biochemistry, it need never be called that.

made her appearance. Thus the second year began — 1922 to 1923.

Almost at once, I found myself at another fork in the road. The professional situation in New York was not as simple as it had seemed a year earlier when Professor Whipple had asked me to join his staff as neurosurgeon.

The Neurological Institute of New York was pushing ambitious plans of its own. It had been founded in 1909 when a group of neurologists rented premises on Fifty-seventh Street near Lexington Avenue, about ten minutes' walk from the Presbyterian Hospital at Park Avenue and Seventieth Street. In 1920, the neurological building was bought for the neurologists, and Frederick Tilney, Columbia's professor of neurology, joined the staff. He began at once to play a dominant role in the transformation that was to make of this private clinic the world-famous institute it is today.

I was a pawn on Tilney's larger chessboard. If he had talked with me about it, which he never did, he would have discovered that I could understand his point of view and might well have sympathized with his eventual purpose. Being a chess player myself, I realized that the master player makes a plan according to the important pieces. When a pawn is in the way, it can be moved or sacrificed. He elected to move me.

In October 1922, I was invited to join the staff of the Neurological Institute, and was appointed assistant surgeon there. Dr. Whipple agreed that I could spend my extra time, when not doing surgery at the Presbyterian, in the institute. There I would work on the neurological service under the direction of Dr. Charles Elsberg. It was agreed, too, that I might transfer patients who came to me at the Presbyterian, and operate upon them in the institute. But the word that Whipple used was "might," not "must." I accepted the change, and for a time, I attended the New York Neurological Institute and took part in their clinical conferences.

The leading neurologists of New York were on the institute staff — Fred Tilney, Foster Kennedy, Ramsay Hunt, Walter Timme, Edwin G. Zabriskie. All of New York's well-to-do patients consulted them when necessary. These doctors came to the institute conferences. They often brought their patients there for diagnostic discussion. It was true enough that I could learn from them. Also, they could, if they should come to trust me, refer their wealthy patients to me for operation. That would mean a large income in time. But Charles Elsberg, the surgical chief, kept a jealous eye on younger men. Nonetheless, I liked him as a person. He was fascinated by the problem of any interesting clinical case and would discuss cases with relish. But he had little interest, and indeed little understanding, of the science that should, it seemed to me, be basic to neurosurgery. In any case, a large income meant very little to me as compared with some other things.

The other assistant surgeon who was working under Elsberg in 1922 was Byron Stookey. He was not happy in this relationship. He himself was an impressive man, a little older than I was, trained at Harvard and in Paris.

I remember the first clinical conference I attended in the New York Neurological Institute. A young neurologist, who was Tilney's assistant, was organizing things along with Stookey. This was Henry A. Riley. He was an anatomist, like Tilney, as well as a neurologist, and he had been coauthor, with Tilney, of the comprehensive textbook used by the medical students. It was entitled *The Form and Function of the Central Nervous System.*

At first, Riley impressed me and gave me a feeling of inferiority, as Stookey had. But, in time, these two men were to become my close friends and delightful companions at meetings in many parts of the world.

Louis Casamajor and others, like Charles McKendree, worked as well in Columbia's free outpatient dispensary in the old Vanderbilt Clinic. It was there among the crowds of poor outpatients, rather than in the Neurological Institute, that I chose to attend faithfully, and I rarely missed my weekly afternoon under Casamajor all through the New York period.

The chief difficulty was that there was not, as yet, a laboratory in the institute where I could do pathology. I found that, while I attended at the institute, my unfinished research at the Presbyterian Hospital called to me and made me unhappy. When I wanted to use microscopes to study pathology, I had to return to the Presbyterian.

I tried to ride the two horses for a month or two. Then I returned to Allen Whipple and made my little speech. I was conscious, I said, of the honor of this appointment to the Neurological

Institute staff. But I preferred to carry out neurosurgery only at the Presbyterian Hospital. That way every hour that I could spare from surgery, I could spend with the microscope. What I needed in the way of further neurological training I could get from continuing contact with the patients in the Presbyterian Hospital and at the Vanderbilt Outpatient Clinic. In neurosurgery, I had much to learn but I wanted a free hand and mind in the choice of what to accept.

A day or two later, Whipple and I walked together across Central Park to the College of Physicians and Surgeons to talk with Dean Darrach. William Darrach was an organizing genius. He had given up a career in surgery to become, in a very real sense, the architect of the reorganization of medicine in the projected Columbia Medical Center.

I remember Dr. Whipple's simple statement to the dean: "Penfield says he can't spare the time to work at the Neurological Institute. He wants, especially, time to carry on his research on the healing of brain wounds with Bill Clarke."

I saw the two men smile at the mention of Clarke's name. They were older than I, but both of them had been taught by Clarke. They understood what I would be about with him.

The real situation was that I could not accept dictation from the institute's chief neurosurgeon, Elsberg, and that the chief neurologist, Tilney, did not want to use me. Perhaps the training I had had in London had given me a different perspective from that of Tilney. It was agreed that I would confine my work to the Presbyterian for the present. And I accepted the understanding that if, in the future, the Neurological Institute should be able to follow the Presbyterian Hospital uptown to the medical center, all neurological and neurosurgical patients would eventually be transferred to the institute for study and treatment and I would then return to the Neurological Institute and begin to operate there.

It must have been clear enough to Professor Tilney by now that the pawn would not interfere with his eventual plans. Still he did not admit me to his confidence or accept me as one of the young men whose fortunes he could so easily promote. He was never rude after our first encounter. He was friendly and passive and I was free to go my lone way and to follow every aspect of neurological interest. But such recognition as I could hope for, in the field of neurology, came from leaders outside New York — among them Stanley Cobb of Boston and Theodore Weisenberg of Philadelphia.

It was all right. I had chosen the third of the three options — to continue with Whipple as neurosurgeon, free to make my own studies. In addition to time for studies on brain healing with Clarke, I wanted to study the pathology that each of my own patients presented. To that end, I worked with Dr. William C. von Glahn, the chief in the hospital's pathology laboratory. In 1924, to my delight, he gave me a small room of my own in his laboratory and offered to pay for a technician.

A strange little orderly, then working on the public wards, applied immediately for the job — a Cockney youngster who, so he said, had done technical work in the laboratory at Queen Square, London. Edward Dockrill had come ashore in New York after several years of sailing about the world as a cabin boy. He needed medical treatment badly, and he needed glasses to improve his vision and correct his squint. These things we could and did provide. But we discovered, all too soon, that he was not a trained technician. Yet he wanted this job. That was something. And he was quick, keen, eager to learn and compulsive in his enthusiasms, and I liked him. When Dr. von Glahn accepted him, which he did with grave doubt, I had my first assistant, a cabin boy. My ship was under way! What was its destination? Who could say?

On Wednesday afternoons, I made it a rule to go to the old Vanderbilt Clinic, which housed another part of Tilney's burgeoning Department of Neurology. In order to gain neurological experience in depth, I accepted eagerly the post of neurologist there — not neurosurgeon. That was already Stookey's role in the clinic. The "old Vanderbilt" was only twenty minutes' brisk walk away from the Presbyterian Hospital across Central Park. It sprawled along Fifty-ninth Street adjacent to Columbia's College of Physicians and Surgeons.

Reporting there, I rubbed shoulders with the neurologists and psychiatrists who came in from various hospitals in New York and Brooklyn and nearby New Jersey. The poor of all descriptions came to that free clinic and crowded along its dark, creaking corridors. Most of the patients lived in the adjacent area, known as Hell's Kitchen.

The clinic chief was Dr. Louis Casamajor, a wise, gentle clinical genius. Bald, smiling, and quick of movement, Casamajor presided over a five o'clock neurological conference every Wednesday, ruling it with a hand of iron. He would select one of us to present to him the most puzzling and instructive patient of the week. After the patient had left the room, each neurologist, in turn, was called upon to discuss, diagnose and recommend. Then Casamajor summarized and made his conclusion. We argued on, after the conference was over, and usually gathered for dinner in a nearby restaurant, returning to the medical school for evening lectures or demonstrations supervised by the excellent neuroanatomist, Oliver Strong.

During those New York years, I learned much more than neurology and surgery. It is the patients who can teach one most. They open their hearts and minds. And the doctor, if only he will listen, comes to understand the inborn nature of man. He discovers the good that is always there, though sometimes very well hidden! And the fears, the loves, the sorrows, the anguish and joy and the hopes the patient harbors deep down inside. I learned what every good physician knows, that healing is of the spirit, as well as of the body, and that compassion brings its own reward. It repays the doctor and the nurse, as they do their best, even before they give their words of guidance or finish the dressing.

The city of New York has its own fascination, even in midsummer, as suggested by a letter I wrote, July 30, 1922: "Here, in the Presbyterian Hospital, there is a greater variety of patients, as regards nationality, than could be found in any hospital of Paris or London. . . . As I walked through Central Park this afternoon on my way to the medical school, many languages could be heard and varying twangs of American speech.

"When I reached Columbus Circle, a man was shouting to a throng of curious passersby that they have only to publicly confess Christ and they will go to Heaven and 'there is no other way.' What must the Hindu and Mohammedan think? and the Jew and the honest agnostic? They don't believe it, of course, and I don't. (Christ who, more than any other, taught the meaning of compassion, could only despair at some of man's interpretations!) . . .

"As I came back through the park I stopped to hear a band playing Schubert. . . . After the Schubert, the leader led his listeners
in 'Swanee River,' and thousands sang. He played jazz, and young
girls oscillated. A young sport accosted a woman of the street
who stood close behind me. Their coarse talk told of another
world that makes up this city too. . . .

"When the towering buildings at the foot of the park began to
light up, it made you think of all the skyscrapers down to Battery
Park. Many of them are beautiful. . . . Yes, if we stay here, we
will learn to love New York in time, especially when we move into
a more livable home. . . . I am doing a good deal of surgery these
days and am trying to speed up as an operator now. . . ."

In the autumn of 1922 we did move into nearby Riverdale, rent-
ing a house among the trees of the Riverdale Country School. We
had friends now. We joined the local Presbyterian church and felt
we had found a home for the family.

In the spring of 1923, I took some weeks off to visit the neurosurgeons Dandy and Frazier and Cushing and to watch them
operate. During two weeks in Boston, I saw Cushing each morning
as he operated on a tumor of the brain. In the afternoons, I worked
with a distinguished pathologist, Frank Mallory, at his Boston
City Hospital laboratory. He taught me better staining methods
for scars and tumor growths. This would help me in my research.

Cushing's brain-tumor material was being studied at that time
by Percival Bailey, a friend of mine from internship days at the
Peter Bent Brigham Hospital. He was doing for Cushing what I
could have done for Dandy had I gone to Baltimore, and had
Dandy wanted it. Bailey's attitude toward the pathology of neurosurgery was much like my own, except that tumors were not
enough for me. I could see now how far our work must go beyond
the patients who came to Cushing. These considerations made me
quite content to work on quietly and hopefully, alone in the New
York environment.

In May of 1923 came an unsolicited "research fund," the first
one: Anna Marie N., age six months, died. I had studied this
lovable baby in hospital and sent her home. It was hydrocephalus
(water on the brain), of the type I could not hope to cure. When
the father telephoned that she had died, I asked the doctor's
question: Would he permit autopsy? He said, "Yes. I would be

glad if you could come and examine the baby. Perhaps," he added spontaneously, "you may learn how to save the life of someone else's child."

Edward, the new technician, and I walked across Central Park to the address of Mr. and Mrs. N. on the West Side. They lived in a clean but very poor apartment. They welcomed us warmly. I remembered how high their hopes had been when they first brought Anna Marie to me. How sad they were when they took her away! There is nothing quite like the joy that a beautiful laughing baby may bring to mother and father; nothing, too, is quite the same as the anguish that follows its death. She mourns for the baby as only a mother can. He mourns for her, and the baby as well.

Edward and I did the postmortem examination in their bathroom. After three and a half hours of delicate dissection and restoration, we left. Very shyly she gave me an envelope. It contained "a letter," she said, that I must not read until we should reach the hospital. I opened it on arrival. It contained fifty dollars!

I wrote her a letter of thanks: "This gift of yours will form a Fund for Hydrocephalus Research. It will buy some books on allied conditions that I have very much wanted."

The study of the scars I had produced in Bill Clarke's laboratory had reached the time for a conclusion, and this became my major concern. I used the methods I had learned from Frank Mallory at the Boston City Hospital. But I could not understand what the microscope showed. I despaired, realizing there was so much that did not show.

We had a delightful vacation in the month of August 1923, at Long Lake in the Adirondacks, living under tents. I took along all the microscopic slides of these brain scars and a good microscope that my wife's father, Dr. Edward P. Kermott, had bought when he was a graduate student in Vienna. I brought along a box filled with all the books that seemed to throw light on the problem — in English, French and German. The authors spoke sometimes as if with authority but never, it seemed to me, could they give sufficient evidence.

I devoted my mornings to the microscope but I made little progress in understanding. The fishing, however, was excellent, and the swimming and boating and the air and the out-of-doors were all that we could desire. We returned to New York in the best of health. But I was dissatisfied and discouraged in regard to my research.

I had been two years at the Presbyterian Hospital. At the suggestion of Whipple I had carried out a whole series of operations for hernia using the fine silk technique of Halsted in order to compare with the cases operated upon by the other surgeons using catgut sutures. As far as general surgery was concerned, I was able now to do all but the most specialized operations in that field.

In November, Allen Whipple announced that I had served out my apprenticeship in general surgery. Henceforth, I would be responsible only for the care of the hospital's neurosurgical patients. He had other men available on the staff to take my place in general surgery.[*]

So I was free, at last, to devote full time to the work of neurosurgeon and investigator. It was wonderful to be free and to live a double life devoted to these parallel, interrelated professions. As neurosurgeon I could claim to be the pupil of many — I had watched Cushing as an intern, and made complete notes. I had learned, quite early, some things from Percy Sargent in London, and through him from Sir Victor Horsley, and I had learned from Thierry de Martel in Paris during my occasional visits there. At present, I was discovering from time to time much I could use in the careful techniques of Charles Frazier in Philadelphia. And I continued, too, to be the distant pupil of Harvey Cushing. I had learned much from the daring and the originality of Walter Dandy. Through these last two men, I would always be the pupil of my first professor of surgery, the man who had taught them the fastidious handling of tissues, William Halsted of Johns Hopkins.[†]

And just at this point I shall add an anecdote that is of historical interest, perhaps, in regard to early British neurosurgery as well as to the evolution of the modern school of neurosurgery in Britain and America.

When, in 1920, I came to the National Hospital and saw Mr. Percy Sargent, Horsley's successor, operating there, I was forced

[*] See note 7.
[†] See note 8.

to conclude that leadership in neurosurgery had already passed to America.

The establishment of British modern neurosurgery fell to others. In 1919, while I was at Oxford, a young surgeon came to Oxford to study our decerebrated animals for a few days. This was the beginning of my lifelong friendship with Geoffrey Jefferson. He was then quietly introducing improved technique into this specialty in Manchester, England. A few years later Hugh Cairns was to introduce the Halsted technique after studying for a year with Cushing in Boston. Norman Dott did the same for the Royal Infirmary at Edinburgh. Thus the modern British school of neurosurgery had no more than indirect connection with the great Horsley. They developed improved operative technique as the rest of us did.

Meanwhile, Percy Sargent (later Sir Percy), whom I found operating at Queen Square (when he was not busy in general surgery at Saint Thomas Hospital), was a very skillful surgeon who handed on Horsley's attitudes and surgical teachings. He had not caught the fire, nor had he the scientific curiosity of his master, but he was an excellent operative disciple in the operating room.

For some months I acted as Mr. Sargent's first assistant in the operating room and I followed his patients after operation, while I was studying the microscopic structure of the tumors of the skull and the brain in Godwin Greenfield's laboratory. During that period, a patient came to Mr. Sargent for operation with an enormous bony enlargement on the skull. It was like a horn. The man reminded one of a mythical unicorn. "This is an endothelioma," said Mr. Sargent when he saw him. "The condition has been called hemicraniosis in France but it is really bony tumor growth. Horsley had a number of cases like this. Under that horn there is a soft tumor pressing on the brain."

To my joy he asked me to assist him in the operation and we went together to the operating theater. "It will bleed," he said, and asked the "theater sister" to get out Horsley's fine steel handsaws. She was a nurse who knew her business and I sensed the sudden excitement in her response.

How well I remember the scene next day, when Sargent removed that bony horn and the tumor under it! We were dressed in old-fashioned Horsley rubber knee boots and rubber aprons with sterile gowns over all. I had pulled my protecting mask up to cover my nose carefully as well as mouth. His covered mouth only. The patient had been put to sleep. I think it was with chloroform.

Suddenly Sargent made the incision with his scalpel and turned a flap of scalp back from the bony horn, working at top speed. We controlled the scalp hemorrhage, as he usually did, with pressure clamps. "Now it will bleed," he repeated, using much the tone of voice one might have expected had he said, "Now it is going to rain."

With trephine and handsaws of different sizes and Horsley's giant rongeur and Horsley's bone wax, he made cuts or trenches in the normal bone all the way around the horn. It bled like a suddenly released fountain. But he carried out his excision with a breathless speed and a dexterity that I had never seen before. In the hands of a slow operator, that patient would have bled to death. But this one came through it, and did very well.

I followed the patient later to his home. Also, I looked back through the laboratory records of Queen Square and found, in all, seven such tumors that had been operated upon by Horsley and two by Sargent. I copied out the history of each and visited the ones who had survived. Alas, I could not show the results to Horsley, now four years dead. But I prepared the study for publication with the permission and the help of the pathologist, Dr. Greenfield. It was a previously unrecognized type of tumor growth that I thought very exciting.

I finished the writing up of these cases in 1921 after reaching New York, during the time of indecision as to whether to move to Baltimore. William H. Welch studied the sections with me. Then, seeing that a substantial cash prize was offered, the Warren Triennial Prize at the Massachusetts General Hospital for a new contribution to science, I submitted the paper hopefully, for we did need the money at that stage. More than a year later, when I had received no notice of the committee's decision, I wrote again to the judges to ask what had been done about the prize. I learned then that it had gone long since to another competitor. It went to one of the two brilliant brother scientists, Cecil or Phillip Drinker. I cannot now remember which one.

My manuscript was returned to me then with the explanation

that it had been forgotten after it was given to Harvey Cushing for his review. I published this paper in England and reported a further study of the same material in the United States. (See W. Penfield, "Cranial and Intracranial Endotheliomata — Hemicraniosis," *Surgery, Gynecology and Obstetrics,* May 1923, pages 657–674.) In an inconspicuous place in this publication, I inserted a footnote (page 660): "This paper, as published, was entered in the competition for the Warren Triennial Prize at the Massachusetts General Hospital in April, 1922."

Victor Horsley and his pupil Percy Sargent belonged to the early neurosurgeons. Cushing, Jefferson, Dandy and others are technically separated from them in the modern school of neurosurgery. It was the transformation of surgical technique led by William Halsted that separated the two schools.

The priority for the recognition that these meningeal fibroblastomas (endotheliomas) grew into the Haversian canal system of the skull and led to the formation of new bone should go to Sir Victor Horsley. He realized what he was dealing with and rescued the patients. Only he did not publish his findings. I am glad to have been, in a sense, his posthumous coauthor.

Looking back at the old Presbyterian Hospital I see it in the golden light of the nineteen twenties. There was in it a fine tradition of human kindness, which, thanks to the new alliance with Columbia University, went hand in hand with the best in medical science. In the hospital lunchroom, quick consultations took place at midday among those who made up the attending staff. Lasting friendships that one treasures were formed there amid a genial din of talk and laughter. Dean Darrach, with the help of the medical and surgical chiefs, Walter Palmer and Allen Whipple, created a splendid clinical center for thoughtful study and treatment. For patients, it was an oasis where they could come for healing or, failing that, comfort and consolation amid the vast turmoil of New York City.

5

Keys to Understanding

Madrid, 1924

In the autumn of 1923 when Allen Whipple, my surgical chief in the Presbyterian Hospital, decided that I had served long enough as general surgeon and could carry on, handling the brain surgery exclusively, I entered the stage in life toward which I had been working since I left the Johns Hopkins with the title of "Doctor" five years before. Those five years of special training were past. Time was now my own, time in which to reflect, to plan and to work.

Now I would care for, or give an opinion in regard to, the patients who needed me throughout the Presbyterian Hospital as before. But now I could find more time for the research that beckoned to me.

Two years earlier, on arrival in New York, I had met William Clarke in his laboratory of surgical pathology and had decided to attempt what he proposed, to demonstrate by cell stains the process of healing in the animal brain after experimental wounds had been made. I hoped this would be the first step toward a better surgical operation for the cure of epilepsy. My results were mediocre. I had come to a dead end and I knew it.

The staining methods I had used up till now were those I had learned in Oxford and London. They were in use in the foremost medical clinics around the world. And yet there were many cells in every section that showed their presence only in ghostly outline.

These were not the nerve cells, not the neurons that flash their electric currents back and forth along delicate wirelike branches as they carry out the actual work of the brain. That neuron network is man's marvelous minicomputer. It discharges the business of the mind. No. These unstained cells were different. They were non-nervous.

It was said that they nourished and supported the neurons but no one could see what they were doing and I could not tell how they might be changing while the brain recovered from injury. Perhaps if I could demonstrate these cells clearly I might understand the healing process in the brain and discover why a healing scar is followed so often by epilepsy in animals as well as man.

I recalled a time, four years before, when I was a postgraduate student at Oxford and had followed another trail of investigation to a dead end. My problem then concerned nerve cells, the neurons themselves. I was searching with the microscope for the evidence of fatigue that others had seemed to see in the voluntary motor cells of the spinal cord.

My results had been negative. But Sir Charles Sherrington had said: "Don't give up until you have tried the methods of Ramón y Cajal. The techniques," he added, "are probably described in Spanish in the *Cajal Transactions*. Cajal was here, you know, in England once, just long enough to accept a doctorate from Cambridge, *honoris causa*. He stayed with me. He sent me some volumes of the *Transactions* of his laboratory after he returned to Madrid. I put them in the library."

So, I had gone to the Radcliffe Library and, copying out some methods, tried them. One of them gave me what I needed. I was thrilled. It was simple and clear. I saw nerve cells as I had never seen them before, and in them, such structures as the Golgi apparatus. I drew them and photographed them, and Oxford University gave me a research degree (bachelor of science) when I submitted the study as a university thesis.

At Oxford, histology was taught in the Department of Physiology, not in the Anatomy Department, as in other medical schools. H. M. Carleton was the histologist. He and I tried out various Spanish methods during that year, 1919 to 1920, using gold or silver in solution to impregnate sections of the brain. Our attempts were not always successful, of course. But sometimes they had brilliant results. We enjoyed these explorations. He called me jokingly, I remember, "Ramón," and I gave him the nickname of "Hortega," the most impressive of Cajal's pupils.

When I moved on to London and worked in Godwin Greenfield's laboratory of neuropathology at Queen Square, I marveled at how little information the standard paraffin and celloidin techniques revealed as compared with my glimpses of the frozen section preparations of the Spanish school of cytologists. Greenfield, however, and other pathologists around the world, seemed to distrust the Spanish methods and found no use for them.

Sometime in the autumn of 1923, Sherrington's words came back to me: "Don't give up until you have tried the methods of Ramón y Cajal." So I turned again to the library — forlorn hope! This time, with Spanish dictionary in hand, I went to the New York Academy of Medicine. I found pictures that seemed to represent the cells I could not stain and a method reported in Spanish for staining them. Returning to the Presbyterian, I set up the techniques as well as I could, and began to teach the little orderly from the public ward how to be my technician. With the very first sections, the outlook changed. It was the Oxford experience all over again. Very exciting, but also very confusing. What I saw was difficult to interpret. Occasionally cells stood out, clear and complete, as I had never seen them before.

Finally — I suppose it was early in January 1924 — I asked for an interview with Professor Whipple. He had, by now, become my understanding friend. But I hardly thought he would listen to the request I was about to make. I began with a little preamble.

"When I arrived here in June 1921," I said, "and you took me on the staff as your neurosurgeon, you said you were doing it because of my experience as a neurophysiologist and neuropathologist and neurologist. I confessed to you that I was no neurosurgeon, not yet, and you said you and the other surgeons would teach me surgery. I'm very grateful to you for that. I like surgery and especially neurosurgery. But I'm going to ask you something now, not because I am a surgeon but because there is a little something of the other three, physiologist, pathologist and neurologist, inside me still. They want me to stop and go off on a crazy expedition." He looked at me quizzically and waited.

"As soon as the medical school opened that first year," I went on, "you sent me to help teach in Bill Clarke's course of surgical pathology. Bill laughed at me, coming here as a brain surgeon, but unable to tell him how the brain heals. I knew he had a secret desire for a set of teaching slides to use in teaching surgical pathology to medical students. But he had another purpose too. He wanted to see me approach brain surgery as a critical scientist should. So we laid out a plan of investigation in his laboratory.

"Well, I've carried out the experiments. We have the microscopical slides. They are stained by the commonly accepted techniques. It took me two years to do it and I've almost finished writing a paper to summarize and analyze the results." Whipple nodded and smiled but said nothing. "I hoped," I continued, "that it would throw some light on the cause of epilepsy. It doesn't. I suspect the trouble lies in the fact that neither I nor anyone else can see the complete microscopical picture. But I must admit now that even if we do come to see it clearly, it is possible that we won't know any better how to treat patients. Nevertheless, I have a plan."

I hesitated. I was afraid he might think I had lost my mind. He looked at me as if nothing from me would surprise him and said, "Well, Pen! Why not drop the other shoe?"

"I want to take six months off from the Presbyterian Hospital this spring," I blurted out, "and go to Spain to learn the Spanish methods and have those histologists explain what the sections show. Can you make it possible for me to take Helen and the two children with me? And go to Madrid?"

"Madrid!" Allen Whipple laughed. "For bullfights perhaps, and for art certainly. But I've never heard of anyone going to Madrid to study anything medical or scientific."

"Yes, I know. No one ever has, as far as I can discover. But, all the same, I would have gone there from London, before returning to New York, if my funds had not run out. You remember, perhaps, that the Nobel Prize went to Santiago Ramón y Cajal in physiology and medicine?" Allen nodded, so I hurried on. "That was eighteen years ago. He shared the prize with an Italian, Camillo Golgi. Golgi refused to speak to him when they presented themselves at Stockholm because Cajal had started his research by using his, Golgi's, method. Golgi evidently thought the whole prize should have been his."

I saw I had caught Whipple's interest now.

"Cajal has gradually gathered a school of Spanish cytologists about him since he received the Nobel award. Their contribution to the knowledge of the brain is vastly greater than that of Golgi or of any other microscopist, in my opinion. They have always hidden the reports of their work away in Spanish journals. But in the drawings published by one of them, Pio del Rio-Hortega, the cells, which are no more than ghosts in my standard preparations, stand out sharp and clear, each cell body and nucleus and fiber and granule.

"The Spanish scientists use silver and gold to impregnate cells selectively. In their hands it's like depth photography. I've tried to make Hortega's method work on the brain scars and Percival Bailey has tried it on the brain-tumor material in Cushing's collection. Neither of us can produce anything to compare with the brilliance of the pictures del Rio-Hortega publishes." *

Whipple was shaking his head now, but I wasn't about to stop. "Perhaps," I said, "if I could use their methods properly, I might do something constructive with these brain scars of mine. But there's more to it than that, much more! The Spanish scientists have been studying normal animals, mostly rabbits. What I want to do is to use their methods to study the brain of man, and then move on to the effects of disease on the brain. And there may be other things we can discover."

But Dr. Whipple held up his hand. "Pen, I just haven't enough money left in my budget." He shook his head again. I waited anxiously. Without his help, I could see no light ahead. Presently he slapped his knee. It was a habit he had, when something occurred to him.

"I operated on the daughter of Mrs. Percy Rockefeller," he said. "It was when we were inaugurating the full-time plan two or three years ago, and I made no charge whatever for the operation. . . . She seemed grateful. . . . If she would help . . ."

He stood up suddenly. "Pen, I think you *ought* to go, as soon as possible. We can carry on here without you, for six months. We will turn over the neurosurgical cases to Elsberg. I'll let you know what I can arrange."

He was leaving the room now, but he turned in the doorway. "I

* See note 9.

only wish Mary and I could go along with you." He laughed again. "Spain! Madrid!" Then he added thoughtfully: "Bill Clarke is right, you know. Each of us should make his own approach to surgery as a critical scientist. This is what Halsted did when he went to Johns Hopkins nearly forty years ago. It is what I am trying to do all over again here at the Presbyterian. If you really *must* go to Spain to do your job — well, I'll arrange it, if I can."

Mrs. Rockefeller did help him. But I do not know to what extent.* When Whipple said "go," that was enough for me. I wrote to Señor Don Pio del Rio-Hortega, care of the Instituto Cajal, Madrid, since I had no other address, asking his permission to study with him. This was the man who had published the method that gave me such startling results.

I began at once to take Spanish lessons at the Berlitz School twice a week in downtown New York and it was typical of my wife's response to a challenge that she journeyed from Riverdale downtown, ten miles through the subway, to the Berlitz School to take each lesson with me. We even invited a young Puerto Rican to dine with us six days a week so we could "talk" Spanish.

Then we offered our house for rent. Although no bidder appeared, we booked passage on a small French liner, the S.S. *Rousillon,* for Vigo, Spain.

But still no word came from Madrid. As the time of departure approached, I cabled Hortega desperately. No response. We sailed on schedule, late in March of 1924, wondering what would come of it all.

When we were halfway across the Atlantic, Hortega's reply was forwarded to us by wireless from New York. One word only, "Venga" (Come). I looked up the word *venir,* to come. *Venga* was the imperative form usually applied to a child or a dog. *Bien*

---

* Others helped Whipple to finance this project privately. I am delighted to record now something that I never knew: Elsberg was one of them. In 1970, I learned from Dr. Fritz Kramer of New York that his reading of Charles Elsberg's correspondence showed that he sent Whipple, at this time, a check for two hundred fifty dollars toward "Penfield's trip to Spain." It is clear enough from my own records that, financially, I was sailing very close to the wind! In my letters home from Spain, this note appears: "Madrid, May 25, 1924: We received a check this week from Allen Whipple, which pulls us out of a very awkward financial hole."

venido was recommended to signify "Come and be welcome." But the wireless message said only "Venga."

There, in mid-ocean, I wrote a speculative letter to my mother in California:

"We spent the night, Monday, before sailing, downtown with Allen and Mary Whipple, and it made the getting-off a simple procedure. I went to the hospital with Allen at eight in the morning and sent off the second paper [for publication] that was to be finished before sailing. This one is on the pathology of brain wounds and adhesions. . . . I can get no farther until I learn something more about neuroglia cells in Madrid.

"Here we are on the high sea, and where are we going as far as the future is concerned? The house in Riverdale was not rented when we left, and we simply must have that income. My ability to build up any private practice is very doubtful. The well-to-do all go to Elsberg. The point is I've done nothing to justify their coming to me. . . . I do not see the way toward a solution of the hydrocephalus problem or epilepsy. There is not the slightest guarantee that any guiding clue lies ahead in the direction I am taking. I am at the height of my power at thirty-three and still reaching out for new weapons . . . using none.

"Anyway," the letter added grimly, "our bridges are burned. If I do get this last weapon in Madrid, shall I be able to see how to use it? Or, will it be the wrong weapon? . . .

"Last night," the letter concluded, "we studied two Berlitz Spanish lessons, danced a little, and read aloud from *Rosinante to the Road Again.* [That was a recent book by John Dos Passos.] It was very pleasant and the storm and terrible seasickness of the day before were quite forgotten."

I remember how the title of the Dos Passos book echoed in my thinking — *Rosinante to the Road Again.* Rosinante was the horse that carried Don Quixote from La Mancha out into the wide world where he was prepared, he thought, to set its wrongs right, just as we were. Rosinante, to quote the description given by Cervantes, was a horse "so lean, lank, meager, drooping, sharp-backed and raw-boned as to excite much curiosity and mirth."

This expedition of ours to Spain had aroused much curiosity among our friends and, I suppose, some mirth. After all, why should a surgeon be the first foreigner to come to the Cajal school as a disciple? Why should I not have been satisfied with neurology as it was, a diagnostic art, and neurosurgery as a treatment for tumors and the relief of pain? Why hope to operate on epileptics? Why inquire into everything? Was I, after all, as mad as Don Quixote? Here I came, riding a western Rosinante back to La Mancha, expecting to be taught as a sober scientist! And Helen was following her mad young surgeon-husband like a credulous peasant girl, like Quixote's lady of love, Dulcinea del Toboso! Allen Whipple's words came back to me: "If you really *must* go to Spain to do your job . . ." Even he had doubts.

This was a lonely project. But perhaps there is, in all research, a time when a man is all alone and must struggle against his own doubts. Even when he holds to his course, doubts go along with him and mingle with the questions at the back of his mind. But, as I have said, we had burned our bridges. I could only explore now. Most explorers are thought to be mad by someone, and all explorers are lonely. Perhaps a touch of madness is a help — that and the knowledge that someone, like Dulcinea, believes in you.

Our landing in Vigo, capital of the province of Galicia, and our onward train travel to Madrid, were described by my Dulcinea herself in a letter to a group of her former college classmates. It showed at least that the mad Quixote managed to be happy as well as grim, and that Dulcinea was always cheerful as well as courageous.

We found temporary lodgings in Madrid in a large *pension.* Here we discovered that Ramón y Cajal was known to everyone. In fact, he seemed to be a national hero. But no one had ever heard of Hortega. On further inquiry, I discovered that Hortega had a laboratory of his own in the Residencia des Estudiantes (a university students' residence) situated in the outskirts of the city.

On the first morning after our arrival, I walked out along the Avenida Castellana, marveling at the beauty of Madrid in early spring. The laboratory was housed in a single, L-shaped room. I knocked. When no one answered, I pushed the door open and saw a series of tables, one after another, placed beside each window in the outer wall. At each table, a man was sitting, with a microscope and small glass dishes and bottles before him. I advanced hesitantly. Not knowing what to say, I said nothing. Turning the corner of the room, I discovered more men at tables. At last, someone rose, a little man who had been sitting at a larger desk placed at the far end. There were no technicians, no secretaries, no doors into other rooms.

Those seated at the tables had looked up as I entered, while the hum of conversation ebbed away and silence fell. Here was a test for my Berlitzian command of the Spanish language! But I made the plunge. The man at the desk smiled politely and came to meet me. This was Pio del Rio-Hortega — a slender man in his mid-thirties, with high forehead, black hair and a small mustache. He had the strong, handsome features of a Castilian noble and the quiet dignity of a gentleman. He seated me at the only vacant table. It was next to his desk. I was heartened to realize that I was expected, at any rate.

From the large laboratory windows, we looked out northward, across the barren plain of Castile to a magnificent mountain range, the snow-capped Sierra de Guadarrama. I took stock of the situation. There were ten of us, each at his own table, the master — they called him "Don Pio" with quiet respect — and nine disciples of whom I was now one. Two of the nine, I learned later, J. Jimenez Asua and C. Collado, had, like Hortega himself, worked in Cajal's laboratory some years, before Hortega withdrew from Cajal to set up this daughter laboratory.

The "master" began his teaching at once, that first morning, by taking me, step by step, through the cutting of sections for the microscope. He carried me through each step of his own silver carbonate technique. This would, he said, visualize the special cells that had baffled me. They were the ones that had shown themselves only as "ghosts" or naked nuclei in my New York preparations. It was for this I had come to Spain. These cells made up most of the "third element." That term had been introduced by Cajal to suggest that these cells were actually different from neurons and neuroglia. In regard to this, I gathered, there had been a difference of opinion between Cajal and Hortega himself.

After this initial demonstration, it was clear that I was on my own — like the other workers in this strange laboratory. But no longer alone. For now I had the means I needed and could ask for the guidance and interpretation I had come for. I could study the question of the "third element" for myself, since Hortega and Cajal seemed to differ.

Don Pio del Rio-Hortega at his desk in his laboratory in the spring of 1924 (Residencia des Estudiantes, Madrid). This was a time exposure photograph taken with my simple box camera. "Al gran artista de la oligodendroglia y de la fotografía y excelente amigo — Dr. Wilder G. Penfield, P. del Rio-Hortega."

I looked about at my companions. They were all Spanish physicians or medical students, men of differing types, from swarthy to nearly blond. Each seemed to be working on his own project, using some application of the Hortega or the Cajal methods.

Let me describe the procedure:

You cut a small block of tissue, from a rabbit brain immersed in the formalin fixative, and washed it. Then you carried the block to the freezing microtome. When it was frozen solid on the stand, you swung the heavy, well-balanced, carefully sharpened razor back and forth, cutting thin sections that fell into the water of your petri dish. With twenty or thirty such slices floating in the water, you carried it back to your table. These were the sections. They were like small, blank squares of white paper.

From that stage onward, the sections were passed, one at a time, through a series of solutions and washings. One of the solutions impregnated the tissue of each section selectively. A glass rod was used to lift each delicate slice of brain from dish to dish until you decided to mount it. The mounting process was always the same. You passed the section through alcohol and carbo-xylol to get rid of the water, placed it on a glass slide, and blotted it with absorbent paper. When it was dry, you put a drop of clear sticky Canada balsam on it. This was Canada's contribution. Then, after you had placed a thin glass cover-slip on the balsam and pressed it down, you had the permanent preparation.

The brain slice was now between two layers of glass and everything in it was clear and transparent except what had been stained by the silver. When such a slide is placed on the microscope stand, you look through the tissue and see only what the silver reveals. If the staining is not satisfactory, the slide is discarded and you carry other sections through the staining sequence, using small modifications or additions. I came to realize that, with care and patience, selective staining might be possible for almost any and all of the cell structures within the brain. This was truly selective photography.

As the days grew into weeks, I wondered why Hortega and Cajal had separated. There was silence and an air of mystery about this. Hortega spoke of his master only with deep respect and admiration. I had heard rumors of jealousy before coming to Spain. But I soon discovered that it was Cajal who had established Hortega in this new laboratory. It was Cajal who had made provision for his support. Cajal had influence with the government, even with the then-dictatorial government of General Primo de Rivera and with the reigning king, Alfonso XIII.

Finally, some weeks after our arrival, it was arranged that I should call on the great man, Don Santiago Ramón y Cajal. When the appointed hour approached, Hortega, who had had plenty of time to go with my wife and me to the theater, or to see the paintings in the Prado, was "too busy" to go with me to make this call. On occasional Sundays, he and his friend Gomez del Moral had even guided my wife and me to Toledo and Aranjuez and to the Escorial to see where Philip II had lived out his life in seclusion like a monk.

Hortega's first assistant, Jimenez Asua, was instructed to introduce me. He had sent reprints of my few publications to Cajal in advance, and I recalled with satisfaction that I had referred to the old master with admiration in two of them, written at Oxford.

Cajal's original laboratory was on the third floor of a building in which there were other university laboratories. The third floor was called the Instituto Cajal. We found him, as the weekly letter to my mother explained, "in a book-filled room," sitting at the end of a long table.

"May 11, 1924. . . . He [Cajal] was slouched far down in his big armchair so that only his head and shoulders appeared. He remained seated while Asua explained to him that I had thought to wait until I spoke the language well, but that I had come without a proper command of Spanish to be presented, as I could wait no longer. Don Santiago got up very slowly and shook hands. He is short and stocky. He has a prominent Roman nose and a strong chin, half-concealed by a very sparse white beard.

"He talked to Asua," the letter continued, "about what a bar language is and then turned to his obsession, of which I had heard before. He passed his hand over a long shelf of books. [I could read the word *Trabajos* on the books spines, which means the Transactions of his laboratory.] 'Look at these,' he exclaimed, 'buried, almost lost, in Spanish. Every day I read something, especially in German, published as new work, and it was done here carefully by many methods, sometimes thirty-five years ago.' Then he added, and his voice broke, 'It is tragic, tragic.' "

When Cajal observed that I was in fact understanding his remarks in spite of Asua's slighting introduction, he brightened up a little and, turning away from Asua, talked to me.

"We changed the *Trabajos*," he said, "last year, to French entirely. I would rather publish it in English as it is now the most widely read language and they are more interested in our work in England and America. But it is not possible to find in Madrid a man who can translate our papers into good English and who also knows biology well."

"After this explanation," my letter continued, "Cajal took me to the outer door where I seized my hat and cane. I thought he was through with me. But then he turned around and took me back into the laboratory and showed it to me and introduced me to Sr. Sanchez, a gray-haired man who showed me, with great enthusiasm, sections of the eyes of insects stained with silver."

When Cajal "turned around and took me back into the laboratory," his manner had changed. He seemed to look at me as a person for the first time. I felt less like an intruder and presently I put my hat and cane down again. But before long his interest in me must have run out for the letter to my mother concluded dryly:

"Cajal looked at his watch and I looked at Asua. But at that moment, a young fellow, Fernando de Castro, came in. Cajal seemed to brighten up and said Castro was master of his (Cajal's) gold method for neuroglia and suggested that I could work sometimes at a table where Castro would teach me."

Cajal left us then and I did stay on to talk with Castro. Dr. Sanchez insisted that I should examine with his microscope the complicated structure of an insect's brain, explaining that the brain of an ant or a bee was just as vast in its complexity as the brain of man or any other mammal. I marveled at what he showed me and at the beautiful sections of mammalian sympathetic nerve cells on Castro's desk.

Finally I took my leave and, walking back to Hortega's laboratory on the outskirts of the city, I wondered again what had come between Cajal and Hortega. Cajal's depression must have been a factor. I realized that the focus of work in his laboratory was on the nerve cell and its connections, while the attention of Hortega and his disciples had shifted to non-nervous cells. It was clear that I had come to the man who could help me most.

I had been astonished to discover Cajal, the Nobel laureate, so slow, depressed and concerned with recognition. It was not true that he was ignored. His great monograph on the microscopical anatomy of the brain, published in French, was in use wherever there were any serious students of the nervous system, all around the world. It seemed to me quite clear that, at seventy-two, he was suffering from a true depression that had come on recently and not from senility or "cerebral arteriosclerosis of the brain," as he himself suggested in a newspaper interview at about that time.*

I did, on occasion, return to the Instituto Cajal during the remainder of my 1924 stay in Madrid. I consulted the books in the library, I asked questions. But I did not work at the vacant table next to Fernando de Castro; no man can serve two masters.

But I worked on, day by day, sitting at the desk beside Don Pio del Rio-Hortega. From time to time, I would show him a section, as did his other disciples. He would nod or shake his head. Then, he might suggest a modification. But the search for clear, selective impregnation was each man's own problem. I carried out most of the Spanish methods at least once and wrote the details down in a card index for future reference. But I wasted little time on Cajal's methods or the study of nerve cells themselves. Cajal had been doing that for a quarter of a century himself, and there was little hope that a neophyte like me would stumble on anything significant there. On the other hand, it was equally clear that if one desired to throw new light on the effect of disease, or injury, and on the process of healing in the brain, the best hope lay in the study of the non-nervous cells, using Hortega's little-tried methods.

Of the non-nervous cells, there are three types: first, the well-known *astrocytes* (or star cells) that men had long called "neuroglia" (*neuroglia* is the Greek word for "nerve glue"). They are the true supporting cells in the brain. Second and third, there are the two types of cells that made up the mysterious "third element," which only Hortega's method would stain. This third element, I could see quite clearly now, was made up of *oligodendroglia* ("few-branching glue-cells") — I like to shorten that word to "oligo" — and *microglia* ("small glue-cells"). They are the little

* I might add that in 1932, eight years later, my wife and I returned to Madrid only to find Cajal working again at high speed. Hortega went with me then to call on him in his home and it was plain to see that the understanding relationship of master and disciple had been restored.

scavengers of the brain that grow big with scavenging immediately after injury of any kind to the brain.

It is always the unexplored that challenges an investigator. By now, I had glimpsed an undiscovered country. There was a spirit of proud excitement among us all. It was, I suppose, akin to the contagious spirit that must activate a group of sincerely dedicated artists at work.

One morning, I was thrilled to see that the "oligo" cells in one of my sections were especially clear, complicated and beautiful. The cells were not "few-branching" but many-branching. I set the slide down and ran more of the sections through the solutions, using exactly the same timing and modifications. When I had mounted them all on slides and examined them, I found the results were equally good. So I made a careful note of the times, the heat used, and the strength of the solutions.

Then I stood up and handed a section to Don Pio. Without a word, he put it on his microscope and examined it, as usual under a low power of magnification. He did not look up. But he whirled the carrier of the lenses on his microscope and set the section under the high-power oil-lens with a magnification of one hundred times. I waited. Finally, he turned and said quietly, handing the section back, "Casi mejor que yo" ("Almost better than I could do"). I might have laughed at his use of the word "almost." But no. I could expect no higher praise.

Later in the day, Don Pio sat down beside me and asked if I would not like to publish a confirmation of oligodendroglia as a cell group in the central nervous system. His pupil Collado had done this for microglia but no one had done it for oligo. I realized, and I am sure he did, that it would mean much more if the first published confirmation of oligodendroglia came from a foreigner.

I agreed, of course. So I began to make drawings of the cells, staining them in different regions of the rabbit's brain. Don Pio lent me his paintbrushes and showed me how to make use of black paint instead of crayon, and how to shade, and how to add highlights. Here was an unexpected art specialty that Cajal and he and Castro had developed to a high degree of perfection.

He showed me, too, another method he had not yet published. I used it and saw the beautiful round granules, the gliosomes, stand

Oligodendroglia satellites. A, adjacent to neuron; B, adjacent to neuron and blood vessel.

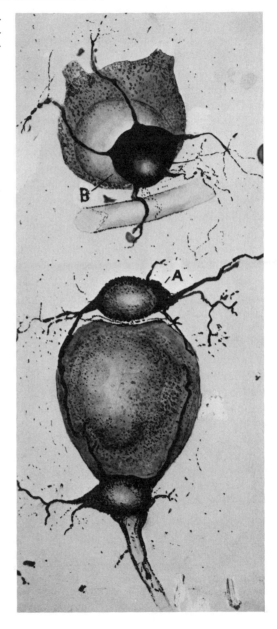

out crystal clear in the body of each cell and extending out along its branching expansions. I sent the oligo paper with the drawings away and it was published in *Brain,* the leading British journal of neurology. The time had come for a fearless, disinterested judgment. Any Spaniard would have found it difficult to criticize Cajal even as mildly as I did.

"Oligodendroglia," I wrote, "has received no confirmation as yet, though accepted by several writers. This is probably due to two causes; first, the difficulty of staining this element, and second, the fact that Cajal, repeating the work of his disciple, was unable to stain these cells, and, although he confirmed microglia as a group, he cast considerable doubt upon the validity of del Rio-Hortega's description of the remaining portion of the cells previously termed by Cajal 'the third element.' " Then came the criticism, sugarcoated as it was: "As Cajal, the great master of neurohistology, has himself so often pointed out, it is extremely dangerous to assign value to negative results." *

I was ready for this which was a clear demonstration of the anatomy of the phantom cells that had baffled me so long. The microscopic study of the anatomy of cells is called cytology. But I was impatient. This was not enough; I wanted to move on. I wanted to make cytology the beginning of better pathology. And also, there was so much more to do. Oligodendroglia made up only half of the third element. There were also the microglia to understand.

I had brought along with me a microscopical section I had prepared in New York by Hortega's microglia method. It showed the brain of a patient of mine. Poor fellow! He had died from the expanding pressure of a malignant brain tumor and had come to autopsy. I had not understood what the section showed in New York; there were so many shapes of cells. As I restudied this section now, with the help of Hortega, it came clear. Suddenly I understood it all. I could see what the microglial cells had been doing. So I wrote another paper, that spring, to explain it to others and planned to publish it in the United States in a pathological journal. Curiously enough, it was based on that one single section.

---

* W. Penfield, "Oligodendroglia and Its Relation to Classical Neuroglia" (from El Instituto Cajal, Laboratorio de Histopatología, Madrid), *Brain,* 47:430–452, 1924.

Microglia cells appear in one form when at rest in a normal brain. When there is injury or destruction at any point within the brain, whatever the cause may be, the microglia cells that are near the disturbance change within hours. Soon they are transformed into amoebalike scavenger cells that actually wander through the tissue and devour the broken parts of the dead cells and their branches.*

What would Cajal say when he should read what I had written? It was an elaboration of Hortega's thinking about the "third element," little more than that. But I was writing frankly, without considering the pride of previous workers. It was joy to prepare these two papers. So many things that had puzzled me seemed simple now. I could understand what happens in the brain after injury and during the healing process. And you, the reader, although you cannot see the drawings, will understand it easily. It is so simple. That is apt to be true in science. When you have the answer, it all seems suddenly so simple.

The fact is, nerve cells that are directly involved in a wound are apt to die. They do not grow again. At the same time, the microglia go into action, at once, as wonderfully mobile scavenger cells. The oligodendroglia cells, like the nerve cells, die if close at hand. Or, if a little farther off, they multiply, increasing thus in number. The nearest neuroglia astrocytes may die at once. The remaining astrocytes subdivide and multiply promptly. They grow larger and form heavy fibrils.

If something breaks through the brain's pia mater lining, the cells of connective tissue from without grow into the brain, intermingling with the astrocytes and forming the scar of so-called healing. But the scar, it seems, never rests. It goes on contracting. And something detrimental, yet to be analyzed, persists.

Hortega and I began to discuss the question that was always at the back of my mind. Why should the healing scar ever become the cause of epilepsy? We decided to make a new experimental series, studying simple wounds made in the brains of rabbits. It was, in fact, a much-simplified repetition of my New York series of experiments. We began at once that spring and studied the scars at short, graduated intervals, using his simple methods. I carried the specimens away to be worked over in New York and be-

* See note 10.

come a combined publication. But Pio procrastinated. This was his old-time enemy. I could not get our results into print for three years, not until 1927.

This was a portentous moment in Spanish history. It was the period immediately preceding the Spanish Civil War. Next door to Hortega's laboratory in the Residencia des Estudiantes was the University Laboratory of Physiology. Juan Negrin was the professor. He was to become the leader of the Communist uprising twelve years later. It was also a time of remarkable renaissance of Spanish culture. The conversations that went on in the laboratories of Madrid had more to do with the promising work of Spanish artists and writers and musicians than they had to do with medicine.

Madrid seemed very far away from the rest of the world in 1924 and, on the whole, the Spaniards we met were quite content to have it so. Not one of the medical men we met could speak a word of English. A few spoke French. But their command of the language was too halting to be of practical use. They showed us delightful courtesy, however, and our own communication in Spanish became meaningful, if never musical.

I never did ask Don Pio why he had not answered my letters, or why he had been so long with his reply to my desperate telegram. It was Fernando de Castro, Cajal's leading disciple, who told me confidentially that a technician in the Instituto Cajal was a bitter enemy of Hortega and was largely responsible for his break with Cajal. Mail addressed to Hortega at the Instituto Cajal, where I had addressed him, he added, would have been forwarded by this technician, if forwarded at all. The suggestion was that Hortega might have received my message after undue delay.

I may add that when I heard from Percival Bailey, working in Cushing's clinic, that he, too, had written to Hortega without a reply (he had written to invite Hortega to visit Boston), I ventured to ask Hortega if he had ever heard from Bailey. He said yes. But he added, "Bailey is dead." I assured him that this was not the case since I had just heard from him. But next day, to my astonishment, Hortega brought to the laboratory a clipping from *The Times* of London, which reported the death of a "Percival Bailey" who had been hanged for some crime that I do not now recall. When I laughed at this, Pio was not amused. Nor was Percival Bailey, quite understandably, but for a different reason, when I told him on our return.

I record this story here only to show how distant the rest of the world must have seemed to those who lived and worked at their microscopes in Madrid during the nineteen twenties. I must add, in fairness to Cajal's "technician," that during the years that followed, Hortega could rarely bring himself to write me a letter, although he sent an occasional tardy telegram.

In any case, I went to the laboratory at eleven each morning and, after we had become well acquainted with Don Pio during our weekend excursions, Pio even suggested to my wife that she should come along with me to the laboratory. So, Dulcinea began to walk with her mad Quixote, each morning, out along the tree-lined Avenida Castellana. We deposited a son of seven and daughter of five in a "modern" Spanish school on the way, where they could at least play the games and sing the songs in Spanish. The spring was lovely, the flowers and the bougainvillea beautiful. From deep in Retiro Park, the mockingbirds made distant music that we shall never forget.

When Dulcinea did appear at the laboratory and when she even remained through the morning session from eleven o'clock to two, it must have shattered certain Spanish precedents. She was introduced to microscopes and before long she was making some of the drawings of cells needed as background for the illustrations in my forthcoming publication. Soon, too, Don Pio asked her to give him an hour of instruction each morning in English. And I chuckled to myself to hear him reading the day's lesson taken from a child's story so soberly in English. Meanwhile his pupils, sitting at their tables, stopped their flow of Spanish conversation to listen with respect, if not with understanding, to the utter nonsense of *John Martin's Magazine*.

In the cool of the evening, we might spend time with Alice (the Swedish maid of all work who had come with us from New York) and the children in the park. The theaters did not open their doors until eleven o'clock. But there was always the Spiedum Café where Hortega and his boon companions gathered for their *tertulia*. One might sit there, after purchasing one small cup of coffee, on into the cool, fragrant hours that follow a summer midnight in Madrid, and walk home under a heaven of stars that seemed to burn with unparalleled brilliance.

In the end, I found that my concern as to Cajal's reaction to the fearless attitude taken in the two papers prepared for publication was groundless. He was not a man of small caliber. If he had been hurt by the fact that I had come to Hortega and not to him, he forgave me. He must have sent for Hortega. At any rate, they arranged together that both papers be published in Spain as well as abroad. When Cajal had one of them translated into French for inclusion in his own beloved *Laboratory Transactions,* I wondered to myself: Was he accepting me as his pupil after all? Or was he putting behind him whatever it was that had come between him and Don Pio?

I recalled the alteration that took place in his attitude during my first call at his laboratory. He had glowered at me without rising during Asua's introduction. He had been increasingly hospitable, and even courtly, when I took my leave. Did that mean he was forgiving me too for something? *

I called on Don Santiago to thank him and to pay my respects, when the close of our Spanish adventure drew near. He smiled at me and gave me his portrait, which he autographed in a clear flowing hand.†

That picture hangs today in the Montreal Neurological Institute, and I like to think that through it a great Spaniard, Santiago Ramón y Cajal, still speaks to us of his past and our future.

Why should the reader of this story have been taken from New York to Madrid and back again when the author's eventual purpose was only to explain the birth of an institute in Montreal? The answer is simple enough. The methods learned in Madrid were to point the way for me, and later for my own pupils, to make a worthwhile contribution to neuropathology and to neuroanatomy and to clinical neurology.

But there was something else that I discovered in Madrid. It

---

* The paper I had sent off to *Brain* appeared also in Spain, in English, in the *Bol. de la Soc. Española de Historia Natural,* 218, 1925. The second paper was translated into French, "Microglie et son rapport avec la dégération nevrogliale dans un gliome," and published in the *Cajal Laboratory Transactions, Trav. du Lab. de recherches biol. de l'Univ. Madrid,* 22, 277–293, 1924.
† See note 11.

had more to do with the spirit than it did with knowledge and yet it was something I could hope to hand on. A change in method or technique accounts for many things in human history.

A new technique can help to mold a man or to make him famous and to create a cause. There is no better example of this truth than the story of Ramón y Cajal himself. As a young doctor, he returned from his military service in Cuba and used his accumulated pay to buy a good German microscope and a few books and dictionaries. This made foreign methods of study available to him, and gave him such knowledge of the cellular structure of the body as there was in 1880.

He happened to try the silver staining method of an Italian, Camillo Golgi. It impregnated nerve cells specifically with a silver salt so that he could see the cells as individuals. He turned to the nervous system with it and began, at once, to think of nerve cells as separate units. This was contrary to the general belief that they were continuous with each other in what was called a *syncytium*.

With his own modifications of Golgi's technique, he soon had in his hands a new and more reliable method. Suddenly, he could see what no one else had ever seen, the almost complete detail of nerve cells and nerve connections. He enunciated the neuron theory of cellular independence and defended it all through his life, the theory that we, today, take for granted in histology.

So it was that this physician appeared unexpectedly in Spain with his microscope and his new technique in a time when Spain had little scientific communication with the rest of Europe. Working alone, he was like a man who had lit a lantern in the dark, one who had a magic key. He opened the doors all along a dark street so others could see into the secret chambers where the brain meets the mind.

It was the brain of animals that Cajal studied. But rabbit and *Homo sapiens* are strangely alike, under the pia mater; one might say they are "sisters under their skins," to paraphrase Rudyard Kipling. Cajal worked feverishly, recording what he saw. More than that, he stated what he could conclude about the working mechanisms within the brain and spinal cord. To this end, his drawings and writings were of far greater meaning than photographs ever could have been.

So it was that Ramón y Cajal became what Sir Charles Sherrington called him after his death: "The greatest anatomist of the nervous system ever known." *

Cajal must have had his true reward all through his life except, perhaps, during the period of his depression. With exploration and discovery, there comes an excitement, a fact that every child knows, but that adults tend to forget. This excitement drew kindred spirits to the young Don Santiago, among them Pio del Rio-Hortega. Nothing is more contagious than the excitement and joy of discovery. So it was that the Cajal school of medical science was born in Spain and flourished there. But strange as it may seem, it was long ignored by medical men and even distrusted. The younger members of the Spanish school of histology devoted their talents to normal structure, or neurocytology, as Cajal had done, not to the abnormal and to neuropathology.†

When del Rio-Hortega devised a new technique of his own that would demonstrate the non-nervous (third element) cells of the brain, he gave pathologists of the world a new key that would fit many locks in the study of the human brain and its abnormalities. It was for this key I had come to Spain.

With the anatomical skills I had learned in Madrid, I could now make my own fundamental scientific approach to problems in neurosurgery. And I longed to apply it to the whole field of clinical neurology. I did not realize then that this application and the excitement of using these new methods would draw kindred spirits and make it easy to form a group of our own and to organize a team for applied research.

Cajal and Hortega were scientists. They could go in their research wherever the techniques took them. But clinicians are different. We have our practical purposes. We must select our weapons and plan our researches with the patient and his unique problems in mind.

My family and I spent four and a half months in Madrid, leaving only in mid-August when even the most dedicated of Spanish neurohistologists had fled from the city's heat. Then, since our

---

* This description was written by Sir Charles Sherrington, when he himself was ninety-two years of age, in a memoir of Dr. Cajal. See Dorothy Cannon, *The Life of Cajal* (New York: Schuman, 1949).
† See note 12.

house in Riverdale had been rented, we could not return home. But, since a check in payment of that rental had arrived, we were happily in funds again, and were able to move on to France to spend six weeks in much-needed reflection and reconsideration, while Alice, the maid, visited her family in Sweden.

We visited Lyons briefly so that I could watch René Leriche and talk with him. He was a fascinating pioneer in operations on the sympathetic nerves, designed to relieve pain and improve circulation. Then we moved on to Paris, where I wrote a summary of his work with a view to publication on our return to New York.

The Spanish interlude was, as Allen Whipple had predicted it would be, a thrilling adventure for Helen and me. Rosinante served me very well in my professional career. And beyond that, all things Spanish from art and music to literature and romance fascinated us and became for us a continuing source of pleasure. We learned to love the land of Don Quixote. We found the true gold of science there, and the treasures of art, to boot.

Yes, Rosinante had served us very well.

6

Laboratory of Neurocytology

We returned to New York in September 1924. As our ship moved swiftly into the harbor and up the Hudson, the wind was blowing from the west. It brought familiar scents and memories. The towering buildings on Manhattan Island rotated silently, one after the other, when we passed them, as if in review. At last the great ship turned in a majestic circle, approaching the dock, and her deep-toned bellow sounded a challenge to this urban stronghold. It echoed all the way from the Battery on the southern tip of Manhattan north to Riverdale and Spuyten Duyvil.

As we motored northward up Fifth Avenue toward our home in Riverdale, we had a passing view of the red brick Presbyterian Hospital, sprawling along Madison Avenue just beyond the Frick mansion.

A few days later, I reported at the Presbyterian in time for surgical rounds at eight in the morning. Hugh Auchincloss, my senior on the Second Surgical Service, was already going from bed to bed. He would be operating at nine. Johnny St. John and Barclay Parsons were doing the same thing on the first service, and John Hanford and Frank Meleney and Fred Van Buren. They were all there. I would see the physicians later — Bill Palmer and Dochez, Loeb and Atchley, Hangar and Lamb and the others. What friends one makes in the fellowship of medical practice!

After rounds, I went to the office of the director of surgery, as I had on my first arrival at the Presbyterian three years before. Allen Whipple smiled his understanding smile.

"Well, Pen, did you find what you hoped to find in Spain?"

"Yes," I replied, "I'm ready for work. I can do the job now."

"Thank heavens," he grunted. "I'm glad you're back. We have plenty of work for you right here. This is a big hospital. It has been hard to get our neurological and neurosurgical work done while you were gone. Now, Bill Palmer [professor of medicine] tells me he would like to have you see the consultations on the Medical Service and in the Medical Outdoor Department. I expect you to take charge of neurosurgery on the wards and in the Outdoor. Purdy Stout wants you to study and report on all the neurological specimens that come to his surgical pathology laboratory. Von Glahn wants you to do the same for the neurological autopsies in the medical pathology laboratory."

I hesitated.

He looked at me in surprise. "I thought that was what you hoped to do."

"It is," I said, "exactly what I want to do. I want to study every aspect of neurology until we move uptown to the new hospital. I'm ready for the neurosurgery, and I have wonderful plans for the pathology. I'll do the best I can with what medical neurology comes along. I want to continue as a neurologist, too, in the Vanderbilt Clinic with Casamajor across the Park. But, I want more than that — a laboratory of my own where basic work can be organized, and I shall need someone to help me."

He smiled. "All right, Pen. I was afraid you would say that! I'll do my best." Then he laughed. "You have a technician now in the pathology laboratory. But you may not have him very long unless you can tone him down a bit. You'd better see von Glahn right away."

I hurried along the hospital corridor and down the stairs to medical pathology. The pathologist, Dr. von Glahn, laughed too when he saw me. Then he shook his head. "Your technician," he said, "has been working day and night to prepare better and better slides to show you on your return, using Spanish methods and all. Every time I pass that room of yours, he comes out and stops me and wants to show me 'something beautiful under the microscope.' But he is a difficult little devil. Yesterday, I understand, there was a fistfight between him and my chief technician. We must have peace. You understand!"

Then he added: "Oh, yes. Something else I must tell you. A National Research Council fellow from Iowa has drifted into the laboratory. He said he was interested in neuropathology so I told him to make himself at home with the specimens of the nervous system until you should return."

I left von Glahn and crossed the section-cutting area. A new and rather ostentatious sign had been placed over the door of "our room." It read NEUROPATHOLOGY. Edward Dockrill was moving about inside. At first glance I could see the boy had changed. He was certainly better fed and he seemed to have come almost to manhood. But I also noticed he had a very black and swollen eye. I ignored this all-too-obvious fact and admired what he could show me under the microscope. It was really excellent, some of it, and I realized that here was a young perfectionist who would learn all I was ready to teach and who might well add something independently. We laughed together and I talked of the future, and the laboratory we might have, someday, which would be all our own. When I saw that he was reassured, I left the room and started toward the broad flight of stairs that led up to the main hospital corridor.

But a young man was coming down the stairs. I guessed this might be the "National Research Council fellow." So I waited. It was. His name was William Vernon Cone, born in Conesville, Iowa, a descendant of a William Cone who had come to the Massachusetts Bay Colony from Scotland in 1646 with his English Quaker wife. Cone had big shoulders and a high forehead. So much I could see as he came down the stairs. When he reached the floor and stood beside me, I was surprised to discover that he was short and stocky — a big man on short legs. He had heavy features and wore a rather sad expression at times. But his face lit up in a delightful smile as he talked, and his eyes shone when we discussed neuropathology.

I discovered that during his vacations, while at the Medical School of the University of Iowa, he had worked in the laboratory of the psychiatric hospital, studying brain pathology under Samuel Orton. Orton was a well-known psychiatrist and an excellent neuropathologist. On receiving his M.D. degree in 1922, Cone had been awarded the National Research Council Fellowship, and so continued in clinical work and neuropathology with Orton.

Coming to New York, he retained the fellowship and expected to take training in neurology under Fred Tilney. But Tilney, Columbia's professor of neurology, was very busy with his private practice just then and with the organizing of the New York Neurological Institute. Since the institute had, as yet, no laboratory of investigation, and since Cone had no taste for the neurology of private practice, he had gravitated to this laboratory of pathology in the Presbyterian Hospital.*

We returned to the neuropathology laboratory and plunged at once, Cone and I, into an argument about neuroglia while Dockrill beamed. This had been Cone's special preoccupation as well as mine. It was a rewarding argument. He showed me a microscopic section that puzzled him. Dockrill had prepared it, using Hortega's method. I saw at once that the oligodendroglia cells were strangely swollen. I had never seen that in the rabbit brains we had studied in Madrid. This section had come from a patient who had died from tuberculous meningitis. We realized with some excitement that disease was producing a selective degenerative change in these delicate little cells. I had come to understand these cells so well when they were normal. But here was something new.

But that was only the first of a long series of arguments that we were to carry out with a microscope between us during the next thirty-six years. With these discussions, there was to come a deep affection, respect and companionship. He asked the National Research Council to transfer his fellowship to the Presbyterian Hospital.

So it was that Bill Cone, whose previous preparation and interest were so well suited to our eventual purposes, became my assistant in clinic and laboratory. He was a simple man of spectacular talent, great drive and unbounded enthusiasm. And how fortunate I was to have him come to me!

Is there not a larger destiny of which each man's career is but a part? It has always been my belief that, for everyone who is

* See note 13.

ready and willing, there is a place. It seems to wait for him or her, in some good human cause. Causes are man-made, to be sure, and, in the long run, I believe man can control the destiny of civilization on this earth. And yet I know that, beyond it all, there is an everlasting purpose, and within each one of us there is that lonely something that links us with Divinity. The link is there, to be used or disregarded. Each must make his own choice.

But I had better get back on the highroad and get on with the story I have to tell. It is enough to say that William Cone, age twenty-seven, came to work with me — whether it was good luck or a kindly providence or a destiny that waits for a man and influences his achievement.

At thirty-three, I had an apprentice who could help me and who must be taught. He learned fast. Soon, he seemed to double my potential. He became my alter ego throughout the hospital. He acquired the art of neurosurgery and patient care as if by instinct. He learned from Whipple and the other masters of general surgery in the hospital as I had done, leaping over the intern and residency sequence, reading widely, and approaching his specialty with the basic understanding of pathology and anatomy that he had already mastered.

So it came about that a few months after my return from Spain, there was another important development: a new laboratory opened its doors to serve our enlarging purposes — the Laboratory of Neurocytology. The title was rather presumptuous perhaps. But we proposed, with the help of the Spanish methods, to apply all that was new in mammalian neurocytology to the brain of man and to the problems of human pathology.

For the new laboratory, we had been given one large room in a tower that jutted out of the Presbyterian's outer wall next to the surgical operating suite. I had the room completely rebuilt. A black workbench ran along under the windows in the tower walls. This bench was subdivided marvelously by half partitions and tall cupboards that projected out into the room and gave a sort of privacy and personal convenience that would have been very welcome to me in Hortega's one-room laboratory. They were like the open-ended cells in a round beehive. This was a modification of the Spanish laboratories, set up so that we could all use the Spanish metallic methods and still carry out other maneuvers. Each worker had a window and bench of his own. The laboratory even had a small cubbyhole for visiting doctors who might, we hoped, come to us to learn technique.*

We added something to laboratory procedure, unheard of in Spain, when we secured a secretary. Fortunately it was Mrs. Laurence Gourlay, a woman of charm and intelligence. Companionship and an enthusiasm for excellence may well develop within any group of workers, small or large. But a superior person in the position of secretary can add to the morale and discipline something unique. This is a fact all too seldom recognized. Mrs. Gourlay was accurate in her own work and capable of directing the affairs of difficult men, unobtrusively and for their own good. She brought to the Laboratory of Neurocytology, crowded as it soon became, an atmosphere of loyalty, gaiety and good manners.

Into this laboratory flowed the pathological material, that had to do with the nervous system, from the whole hospital. But also, by happy arrangement with the chief surgeon of the New York Neurological Institute, Dr. Elsberg, all tissue removed at operation in that institute was sent to us by messenger. It followed, of course, that prompt reports must be made on every specimen to the department of origin. These I dictated into a dictaphone by day or by night, and Mrs. Gourlay did the rest.

The laboratory proved to be a good workshop for each of us. A grant for its budget, that first year, came as a gift from Mrs. Percy Rockefeller to Dr. Whipple, as a sequel to her donation for the travel expenses of the Penfield family to Spain. Before the year had ended, she invited me to lunch. I found that Mrs. Emmet Holt, wife of a very well known pediatrician, had been invited to be present, no doubt to serve as critical consultant to my hostess.

"I was much struck," I wrote to my mother on April 10, 1926, "by their simplicity in dress, and manner. . . . They were much interested in the work of the laboratory and made me talk at great length about neuroglia cells and the Spanish investigators." Then the beggar that I was learning to be spoke out as the letter

* See note 14.

continued: "Mrs. R. seems willing to back the work a little longer and I am writing today asking for $24,000 to carry on the work for the next two years."

In retrospect, I am astonished at my own temerity. She could not do it all at once. But in the end she gave what was needed to carry our laboratory project through all three years of its life, paying the money out with quiet anonymity. Why? I can only say that true compassion does not know the meaning of "ulterior purpose." She understood, somehow, the nature of our project and she wanted to join the cause, I suppose.

Why had the poor mother of the hydrocephalic baby given me money in a sealed envelope? She hoped, you may say, that her child might not have died in vain, hoped we might win the next therapeutic encounter. She understood it all before I told her. She said simply that she wanted to help save another woman's child. Doctors can learn the nature of compassion from their patients. This streak of kindness, this desire to help others, is born in all men and women. It lifts mankind and gives us hope for the years that lie ahead.

A week after the luncheon with Mrs. Rockefeller, my Sunday letter to Mother throws a little light on two other young neurosurgeons of the period, each making his own basic approach to the profession:

"April 18, 1926. . . . I have been in Chicago to talk to the Neurological Society about brain wounds. The invitation and the very generous payment of expenses came as very much of a surprise. It was probably due to Loyal Davis, who is the secretary of the society and is a brilliant young neurological surgeon. He is the only one specializing entirely in that in Chicago. He and Percival Bailey and I all graduated [in medicine] in 1918. Bailey is in Paris studying psychiatry and grooming himself for the chair of neurology at the University of Chicago. . . ." *

Cone and I were working very hard in 1926 and 1927 with long hours in hospital and laboratory, and there was always an unfinished manuscript on my desk at home that called to me in the evening. Sometimes I was very tired and my memory seemed to go blank. On such occasions, we broke off, when we could, and

* See note 15.

went away for a few days, my wife and I, to sleep long hours and laugh at life. I returned to the struggle, each time exultant and full of drive. Cone, on the other hand, did not seem to tire. He could rarely be induced to turn aside for diversion. My projects in neurology and neurosurgery became his projects, and his evening hours often found him in the hospital, carrying out some kindly act for a patient with the help of the intern, or working in the laboratory.

Although I was never without an unfinished manuscript, my publications were not numerous, nor were they very important. Among them, at this time (1925), was "The Career of Ramón y Cajal" (see note 12), and I discovered that authorship of this sort was a pleasant change from the writing of scientific papers. I was astonished too, and pleased as well, at the interested response this biography called forth.*

In May 1927, our little Laboratory of Neurocytology, now two years old, was recognized by the American Neurological Association at its annual meeting in Atlantic City. Cone and Richard Buckley, who had come to us as a volunteer worker from Yale, and I, read papers there in a symposium on neuroglia. Following the symposium, we had three applications from workers who wanted to come to our laboratory to learn the methods.

A combined meeting of neurologists from the United States and Great Britain was being planned for July in London. When an invitation came from one of the organizers, Theodore Weisenberg of Philadelphia, to present a paper there, I was delighted, of course, and Allen Whipple was pleased. He said I must go and he would find the money for the costs of travel, this time without my wife.†

So, I outlined another paper hurriedly, a study of how the brain heals after an injury, this time using the new Spanish methods. It was now six years since I had undertaken to get a clear picture of that process. I still hoped it would throw light on the cause of epilepsy. But I was beginning to realize that an investigator may not himself know the full significance of his

---

* See note 16.
† This British-American meeting proved to be the forerunner of the First International Neurological Congress, which was to take place in Berne four years later, in 1931.

work until he analyzes it and tries to prove his conclusions to others.

It was while I was preparing to go to London that I first heard from Montreal. I had begun to operate early that morning of June 25 in one of the operating rooms of the Presbyterian Hospital. The patient had been anesthetized by Miss Anne Penland, the anesthetist. With the help of my assistant, William Cone, I had exposed the cerebellum, preparing to remove a brain tumor. It was, we suspected, a benign growth, not a malignant one, but placed so deep beneath the surface that its removal would be difficult and perhaps dangerous to life.

A nurse came behind me and spoke quietly in the stillness:

"Dr. Edward Archibald of Montreal is here. He says you expected him."

I did expect him. He was the professor of surgery in McGill University. He had written that he would like to spend a day with me and he hoped that he would be able to watch me carry out an operation.

I turned. Another nurse was opening the door of the operating room as a man entered, gowned and capped and masked.

"Sorry to be late," he said. "What is your problem?" I told him the patient's story briefly. She was a young woman of thirty-three with everything to live for. She had a tumor within the skull. Because of its position, it had been taking from her, slowly, the control of her face and the ability to balance her body. Obviously, it would in time, if not removed, take away eyesight and life. Because of its position, I explained I was not sure whether I ought to try to remove it completely, or whether it would be kinder and wiser to settle for partial removal and temporary cure. She wanted me, especially, to bring back the movement of the left side of her face. She didn't entirely realize the gravity of the situation.

Archibald nodded, and I turned back to the problem and operated in silence. I have never been able to concentrate on more than one thing at a time. Consequently, conversation in my operating room, unless it has a practical purpose, is always a menace. Dr. Archibald watched over my shoulder silently all morning long while I removed the growth to the best of my ability.

It proved to be benign, growing within a capsule from a deep attachment to the auditory nerve. It had stretched but not broken the adjacent nerve that controls the movement of the left side of the face. It seemed likely that the control of facial expression would return. At last, when the job was done, I asked Dr. Cone to carry on. He would close the incisions and, with Miss Penland, would shepherd the patient back to consciousness.

Archibald and I dressed and emerged into the sunshine on Seventieth Street. We hailed a taxi and were taken down Fifth Avenue to have lunch together on Fifty-seventh Street. There was nothing unusual about this meeting, nothing to make it memorable, except that I was thirty-six and Archibald was fifty-five. The age relationship of operator and viewer is usually reversed.

When we reached the restaurant, we had lunch and sat there after the meal to talk. Professor Archibald was a quiet, polished, amusing man, quite distinguished in appearance, even handsome. He was partially deaf and spoke in a very low voice, almost in a whisper. He proved to be a fascinating talker — perhaps I should say whisperer — about things that carried us beyond the field of our profession to philosophy and anecdote and back again to details of surgical technique. In this urban environment, he seemed a gentleman of the old school who might have stepped out of the culture of New York's own colonial past.

He described Montreal and his own plans for building a strong Department of Surgery there in the Royal Victoria Hospital. He listened too as I told him of my ambitions and my plans for neurosurgery and neurology — plans that had been so long developing. Finally, he apologized, saying he would have to catch a train. (It was after seven o'clock in the evening by then and we had come to the restaurant for lunch!) I suppose he had been making up his mind about me. But at last he spoke to his purpose.

"I want you to come to Montreal," he said, "and take over my practice in brain surgery. I can't continue to specialize in that if I am to carry on as a specialist in chest surgery as at present. I must find time to modernize and to rebuild our surgical department in the Royal Victoria Hospital."

We left the restaurant and he hailed a taxi. As he opened the door of the cab, he turned back to me, speaking in perfect French: "A Montréal, on parle français. Vous parlez . . . n'est-ce pas?" I hesitated for a moment. Then with more assurance than was justified, I exclaimed, "Mais, oui." He smiled and nodded.

Then he added: "You have very large ideas, plans for much more than I had in mind. Well, let me know what you would need to make your dreams come true. I'll write what I can promise you." He smiled again and looked at me for a moment. Then he entered the taxi, closed the door, and drove away, leaving me to my thoughts. How long I remained there, standing on the curb, I have no idea. Two dreams, not just one, had been discussed that afternoon, and "dream" is not quite the word. A night dream is never planned. But a daydream may be. Daydreams, they were.

Archibald had *his* plan: to strengthen his surgical team by bringing a neurosurgeon to Montreal, a man who would pull his share of the load. He wanted me to be the neurosurgeon in a department of surgery. But, I was that already. And I saw the need of being and doing so much more than that. He had need of a horse. He was not prepared to bargain for the team that I wanted to propose, or for a racing stable. At least, not yet.

His plan and mine did not fit, I thought. Perhaps they would never fit. But, I had been charmed, even inspired, by the man and what he told me of this great bilingual city. Montreal, as I saw it then, was aloof, aristocratic — a cosmopolitan crossroads for European and American culture and learning, a place where one might, perhaps, gather a group, work quietly, and be able to escape at times to the vast wilderness just beyond it.

My purpose and the plan were not born that afternoon, of course. But the idea that such an establishment could be created to advantage in Montreal *was* born then.

Next day was Sunday and, as usual, I wrote the weekly letter to my mother in California:

"June 26, 1927. . . . Dr. Archibald came down from Montreal. He watched me remove a cerebellar tumor. Then we went to lunch and, when we had finished, it was 7:15 P.M. and almost time for his train. . . . In some ways, the thought of changing to Montreal is tempting. He came with a sort of informal idea of getting me to come up there to practice, and proposed a guarantee of a minimum of income for a few years. I told him I would not come simply to practice. But if there was an opportunity to build up a neurological clinic along proper lines, along with practice, I should be very much interested. . . . There is only one other neurological surgeon in Canada and he is just beginning in Toronto." *

On the following Sunday, July 3, 1927, I wrote my mother again: "It is now the small hours of the morning and I have finished enough of my London address to incorporate the illustrations. Helen is well. I do hate to leave her." The next night I took the train to Montreal and spent the day visualizing the possibilities with Archibald before taking ship from there for England.

On July 15, 1927, I wrote from England: "Here I am again in London. How familiar things seem and how intimate and small after New York! . . . I walked out across London and a host of memories came thronging back. It is only six years but I seem to remember myself as much younger. I watched the people. They are just the same, although the skirts have risen with those in New York . . ."

From London, I sent a letter back to Archibald. "Canada needs a well-developed neurosurgical clinic," I said, "and Montreal is a suitable place to develop one. The heart of the clinic would be a neuropathology laboratory for both neurology and neurosurgery . . . four or five rooms, a technician and a secretary. This laboratory," I pointed out, "would be the place to which men, wanting postgraduate experience, should be attracted, and it is here where most of the investigation should be done." The letter included other detailed conditions, for I expected academic standing equal to that of the neurologists I had met in each of the two large university hospitals. I wanted to deal with the neurosurgical patients from both hospitals, the Montreal General and the Royal Victoria, but to develop an operating team in only one. That must be in the hospital that was able and willing to provide the laboratory. I hoped to bring Cone with me, and he would require a full-time salary. For myself, I would need no more than a temporary guarantee to cover my possible failure to make a living from practice limited to office and hospital.

I had landed in England well before the symposium to take in another meeting. At the end of two weeks, I had finished writing the address. It was typed at the last moment. This is a bad work-

* Kenneth McKenzie was returning to Toronto after a year of work with Harvey Cushing in Boston.

habit, no doubt, but it is one from which I have never managed to escape. Addresses have a way of blossoming for me with new ideas in the excitement of their approaching presentation. They seem to take command of the writer and his unfortunate typist.

While in England on this occasion, I could observe neurology and reflect on what makes for leadership in our profession. "Monday evening," my weekly letter reported, "I dined with Gordon Holmes. . . . Holmes acts interested and always insists on doing something for you. Kinnier Wilson, the other leading neurologist in London, acts the same way but it never goes any farther. The younger men are consequently disciples of Holmes. . . .

"Montreal," the letter concluded, "looks better all the time. If they will meet our terms, I think we shall have to go. There are many, many things I want to do. I've some ideas on epilepsy now that I can't wait to work on. It's no use tackling anything without a complete, smooth-running experimental and clinical machine."

It is obvious that, by the summer of 1927, the main features of my projected plan were clear to me. And I could see, from this vantage point, how important was the personal relationship between the senior and the juniors in any group, whether this involves professor and students or chief and assistants.

During the time abroad, I visited Sherrington, the physiologist, in Oxford, and Greenfield, the pathologist, and Holmes, the neurologist, in London, rejoicing to meet them, their wives and children again. These were the men who, like Sir William Osler, had given their friendship and personal interest while they were teaching me. The others, who had only lectured or operated, making no gesture of personal concern, were little more to me now than the books I had read.

I saw Lady Osler, who was about to make another pilgrimage to Revere's grave in Belgium. She had the same delightful laugh and her eyes softened as she recalled the far-off undergraduate days when she and Sir William were so kind to us all.

During the days of this British-American neurological congress, I lived in the home of Gordon Holmes in Wimpole Street and attended the meetings from there, discovering with pleasure that I could introduce my new American friends to their transatlantic colleagues.

On my return to New York, Bill Cone had problems waiting on the wards and a baffling autopsy case to show me in the Laboratory of Neurocytology. And then there was the problem of what to do with Dr. Laidlaw.

George Laidlaw had been using my desk and microscope while I was abroad. He surrendered them when I entered the laboratory now. Then he handed me one microscopic slide with an air of ill-concealed excitement. As I sat down to examine it, I realized that Bill Cone and Edward Dockrill had come to watch and Mrs. Gourlay had stopped her typing to listen. The section he had given me demonstrated the wirelike fibrils within the connective tissue as I had never before seen them. The picture was beautiful. I shifted the lenses of my microscope to study it under the oil immersion, in silence for a time.

Laidlaw was a successful middle-aged New York doctor. Not long after his wife died, he himself had an operation for the removal of what he called a "tumorous growth." After the operation, when the surgeon and the pathologist told him the growth was malignant cancer, incompletely removed, and that he had at best a year to live, he closed his office and gave up his medical practice forever. He traveled then through the world, visiting famous laboratories and asking permission to study for himself their microscopic preparations of cancers like his own. He returned to New York, the year ran out, and he did not die.

One morning he had come to see me in the Laboratory of Neurocytology. He showed me a section of his "cancer." Its appearance suggested cancer. But this was not a growth that came from nervous tissue, so he and I took the section upstairs to Purdy Stout. Stout would not venture a diagnosis but, speaking frankly, he feared it might be malignant. So Laidlaw and I returned to our laboratory and sat down.

I told him that the pathologist who predicted his death obviously made a mistake and that if he had had at his command a better method of staining the connective tissue in the growth, he might have seen clearly enough to avoid such mistakes. Why didn't Laidlaw himself try to devise a better method? I suggested that he might begin by modifying, in one way or another, the method of del Rio-Hortega. That technique brought to light the oligodendroglia cells within the brain, and I had noticed that it did at times show the connective tissue outside the brain selectively.

Then I had to tell Laidlaw that we had no room for another worker in our crowded one-room laboratory. He begged to be admitted. When I refused, he said: "My time is running out. What you have described is exactly what I want to do with what may remain of my life. I can only do it here and I want to do it now." But I had shaken my head, thinking that what he had said was equally true of us all.

This was the thinking of Hippocrates, the Father of Medicine, four centuries before Christ, when he wrote: "Life is short, the art so long." And Geoffrey Chaucer phrased it again in Renaissance times: "the lyf so short, the craft so long to lerne." Should we admit a practitioner with no special skill, in his late fifties, to work on the corner of another man's desk? No.

Laidlaw took his leave. But when he returned the following morning, Cone proposed a compromise. He would make room for him on his own bench until I sailed for England. Then he could work at my bench until I returned. After that, having learned our technique, he might move on to another laboratory. So I had agreed. Now I was back from abroad and needed the bench and the shelves in my cubbyhole.

But the section Laidlaw had given me was a triumph. He had done, in two months, what I hoped he might accomplish in a year. I looked at him. He was smiling expectantly. He looked well. No suggestion of recurrence of cancer in that face. I glanced at Mrs. Gourlay. She smiled. As I had entered the laboratory that morning, she had said quietly: "Dr. Laidlaw wants so much to stay. He works quietly and methodically every day and far into the night. He is always cheerful. We like him." I recalled too the moment three years earlier when Hortega handed a section back to me and said, "Casi mejor que yo." I handed the section back to Laidlaw now. But I looked at Dockrill, the technician. He nodded his head and offered to make room for him where there had been no room before. Bill Cone laughed in his rumbling bass and clapped Laidlaw on the shoulder, saying, "Yes, yes." So Laidlaw stayed on and his own laugh continued to be heard there in the Laboratory of Neurocytology until the lab was closed six months later.*

* Armed with a new technique, Laidlaw carried on for years in what was for him a second career, as pathologist, seemingly young, keen, vibrant. His

But I was facing a problem of my own, whether to continue the writing of a book that Cone and I had undertaken, or whether to abandon the project. The decision to undertake it had been reached six months earlier in January of 1927 after discussions with those whose opinions we valued. W. G. MacCallum, the pathologist at Johns Hopkins, was particularly encouraging. So we had undertaken to write a textbook on the general principles of neuropathology without describing specific diseases.

In the months that followed, we had set to work, using the added information that had come to us by application of the Spanish methods. We took a publisher, Mr. Paul Hoeber, into our confidence. Indeed, I think it was Mr. Hoeber who had first suggested the plan to me. It was to be the best book ever written in this field. Why do it at all if it was to be anything less?

We outlined the chapters, but, as we began to write and to read the relative literature, we realized, far too often, that someone else, somewhere in the world, could write a better chapter. I wrote to several to see if they would do a chapter for us. I was surprised when the invitations were readily accepted, since my name carried no prestige as editor.

And there was another difficulty. To my surprise, Bill Cone found writing difficult. He would turn, with evident relief, away from the half-written page and focus instead on the care of our patients. This he carried out with tireless enthusiasm. Or he applied himself to the perfecting of technique in laboratory and operating room and he did this with equal delight. In short, Cone was a doer and a reader, not a creative writer, and I was left alone at last with little more than a book plan on my lap.

On August 14, 1927, I wrote in the weekly letter home: "During the past month I have gone over and over the question of writing a book. It would embody our work on glia and the basic princi-

method helped us greatly in our own studies of tumors and scars. After the Laboratory of Neurocytology closed, he continued to work with Professor Stout as a respected member of his Department of Surgical Pathology. Meanwhile, the "Laidlaw stain" came to be known and used by pathologists everywhere. It threw light on the difference between malignant and benign growths and it helped pathologists to avoid the mistake in diagnosis that had led Laidlaw himself to close his office.

ples of neuropathology. Last week I decided to write it, but today have decided not — I think definitely."

This had been an exercise in humility, forcing me to recognize the limits of my own capacity. But the book should be written. No one had done it. It was important for the future of neurology, or so I thought. I began to consider changing from author to editor. I did not really want to be an editor but I had already written to several authors and Paul Hoeber made it harder to give it up. He wanted to publish a big cytology and he described it to me as a duty not to be shirked.*

At last I undertook the editorial project, which became, for me, a labor of love. The title eventually selected was *Cytology and Cellular Pathology of the Nervous System.*

But why a labor of love? Love of what? That is a difficult question to answer. I did not enjoy the work of editorship. It was not "love" at all but rather a sort of fierce and persistent loyalty to an ideal. Perhaps it would be more accurate to say that it was a part of my contribution to a cause I had joined, a cause far bigger than myself. I did write one chapter for volume three, "Tumors of the Sheaths of the Nervous System," because I thought I was right and that others had been wrong in regard to the classification of these benign growths. Also, I wrote the chapter in volume two on neuroglia, normal and pathological. But if Cajal had accepted the invitation I sent him, I would have dropped out of that also, at least in part.

In the end, there were twenty-six contributors. The three volumes were dedicated to Ramón y Cajal. Among the authors of different chapters, some had once been my teachers, such as del Rio-Hortega in Madrid, Godwin Greenfield in London, Jean Nageotte in Paris, Max Bielschowsky in Berlin. Being an editor, I used to reflect, was a little like being the playing captain of a football team composed of star performers, most of whom were speedier than oneself.†

When I look back, I realize that the experience of creating the *Cytology* brought me — what shall I say? — humility with understanding. No man could master all the current knowledge of the nervous system by himself. No one can make the best use of that knowledge working alone in the vast field of neurology. Only a

* See note 17.
† See note 18.

team could hope to accomplish that, a selected team in a planned setting.

My trip to Spain and the evolution of the Laboratory of Neurocytology, now about to close its doors, had introduced me to a new world of exploration. This was basic science. But the boundaries of the basic sciences, I discovered, are like the horizon, which recedes as one advances, no matter how far he may travel or in what direction.

In Hortega's laboratory, I had been dazzled. I thought I could shed a little light on all the microscopic structures of the brain, particularly the human brain. But my patients in New York had their own special problems that called for solution. They taught me the fact that clinical medicine will always need purposeful and more restricted planning of research. I know now that the clinician's research may be basic, but it must be applied. Discoveries are as unpredictable as the goals that are scored in each game, but the playing schedule for the season is established for you in advance by the patients who present themselves.

Suburban life for us became pleasant and stable, and so my wife decided we should balance our family by having two more children. Thus our third child arrived February 6, 1927, a golden-haired daughter, named Priscilla after the charming wife of my Princeton classmate Dr. Francis Hall of Boston.

On December 19, 1928, our fourth child arrived, a lusty red-haired boy. We called him Amos Jefferson after my generous grandfather. We thought of him as our "good-luck piece" for, with him, came a turn in the tide of our personal affairs. On the very day of his birth, the Congress in Washington passed a long-awaited bill, authorizing payment from German securities of claims against the German government, arising from German action before the United States entered the war.

This promised eventual payment to me of nearly twenty thousand dollars, a welcome windfall. A friend of my Princeton undergraduate days, Paul F. Myers, was a law student in Washington, D.C., in 1916 at the time my leg was shattered by the torpedoing of the cross-Channel ship, the *Sussex*. Without my knowledge at the time, he had put in a claim for me against the German government.

Suddenly, too, my private practice actually began to prosper.

Part of this improvement was due to a strange accident. Two married couples were carried in from Park Avenue and placed in my care. While walking home from the theater, they had all been run down by a speeding car just as they were passing the Presbyterian Hospital. Three of them had suffered head injuries and really needed my care. The fourth proved to be dead, alas. The surviving three were in no position to choose a better neurosurgeon since they were dazed or unconscious. The good part of this extraordinary affair was that the survivors recovered completely. And, furthermore, they proved to be wealthy, as well as grateful to their surgeon. Indeed, they recovered so completely that I watched a marital triangle developing before my very eyes. The one surviving male had become the focus of the affection of both women. As the years pass, I have been tempted to write a series of true-life stories drawn from the astonishing plots my patients give me.

In any event, it was clear enough now that such added income from private practice would be enough to support and educate our growing family, even in New York. I could do the standard neurosurgical operations well enough now. In addition to that, I had been prompted to devise other varied procedures. The patients who flowed through the Presbyterian Hospital in an unselected stream brought many varied unsolved problems with them and the alert physicians of Walter Palmer's medical staff presented them enticingly. I began to carry out maneuvers and operations for the relief of certain kinds of headache, heart pain, high blood pressure, spinal deformities and unusual conditions that produced epilepsy.

But, nonetheless, I was dissatisfied and restive. All this seemed to be worthwhile from the patient's point of view. But it did not lead toward my major objective. When I stopped long enough to look at what I was accomplishing in New York, I was unhappy. I had turned from experimental physiology, in my Oxford days, toward neurosurgery, because I thought the neurosurgeon might become a neurologist-in-action. Since he could expose the living human brain, he should be able to study and even to influence the brain's physiological activity.

But these operations that I was carrying out made little approach to brain physiology and the others, as well, fell far short of that. Even the studies with the microscope in the Laboratory of Neurocytology stopped short of my true objective. They threw a brilliant light on the anatomical structure and on the alterations wrought in the brain by disease and injury, but not on brain physiology. I had yet to find a way of understanding what the brain was doing and *how* it did it.

No one in the New York Neurological Institute shared this point of view with me. They had other preoccupations and, of course, rightly so. Except for Cone, I was much alone there. I had seen the need of teamwork in a scientifically adequate neurological institute ever since I had refused the invitation to go to Baltimore five years earlier.

I had acquired the skill of neurosurgery in the succeeding five years, and I had made an effective approach to the nervous system of man with new techniques for the microscope. I was ready for something else. But I didn't quite know what. I could operate, thus laying bare the brain, and I did so always with a certain sort of reverence. What was going on within the pia mater of this living, thinking human brain on the operating table below me? There was reflex action in it and there were various partly separable functional mechanisms. How were we to learn more about them?

I stood before the functioning brain of man as if before the great Sphinx, and was dumb. I had no way of asking the critical question. I had no clues. Would I ever have?

To express it another way, brain-tumor surgery seemed to give us few ways of studying the brain and few clues to understanding. I'd gone as far as I could go taking Cone with me. Doors were closing around us now. Where was our work in the world to be carried out? The time had come when the faith of a scientist would be put to the test.

What about Montreal? This invitation had come to me first when Dr. Archibald visited New York in June of 1927. But four months later, October 1927, he had written that he had not yet been able to secure the necessary financial support for a laboratory, or for Cone's salary. I concluded he probably never would be able to deal with what he had called my "large ideas." At the year's end, nothing had materialized.

It was obvious in my weekly letter of Sunday, January 9, 1928, that I had given up all expectation of Montreal:

"The time draws near," I wrote, "for our move up to the new hospital and school. . . . I must go ahead now and plan on staying here in New York. . . . Elsberg," I added, "opened up a little before he went abroad, not a great deal, but it made me feel he might have a place for me where I could be moderately independent."

He "*might* have a place for me." That was his attitude. It was quite understandable that Elsberg should wonder vaguely what to do with me when the time should come for the New York Neurological Institute to take over neurosurgery at the new medical center. During the transition period of the past six years, 1921 to 1927, I had served a transitory purpose to the Presbyterian. Even at the institute, while I had taken no clinical responsibility, I had been their neuropathologist for almost three years, and this was, of course, without pay.

I liked Elsberg for his enthusiastic interest in each clinical problem. But that was all we had in common. Somehow, I felt shy with him. I was like a horse left free too long to gallop in the pasture.

So it was that, as the year of 1928 was ushered in, I was laying plans to move in three months' time, with my surgical and medical associates, from the old Presbyterian Hospital to the new medical center uptown at 168th Street and Broadway. The Neurological Institute was scheduled to follow, moving into their own neighboring, newly built institute a year later, March 1929. Until that time, the freedom I had enjoyed for the past six years at the Presbyterian would continue to be mine, freedom to study patients and to treat them, freedom to make the new approaches to the unsolved problems of neurology that occurred to me.

After that date, it was intended by those who had overall control of the hospital and medical school that Cone and I would shift our allegiance to the institute. But, since no one in the Neurological Institute who could speak with authority (least of all Professor Tilney) had taken me into his confidence or suggested that he needed me, my departure from New York was inevitable. There seemed to be no hurry. I was content to wait.

Then came the surprise. On Monday, January 10, 1928, came the following telegram from Edward Archibald: "All arrangements made. Could you come to Montreal on Wednesday for a day of discussion?"

I wired back that I would come. But, when I took the night train to Montreal Tuesday evening, I had many misgivings. Although I knew and admired Dr. Archibald, I had discovered enough about the Royal Victoria Hospital and the attitude of its board of governors to make me cautious, to say the least. I decided to make the visit, however, keeping an open mind, asking many questions.

I had learned something by talking to Archibald and from other sources about the Montreal scene. Archibald was, I discovered, professor of surgery. But he was only acting chief surgeon of the Royal Victoria Hospital with the backing of the hospital's medical board. He had never been appointed chief surgeon by the board of governors.

In 1923, four years earlier, the man who had been chief of the hospital's Surgical Service and professor of surgery at McGill, Dr. George Armstrong, retired. It was expected that the hospital medical board would consider the situation, consult with the university, and nominate a single candidate as Armstrong's successor. After this, the hospital and university governors would be able to agree on one man to be in charge of both the surgical care and the surgical teaching in the Royal Victoria. Archibald and C. B. Keenan were the two senior surgeons next in line.

Armstrong, however, seemed to feel that there was no one on his staff fit to succeed him. Sclater Lewis, who eventually wrote the hospital's history, quoted Armstrong thus: " 'Archibald is too active in research to be placed in charge of a busy, routine, surgical service.' Oertel, the hospital pathologist," Lewis added, "was Armstrong's chief supporter in this opinion." *

When the medical board delayed action and no nomination was forthcoming, Sir Vincent Meredith, president of the hospital board of governors, took the initiative. Here was the beginning of trouble. He seems to have ignored the university and the hospital's medical board completely, except for Horst Oertel, the pathologist. He sent Oertel to New York to look for likely candidates. This is information I can, myself, add now to the story.

* D. S. Lewis, *The Royal Victoria Hospital, 1887–1947* (Montreal: McGill University Press, 1969). This is an excellent history of this remarkable hospital.

Although it seems a very strange coincidence, I was one of the two whom Oertel interviewed at the Presbyterian Hospital in New York. Whether he went to other hospitals there or elsewhere, I do not know. Perhaps he turned to New York's Presbyterian because it was the only university hospital in that nearby city.

Early one morning in the spring of 1923, when I had remained at home convalescing from the flu, Professor Whipple telephoned to me. He had made an appointment for me in his office, he said. Could I come down to the hospital? He explained that he had been asked in earlier correspondence to suggest two possible members of his staff who might be considered suitable candidates for the position of chief surgeon at the Royal Victoria Hospital in Montreal. He had submitted the names of Dr. Fordyce B. St. John and myself. Now, it seemed, Professor Horst Oertel, pathologist and member of the Royal Victoria Hospital board, had arrived to interview us without further warning.

I was not feeling well, but I dressed and came downtown to the hospital at once. The idea of suggesting me for such an important post, when I was only thirty-two, surprised me very much. Indeed, I thought it was absurd. But I said nothing about it. We talked, Professor Oertel and I, and he must have taken my measure, so to speak. At the end of an hour, he seemed to agree with me, since he did *not* suggest that I should apply for the post!

Oertel had a thick German pronunciation that muffled the English accent he had obviously acquired in England, rather than in the United States or Canada. He was quick-minded and completely sure of himself. When we met he had said, ponderously, that he was director of the new Pathological Institute of McGill University; I asked him quite innocently what that was. Finally, I understood that the Royal Victoria Hospital and university were, at the moment, building a pathological institute with help from the Rockefeller Foundation as well as the Province of Quebec. He was to be its director.

What he told me was this: The chief of the Surgical Service of the Royal Victoria Hospital, Dr. George E. Armstrong, was well past the age for retirement and the medical board could not make up its mind about the nomination of his successor. Consequently, the House Committee of the Board of Hospital Governors had decided to seek out candidates for themselves.

I asked about Edward Archibald, whose reputation I knew, even then. Oertel replied that Archibald would not do. He was "deaf and always late to his appointments." The Royal Victoria needed someone who could build up a suitable private practice in surgery.

Dr. St. John, I learned later, drew higher marks in his interview. Oertel ended by inviting him to apply for the position of chief surgeon. But St. John, who knew something about the situation in Montreal, refused. He knew "Eddie" Archibald very well and considered him a friend and a very able surgeon. He would not be willing to compete against him.

Shortly after this, the president of the Royal Victoria Hospital invited a surgeon from Aberdeen to Montreal, Sir Henry Gray. He became chief surgeon for a period of two years, although the university had appointed Archibald as professor of surgery.*

Now as I was about to make this visit to Montreal in January 1928, only a little more than two years had passed since Henry Gray had withdrawn from the Royal Victoria. I had much to learn about that hospital, the city, the university and the people. I know now from long experience that an American, going to Canada for the first time, should acknowledge his ignorance on crossing the frontier. Canadians have their own history and, in each province, their own way of life. Canadians are different from the British, the French and the Americans — very different. Certainly, in the Province of Quebec, there are proud traditions that can be appreciated only when one knows the history of both founding races, and after one has lived with them and, one hopes, come to be accepted by them.

* See note 19.

7

The Royal Victoria Hospital, Montreal

A Day of Decision

In 1887, the Golden Jubilee of Queen Victoria's reign was celebrated throughout the British Empire. In this year, two public-spirited citizens of Montreal offered to donate a million dollars to build a hospital. It was, they said, to be "for relief of the sick poor . . . and the provision of increased facilities for . . . medical education and for training professional nurses." The Montreal City Council appropriated a beautiful building site for it, high on the shoulder of Mount Royal, and the Queen gave permission to name it the Royal Victoria Hospital.*

Six years later, in December 1893, the Royal Victoria was opened by the Governor-General of Canada, the Earl of Aberdeen, in the name of Her Majesty. An admirable citizen, R. B. Angus, was elected president of the board of governors, which undertook to control and to support the institution. Appointments to the staff, it was stated vaguely, were to be made "by merit only." Thus, Montreal's second large English-speaking hospital was born at the close of the Victorian era.

It was housed in a ponderous castellated building of cut stone in Scottish-baronial style. Its close resemblance to the Royal Infirmary of Edinburgh must have pleased the donors. From above Pine Avenue, the Royal Victoria looked down on the medical school and across the other academic buildings of McGill Univer-

* See note 20.

sity to the city and the mighty Saint Lawrence and, on a clear day, even beyond that to the Adirondacks and the Green Mountains in the neighboring states of New York and Vermont.

A quarter of a century earlier (by Confederation in 1867) the British colonies of North America had begun to establish their independence as a nation. Thus, without a war, Canada was doing what the United States had done in 1776 by means of armed revolt.

The Canadian way of progressive establishment was different from the American, in many ways. North of the international boundary there was, one may say, no formal "melting pot." In the city of Montreal and in the whole Province of Quebec the great majority of Canadians were French-speaking.

Thus, the history of the care of the sick in Quebec was a double one. It went back a long way to the time, three centuries earlier, when that heroic French gentlewoman, Jeanne Mance, opened her home as a hospital to the first settlers and to the Indians alike. This was the real beginning of the first Montreal hospital, the Hôtel-Dieu. It was, of course, French-speaking, and the date was 1644. The Hôtel-Dieu was maintained by courageous, long-suffering French-Canadian nuns, now called the Sisters of Saint Joseph. With the eventual establishment of the Medical School of the University of Montreal (l'Université de Montréal) the Hôtel-Dieu became one of its teaching hospitals. By 1928, when I visited Montreal, the Hôtel-Dieu had come to its final building site, not far away from the Royal Victoria, on Pine Avenue. There it stood, its elegant dome behind high cloistering walls, recalling Paris and the Salpêtrière to the many Montreal physicians who had done their graduate work in France. Thus there were in Montreal two separate systems of care for the sick: first, the French-speaking hospitals associated with the French-speaking University of Montreal, and second, the English-speaking hospitals associated with the English-speaking McGill University.

With the opening of the Royal Victoria in 1893, it was clear enough that McGill faced a problem in her second teaching hospital. The university's formal relationship to this proud and well-appointed institution was not at all clear.

Montreal's first English-speaking hospital had been the Montreal General. It was founded, in 1819, as a "house of recovery" by the Female Benevolent Society of Montreal. Three years later, it had its second formal opening, in larger quarters, as the Montreal General Hospital.

The four founding physicians on the medical staff of the M.G.H., all of them trained in Edinburgh during the heyday of that great center of medical teaching, formed the faculty of medicine immediately. It was McGill University's first faculty. In a sense, the hospital and university came tumbling into the world under pressure and almost simultaneously, like twins in a precipitate labor. The haste was necessary in order to allow the university to inherit the estate of the Scottish fur-trader James McGill, and to acquire his pleasant pasture land on the slope of Mount Royal for the purposes of higher education.

On the day of my visit in 1928 I discovered that the Montreal General was more than a mile away from Mount Royal and was thus far removed from the university and the Royal Victoria.

Although the "General" was difficult of access through the city's business district, it was remarkable in many ways. It had been the early excellence of clinical medicine in that hospital that had drawn young William Osler to it from Toronto in 1870. He completed his medical studies at McGill and in the General Hospital. Later, he had returned to teach medicine there and to do pathology during the decade of 1874 to 1884. By 1893, when the Royal Victoria began to admit patients, Osler had become the first professor of medicine at Johns Hopkins and was demonstrating to the medical profession of the world the value of bedside teaching as it had come down to him from Edinburgh through the Montreal General.

In the Royal Victoria Hospital, good clinical medicine and surgery were practiced from the start. But it was not until the 1920s that true distinction and academic leadership came to it. That was when Charles Martin became dean of medicine and Jonathan Meakins returned to his own hospital from Edinburgh to be professor of medicine, and when Edward Archibald emerged as a distinguished leader among the surgeons of North America. Curious as it may seem, it was during this very decade of the Royal Victoria's professional ascendancy that intramural rivalries appeared and, all too frequently, a lack of effort on the part of the hospital governors to cooperate with the university.

I referred to the breakdown of cooperation (1923–1925) between the Meredith regime in the Royal Victoria Hospital and the Medical School of McGill University in the previous chapter.* There is more to be said, however, about both Archibald and Sir Vincent Meredith.†

After the resignation of Sir Henry Gray as chief surgeon of the R.V.H. in 1925, Meredith made no further independent appointments, and so Archibald continued quietly to enlarge and develop the Department of Surgery in the Royal Victoria, taking over the virtual leadership, without formal appointment as chief. Thus, in March 1927, Archibald and C. B. Keenan, as senior surgeons, together recommended that a subdepartment of neurosurgery should be established. This was approved by the medical board, the hospital governors and the university. Archibald then began to look about for someone who could take over his practice in neurosurgery. It was apparently Dr. Archibald Malloch who suggested my name to him.‡

On January 12, 1928, Dr. Archibald met the early train from New York and took me home with him to breakfast in his house in Westmount, a very pleasant residential section of Montreal. He was dressed in his fur hat and big fur coat. Fresh snow had been falling on the city and children were on their way to school, well bundled up. Archibald outlined the day's program for me. As seen now in retrospect, the visit of this naïve young specialist from New York had its amusing aspects and even its absurdities.

A lecture to the senior medical students on the diagnosis of brain tumor had been planned to start the day. The students had never seen Dandy's procedure of air encephalography. Archibald had a patient who, he thought, should have the test. So I said I would carry it out before the class and proceed with the lecture afterward.

The large operating room of the Royal Victoria, walled and floored with slabs of white marble, with its amazingly steep amphitheater seats, had been chosen for the event. All the seats, and the stairs as well, were filled with curious students when we arrived, and I could see many standing at the back, their heads almost touching the ceiling as I looked up in consternation.

At the start of an encephalogram, one carries out a lumbar

* See note 19.
† See note 21.
‡ See note 22.

Edward Archibald

puncture, usually a simple enough matter. The patient was wheeled in and placed in a sitting position. I injected novocaine to avoid pain, and then slipped a long, hollow lumbar-puncture needle in between the tips of the lower spine, expecting to draw off spinal fluid and to replace some of it with air. The bubbles were to rise within the spinal canal and enter the cavity of the ventricles deep within the brain. Meanwhile, the head was to be postured, as I would show them, in such a way as to guide the bubbles along that pathway.

But spinal fluid refused to come from my hollow needle. I was exasperated but, finally, in order to spare the patient further discomfort, I gave up the attempt, telling him I would try again later in the day. Then I began the lecture, hiding my embarrassment as well as I could.

The professor of medicine, Jonathan C. Meakins, and the dean, Charles Martin, had done me the honor of coming to watch and listen, as had Professor Archibald. They sat in the front row. Before I had finished the lecture, a nurse came in. She announced, in a voice that, it seemed to me, was far too loud, that the surgical resident had done the lumbar puncture successfully. Did I wish to carry on with the encephalogram? It was the last thing I wished to do, but I could not desert the patient now, so I said yes. They wheeled him in again and I told the audience that the lecture was over. They might leave while I completed this job. But no one stirred.

As far as I remember it, the rest of the procedure went off smoothly. The patient was taken to the X-ray department, where the radiographs of the head were taken. They would show the shape and position of the air collection and so prove the presence, or absence, of a brain tumor.

At last, when the patient had disappeared and the students had filed out, I turned ruefully to the professors in the front row. Archibald introduced me then to "Jack" Meakins, a tall, handsome, impressive man, the professor of medicine, and to "Charlie" Martin, the dean of medicine, a small, quick-moving man who was not at all impressive at first — not until you talked with him and discovered the keen mind, the quick perceptions, the unyielding strength and the human kindness always served up with a quip or a laugh.

We four made our way from the surgical amphitheater to Meakins's laboratory and office on the other side of the hospital. There, I listened while they told me much that I had not known about the past and the present of the Royal Victoria Hospital.

It was evident that the old order was changing rapidly. Modern, scientific medicine had come to this conservative university hospital. Charles Martin had been, in many ways, the moving spirit in the change. He had himself been professor of medicine and, with Dr. W. F. Hamilton, one of the two senior physicians. But in 1923 he became the dean of McGill's medical faculty and succeeded in his effort to gain the promise of assistance from the Rockefeller Foundation. With that help, a full-time chair of medicine had been created and a scientific university clinic endowed within the hospital.

Richard Pearce was director of Rockefeller medical philanthropy in all countries outside the boundaries of the United States. Pearce agreed to Martin's scheme, provided he could induce the young Canadian Jonathan Meakins to return from Edinburgh, where he had become the Christison Professor of Therapeutics following the First World War. Meakins had had his early training under Martin and, later, in the pathology laboratory of the Presbyterian Hospital in New York.

This proviso was exactly what Martin had been working for, ever since Meakins left. Thus in 1924 Meakins, who, Sclater Lewis points out, had become a great success as professor in Edinburgh, came home. He was made professor, physician in chief, and director of the newly endowed University Medical Clinic in the Royal Victoria Hospital. Meanwhile Martin, who was married to the charming daughter of the hospital's first president, R. B. Angus, had withdrawn from the professorship of medicine and from active medical practice to devote his full time to the dean's responsibilities.

After our discussion, the dean thought best to leave us. Archibald, Meakins and I crossed University Street to call on Horst Oertel in his Pathological Institute. I recalled my interview with Oertel in the Presbyterian Hospital five years earlier. But my companions did not seem to know of Oertel's visit to New York. So I kept his secret to myself.

This building had been, in a sense, Oertel's own creation — an impressive structure of gray stone. To the left of the entrance was carved a crest from which a human skull emerged menacingly. Below the crest were the words *Fiat Lux,* Let There Be Light. In the entrance hall, also in Latin, the following injunction was inscribed. To translate it was to feel a cold chill pass down one's spine: "This is the place where death rejoices to come to the aid of life. Nothing recalls one from sin so much as the frequent contemplation of death!"

I began to realize that this second meeting with Oertel was to be a crucial encounter. I had asked for three or four rooms and they must be fully equipped for everything that goes with the use of the microscope. Unless he would make it possible to reproduce and to develop further what had already begun to grow in the Laboratory of Neurocytology at the Presbyterian Hospital, I had no desire to move to Montreal or anywhere else. Oertel's Pathological Institute was, it seemed, the logical place, if any, for our laboratory in Montreal.

He received us. He shook hands with me without referring to our previous meeting. Archibald explained that he had managed, at last, to secure promises of financial support for a laboratory of neuropathology as well as a full-time salary for my assistant, who, we hoped, would be the neuropathologist and neurosurgeon William Cone. Archibald explained further that Cone and I would expect to carry out our own autopsies, although under Professor Oertel's general supervision. We would also be responsible for the examination of pathological specimens that were of neurological interest, removed in the Royal Victoria operating rooms.

This, Archibald added, was according to the plan I had submitted. He hoped, as I did, that this laboratory could be established in the Pathological Institute as "the heart of our neurological clinic," a center for work in neurology, both medical and surgical. I realized suddenly that Oertel had not yet agreed to the proposal although it had been laid before him. I surmised that Archibald hoped for a favorable reception if he came thus, accompanied by the professor of medicine and with the promise of financial support in hand but without the dean of the medical school, who seemed to be persona non grata.

Oertel replied briefly that he could give us only the two rooms that he would now show us. There were, I noted, other vacant adjacent rooms, but he made no mention of them. One of the two rooms was already being used by Dr. Arthur Young, a promising young neurologist. The other room would be for the neurosurgeons, he said. Young was waiting for us, standing beside some formalin specimens. I was delighted to discover his interest and I would have liked to talk with him. But Professor Oertel cut us off. He was talking rapidly now, and I had to concentrate, since I still found his German pronunciation difficult to understand. He did not seem to feel any need of help from Young or me. Pathology was his own field, a subject to be taught by well-trained pathologists. It was not a field for investigation by clinicians.

As I listened, the whole Montreal project seemed about to vanish. So I made an effort to find out what Oertel himself was doing and what interested him as a scientist, hoping that he and I might discover a common subject of interest. At that time, he was trying to stain nerve fibers that others had reported growing in tumors and neoplasms of various types. His technician was using a silver impregnation technique and having some success. I realized that, here, I could help him. But he was not interested in my experience any more than he was in my ambitions. He did not care to discuss Archibald's presentation of my plan.

Again, he cut off discussion. He would be glad to make two rooms available to us. He might find time to teach us, too. Something beneath his shallow hospitality angered me. I wondered if he realized that he was holding the trump card. With it, he could block Archibald's plan. He played the card cleverly. It would indeed have blocked the whole undertaking, had not Jonathan Meakins been listening.

How different, I reflected, was Oertel from William von Glahn, who had welcomed my first faltering attempts to do neuropathology for the pathological conferences at the Presbyterian Hospital, and Purdy Stout when I began doing surgical neuropathology there. How different from the professor of pathology in Baltimore, William MacCallum, who had wanted me to develop a subdepartment of neuropathology in the Johns Hopkins Medical School and had later urged me to write a special book on brain pathology.

But I do not want to be unfair to Horst Oertel. He was, I am told, a dramatic classroom teacher who spoke with eloquent authority. And his life and career are worth describing.*

Professor Oertel bowed, stiff and formal. Meakins, Archibald and I left the Pathological Institute and recrossed University Street. Going to Meakins's office again, we sat down. I was bitterly disappointed. Unless I could re-create and expand the Laboratory of Neurocytology, why come to Montreal? The question echoed in my mind.

"Professor Oertel," I said, "does not want me. For my part, I see I could not work under him in the Pathological Institute." My companions did not reply. I was wondering about the other university hospital, the Montreal General.

"Would the pathologist," I asked, "at the Montreal General care to take us in?"

"Professor Lawrence Rhea is the pathologist there," Archibald answered. "He would welcome you, I think, and he might be able to squeeze you in. You would like him. Everyone does — a delightful fellow, an American gentleman from the Deep South, and a very good pathologist. But," he added, "could you set up the laboratory there and still do the operating here?"

I shook my head. "No, one must be able to go back and forth quickly from laboratory to operating table. We would certainly have to do most of our operating in the hospital that provides us with the laboratory."

Meakins had said little up to this moment. Now he spoke. He spoke to Archibald as if he had just made a decision. "No, Eddie," he said, "the laboratory must be here in the R.V.H. I can shift people around in my University Clinic. I could give you," he said, turning to me, "three rooms. They might even be subdivided with a partition or two." Then he said something that really thrilled me: "I'm ready to do this because you say you hope to serve the future of medical neurology as well as surgical neurology." †

Meakins and Archibald exchanged glances and neither spoke for a moment. I realized then that this was something quite unrehearsed. They understood and respected each other. And I realized, too, that here in Montreal there was no rivalry between the two major departments, medicine and surgery. But I realized some-

* See note 23.
† See note 24.

thing else as well: Meakins could do what he liked in his own endowed laboratory. But Archibald had no endowment, and no laboratory in the Royal Victoria, and Sir Vincent Meredith was its president. If Meredith was still opposed to Archibald, as Oertel certainly seemed to be, would he not also be opposed to my working as a surgeon under Archibald? I put that thought out of my mind for the moment.

Meakins's laboratory had been created for him by renovating what had been the hospital's Ward K, and by building an addition, at the end, for laboratory animals. He called it the "University Clinic" since it was supported by a university endowment. We walked now down the central corridor. The rooms on both sides hummed with the activity of medical research. It had to do with respiration, metabolism, endocrinology. I was introduced to the workers — probably Edward Mason, Hugh Long, John Beattie, Ray Brow, Walter and Jessie Scriver and David Slight — keen, young, spirited physicians, trained in science. I sensed their high morale and their urge to excellence.

At the end of the corridor, next to the animal quarters, Meakins showed us where our laboratory of neuropathology might be set up after minor alterations. I was content at once. To be crowded, I realized, was nothing. The advantage of working in such an environment of quality and scientific excellence was everything.

A luncheon was given in my honor that day in a large upstairs room with an oval ceiling at the Mount Royal Club. The university's principal, Sir Arthur Currie, was toastmaster, and I counted twenty-five guests. I had not expected anything like this. But the old-world British formality in the club and the easy hospitality of my hosts were familiar enough to me after my years in Oxford and London, and reassuring too. I had a sudden sense of being at home with men I liked.

This was essentially a university affair with the department heads of the teaching hospitals present, from the Royal Victoria and the General. Meredith was not present and not represented, I noticed.

There were gestures of welcome and a toast to the King. Then there were speeches, described in the weekly letter to my mother. The letter noted, "Fred MacKay, the neurologist from the General Hospital, spoke and said the physicians of that hospital would cooperate to the maximum if I came." This gesture of friendship and cooperation from the great sister hospital was, as Archibald whispered to me, "very gratifying."

After the luncheon, I talked, in something of a haze of bewilderment, to a succession of people. But I remember very clearly some reassuring words from Dr. Lewis Reford. He was a handsome, likable fellow — a sportsman, a gardener and a stamp collector as well as a doctor. After his medical qualification, he had spent a year of graduate study at the Johns Hopkins. There, in the Hunterian Research Laboratory, he had come into contact with Harvey Cushing before Cushing left for Boston. Reford was at that time considering neurosurgery as a career for himself. That was fifteen years before this luncheon. Since then, he had married, and decided he would give up practice. "My family and I," he said, "are helping Eddie Archibald in this undertaking. We hope you will come." I surmised then that these friends of Archibald must be supplying money for Cone's salary and perhaps for the laboratory.*

After the luncheon, Professor Archibald and I left the club and walked along Sherbrooke Street. It had been snowing but now the sun was coming through. The street and sidewalk had been cleared, except for this last fall of snow, and traffic was moving along at a leisurely pace. But, as we turned up Peel and began to climb the shoulder of Mount Royal, the cars were racing past to make the hill while snow chains beat their rapid tattoo against the mudguards. On the sidewalk, only a narrow path had been shoveled. The walls of snow were so high on each side that we could hardly see the cars on the one hand and the houses on the other. Slipping and struggling to keep our footing, we reached Pine Avenue and paused there.

Archibald pointed to an imposing residence. "The home of Sir Vincent Meredith, the president of the Royal Victoria Hospital." The house was a little withdrawn from the street and built of red brick with multiple gables. There was a projecting turret and a bulbous greenhouse for plants.

"I want to meet him," I said.

"Yes," Archibald replied, "I tried to arrange it through David MacKenzie. He is the urologist, you know. He operated on Sir

* See note 25.

Vincent recently. He said Sir Vincent was surprised and pleased when he told him you had been a Rhodes scholar, but he would not have time to see you."

There are moments in life that stand out clear and vivid while other memories fade. This was such a moment. I can see the house now and my companion. I remember my awareness vividly as if it were yesterday.

Edward Archibald, one of America's most distinguished surgeons, professor of surgery, could not approach the president of the Royal Victoria Hospital with so simple a request as the introduction of his protégé. Meredith had defied the university and blocked Archibald's plans before. He was in a position to do it again. It was, after all, only three years since scandal and tragedy had led him to withdraw his support of Gray.

Meakins had succeeded in setting up his University Clinic. But Meakins came back to the Royal Victoria with the generous endowment that Martin had secured for him and Sir Vincent was a banker. Archibald and I were beggars. Oertel had been Sir Vincent's agent when I met him first, and this morning he had treated me and my plan with contempt. Now, I was told the president had no time for me.

"I'm not going to make a decision about coming to Montreal," I said, "until I have met Sir Vincent Meredith and talked with him." We stood facing each other for a moment. Archibald looked at me with his quizzical smile and raised his eyebrows. But he said nothing. We walked along in silence. Presently he remarked, as if it had nothing to do with the matter, "You will find that Lady Meredith is charming."

I was to discover, in the years to come, that Edward Archibald never spoke ill of anyone. He made no reference to Sir Vincent now. But the direction of his thinking became apparent later in the afternoon when David MacKenzie brought me a cordial invitation to tea from Lady Meredith. Archibald did not come with me to the Meredith home at five o'clock that afternoon, but MacKenzie did, an intriguing Prince Edward Islander with an excellent sense of humor and an accent in which there were recurring echoes of the Scottish Highlands. Lady Meredith made me feel welcome. I looked about, observing everything. The culture of English-speaking Canadians in Quebec, as we were to discover on many occasions, has a distinctive character and a delightful charm all its own.

"Sir Vincent," she said, "will be a little late." I felt hopeless, as if I had come to the end of the road. What chance was there that this charity-minded autocrat would change his attitude or make a bargain with me, however well I might describe to him my purpose and my dream of a new approach to an understanding of the brain and mind of man?

When Sir Vincent entered the room, he seemed to be just what one would have expected of the president of the Bank of Montreal — confident, well-groomed, handsome, gray-haired and mustached. But on closer approach, I was startled to discover that here was an old man, confused and unsteady. During our conversation, he tried, quite unsuccessfully, to discuss the Royal Victoria, past and present. He was not clear, at least not now at the end of a day's work. Standing there, close to him, I made what any medical practitioner would have called "a snap diagnosis."

This was a case of cerebral arteriosclerosis, probably of some years standing, but now, at seventy-eight, advancing rapidly. The transient attacks of forgetting and confusion, one of which I was witnessing, probably would occur more and more frequently. A paralyzing thrombosis might be feared at any time.

As president of the Royal Victoria Hospital, the man I saw before me had been a stubborn, hardworking, well-meaning man. He was also an opinionated dictator, but, nevertheless, he made his kindly rounds through the wards of his hospital every Sunday morning, I had been told, accompanied by Miss Mabel Hersey, the very impressive superintendent of nurses, while Lady Meredith went to the Anglican cathedral, and prayed for him, no doubt, and all his good works.

Having made up his mind that Archibald, the surgeon who was "somewhat deaf and usually late for appointments," should not be made chief surgeon of his hospital, Sir Vincent was not likely to change his mind or to favor Archibald's proposals in regard to neurosurgery.

At seventy-four, he had brought in a chief surgeon more to his liking, Henry Gray, with the result that I have described. Now, a sudden change had come upon him. He was, I thought, conscious of his own confusion. He was making a gallant attempt to preserve his dignity and to do the things he had thought right. If my diagnosis was correct, this was not a man to be feared, not for long at any rate.

My heart leaped up. Twice that day I had concluded that Montreal was not the place to put forward my plan. And now, for a second time, the threat had crumbled and vanished before my eyes. I felt sorrow for Lady Meredith and a certain admiration for Sir Vincent, the strong, stubborn actor, so suddenly overtaken by senility. Father Time, who, soon or late, will call for us all, was ringing the curtain down on his act. Or so I thought. I did not then suspect that I was still to receive a giddy blow from the aged warrior.

All during that day of decision, I had been impressed increasingly by the quality of the physicians and surgeons I had met: Martin, Meakins, Archibald, of course, but many others too. They were reserved and civilized in a way that made them different from the doctors I had met in other parts of the world and I felt at home with them. I had had a frank and illuminating discussion of the whole situation with three Royal Victoria physicians. They were friends of Archibald Malloch and, like me, were not yet forty years of age — Sclater Lewis, Arthur Henderson, and Graham Ross.

I had yet to meet the French-Canadian members of our profession. I realized how important their reception of the proposed medical adventure would be. It was essential, for my ulterior purposes, that the neurologists of both languages should join us and form one group with us. The English-speaking neurologists, I observed with some surprise, had not figured in the preliminary discussions. In spite of that, it was true that Fred MacKay, neurologist in chief at the General Hospital, had voiced the welcome from that venerable institution. But Dr. Colin Russel, neurologist at the Royal Victoria and associate professor of neurology at McGill, was gruff and a good deal less than enthusiastic. I had liked him, nonetheless, in our brief meeting, and I knew he would soon find that we were bringing him much more than we could possibly take away.

It should be easily possible, I thought, to assemble a team of neurosurgeons and to develop for myself a neurosurgical practice, with Dr. Archibald's approval. I was ready with the technical know-how of the day and was keen to use my hands. That was what he wanted. For me, that would only be a beginning. So I promised to move to Montreal, and hoped to bring Cone with me.

After the sun had set behind the shoulder of Mount Royal that afternoon, its rays continued for a time to cast a wonderful warm light on the great buildings of Montreal below us. The cathedral and the Sun Life Building, rising alone above the other roofs on Dominion Square, were bathed in gold. I have seen this beauty often since then. But that afternoon, it seemed to me a promise, perhaps, for great things in the years to come.

8

Interlude in Germany

On the following morning, January 13, 1928, I woke early, as the Montreal–New York Express was throbbing its way southward. I dressed and sat at the window of my compartment, switching off the light and looking out into the darkness. The doubts that had awakened me must be faced. Why should anyone care to join me in Montreal? I wanted to plan the research and clinical organization of a team. But the team did not exist. And was I ready to do even my own part of the job? Had I the skill and the wisdom?

The tracks of the Delaware and Hudson Railroad run along the east bank of the Hudson River after they pass through Albany. I could be home in time for breakfast if I left the express at Yonkers and walked to Riverdale. As we were approaching the Yonkers stop, I saw, beyond the darkness of the river, a golden light that touched the tops of the lofty palisades.

It was a strange place for dawn to break — over there to the west. But I had seen dawn come like that before, on many a winter morning, as I walked to the seven o'clock commuter train in Riverdale. As the sun approached the rim of the world behind the watcher's back, its first rays touched the tops of the distant palisades with gold, moving down the face of the cliff until they reached the swiftly flowing flood of the Hudson. Then, day dawned and the gold was gone.

Able men would be ill-advised to join me, I mused, unless I had real clues that promised them a better understanding of the unknown mechanisms of the human brain. I had new methods for the microscope, it was true. But, it was not enough to grope with them blindly through the darkness. One must know where dawn will break and the gold appear.

I had told her not to come. But I found Helen waiting for me in the dark outside the Yonkers station. We drove home slowly, while I described the day in Montreal. We talked of the four children and of the schools, the culture and the way of life in that bilingual Canadian city, and what it would mean to become Canadians.

On the second day, realizing that I had, as yet, no promise in writing, I wired Dean Martin: "Is it safe to let my bridges burn?" His answering telegram came back at once, three words: "Burn your bridges." A detailed letter arrived from him the same day.

So, we did let the bridges burn. But, watching them go, one by one, my wife and I felt lonely and prematurely nostalgic. After all, we were saying good-bye to our native land — the lovely Wisconsin countryside of our youth as well as the professional world of later years. We were parting from neighbors and friends. We would miss the hospitals, the theaters and the opera. Even that giant, the thundering city itself, had cast its spell on us. Yes, although there was much in New York from which we were glad to escape, there was much we would miss.

"Why do you do this when we can give you every facility here in New York? Why look elsewhere?" Many asked me that. Some thought it madness. They had said something like that four years before when we went to Spain. We began to wonder ourselves. But, we continued to pack our lares and penates, not daring to look back.

I told Bill Cone the story and gave him an invitation to come with me to Montreal. He was delighted at first and laughed with excitement at the very thought of being a partner in the project. But counterproposals were made to him that same day — a laboratory of neuropathology of his own in the new New York Neurological Institute and "all the neurosurgery you can do." Elsberg joined Whipple in urging him to stay.

During the three and a half years since I had found Cone waiting for my return from Spain, he had grown in stature. He was now much more than an expert in neuropathology. He was a good clinician and a very promising operator. Added to that, he loved patients and he had a driving enthusiasm and a keen mind and singleness of purpose that are rare indeed. It seemed to me inevitable that he would decide to remain in New York. I cast about for someone who could replace him, but I found no one.

I had told Archibald impulsively to expect me in Montreal in March 1928. My family would follow in June, after school was out. But now, I was unsure and undecided. I knew I was not ready to make the plunge. Like one who would be a swimmer, I shivered instead at the end of the diving board.

Then it all changed — I am not quite sure when that was, sometime in the first week after the day of decision in Montreal. Our whole plan was altered. We postponed the plunge for six months, deciding to go to Breslau, Germany, and to take the family with us.

What brought about this sudden change of plan? A Frenchman, seeking a clue to the unexpected behavior of a male friend, is apt to shrug and say, *Cherchez la femme.* Not so here. It was a patient, a young man of eighteen years, William Hamilton, who triggered our decision to go to Germany and to the city of Breslau. And, because his case was one of those that were to chart my future course, I shall describe it in detail.

At the age of fifteen, Hamilton had been struck on the forehead by a brick that fell from a high chimney. He was taken at once, unconscious, to a hospital in New Jersey. There, a surgeon removed fragments of the broken skull and scraped out bits of brick from the wounded right frontal lobe. After that, he sutured the scalp and hoped for the best. The wound did heal, and the patient seemed to recover, although he had a soft pulsating place in his forehead.

Some months later, he began to have epileptic attacks. In each of them, he stiffened, lost consciousness, and fell to the ground, giving vent to a scream. He did not hear the scream. But others heard it and saw him writhing on the ground with convulsive movements of the arms and legs. When the movements stopped, he lay unconscious, and those about him discovered that he had bitten his tongue and soiled himself.

This was a fit, a generalized convulsion. The Romans called it "the falling disease" and the ancient Greeks named it "epilepsy," the curse of the gods. This so-called curse has many forms, depending on what part of the brain is the focus of trouble. Sometimes the patient does not lose consciousness but is aware of a numbness of a hand, an involuntary movement of a foot, a flashing of lights, or perhaps a dreamy state in which he relives some minutes of his own past. To Hamilton, however, epilepsy came in its most dreaded form, as an immediately generalized convulsion.

What was happening to him that could strike him down so suddenly? Within the brain, where it had been hurt by the falling brick, a sudden electrical discharge occurred at the time of each attack. It blocked the action of the delicate mechanisms that must be active if a man is to be conscious. It is in the nature of nerve cells to be electrically active. Indeed, each cell seems to develop its own individual electrical charge, and may be discharged as messages reach it and it plays its specific role in the business of the brain. This is normal. But in the epileptic state many cells discharge at once in what we call an epileptogenic explosion. The timing of such an explosion is as unpredictable as the lightning that flashes unheralded from a thundercloud.

Hamilton had been referred to me by his family doctor, a close friend of Professor Clarke, who had induced me to undertake the experimental study of brain scars on my arrival in New York. I had learned, during the years of that study, what happened in the brain after it was wounded. I had learned, too, how to remove the scar and not leave a second scar. If the operation was properly carried out, only a fluid-filled space was left, surrounded by normal brain.

When Hamilton entered my office, I decided the time had come at last to convert my research conclusions into therapeutic action. Bill Clarke, I suppose, was waiting for me to do just that. In any case, I operated on Hamilton three weeks before my January visit to Montreal. As the operation progressed, I discovered that in order to leave only normal convolutions, I would be forced to remove more than half of the right frontal lobe, a very radical procedure. But that is what I did.*

On my return from Montreal, Hamilton was up and about but still in hospital. He begged to be sent home. He seemed well

* See note 26.

physically, and I was much relieved to discover that the psychological tests, as far as they could go, showed no loss of mentality in spite of the wide removal of right frontal lobe. How could that be, if each convolution of the brain has a useful function? That question was to be a recurring one and a subject of much future study.

But *was* Hamilton cured? How could I tell? When he asked me that, I replied simply, "I hope so." But I wondered. Would the fits not return in the months or years that lay ahead, even if no further scar did form? If the attacks did return or if, somehow, he was worse off, the radical removal of brain would become unpardonable. But one patient would not provide adequate proof that this operation would succeed in other cases, even if I did wait, and even if he was cured of his attacks. Without such proof, would I be justified if I were to repeat this radical procedure in a series of patients?

The Father of Medicine knew the meaning of such dilemmas long ago: "Life is short," Hippocrates wrote, "the art so long, opportunity fugitive. Experience is deceptive and judgment difficult."

During the next few days, these questions spoke out from time to time in the shadows of my mind, the way research problems so often do. They went about with me, until a chance occurrence switched on the light. That happened when I stopped to speak to a general surgeon in the corridor of the Presbyterian Hospital. He had just returned from a journey to clinics abroad.

"By the way," he said, "I heard of a man in Breslau, Germany, who might interest you. He admits patients who have epilepsy to the hospital and keeps them there until he finds the cause of the fits in the brain. Then he removes the cause at operation." The doctor paused and shrugged, then added, "At least that is what they told me. I was never able to see him work."

"What's his name?" I asked.

"Foerster," he replied.

"Foerster? The name is familiar. Oh, yes," I exclaimed. "I read a paper by a man of that name. He showed that, years afterward, there is a wandering of the ventricles toward the site of a gunshot wound of the brain. *Ventrikel Wanderung* he called it."

"That must be the same man," the doctor replied. "He operates mostly, I'm told, on patients who were wounded in the war."

"But, as I remember it," I objected, "Foerster doesn't operate. He is a neurologist."

The doctor laughed. "He *is* a neurologist. He's the professor of neurology in Breslau University. You see, I went there to watch Kütner, professor of surgery. He told me that before the war, when Foerster wanted a craniotomy done, he brought the patient to the surgical clinic. Kütner would operate and Foerster would assist him. Since the war, Foerster operates on his own patients and Kütner never sees them anymore. Somehow, Foerster made himself into a neurological surgeon during the war. He didn't seem to want me around although I wanted to see him operate. They say he is bad tempered in the operating room."

This chance conversation stands out in my memory. I remember, even now, where it was. We were standing in the hospital corridor, beside a door that opened out on the old cement tennis court. What an impossible court that was to play on! Although I remember the doctor's words, I have forgotten his name and all else that followed.

Suddenly Hamilton's question, and the problem he presented, had moved forward onto the stage of my thinking. Did this neurologist have the evidence I needed? Had he done the series of cases that I was tempted to undertake? I must find that out. Somehow, I must go to see him.

I left for home early that afternoon and stopped at the library of the Academy of Medicine. There, Archie Malloch helped me to look up everything that Otfrid Foerster had published. He was, we discovered, at that time president of the exclusive German Society of Neurology and Psychiatry. He had written excellent articles on the surgical control of intractable pain and on the anatomy of the nervous system. But he had published nothing on the subject of surgery for epilepsy. Perhaps, if I were to visit him, he would tell me his results. Perhaps I might even examine under the microscope whatever it was he had removed. Whether he was doing what I had done or whether it was something different, I must discover what it was.

The problem of epilepsy had fascinated me from the time I had seen, and first studied, the brain. I had read and filled my index cards with notes from the writings of Hughlings Jackson. He believed that each seizure was the result of irritation at some particular focus in the brain.

That night, at home, we made the decision. Helen only laughed with excitement when I proposed another trip abroad. We would take the four children with us for six months and she would teach them herself, keeping them abreast of their classes, and they would learn German. We would, ourselves, improve the meager command of that language that each of us had acquired in college.

There were millions of epileptics around the world, I reflected. And they were waiting for help. Some of them, at least, must have brain scars. Some had seizures due to other causes. The drug treatment, which was, at that time, chiefly bromide and phenobarbital, was not very satisfactory.

I wrote to Foerster, asking his permission to visit his clinic as a graduate student, and to Archibald, asking permission to postpone arrival in Montreal until September. But we did not wait for answers. I managed to get a Rockefeller Fellowship from Richard Pearce, who was in charge of the foundation's medical philanthropy for Europe and Canada. It amounted to only one hundred eighty-two dollars a month but it added a grant for travel expenses for me. That would enable me to take trips to all the medical centers of Europe. When I wrote to Dean Martin at McGill to tell him the change of plan, he sent an immediate check for a thousand dollars toward our expenses. He thought highly of medical science in Germany, remembering his own graduate years there.

Thanks to the recent improvement in my private practice, I was able, at last, to pay off all the loans that had helped me through my graduate study period, and I put the remainder into the family travel budget. This would, I thought, get us safely back to Montreal, although we would certainly arrive there with no reserve in the bank.

Archibald agreed to the change. It was true that he had come to New York in June of 1927 to find a young man who would take over his neurosurgical practice, and only that. But when he found that I had what he called "large ideas," he understood. He had had "large ideas" himself and he needed financial support for them badly. But he too sent me an unsolicited check. It was for five hundred dollars. It followed me to Germany.

This trip had become a great obsession from which I did not want to escape. I realized how much I wanted to be alone, to think things out, to make a realistic approach toward understanding the human brain, to find a clue that would show me where dawn would touch the palisades of darkness.

But I had to have at least one teammate. I invited Cone to accompany me on a visit to Montreal and introduced him to everyone I knew — everyone, that is, except Professor Oertel and Sir Vincent Meredith. Columbia University was "making a terrible drive to keep Cone," I wrote to my mother, "and he has received an invitation from Percival Bailey to join him in his newly established neurosurgical department at Chicago University. The rivalry for him will be a good thing if I can get him in spite of that. . . . But anyhow, we're off, Helen and I, on the biggest adventure yet."

Two weeks later, I wrote my mother again: "Bill Cone has decided to throw in his lot with me in Montreal. He is turning his back on a big opportunity in New York. As Byron Stookey expressed it, 'the biggest opportunity I ever saw a man turn down.' "

Our fellow neurosurgeon Byron Stookey was somewhat wistful as he saw Cone and me leaving New York. If I had remained there, I would have enjoyed working shoulder to shoulder with him in the New York Neurological Institute. He was an able neurosurgeon who found himself blocked by the senior neurosurgeon, Charles Elsberg.

That is in no sense a criticism of those who were planning the enlarged institute of neurology in New York. My approach and my orientation were different and my departure inevitable. Elsberg had, no doubt, his own plans for neurosurgery in New York, and he was loyal to the institute's ambitious medical director, the professor of neurology, Frederick Tilney, as were the neurologists.*

Seeing it all in today's perspective, I have only a deep sense of gratitude to all those who were building the great institutions in uptown New York — gratitude for so many lessons and so much friendship.

Our Laboratory of Neurocytology was closing its doors in the old Presbyterian Hospital. Cone and I speeded up the work in order to finish off every detail. A set of duplicate reports was sent to the Royal Victoria Hospital and many hundreds of precious specimens and microscopical sections were packed lovingly in an enormous barrel and shipped to Montreal. Thus, the new Mon-

* See note 27.

treal laboratory would start as a continuation, not as a beginning.

There were dinners and other occasions of farewell. At one of them, the neurologists of the Vanderbilt Clinic gave me what the weekly letter described as "a nice leather traveling bag" provided with a special snap-lock that fastened the two halves of the bag together mysteriously. I put the kindest interpretation on the gesture.

So the Penfield family sailed for Germany on the twenty-first of March, 1928, the very day on which the rest of the staff of the old Presbyterian moved uptown to the new medical center.

From mid-Atlantic, I wrote to my mother: "Well — seven years in New York! I wonder what Montreal has in store. Whether we shall be permanent there depends on whether or not they will back a combined neurological and neurosurgical clinic. Already the Royal Victoria Hospital has *withdrawn their support* from the laboratory, $2200 yearly, which was about half enough. This," my letter continued, "has been withdrawn by Sir Vincent Meredith. However, there is some money available and I intend to use it for everything needed in the first year, regardless of the future. If they will not then back the undertaking, I shall hope to be able to leave." *

This loss of support was indeed a blow to me. It came directly from the hospital president through W. R. Chenoweth, the superintendent. It confirmed my initial conviction that, unless something happened to force that aged dictator into retirement, my future in that hospital held no great promise. I had gambled on the probability that age and sclerosing arteries would be on my side. But I seemed to have lost.

Nevertheless — in spite of this news and despite the fact that, up to the time of sailing, Professor Foerster had not replied from Breslau, the letter written to my mother from shipboard was actually exuberant:

"Our getting away from New York went very smoothly although Helen and I had only four hours of sleep on next to the last night and only two hours the last night. [We were packing what had to be packed for Europe, on the one hand, and for Montreal on the other.] You may imagine," the letter added, "that without Helen's

* See note 28.

courage, ability and patience, I should never have dared to undertake these trips." *

When we docked in Bremen, a telegram was brought aboard ship. It was signed "Otfrid Foerster" and written in English. He welcomed us to Germany and invited me to his clinic. Thus, my letter home concluded: "Just pulling in. All packed. Twenty pieces of luggage! Excitement high and all happy. A busy trip . . . and yet I think I have never enjoyed one more. Hope we can make it across Germany in one jump. It is fourteen hours of train-travel to Breslau."

We did make it, although there were incidents that were amusing and even terrifying. The terror really hit me while we were changing trains late at night in Berlin's vast and gloomy station. I stood on the edge of the high arrival platform with Baby Jeff on one arm and the new neurological traveling bag gripped firmly in the other hand. At that moment, the two halves of the bag burst open, spilling bottles, toilet articles, diapers and freshly written manuscript onto the dark track below. Giving Jeff to his ten-year-old brother, I climbed down to retrieve the lost articles. If a train had come through then . . . well, it didn't.

Most of our first month was to be devoted to learning German in the village of Obernigk, an hour's train journey outside Breslau. It was a health resort on the edge of a dark forest where the trees were planted in orderly rows. Fräulein Bergmann entered the family here as our German governess, an event of some importance since she was to remain more than ten years with us. Since she spoke no English and no one in the *pension* and village spoke anything but German, the setting was perfect for learning spoken German.

The first letter that reached us from Montreal brought further startling news. Sir Vincent Meredith, seventy-eight, had suffered a very severe "stroke" and was, the letter stated, completely incapacitated. The picture of the man, and his charming wife at tea, came back to me. My prognosis, it seemed, had been correct after all, except for the timing. I could only heave a sigh of relief, and reflect that dictatorial power in the hands of any man, however well-meaning, may be a threat to the common good.

* See note 29.

The time that I could devote exclusively to learning German was brief. The weekly letter home described the interruption as follows: "A telegram came from Foerster in Breslau to say he would operate, next day, on a case that would interest me. He did a splendid operation, removing a sixteen-year-old gunshot-wound-scar from the brain. It had caused epilepsy, and had pulled the whole brain toward the scar in the way I described and discussed in London last June [1927]."

It was for this I had hoped. So I stood in the Wenzelhancke Krankenhaus operating room, watching Foerster carry out his operation from start to finish, as Max Peet and Eddie Kahn had watched me. Throughout the long procedure, his attention to his task never faltered. His methods were fussy and awkward and his patience, with his assistants, very short. But he adhered to proper basic principles and he treated the brain with a sort of reverent gentleness.

In the end, although his technique was different, very different, from mine, he did what I had done in the case of Hamilton. He removed the scar and, with it, the surrounding partially injured convolutions. He looked tired when, at last, he turned from the patient late in the afternoon and, taking off his mask, handed me the specimen, a brain scar and the adjacent convolutions delicately excised.

"During the next three or four days," to quote again from my weekly letter, "I worked hard at the tissue and succeeded in getting some very pretty stains of different kinds of neuroglia cells. In such tissue," the letter concluded hopefully, "lie hidden some of the secrets of epilepsy, if not the whole story."

Foerster was not, himself, an expert neuropathologist. Consequently, after each of his previous operations for the radical treatment of epilepsy, he had divided the specimen in half, sending one half to Professor Wilhelm Spielmeyer, the celebrated neuropathologist in Munich, and keeping the other half in reserve. If Spielmeyer ever did make reports to him, I never saw them. But I suspect that he found the standard German techniques of that period as unsatisfactory to the purpose as I had, before I ran away from New York to learn the Spanish techniques.

Foerster had secured the special chemicals I knew I should need, and had equipped a little laboratory for me in the corner of *Abteilung Acht* (Ward Eight). There I was separated from the patients, in their beds, only by a wooden partition seven feet in height. Sitting at my bench there, the voices, the sounds and the smells of busy hospital life came to me. But I could work undisturbed. Oblivious concentration has always come easily to me. At about eleven o'clock each morning, I would hear the head nurse — they called her *Schwester* — cry out, "Der Herr Professor kommt." Her cry was followed by an outburst of scurrying followed by a sudden respectful silence as the door opened and Professor Otfrid Foerster entered, followed by white-coated assistants and students in the sober Germanic sequence of seniority.

I suppose it must have been the third or fourth morning before I was ready for him. That morning I stood on a stool and peered over the partition as he made his clinical rounds. He passed from bed to bed, stooping above each patient in turn, examining and listening intently, nodding, shaking his head. The chief resident described each patient's history and the findings. The patients themselves, it seemed to me, were strangely silent. Something about the relationship disturbed me. The expression on the professor's thin, strong, deeply lined face was often kindly as well as intent. But, something was missing, something that had to do with friendship. There was no laugh, no spontaneous talk between doctor and patient.

I was to discover later that his patients feared him and sometimes hated to return to report their progress after operation. They failed to discover the kindly human being that lurked behind his professorial façade, and I suspect that they hid from him some things a doctor should know. These people of Prussia had a deep respect for learning. They believed in authority and liked it. It gave them a sense of security, no doubt, and yet something of great value was missing — affection on the one hand, understanding on the other.

At last, the ward visit was over and the professor turned from his white-coated followers while they stood erect and clicked their heels. Then came his curious transformation. The man who entered the doorway of my laboratory had changed, as if a cloak had fallen from his shoulders. He was impulsive and unpretentious. When he saw that I was ready for him, he laughed with

boyish excitement and sat down to examine the microscopical
sections spread out on the table, he with his ponderous Zeiss
microscope and I with mine. It was only three weeks since I had
arrived in Breslau, wondering what I should find, how I might be
received in a strange Germany.

This was one of the great moments in my life, one for which I
had prepared hopefully. I had used the Spanish methods of impregnation. The results were satisfactory. Foerster and I seemed
to share an awareness that something hidden was close at hand.
The brain cells were clearly shown with all their complicated
branches — neurons, neuroglia and microglia. The connective tissue cells, too, outside the meningeal sheaths were distinct (thanks
to the Laidlaw stain). In the scar, cells were mixed and inter-
mingled. And in the adjacent half-destroyed convolutions, there
were remarkable changes. I had come to recognize them in my experimental series. But this scar was sixteen years old. The changes
had gone much farther and the man was subject to epileptic fits.

We were seeing the anatomy of the cause, under the microscope,
quite clearly now. The cause itself must be there during life. It
must be part of the abnormal physiology. That, we could not see.
But we might begin to guess its nature. We could create hypotheses now based on valid clues. In the darkness of this mystery, the
clues would point to where dawn might break.

Foerster hurried off and brought back jar after jar of formalin,
each one with its careful label, until he had placed on the workbench all the other specimens, or rather the half-specimens, in his
series of operations for epilepsy. "I'd like to have you study them
all," he said.

Then he proposed that we should publish, together, his whole
operative series with his results and with my microscopical findings. I agreed. Once again a door had opened and I was in a room
that no one had entered before me. The tools I needed were here
to hand, and from distant doorways, opportunity seemed to
beckon, as if I were moving on through a labyrinth like the mythical one that Daedalus built in ancient Crete.

There were twelve cases in Foerster's series. The patients had
survived, and they could now be reported, from one to five years
after operation. The results were excellent from the patients' point
of view. It was clear that Foerster was carrying out the right opera-

tion. My experimental studies showed why it was right. Together, we could see ways of improvement now. There were details in his procedure that I would adopt. Some I would change, I thought, as I looked into the future.

In the weeks that followed, I worked out the story of healing and scarring in the human brain, a wonderful sequel to my animal series. I wondered what Bill Clarke would say if he could stoop above me and look over my shoulder, as I had seen him do so often in his class of surgical pathology in Columbia's medical school.

I recalled his knowing smile when I met him first and when he asked me to help him teach the medical students. "We can show them," he had pointed out, "the healing of all the tissues in the body except the brain and spinal cord. Every surgeon must learn to understand for himself the healing process in his own field." Then he had asked his questions: "What does go on in the brain? How does it heal? I want you to show me here," he had said, as he pointed his crooked finger at the microscope between us.

Professor Clarke knew I couldn't do it, fresh though I was from the laboratories of the world. He knew, too, that there was no better place than his own efficient laboratory in which to set up the initial experiments that would perhaps answer his questions.

"Wouldn't you like," he had added as if he were speaking to himself, "wouldn't you like to see how the nerve cells and all the supporting cells behave after the blood supply is shut off by a blood clot or a stroke, or when the brain is injured in other ways?" And then had come his final question: "What is the cause of epilepsy?"

Well, after seven long years, I could answer his questions — all but the last one. To that I could offer partial answers now. I could suggest exciting approaches to epilepsy and to the mystery of its ultimate cause.

Having done that, I thought as I sat there at my bench in Breslau, I was free, at last, to turn back to neurophysiology, to study the living processes that lead to epileptic discharge and to study the changing circulation of the brain.

And there was another great gain that I only vaguely perceived. Now that I was justified in operating on the brain of conscious men and women, a new field of exploration was calling and a new approach to the general anatomy and physiology of the brain was opening to me as well. All this would be a side issue while treating epileptics. But I knew, now, that many doors would open provided I had the wit to take advantage of each opportunity as it appeared. To put it all another way — the patient's advantage and the desire of a team of workers to study the physiology of the brain could well be served at the same time.

The prospect of operating, under local anesthesia, on a long series of patients who might be cured of their epilepsy had another very exciting aspect. The electrical stimulation that must be used to guide the surgeon in his removal of the cause would perhaps tell the thoughtful surgeon many secrets about the living, functioning brain. He could learn what the conscious patient might tell him. This would help the neurosurgeon to understand the interrelationship of the mind to localized functional mechanisms in the brain.

The relationship of electricity to knowledge of brain function is part of a fascinating story. Electricity was first discovered as a form of energy in 1792. They called it animal electricity at the start. Its discovery came when Luigi Galvani in the University of Bologna and Alessandro Volta of Pavia realized that energy was being conducted along the nerves of a frog to its leg muscles. That energy made the muscles contract. Almost eighty years later, two German physiologists exposed the brain of a dog, under a light anesthetic, and touched the cerebral cortex, in what we now call the motor convolution, with an electrode that delivered a gentle electric current.

Behold! The dog moved its paw on the opposite side of the body as if he were making a voluntary gesture. The experimenters, Gustav Fritsch and Edouard Hitzig, published their findings in 1870, stating that they had found the place where "the spirit enters the body." What they had done was to prove that there is, within the brain, a separate mechanism that must go into action during the animal's voluntary use of the leg, a motor mechanism in which the activating energy is electrical.

They had given the world a clue as to how the brain worked. Physiologists could now proceed to localize, little by little, discrete functional mechanisms, electrically activated, within the brain. Also, Charles Sherrington could identify the involuntary reflexes that served the overall integration of function within the brain, and Ivan Pavlov could show that new skills were learned by the establishment of acquired or conditioned reflexes within the nerve circuits of the cerebral cortex. After the discovery of electricity, men came to understand that all the pathways of the brain and spinal cord and nerves are being normally traversed at lightning speed by electrical potentials.

It is easy to see, now, that the six months of making ready to launch the Montreal project would have been well spent if there had been no other gains than we had made at the workbench in this German hospital. But there *were* other gains, real ones.

On May 14, 1928, the weekly letter to my mother referred to a gain in the direction of editorship: "Our German has improved and we are very happy and well situated here," it began. "I am sending off letters to the authors of the various chapters in the *Cytology* that I have undertaken to edit. I can't believe that Cajal and Hortega and Bielschowsky *et al.* will write for it. I have selected the world's best as nearly as possible. My editorship seems rather preposterous. It *will* be a sorry joke if they all refuse."

Another gain came from Otfrid Foerster himself. As the professor of neurology and the neurosurgeon in the University of Breslau, and as perennial president of the German Society of Neurology and Psychiatry, he was a rather awe-inspiring phenomenon. But he seemed a simple man at home, or in the laboratory, or sitting over a cup of coffee, or sipping a glass of beer. He was a talker and teacher who loved to talk and teach. He wanted to improve his own command of English. But he would listen, too, and so we were good companions. Helen and I dined with him and his wife in Breslau and they came to us in Obernigk. Their little flaxen-haired daughters, Ilsa and Lorchen, came for longer visits that contributed to the language-learning project of our own children in that best of all classrooms, the playground where they joined the other village children.

Foerster had a remarkable memory and a fund of great experience on which he could draw with vivid accuracy, when stimulated to it by a congenial listener. Only a few years earlier, when Lenin had been struck down by a sudden paralysis in Moscow, it was Foerster who had been selected from all Europe and called to his bedside for consultation. And during the subsequent two years of that mighty Communist leader's life, Foerster had been flown back and forth regularly between Breslau and Moscow.*

Rumor had it that the Soviet government paid Foerster a prince's ransom for his medical services. Perhaps that was how it came about, as one of the Breslau medical students informed me, that Foerster alone among the professors in the medical school could afford to make no charge for the formal series of lectures he gave. It might explain also how he was able to give a grand banquet at the close of the lecture series. I remember the banquet well. It was held in the Nord Hotel, and goblets of champagne, at every place along the white tablecloth, held freshly peeled peaches that turned impressively under the gentle bombardment of bubbles rising from the bottom of the glasses!

Cone came from London with his wife, Avis, to attend Foerster's university lectures, and then continued on his visits to other neurosurgical clinics. He was making his own gains since this was his first trip abroad. He was watching surgeons operate, following neurologists in clinics, seeing the world.

After the lecture series was over, Foerster and I went on our own week-long tour to medical centers. When we crossed the frontier into France, it was the first time for him in the fourteen years since the outbreak of World War I. Before we left Breslau, his devoted assistant, Dr. Schwab, came to me in consternation: "The professor has had a haircut! Is he really going to other clinics with you?"

In Strasbourg, Foerster and I visited a famous surgeon, René Leriche. Each morning, for three days, we watched him operate and, each evening, we dined with him and his German-born wife. I had seen Leriche operate four years before, as I was on my way home from Spain. Indeed, on reaching New York, I had published a critical review of his work on the nerves that control blood vessels. We hoped, Foerster and I, that Leriche's procedures might suggest to us some way of altering the circulation of cerebral vessels for the benefit of epileptics. This proved to be a vain hope, but we stayed on to admire his dexterity. We listened to his fascinating peroration while he was scrubbing his hands before the first

* See note 30.

operation on the first morning. On the second day, to our astonishment, he repeated it with unabated eloquence, as South American surgeons came crowding in to watch him. And on the third day, word for word, he made the same speech.

At midday before our departure, Foerster and I took lunch alone in the sunshine on the gay terrace of Strasbourg's Maison Rouge. It was a holiday in Alsace. When my companion was somewhat mellowed by the surroundings and the wine, he reproduced Leriche's introductory speech, word for word in perfect French, complete with gestures, and we laughed and laughed together, not thinking the less of our friend, René Leriche.

Surgeons may standardize their surgery and laboratory men their techniques, but they differ amazingly as human beings. The best of them, in my experience, are apt to be the most colorful, variously cultured, and, above all, entertaining individuals.*

From Strasbourg, we returned to Germany and went on to Berlin to visit a very remarkable neurological institute and to meet a distinguished man and wife who illustrate very well what I have just said. I refer to Professor Oskar Vogt and his wife, Cécile. But my letter home, June 4, 1928, describes them. Foerster and I were guests in their home at dinner and the following day at lunch.

"Oskar Vogt," I wrote, "is the director of the Kaiser Wilhelm Institut für Hirnforschung, which means 'brain research.' He is, I suppose, the intellectual leader of German neurology. His wife, Cécile Vogt, is almost equally famous. They sign their scientific communications 'C. and O. Vogt' always. Their work is always *profound* and I was curious about them, but feared I would not be able to meet them.

"She," the letter continued, "is French (they met in Paris when he was a student there) and he is a roaring German. What a household! . . . Into the father's rumbling speech comes, often, a reference to *meine Tochter* and then he smiles.†

"Professor Vogt," the letter went on, "talks all the time, always with spirit and feeling and wisdom and complete assurance. When he is excited, which is often, his old dueling scars stand out on the left side of his face and he sends out a fine spray over his short

* See note 31.
† See note 32.

white beard. I intercepted this spray several times. But it did not burn as you might have expected.

"His wife listens, leaning forward, with a faraway look in her wide-set eyes, and a smile. She is tall and smiles most of the time. She seems oblivious of the fact that her glasses are about to drop from her nose, that the maid bungles things at the table, that her husband sets the maid right. One thing she follows with eager comprehension and that is his steady flow of erudite conversation.

"The Russian government," my letter added, "called him to Moscow at Lenin's death to take away his brain for examination, as they had called Foerster, hopefully, to save Lenin from death.

"Complete sections are made routinely through each whole brain in the institute laboratory. It takes one technician one year to do it. Each section is photographed by one of [Vogt's] four photographers. He has set himself the overwhelming task of mapping out the arrangement of the nerve cells in every area, and of allotting to the various types of cells the role they play in mental processes."

The unusual detail that appears in this letter to my mother shows how deeply I was impressed. The Kaiser Wilhelm Institute had plenty of funds and an all-embracing purpose. Alfred Krupp, Germany's great industrialist, was Vogt's friend and financial supporter. There were more technicians than I could count in room after room of this beehive of science. They prepared perfectly standardized sections of reasonable quality taken from the brains of man, mammal or insect, under the all-seeing eye of the director.

The work was basic and careful. But the approach was toward all knowledge of brain anatomy. Vogt was using animal experimentation as well as the microscope. And he was making many conclusions about the cellular architecture and the function of the brain. It was too far removed from patients and diseases and human physiology to suit me. They were working, it seemed to me, in the dark without the help of clinical clues that might show where the dawn would break.

This was not the sort of institute that had been building itself in my mind. Here was efficiency, accuracy, great industry. But here also was an attitude of unimpeachable authority. That made me uneasy.

Vogt, I discovered, had studied the brain of Lenin exhaustively.

Concurrently with that, he was, at that time, making a comparative study of the brains of intellectuals, using the brains of low-grade German criminals as controls for this study. So, the three of us sat down, as I remember well, to spend some time, each with his microscope. Vogt pointed out that Lenin had the brain of a genius. His evidence showed what he had expected, and just what someone in Moscow hoped it would. The Moscow hope, it would seem, was to discover in Lenin a superior being.

In the brain of Lenin, we were shown many giant nerve cells. We could see them in the third layer of the gray matter. "Vogt compared this," to quote from my letter again, "with the brain of an ordinarily intelligent Russian and the brain of a murderer, and he stood up and roared out long sentences of rumbling German."

But I grew fatigued at last and my mind wandered. I am not a genius at foreign language, or at anything else, alas. Neither Foerster nor I was convinced with regard to the brain of genius. We saw the giant cells and agreed that they were not there in the control sections. But — Foerster expressed his doubts when he wondered if this could be a normal characteristic of the Oriental brain. Lenin, he said, had had some Chinese ancestors. On the other hand, my doubts were different. I wondered about the technique of fixation that had been used in the preparation of Lenin's brain.*

There was much to learn in this splendid laboratory complex, dominated by the Vogts and dedicated to the broad field of neurological science. But it seemed to me dangerously isolated, too far removed from patients and from general medicine and surgery. The New York Neurological Institute, I reflected, suffered from the opposite form of isolation and the National Hospital at Queen Square, London, likewise. They were concerned with neurological patients but were too far removed from basic science and the other disciplines of medicine, too far away in space and in awareness.

---

* This is not the place to discuss scientific evidence. It may be stated, however, that critics of Vogt have since suggested that the difference in brain cells of these two classes of men, the genius and the ordinary citizen, is due to the fact that there was a period of days between death and autopsy in the case of the great men he studied. In contrast to this, there was immediate autopsy in the case of the criminals. Thus, the "giant cells" might be no more than evidence of the swelling that occurs when there is delay between death and postmortem examination.

Oskar Vogt was all alone in one sense. He had every facility that he could use. He had associates, like his wife and the neurocytologist Max Bielschowsky, but no one to compete with him. When one is alone, it is so easy to go off on a tangent.

I wanted to see neurology and neurosurgery united in one academic department. I had struggled to make myself a little of everything — surgeon, neurologist, laboratory man. In the end, I had learned that I could not master it all well enough to trust myself to be a lonely dictator, as Vogt was, or Foerster for that matter. It seemed to me there was only one way to give the neurological patient the best in every aspect of diagnosis and treatment and one way to plan research through the years. That was by means of a working fellowship arrangement, the establishment of a team that could work near the bedside of the patient.

There had to be a captain of the team. He would have to organize, it is true, and plan for the future. But he could also dream and carry out his own work quietly. He need not strive to do and be the impossible, the lonely authoritarian. This, I suppose, was the substance of my thinking on leaving Berlin.

"During that week of travel," my letter of June 4 continued, "I found Foerster to be a remarkably good companion. . . . I am learning how to sit and talk, or not talk. Foerster has the best mind with which I have come in contact, with the exception of Sherrington. They are of the same mental type as far as simplicity, accuracy and logic are concerned. Neither makes any pretense. I get more from Foerster, for he has done what I want to do and deals with the same problems. He doesn't operate as well as we do in many ways."

The letter closes with a sentence that shows how far our discussions ranged, not leaving out philosophy and religion: "Foerster believes that the soul of each of us is not, in any sense, a product of the brain."

During these visits in Europe, I was able to introduce myself to some of the men who had agreed to prepare chapters for the *Cytology and Cellular Pathology of the Nervous System*. I was editing it actively now and I learned a good deal from each of them. And I was able, also, to coordinate their work — Bielschowsky in the Vogt Institute, Ariens Kappers in Amsterdam, Phillip

Stöhr in Bonn, Jean Nageotte at the Collège de France in Paris.

I bombarded del Rio-Hortega with letters and finally, after a long silence, received a telegram from him followed by a letter. "Of course I will write for your book. How could you think otherwise." Cajal alone refused, saying he had advancing arteriosclerosis, the histologist's way of describing old age. Nageotte took over part of Cajal's chapter, and I planned to do the other part.

In the quiet intervals of the summer, I studied Foerster's excised specimens in Breslau and thought about the cause of epilepsy, building up hypotheses that could be tested in the future. There was microscopic evidence that the scar exerted an advancing pull upon the brain and upon its blood vessels. Sometimes, when Foerster tugged on the scar with his forceps at the time of operation, the patient had one of his typical attacks right there on the operating table. But, the question arose: Was that pull, necessarily, to be considered a cause of the subject's habitual spontaneous attack? I wondered about these things.

Something more was happening within the atrophic convolutions near each scar. Here and there in the gray matter were tiny areas of recent cell death. Each area was located about one of the smallest arteries as if the blood flow through it had been, at some time, too long shut off. This same phenomenon had been described by Wilhelm Spielmeyer in Munich. He had found it in the brain of epileptics of various types as well as in the post-traumatic cases. I went to visit Spielmeyer. He was head of an institute of neuropathology. Thus, his field of interest was restricted to what could be seen through the microscope.

To my great pleasure I found an American neurologist, Stanley Cobb, working in Spielmeyer's laboratory. I had known him from the time when he was a graduate student under the great psychiatrist Adolf Meyer, at Johns Hopkins, and I was a medical student there. He was now preparing to launch his own project in neurology and he was to have the help of the Rockefeller Foundation. His plan was to return to Harvard as professor of neuropathology and to the Boston City Hospital as neurologist in chief. Cobb had been, some years earlier, a student at the Vogt Institute.

When I visited Vogt with Foerster, I had informed him that I was a friend of Cobb. Vogt had looked at me then with interest and exclaimed, "Oh yes, the handsome American, an excellent fellow." Cobb *was* an excellent fellow. I had found in him a kindred spirit — contemptuous of pretense, almost naïve in his hope of what might be done by research in the field of neurology.

Returning from a later visit to neurological centers, this time in the Scandinavian capitals, I remarked in my weekly letter: "Berlin, Aug. 26, 1928 . . . and now I have a complete picture of neurology in Europe. Helen is in Obernigk, typing out my report of the other clinics. When this supplement is finished, the whole report will be sent to the Rockefeller Foundation.*

"They asked me for something," the letter continued, "but they don't expect the exhaustive report that I shall send. It is the least I can do to repay them for paying my traveling expenses, and it may also serve an ulterior purpose."

The castle-in-the-air was clear in outline now. It had grown into a project and a purpose. My report was, in fact, an extensive survey, rather a presumptuous one for a young man to make.

The men I have admired most were always simple men — honest in attitude and still learning. Foerster proved himself to be such a man. Others were Osler and Sherrington at Oxford; my teacher of neurology in London, Gordon Holmes; my teacher of surgery, Allen Whipple in New York; and, fortunately for me, the man who was to become my new chief in Montreal, Edward Archibald. These were all open-minded, simple men.

During these early years, the poems of Edna St. Vincent Millay were often on my bedside table. I took delight in her imageries, but applied them to my own thinking in ways that might have surprised the poet.

> *Spring rides no horses down the hill*
> *But comes on foot, a goose girl still.*
> *And all the loveliest things there be*
> *Come simply, so, it seems to me. . . .†*

My personal heroes rode no horses down the hill. They moved through their lives on foot.

The next letter home was written in Obernigk, September 2,

---

* See note 33.
† "The Goose Girl," from *The Harp-Weaver and Other Poems,* by Edna St. Vincent Millay (New York and London: Harper and Brothers, 1923).

1928: "I am straining to finish the paper on epilepsy, writing out my own part and all that I understand of Foerster's. I shall leave it with him to translate and amplify. He is full of ideas and determined energy. I stayed in Breslau late yesterday to sit with him, after supper, until train time at 10:30. He becomes a philosopher at that time in the evening." Foerster was fifty-five, eighteen years older than I was at that time.

On September 9, 1928, I wrote: "Wednesday night, Helen and I worked till 2:30 in the morning on my paper with Foerster. She, typing, of course. It was finished. . . . There will be fifty illustrations! In some of them, I tried my hand at drawing, as his artist is not very good. . . .

"Thursday evening," the letter continued, "Helen and I dined with the Foersters very quietly. He is proud of his wines and they had beautiful glasses of Bohemian colored glass which rang out in remarkable soft tones when they were clinked together."

In our Obernigk *pension,* the large bedroom on the second floor, used by my wife and me, was also our workshop. It opened pleasantly through a French door onto a balcony where she and I had rolls and coffee alone each morning and where we competed for the marmalade with German hornets. A tile stove was placed in one wall of the room. There was a large desk against another wall and an enormous typewriter we had borrowed, against the third wall. My wife was not a trained typist. But she made herself an accurate one. And so the many pages of the Foerster paper could be completed for publication, and the long report sent off to the Rockefeller Foundation.

It is not by dreaming, nor by withdrawal from the world into narrow monastic isolation, that one can best prepare for his work in the world. The busy months of postponement in Germany served their purpose well for me. So many elements entered into this reconsideration, philosophical and cultural as well as intellectual and technical. I had the new ideas and the criticism that can come from contact with many minds. And I had help, companionship and contentment.

Years later, when my mother typed out the letters I wrote to her in 1928, she inserted a letter written to her by my wife. Then Mother added her own assessment: "I have inserted this letter, that Helen wrote to me, so that her children may have a glimpse of their wonderful mother who, through all the hard years of their early married life, has stood shoulder to shoulder with their father, strengthening him, working with him and for him, with never a thought for herself. A man with such a wife is blessed beyond measure."

It was my great good fortune, just before the end of the time in Germany, to spend a week with the man whose reasoned criticism I needed most at this time. It came about in this way. As we were to sail from Hamburg following the meeting of the German Neurological Congress in that city, I left the family behind in Obernigk, preceding them by a week. Sir Gordon Holmes came to the congress and he and I were constantly together throughout the meeting. We watched Foerster acting as president, seeing him thus at a distance. We discussed the scientific presentations. But, most important to me was this: I could tell Holmes what I had learned and what I had come to think and plan, and could hear his sometimes caustic comments.

Holmes had become, by that time, London's foremost neurologist. (This claim is borne out by the fact that, when the International Neurological Congress met in London seven years later, Holmes was its president.) He had received his early training in neuropathology and neuroanatomy in Germany. During the 1914–1918 war, he had been neurological consultant to British troops abroad. This was his return to Europe after ten years of peaceful reorientation. By nature, by training and by experience as editor of the leading neurological journal, *Brain,* this rugged warmhearted Irishman had acquired a remarkable capacity to evaluate and criticize.

He studied the plan I had drawn up as editor of the *Cytology and Cellular Pathology of the Nervous System* and suggested changes and rearrangements of chapters. His reaction to this and to German science in general was, for me, a bracing wind that I needed and could use. As my weekly letter expressed it, his willingness to spend the time with me was "flattering and surprising." Foerster was anxious to meet him, as were many others, and I could sometimes be the one to bring these men, once official enemies, together as colleagues with a common interest in neurology.

One afternoon, on the impulse of the moment, we decided to

stay away from the formal dinner of the congress. We "played hooky" and hired a double-oared rowboat and rowed all the way around Aussen Ulster and had dinner in a pleasant restaurant where we talked of many things. "The Aussen Ulster," as I wrote to my mother, "is one of Hamburg's two lakes that redeem an otherwise very busy and businesslike city. They are alive with sailboats and canoes and surrounded by lovely residences."

One morning in August, when I was working quietly in Obernigk, a message was brought to our *pension* by a neighbor who had a telephone. It came from the mother of one of Foerster's patients in a private hospital in Breslau, asking me to come to see her. Foerster had said nothing of this to me, so I ignored her summons. Two days later, there was a stir in the village as an impressive member of the Breslau police arrived. He came to our *pension* and announced to Fräulein Leitloff, our hostess, that Professor Penfield was to come to a certain clinic as soon as possible.

This summons produced a disturbance in Pension Leitloff that was quite extraordinary. Our children's nurse, Fräulein Bergmann, came rushing upstairs. "Aber, Frau Professor," she cried, calling my wife that for the first time, "you did not tell me your husband was a professor. I am so sorry. I did not know." She, herself, it was easy to see, was highly pleased. She was now governess to the children of a "Frau Professor." The deference, respect and social standing accorded to a professor in Germany was, and still is, unknown and difficult to appreciate in the New World.

I must admit that I was secretly delighted with the change. From that morning onward, I found that my opinions were clothed in the splendor of an authority I had never known before. My merest suggestion was law. Here was another view of the authoritarian regime that I had not considered!

Next day I took the train to Breslau and found my way to the "nursing home" in which Professor Foerster treated his private patients. The attendant, who opened the door, did so as if I had been long expected. She took me up to the second floor. "The New York lady [Mrs. William Ottmann]," she explained, "has a room of her own. Her son is the patient in the front room at the other end of the hall." The mother of the patient was waiting in her room.

"Your friend," she said, "Dr. Rawle Geyelin, sends you his regards. Did he not write you? Perhaps he thought it was enough when he wrote to Professor Foerster." Geyelin was indeed an old friend, a clever and very well informed attending physician at the Presbyterian Hospital with whom I had worked on many occasions.

"My son," Mrs. Ottmann continued, "has had epileptic seizures for three years. At first, the attacks seemed to be well controlled by Dr. Geyelin's high-fat diet. But not recently. Perhaps you did not know that Dr. Geyelin is himself not well. He has stopped seeing patients. He told me he was going away for a long period of study. When I asked him what I was to do with William, he said you had told him about Foerster and his operations on epilepsy here in Breslau. I suppose he didn't know what more he could do. So he sent us here.

"But, the attacks," she continued, "are much longer now and more severe. I live in terror of them. I think, each time, he is going to die and perhaps it's all my fault. Poor William! He has no idea what happens. The attacks are dreadful. We have to carry him and everyone stares." She turned away for a moment. When she turned back, she was in full control, but her voice had become husky.

"Well, here we are. I have to make the decisions for my only son and for his future — and for mine. I am all alone, you know. But of course you don't know. You don't read the papers. My husband and I are divorced.

"Now," she continued, "Professor Foerster tells me that the X rays, taken after air-injection, show that William has an abnormality in the brain. He says it could be the cause of his attacks. He wants to do what he calls 'a small operation' to study the condition further. But I am afraid to let him operate. Dr. Geyelin said you would help me decide. I want you to examine William and tell me what you think of it all."

I saw her predicament clearly enough. But I shook my head. "I cannot advise you. I can only tell you what a wonderful friend and teacher Professor Foerster is and what an excellent neurologist. He is eighteen years older than I am, and I came here to study under him. You told him you wanted to see me, I suppose? If so, he decided not to mention it to me."

The "New York lady," as the attendant had called her, took me to her son's room. William was a big, lively, handsome boy (or man) of sixteen years, ready to face anything if it would free him from the strange condition that had come upon him. I talked with him about life and sport but I did not examine him.

When Mrs. Ottmann and I returned to her room, she smiled a little sadly but she did not repeat her request for medical advice. She was a woman of charm and culture and wealth. But she was also one to understand quickly and make her own decisions.

"I suppose," she said, "I should let Dr. Foerster do whatever he suggests. But, I'll tell you now why I began to hesitate and why I sent you word. When you didn't come, I even induced the Breslau police to summon you. I won't tell you how that was done." She laughed and then became serious again.

"I saw Professor Foerster hurrying down the corridor to another patient's room with a full syringe in his hand. There was no cover over the needle. I have been a patient myself and I have noticed that the nurses place a sterile sponge over the needle point."

I made light of her criticism of Foerster's surgical technique and took my leave, realizing that she had placed her finger on what I, too, felt was Foerster's greatest weakness as an operative surgeon. I felt this, and yet, since I had seen no catastrophic infection, I had no proof.

In the medical profession, there are certain rules of behavior that are not included in the ancient Oath of Hippocrates. The Golden Rule of etiquette among physicians is this: Treat the other doctor's patients as you would have the other doctor treat yours. And here is a corollary to that: Judge not a fellow physician until you have all the facts and until he has told you his plans.

The reader will understand that if Professor Foerster had asked me to see young Ottmann, I could have come to the boy as a consultant. I might, or I might not, have been of help then. Since he did not, I might come to the Breslau nursing home as a friend, but not to interfere as a physician. Mrs. Ottmann could take her son back to her physician in New York but she could only make trouble by trying to force me to interfere in Germany (either with or without the help of the Breslau police). She saw this and realized that if she wished to consult me, she could do so only when, and if, I had a clinic of my own.

Returning to my task of authorship in Obernigk, I forgot the whole affair. No premonition came to me that I would ever see this New York woman again, no suspicion that she and her son would play an important role in my life, and I in theirs. It may be true that Fate points the way, but we so rarely recognize the pointing finger. Instead, we blunder blindly onward only to discover at last, in retrospect, the truth of Hamlet's words: "There's a divinity that shapes our ends, / Rough-hew them how we will."

All during this time in Breslau, my reluctance to make the Montreal plunge was lessening. Doubt and fear were giving way to zest and the urge to get back to neurosurgery and the busy life of medical practice.

I discovered an expert artisan in the old part of Breslau. He was willing and able to fashion new surgical instruments for me according to my drawings. Among other things, he made a set of delicate dissectors that I numbered 1, 2, 3, 4, and 5. He did this patiently, at a small cost, and I visited him from time to time until the dissectors suited my hand exactly and I longed to use them at the operating table.

And so, in mid-September, we sailed from Hamburg. Sir Gordon Holmes sailed with us, and when he left the ship at Southampton, we realized how good a friend he had come to be and how wise a teacher. The Cones, too, in another ship, were on their way toward Montreal and at least two research fellows were preparing to join us, by arrangement, the one in London and the other in San Francisco — Dorothy Russell, a young English pathologist in the neurosurgical clinic of Hugh Cairns at the London Hospital, and Ottiwell Jones, a young neurosurgeon in the clinic of Howard Naffziger at the University of California hospital. They were coming for a year of work in neuropathology.

The laboratory that we would establish must be a place for applied science. That is what pathology is. But beyond that, another applied science might now be possible, neurophysiology. Other doors had opened toward this neuroscience during the six months in Germany. Epilepsy beckoned and new techniques of operation and stimulation and recording were waiting to be devised. If only we could assemble a group of able enthusiasts and give them a place to work. I knew now which way to move through darkness toward the dawn.

9

1928: The Montreal Adventure

"Come unto these yellow sands,
And then take hands"

— Ariel, *The Tempest*

Our ship entered the Saint Lawrence River and began its smooth two-day approach to Montreal. The shores were colored in all the glory of a Canadian autumn. Charming villages seemed to move in silent procession past the ship, each with the white spire of a Catholic church, and houses clustered about it with their low-curving roofs. Only French, one knew, was spoken there.

We came at last to Quebec City and saw the Citadel and the Château Frontenac towering above us on the historic Plains of Abraham. It was the flags in Quebec that startled us. We realized suddenly how foreign we would seem, like all the other immigrants who had come and settled here before us.

Canada had not yet adopted a flag of her own. The Fleur-de-lis and the Union Jack still fluttered their competing independence. In this land, there was no melting pot for those two cultures. We knew how rich and how distinctive was the Canadian version of each and we resolved, for our children and for ourselves, that we would live our lives, as far as possible, with those whose culture was that of French Canada as well as with those who spoke English. Would they accept us and let us belong?

When I looked ahead to Montreal, I realized that Cone's decision to come had been crucial in the career of each of us. What had brought him to his decision? The answer to that question was important. At the age of thirty-one, he was a doer by choice, not an administrator, and certainly not a writer. At the age of thirty-seven I was doing these things for him. Was it this? Or was it friendship, or the challenge of an ideal, or the promise of team-work? All these considerations must have influenced him. We had pulled happily together, in a double harness, as friends with a common enthusiasm. Now we could continue that relationship and boast that we were the beginning of a team, something more considerable than any individual can be.

But there was, I believe, another reason for his eagerness to come. We had heard, together, the everlasting whisper that experienced explorers hear. We had heard it together, Cone and I, at the very beginning of our association. It was that day when we sat down together with our microscopes for the first time. We saw an alteration in certain cells. It was clear that disease had produced it. Cajal and del Rio-Hortega had never used their own methods in the study of disease. What we were discovering was something no one else had ever recognized. That made it, for the moment, as precious as the nugget of gold in the pan of a prospector.

We drew up a plan to publish this finding then, and did it eventually after much study. Publication brings pleasure too. It is like the spending of your gold, or like giving it away. But it is not the same, and not to be compared with the happiness of hunting on a hot trail or the excitement of finding.

An angler should understand this, if he is one who has loved the thrill of fly-fishing along a mountain stream recalling absent-mindedly, as he makes each cast, some speckled beauty of the past that rose and struck and splashed its way to shore. He should be able to understand how it is that a scientist, who has been involved in a significant discovery, becomes an altered man thereafter. And those who were involved together have a sense of brotherhood. Such a scientist has a feeling of suppressed excitement as he goes about his work carrying the still-unanswered questions at the back of his mind. I have tried to describe this urge because it is contagious. It can be felt by a team of men and women, as well as by an individual. Nothing that we could bring to our task would be more important than this.

Cone and I could have lived on in New York in security and even affluence. What led me to leave and what really induced him to come along? The answer is that we were fellow explorers.

Rudyard Kipling was, among poets, the keenest of observers.

He had a remarkable understanding of human nature. He seems to have understood and put into words the psychology of an explorer:

"There's no sense of going further — it's the edge of cultivation,"
So they said, and I believed it — broke my land and sowed my crop —
Built my barns and strung my fences in the little border station
Tucked away below the foothills where the trails run out and stop:
Till a voice, as bad as Conscience, rang interminable changes
On one everlasting Whisper day and night repeated — so:
"Something hidden. Go and find it. Go and look behind the Ranges —
"Something lost behind the Ranges. Lost and waiting for you. Go!" *

My father began his professional life as a surgeon. The wilderness, in which he was forced to live alone so long, changed him into a hunter. The call of the wild came to him in later years. He was drawn away by a "voice as bad as conscience." It called to him and changed his life. The psychology of the hunter and the fisherman is somewhat similar, I suppose, to that of an explorer. In any case, I had become an explorer. This explains why I had taken six months in Germany to lay a plan. I would strive now to mount an expedition that could discover the answer to the "everlasting whisper" that I had heard repeated day and night. I would try to do what I knew no man alone could do.

So, the Cones and the Penfields converged on Montreal and with us came a plan and a feeling of assurance that great things lay ahead — if not here in Montreal, then elsewhere. For me, arrival in Montreal no longer seemed a plunge into unknown and perhaps unwelcoming waters, as it had before I ran away to Germany. It was more like struggling up the river's bank to a beckoning land where we would be free, at last, to settle and build with plans of a new dimension. Or else be free to move along, following fortune like the voyagers and the priests who

* From *Rudyard Kipling's Verse, Inclusive Edition, 1885–1932* (New York: Doubleday, Doran, 1934).

came to Canada, long ago, to discover a new world and to build a better society.

The rooms we occupied after our arrival in Montreal were in a house on the south side of Sherbrooke Street, near Mackay. It was one of a series of houses in solid city blocks along that street. Most of the others were still occupied by their original, more affluent, owners. Each had a short flight of stairs that ran up to a landing and an entrance that was quite pretentious in a Victorian style. These rooms, to which we came with four children and the German governess, who was quite content to go anywhere with the family of the "Frau Professor," occupied the whole top floor at 1434 Sherbrooke Street West.

The rooms were waiting for us, thanks to Mrs. Hugh Russel, whom my wife and I had met quite by chance, on the top of a bus, a few weeks earlier in Vienna. Mrs. Russel proved to be the widowed sister-in-law of Colin Russel, neurologist at the Royal Victoria Hospital. She did so much for us during the early months in Montreal, and did it all so mysteriously, that we came to call her laughingly "Aunt Ariel."

I walked along Sherbrooke Street each morning on my way to the Royal Victoria Hospital, looking at life with the eye of an immigrant.

"Can I build up a clinic and practice here in this narrow, unrecognized specialty?" I wrote to my mother only a few days after we arrived in Montreal. "I'm on my own, in a smaller world. . . . I hope the time of organizing will not be too long so that I can get to curing people who would otherwise not be cured, and get close to the clinical problems."

On one of the first mornings, as I swung along on my way to the hospital, I was startled to see an automobile draw up before one of the Sherbrooke Street houses with the enormous antlers, head and neck of a decapitated moose strapped on the hood of the engine. I stood and watched in astonishment while the driver of the car removed the head, assisted by a white-coated houseman who had come running down the steps. Together, they carried this trophy of the chase into the house.

What other metropolis was there in all the world, I mused, so close to the deep wilderness as this unique bilingual city to which we had come? My father's spirit stirred within me. What streams and lakes and forests there must be that could be visited before breakfast! Places where sportsman and angler and swimmer and sailor could find a summer home for himself and his family! Places for summer expeditions and for winter sports! These were boasts that Montreal could make. They were things in which even a busy surgeon could take delight for a lifetime.

The Cones had arrived in Montreal four days before us and had found a small apartment in Lorne Crescent, near the Royal Victoria Hospital. They had enjoyed the six months of travel in Europe. His studies there, which began and ended in London, had been rewarding. It was the teaching of neurology at Queen Square and the neurosurgery of Hugh Cairns at the London Hospital that impressed him most. Since I had left Boston and worked in London, Cairns had had a year as resident with Harvey Cushing in Boston and he was now introducing fastidious neurosurgical technique in the London Hospital, as Norman Dott was doing in the Royal Infirmary in Edinburgh.

Avis Cone was tall and blond and vivacious, a graduate of the University of Iowa, like her husband. When the Cones had come to Breslau to join us a few months earlier, during Foerster's lecture series there, the four of us had enjoyed the time together very much. Like my wife, Avis had taught school a few years before marrying.

At the Royal Victoria Hospital, Jonathan Meakins, the professor of medicine, was expecting me since Archibald had just left Montreal on a trip to Europe. Meakins had been as good as his word. Three rooms in his University Clinic had been cleared out and partitions added according to my suggestion. This had produced a suite of six rooms.

On the first morning, Meakins walked again down the corridor of the University Clinic with me to our laboratory at the end of the hall. In the new laboratory I found Bill Cone investigating the boxes that had arrived from New York. They were filled with reports and transactions and microscopic sections from our former Laboratory of Neurocytology. The giant barrel, filled with little samples of all our treasured New York specimens, was standing on the floor. Dr. Lewis Reford, Archibald's backer, had sent us his Zeiss microscope. It glistened on the table and I had bought wonderful new lenses for it in Germany with money he had forwarded through Archibald.*

Bill Cone was just as delighted and excited as I was. We stood there and talked amid the unopened boxes. There was a gleam in Bill's eye and his rumbling laugh echoed through our unfurnished rooms. Pathology of the brain had fascinated him from his student days onward. Meakins smiled to see our pleasure and left us. This was the beginning of a very happy relationship with the medical staff of the Royal Victoria Hospital. It was to continue for six fruitful years, 1928 to 1934.

Four years earlier, in 1924, Cone had come, uninvited, onto my little stage bringing with him his great strength and drive and enthusiasm for pathology. With his advent, it had become *our stage* in New York, and I became the acting director. A few months later, we had opened our own laboratory in the Presbyterian Hospital but we called it neurocytology. We had yet to apply the Spanish methods of silver and gold to the cell structure of the normal human brain and to the study of the changes that occur in these cells in disease, which was neuropathology.

While Cone was learning to be a neurosurgeon as my assistant in the New York clinic, I had acted as the laboratory's chief and had learned to be a neuropathologist. For three years, I had made all the reports as neuropathologist to the two hospitals, the Presbyterian and the New York Neurological Institute.

Now that we were in Montreal, the picture changed. Our laboratory, which Horst Oertel, the McGill professor of pathology, had spurned, was to be housed in the more stimulating environment of the Department of Medicine. Cone and I were ready to call our workshop of applied anatomy and pathology of the nervous system the Laboratory of Neuropathology. But it was

---

* An unexpected letter had come to me from Mr. Acosta Nichols, who wrote from his Wall Street office in New York, enclosing an unsolicited check for seven hundred fifty dollars for me to use in research, and another for five hundred dollars as a gift to Dr. Cone, who had worked so hard during our fruitless effort to save the life of his little son. The boy had died of a brain abscess shortly before we left New York. Bill refused to accept his check as a personal gift and turned it over to the laboratory. So I bought a microscope to match Dr. Reford's beautiful instrument and placed it in Cone's office.

more than that, for it was to be the center and headquarters of a project in neurology.

Cone would now become the neuropathologist and the chief of the laboratory and I would develop other approaches to the brain, according to plan. What Cone did not seem to realize then, and what he regretted in the years to come, was that I would inevitably have to work more and more with other men who had other skills and interests (such as Herbert Jasper and Theodore Rasmussen).

Cone and I were different, of course. Perhaps that, in part, accounts for the strength of our friendship. He read current literature and he made intimate contact with our patients and our colleagues. He told me much that I needed to know. He watched over my patients. I made no policy decisions and no important personal ones without first consulting him. For him, the care of patients and the perfection of neuropathology made up the world in which he worked so incessantly and so brilliantly. But he would not follow me into extraprofessional life and sport and literature. He could not, it seemed, approach with me the art of creative writing. Physiology interested him not at all. His mind was constantly occupied with a restless concern for perfection of technique, microscopical and surgical, and the care of patients.

During the previous six months in Germany, I had reached out for quite a different set of keys to knowledge. With them we could extend the field of surgery and begin a planned attack on problems beyond the field of brain tumor and intractable pain. I could return, at last, to my first obsession — the study of the physiology of the human brain. But to enter this unexplored territory effectively, more equipment and more skilled help would be needed. Nothing, I realized, would serve my ultimate purpose short of a specialized neurological institute — the old, recurring dream.

I thought of these things walking home to our rooms on Sherbrooke Street. And on the second or third evening, I climbed the steps and rang the bell as usual. But when the door was opened, I was astonished to find a young man sitting on a chair in the hallway. He had waited for me all afternoon. It was our former technician, Edward Dockrill. Bill Cone had decided that Edward should *not* come to Montreal with us. We planned to find, and train, a new technician with a less difficult temperament. Cone had, indeed, managed to find other employment for Dockrill. But Edward had decided to come regardless of that.

"You're sure to need me," he said. "You won't have time to train a new technician now."

I shook my head, realizing I must not reverse Cone's decision. Then I laughed. The boy was looking at me so soberly. I laughed because I saw, suddenly, how absurdly right he was. He smiled uncertainly. I think he understood my dilemma. I told him to talk to Dr. Cone in the morning. He squared his shoulders and walked away with his head held high.

Next morning, Cone did decide to accept him as the technician in the new Laboratory of Neuropathology. "I think," Bill explained to me afterward, "Edward has matured and mellowed. At least I hope so. We do need him right now, and it's going to be different here. We will have more space and Edward will have a technician's room of his own. With his help we will have things humming here before you know it."

Then Bill showed me clearly what my role would be: "There is a great deal more equipment we need. And I hope you can find a secretary even half as good as Mrs. Gourlay. And the graduate students will be here very soon and we must have good microscopes for them." I was condemned to be the procurement officer in addition to other things, and Bill would never be satisfied with anything but the best and always the most expensive. But how happy I was to have him with me to take the detail of laboratory and patient care from my shoulders.

I remember that autumn morning in 1928 when Dockrill rejoined us. Somehow, excitement seemed to breathe through the empty rooms, excitement because of what was about to be born. As Cone and I stood in the laboratory, Dockrill came in, his hands thrust in behind his white apron in the gesture that was so familiar to us. His slightly crossed eyes, behind heavy glasses, always gave him an intent expression. But now there was triumph and excitement too in them and the smile he could not hide.

"Come on, Edward," Bill Cone said, "we might as well unpack the specimens from the excelsior in the big barrel." As they worked together and I set to work placing the transactions and the records on the shelves, even though the shelves were not yet painted, the bare rooms echoed with laughter and talk and I reflected that a team had gone into action again.

So it was that the heart of a laboratory began to beat again. And this transplanted laboratory could develop now into a living, growing project as never before. We hoped the neurologists and psychiatrists of McGill University and also of the Université de Montréal would use it and make it their scientific rendezvous, a place where each might bring problems of his own and hope to see them solved.

But, that morning, I had other creative plans. I left the laboratory and moved on to the operating rooms for a discussion of instruments and the operating table and nursing skills with Miss Margaret Etter. She was the operating supervisor, a highly efficient nurse, but something more. Her welcome, her smile, the glint of gold in the hair beneath the nurse's cap and her quick understanding made the Royal Victoria operating room, at once, a warm and reassuring place.*

On October 18, 1928, the weekly letter to my mother bore a more permanent address, "200 Côte Saint Antoine Road." We had rented a sunny house that faced Murray Park across Côte Saint Antoine. The hillside of the park beckoned to children, young and old, especially when snow was in the air and on the ground, as it so often was from December onward. And we were surrounded by the homes and the schools and the churches of Westmount.

"Helen is unpacking," I wrote, "and sorting around and I am running circles in the two hospitals, feeling my way and ordering instruments.

"Today, I did the first operation. It was on a private patient with a pituitary tumor. She [the patient] was going blind very rapidly, so I had to operate before I was really ready. But it went well, and she is in good shape tonight, with a good chance of recovering her sight."

* Miss Etter informed me that Dr. Archibald had asked her to make available the nurse he thought to be the most skilled of all on the staff for my operations: It was Miss Kathleen Zwicker from Lunenberg, Nova Scotia. I was soon to learn that many of the most remarkable nurses who brought strength to the McGill teaching hospitals came from the Maritime Provinces of eastern Canada. They made it possible for us to do so much more for each patient at the operating table and at the bedside.

In the following week, I went to Ottawa to speak to a gathering of the medical practitioners there. Archibald had scheduled this address for me and, as there were three other speakers from Montreal, "I made some friends on the trip." Then I added in the weekly letter, "I like Canadians and feel at home with them." My talk was on one of my special interests, the radical treatment of severe headache by surgery. I made what many would think an overbold statement: that all pain, wherever located, can be cured by cutting the related nerves, provided, of course, that the pain is bad enough to justify an operation. They were very friendly, whatever the doctors may have thought of this radical young arrival in Canada.

After the meeting, I was taken to see a patient who was in a desperate state. I recommended immediate operation. The patient followed our train to Montreal in an ambulance and I operated on him in the morning.

I had expected that Archibald would help me solve all my problems. Not at all. When Professor Archibald did return from Europe, he was swept away by patients, doctors and hospital calls. He turned again to his preoccupation with his own research problems that had to do largely with surgery of the lungs. He was himself moving forward rapidly in his own career. He went about as if in a dream, often late, sometimes very late, but always kind, amusing, reasonable and just. He almost never had time to see me. When I had to have action from him, I wrote him a letter and he acted helpfully at once, often through his secretary, Miss Pickles.

I realized that, during the past ten years, he had done very little to develop surgery of the brain in Montreal. That was now my responsibility. He invited me to use his office and his desk, at 900 Sherbrooke Street West. I did so for some months, seeing private patients there once or twice a week.

As I viewed the situation realistically, I saw that neither the hospital nor the medical school had any extra funds to finance my project. I managed to support my family from private practice and paid back what was advanced to me by sympathetic members of the medical board like C. B. Keenan and David MacKenzie.

But, for the future of our project, I would have to depend on what we could achieve in surgery, and let that do the begging for us. Archibald had his own projects and could have used far more money than he had. Consequently, I asked him for nothing more. He handed on to me the goodwill of the Hodgson-Reford-McIntyre family and, for no good reason, they did become my friends.

Edward Archibald had given me his discarded mantle, so to speak, and his blessing, while he wore the mantle of new leadership. The future in neurosurgery was to be *my affair*. But I would make it more and more *our affair* if others would join me. He had withdrawn at once into the role of a proud but preoccupied parent.

But how was I, a surgeon, to involve the neurologists of Montreal in our project? A surgeon must admit that any highly trained physician has still some reason to be "proud." Their predecessors looked down on the barber-surgeons of the old days and we, who are the surgeons of today, still have our inferiority complex. And they? Well, they sometimes betray evidence of the reverse inheritance. Or, perhaps it is only that they recall the fact that when they graduated in medicine, nearly all the bright students in the class became physicians. The others went in for surgery.

It must have been apparent to Montreal neurologists that the newly arrived neurosurgeons from New York pretended to have some knowledge of neurology as well as some familiarity with the basic neurological sciences. Did they — the surgeons — also propose to practice clinical neurology? And would they then compete with medical neurologists whose bread and butter depended upon their neurological expertise? That question called for an answer.

Colin Russel did ask me that question bluntly. He was the senior neurologist in the McGill school of medicine and chief neurologist at the Royal Victoria Hospital. He was very well trained, socially well connected, a veteran of the First World War, an experienced clinician.*

My answer to Russel's question was, "No. I propose to accept, as my own, only those patients for whom I, alone, hold the keys to treatment. Cone will do the same when he begins to practice. But, we want to feel free to study the whole field of neurology just as any medical neurologist might. Our laboratory is your laboratory,

* See note 34.

if you will join us. We want to join you in the 'rough-and-tumble' of the public clinics. The time has come when we could all join together to make a more scientific approach to the unsolved problems of the nervous system, and this should include psychiatrists as well."

I described the five o'clock Wednesday clinical conferences that Casamajor had organized so successfully in the Vanderbilt Clinic, New York, for neurologists and psychiatrists, admitting Stookey and me who were, in our private practice, exclusively neurosurgeons.

Dr. Russel's response was immediate. He jumped to his feet. "By gad! I'd like that. That's just what I have always wanted to do, and I have specimens for the laboratory. Bless you! I have a lot of teaching slides. I'll bring them to the hospital and I have a good microscope at home."

I interrupted him to ask a question. "Would the French-Canadian neurologists care to join us in our clinical conferences?"

He shook his head. "No, I don't think so." Then he spoke with the authority of the old army medical officer. "The English neurologists will come. I'll see that they do. They'd jolly well better come. We have beautiful cases to discuss in the outpatient clinic at the 'Vic.' They have even more of such cases at the General.

"But no. We've never mixed that way with the French-Canadian neurologists. Their patients rarely come to our offices for consultation. They'd rather die."

He chuckled and stood before me with his feet wide apart in an attitude that was to become very familiar, a freshly lit cigarette in his hand, his left eyebrow elevated by the pull of a small scar in his forehead.

"Bless my soul! They're just as narrow-minded as we are in the other direction. We live here in separate and independent professional worlds."

He had summed up the situation. Colin Russel himself was well acquainted with the neurologists of London. He was familiar with the teaching of leaders in neurology in Great Britain and the Continent, including, of course, Paris. In the United States, he was a respected member of the American Neurological Association. He attended their annual meetings in Atlantic City. But he did not know the neurologists of the Hôtel-Dieu and the Notre-Dame hospitals in Montreal. Their orientation was to France.

Russel had been educated at McGill and he spoke a little French but he had not bridged the language barrier that separated McGill from the ancient University of Laval in Quebec City and Laval's daughter university in Montreal. The latter had recently changed its name from Laval à Montréal to l'Université de Montréal.

The other neurologists of the Royal Victoria and the Montreal General hospitals were just as enthusiastic about the idea of a weekly conference as Russel had been. They helped to start up the Wednesday five o'clock conferences, imitating Casamajor's standardized procedure. They staged each conference in an outpatient clinic room after the clinic had closed for the afternoon and the room was empty. Lines of patients had sat on those chairs all day, waiting to be seen and to get their medicine. But, at five o'clock, only the patient to be presented and members of the family, perhaps, remained. The chairs were rearranged for conference. Nurses came to watch and listen.

The Wednesday conference, which alternated, at first, between the two McGill hospitals, dealt with a patient whose problem was particularly baffling or interesting. His case was presented completely before the members of the conference. When all the evidence was in and the patient had been examined, and had answered questions, he left the room. Then each member of the conference was called upon, in turn, to sum up the evidence and make his own diagnosis, beginning with the less experienced and ending with the chairman and the neurologist who had presented the patient.

When the Casamajor rules were observed, leaving each man to prove what he could do without interruption, it became an intriguing game. The discussions were often excellent and I discovered, to my delight, that these neurologists were just as clever and well informed as those one could meet in New York or London or Paris or Berlin.*

There were neurologists and psychiatrists in every hospital but

* See note 35.

there were no other specializing neurosurgeons in the Province of Quebec. We were on trial before the medical profession. Had neurosurgery, at last, become a reputable specialty in general? Could doctors trust their patients to these neurosurgeons in particular? Or were the risks too numerous and the mortality too high? Montreal was the largest French-speaking city in the world after Paris.

I saw that the institute we hoped to create for neurology and neurosurgery must serve all the people equally. We must practice in the "two worlds." For me, in coming to Montreal, this was "the writing on the wall." Somehow the wall of separation must be made to disappear. It was not enough to serve the staff and clientele of the Royal Victoria and the Montreal General. I must understand French and English Canada and must serve those who needed me in two worlds.

Language alone was not enough to explain the separateness of French Canadians from the rest of Canada. There was a basic difference in the system of education. French education in the Province of Quebec was classical and, to some extent, ecclesiastical. It had been established, and was supported, by the monastic orders of the French-Canadian Catholic Church.

I am not one to admit that the classical teaching of Plato and Aristotle was in any way inferior as a preparation for the study of medicine. In fact, I believe quite the opposite. And the high quality of the French-Canadian neurologists I was soon to meet would support me in this view.*

Archibald, being the man he was and speaking French with graceful ease, was at home with all physicians. He served patients with lung problems in both "worlds." But he was unique. Damien Masson, a distinguished physician at the Hôtel-Dieu, was also easily bilingual and moved across the professional language barrier with ease. He called me to consider problems with him from the first. But he was not a specializing neurologist.

And then there was Pierre Masson, a renowned neuropathologist. I had come to know him in France at the University of Strasbourg during my studies abroad. After that, he had been called to Montreal by l'Université de Montréal and the Hôtel-Dieu to be

* See note 36.

professor of pathological anatomy. He was a neurologist in the broadest sense and a member of the Académie Française and a charming human being, but he was not a practicing neurologist.*

But how was I to come to know the neurologists in the French-Canadian world? Who would introduce us? I need not have worried about the answer to this question. Since I had a skill not available elsewhere in the Province of Quebec, patients brought us together. Indeed, it was the patients who presented themselves and the nature of the problems that they presented that shaped the future of our Montreal project.

Let me describe the case reports of certain selected patients who came to me during the early months in Montreal. I must do so if I am to analyze the forces that determined the course of events. And, if this account should come to the attention of such a patient, I hope he or she may nod and say, "Yes, it is true. He has told my story as it was."

Shortly after our arrival in Montreal, a well-to-do French-Canadian woman was admitted to my care in the Ross Memorial Pavilion of the Royal Victoria. She spoke no English. The medical problem she presented baffled me. I was determined not to use an interpreter and never to recognize the French language as a barrier between me and a patient. As Archibald had said at our first meeting in New York, "A Montréal, on parle français," and I had told him then I spoke the language. I did not confess how badly!

So I took the history of this first French-Canadian patient carefully myself — a long, slow procedure and probably a painful experience for her. I examined her, using such skill as I possessed. In the end, I was still puzzled. Something was wrong with the nervous system. That was clear. What was it? I told her husband I needed a neurological consultation and suggested the names of the two who were, I had been told, the most highly considered French-Canadian neurologists: Jean Saucier, who was attached to the Hôtel-Dieu, and Roma Amyot, who was on the staff of l'Hôpital Notre-Dame. The patient's family doctor was consulted and Roma Amyot chosen. I remember the consultation that followed very well.

Dr. Amyot came to "the Ross." I was waiting for him there.

* See note 37.

Amyot was a young man — quiet, reserved, sure of himself. He had been the disciple of a distinguished French neurologist whom I admired, André Thomas. Amyot talked to the family and then took the history over again from the patient for himself. I was impressed by the skillful examination of the woman that followed. It was obvious to both of us that the answer to her problem was not neurosurgery. When we withdrew and he summed up before making his diagnosis, I realized that here was a man from whom I could learn. Soon I began meeting other French-Canadian neurologists on a regular basis.*

When opportunity presented itself, I suggested, again and again, to these men that we might stage a formal discussion of some problem that they had discussed with me at the five o'clock Wednesday conference in the Montreal General or the Royal Victoria. It was quite easy to bring private patients to these conferences when the patient himself recognized the value of such consultations. Thus the French-Canadian neurologists did begin to attend the conferences occasionally and joined in the discussions while all of us used French or English as best we could.

Before very long, one of our Wednesday conferences was held in the Notre-Dame Outpatient Department with Amyot as chairman, and then another at the Hôtel-Dieu chaired by Saucier. Gradually, over the years, the conference has become a bilingual affair attended by all Montrealers who are interested in neurology. No one did more to establish the success of this institution in the early days than Colin Russel, the senior English-speaking neurologist, and Fred MacKay, the chief neurologist at the Montreal General Hospital. Eventually, those who attended these conferences created the Montreal Neurological Society, Société neurologique de Montréal. Before it, and since then, many distinguished speakers have presented their work, in English or in French, at five o'clock on a Wednesday afternoon.

The Laboratory of Neuropathology was, of course, a place for the study of brain tissue and tumor growth. But it did become almost at once the heart of the Montreal neurological project, as I had hoped it would.

* See note 38.

Messages, mail and requests for consultation came to us there. The largest room with its benches for microscope research and its chairs for discussions was a place in which neurologists were at home and visitors could be welcomed. Cone and Dockrill had small rooms of their own in which to work. I had the smallest room of all, just large enough for a desk, a microscope and bookshelves. But to reach me there, one had to pass through the secretary's room, where records were kept and telephone messages received. This gave me protection and comparative privacy.

The advent of Miss Hope Lewis as our secretary was an event almost as important as the coming of William Cone. She arrived from England on a ship that docked in Montreal a day or two after our arrival from Germany and I like to consider that providence was taking a hand in our affairs. Her older brother, a Montreal businessman, suggested to her that the newly arrived brain surgeon, about whom there had been some public notice, might need a well-trained secretary. And so she came to see me.

Unfortunately, she came a little late. I had engaged a secretary a week before, an experienced, mature, well-trained woman. But she knew too much. She began by telling me, and the others, what to do. Miss Lewis, on the other hand, was young, a little lame from birth, and inexperienced. On paper, not a likely candidate. But she was gently bred and had the quiet understanding that makes some people wise beyond serious reasoning. I caught the flash of her sense of humor and liked her dignity, her delightful voice and her clarity of speech and thinking. Somehow, I extricated myself from the clutches of the other woman with her maddening approach to duty.

So it came about that, on October 18, 1928, Hope Lewis became our secretary and, like Mrs. Gourlay, she introduced a gentle discipline into the human relations of our laboratory. She answered my telephone, understood my hopes as well as my plans, protected me from the troublesome and the self-important, and brought to me quickly the hesitant student who had a question. She told me the rumors, too, about which she thought I should know. Her advent did indeed seem to be providential.

But in these early years in Montreal so many happenings seem, in retrospect, to have been providential.

At the end of November, the first postgraduate student arrived,

Dr. Ottiwell Jones. I had asked him to wait until the paint was dry on the shelves and benches. On December 3, Dr. Cone and I sat down in the laboratory to talk with him. He had been trained in neurosurgery by Dr. Howard Naffziger, a very skillful pioneer neurosurgeon at the University of California in San Francisco. He was to return to Naffziger as neuropathologist and neurosurgeon.

For a beginning, I suggested that he might take the blocks of selected brain tumors that had come with us from New York, cut sections from them, stain them, and study them under the microscope.

I looked up to the shelves. "There are my reports."

Then I turned to Edward Dockrill. "Where are the specimens from New York?"

His face went blank. "Didn't you or Dr. Cone have them taken away to a storeroom?"

He looked at me and then Dr. Cone, incredulous. "I took them off the shelves," he explained, "when the painters came and wanted to paint the whole laboratory. That was two weeks ago. I piled them carefully into the big barrel that was over there in the corner."

Bill Cone and I looked at each other. "How many bottles are there?" I asked.

He shook his head. "Three or four hundred, I should think. They were all well stoppered and sealed with paraffin and labeled. The paraffin covered the label as well as the cork. The formalin won't leak out unless the bottles are broken."

These were our treasures. Each block of tissue in those bottles had a story of its own. But no one would care to steal them. Where were they? Miss Lewis had joined the circle. She confirmed Dockrill's story.

"The barrel disappeared about a week ago," she said. "Edward and I talked about it then. We thought you must have put it in a storeroom."

No further discussion was necessary. The barrel had been taken by some very strong person or persons. Each of us went out through the hospital then, asking questions. I made contact with those responsible for carrying waste materials from the laboratories. No one knew, or would admit he knew, anything. "Too bad" — that was the phrase we kept hearing. "Too bad."

I went alone to discuss the matter with the hospital superintendent. Mr. Chenoweth was busy. So I waited in the drafty front entrance hall. The weather had turned cold with flurries of snow. I had a "gone" sensation in my stomach and I had been sweating. Each time the front door opened, I was chilled.

A seated statue of Queen Victoria in white marble looked down from the landing of the grand staircase. Her hand was on the shoulder of a small boy who pressed against her knee. The boy symbolized a loyal dominion, no doubt. That boy had grown to manhood. The time had come for leadership here in the West. Meakins and Archibald and Martin were bringing progressive academic medicine and surgery to this hitherto very conservative hospital. Something similar was afoot at the Hôtel-Dieu.

No one had made a balanced academic approach to the mind, as I thought it could be made, through studies of the brain of man. This had yet to be done. This was my project. I would do it somewhere on the North American continent. Our collection of three or four hundred bottles with brain tissue in them had been all we had to show for our beginning in New York.

On the wall beside the superintendent's closed door was a long bronze tablet, a handsome tribute to Dr. John McCrae. On it was inscribed all three stanzas of his poem "In Flanders Fields." If he had not died, as he seemed to know he would, I would have become a colleague of his and now be proud of that fact. How admirable that this Canadian physician could speak to the whole world through such poetry. Montreal physicians were different. Edward Archibald seemed to personify this difference. Indeed, Archibald and McCrae had been close friends and kindred spirits. Before the war, McCrae had lived in a room of his own, for quite a time, in the home of Dr. and Mrs. Archibald.

Yes, the world had changed since McCrae wrote these words in a period of desperation during the First World War:

> *In Flanders fields the poppies blow*
> *Between the crosses, row on row,*
> *That mark our place; and in the sky*
> *The larks, still bravely singing, fly*
> *Scarce heard amid the guns below.*

> *We are the Dead. Short days ago*

> *We lived, felt dawn, saw sunset glow,*
> *Loved and were loved, and now we lie*
> *In Flanders fields.*

But now, ten years later, the war was over. The threatening foe had vanished. Germany was friendly again. The third stanza had lost its meaning. We could be grateful for that. But the words could be given new meaning:

> *Take up our quarrel with the foe:*
> *To you from failing hands we throw*
> *The torch; be yours to hold it high.*
> *If ye break faith with us who die*
> *We shall not sleep, though poppies grow*
> *In Flanders fields.*

The torch to which McCrae referred had served its purpose. It had flickered and gone out. In Woodrow Wilson's hopeful words, those who had fallen had helped *to make the world safe for democracy.*

But there was a torch that was burning still. It had been handed down from medical man to medical man through more than two millennia from the days of Hippocrates of Cos. It had flickered and burned low at times but had never been extinguished. And still there was a foe for us to overcome — ignorance, disease, wrong thinking. The foe would face us always. And there were promises that many a physician had made to those who died.

I thought of the bits of preserved human tissue in the vanished barrel. We needed them for comparison in future studies. I had removed some of those blocks of tissue at grueling operations. Others I had taken, at autopsy, from the patients I could not save. The men and women and children who died were my friends, as well as patients. I had made a promise to their loved ones.

I thought of the malignant tumor from the little Italian boy, the brain abscess from the son of Acosta Nichols, the many abnormalities that had produced epilepsy — in the case of William Hamilton and in Foerster's German patients — and the scars from the New York experimental animals. They were all there. I remembered brave little Jennie Hummel, whose seizures taught us where it is the brain controls the heart and the respiration. She died in one of her strange seizures while I was preparing to operate, hoping to cure. I did the autopsy, instead of the operation, at the scheduled time. Her husband himself asked me to do it, saying, in his anguish, he had to know *why*.

At last, the door before me opened. Someone was coming out. Beyond this person, a secretary beckoned. I entered. Mr. W. R. Chenoweth, the superintendent of the Royal Victoria Hospital, was businesslike. He had been brought to this post by Sir Vincent Meredith, who had found him efficient and useful in the Bank of Montreal. He listened to me and used his telephone to talk to various people. At last he summed up the situation and after pigeonholing it in his own mind, said to me:

"Waste is removed from the laboratories every night and hauled away by truck twice a week. No one has seen such a barrel as you describe. If the trucker did take it, which he denies, it probably went to the Rosemount Dump. But it could have gone somewhere else." He stood up and shook my hand. "Too bad. I hope Mr. Hartley has completed the painting in your laboratory and finished the tabletops to your satisfaction."

I left his office. I was angry. I had already seen and talked to the people to whom he telephoned. I had been told that no one would dream of removing such a large barrel. Someone was lying. Certainly it was not in the hospital now. "If the barrel ever did exist," I must not blame them for its disappearance. No one among this superintendent's people offered help, the sort of help I needed.

Well, we would find it somehow. First, I must make sure the patients would be all right. I sent for the intern, Dr. Maurice Brodie, who cared for our neurosurgical patients as well as the neurological ones, scattered as they were through the male and female public wards, as well as the children's ward and the rooms for private patients in the Ross Pavilion. Brodie was small, dark, eager and undaunted. He had had far too little sleep for the past month. He wrote up his histories in the dead of night with never a complaint. He had an inquiring mind and had confessed to me that to do neurosurgical research had long been his dream. We visited the neurosurgical patients together and I told him that Dr. Cone and I would be out of reach the next day. But, if he should be in doubt what to do, Dr. Russel would advise him.

Next morning early, Cone and Dockrill and I drove to the entrance of the Rosemount Dump. It was on the outskirts of Montreal. Leaving my car outside the gates, we entered the precincts of the dump on foot. It was below freezing. A cold gusty wind was blowing. We followed the tracks that trucks had made out to the brow of a hill — a dreadful place! How little like a rose mount!

As we stood there, a truck followed along the way we had come. It backed around to the brim and, rearing its body upward, disgorged its jangling contents like an enormous dog at stool. We watched the objects cascading down the slope and our hopes rose. It was easy to imagine the barrel and its contents hurtling down from some point along the brim of that hill. But what a big place it was! And where should we begin to hunt? An enormous rat emerged from a crevice, as we stood irresolute, and ran over cans and grapefruit rinds to vanish under a box.

Far down the hillside, three men were moving. They carried bags and probed about, hunting for what they might salvage. If these "professionals" could do it, so could we. Edward's coat, I observed, was not warm enough in spite of the woolly English scarf, the tails of which were blowing in the wind. But he made light of the cold and we descended to the assault.

There were pockets of snow here and there but one could scrape it away with a stick. I climbed down the hill to talk to each of the professional junk collectors. No. They had seen "no barrel, no little bottles."

I remember one of them still, an old man who carried a large sack. He was tattered and stooped. A small icicle had formed on his mustache and his hands were too dirty to wipe it away. My heart ached as I talked with him and tried to imagine what life was like for him.

Bill Cone and Edward, in the meantime, had drawn up a plan of campaign. Beginning at the far right, they were working around the surface of the slope toward the left. I joined them. Bill stationed me near the top and Edward at the bottom. He always seemed to take charge whenever there was real work to do. In spite of the nasty items we encountered, he laughed and made light of the whole affair, helping me to lift some large object and to look under it, for he was very strong. A moment later, he was doing the same thing for Edward down the slope.

"We'll find those bottles," he said. "There are so many of them, one is sure to appear somewhere on the surface and the barrel will be easy to recognize."

I agreed, aloud. But I thought to myself, the barrel has probably been saved and the bottles may well be covered over, and anyway they might all be hiding in some other dump. And what a fool I was. I should have questioned more carefully, and finding the stupid culprit, I should have made him confess. What an absurd undignified picture we made anyway, grubbing here.

The day wore on. My hands were very cold and wet. My left knee was beginning to pain. It had been badly set after it was smashed by the German torpedo twelve years before. It often gave me trouble. The time for lunch had come and gone and we were no more than three-quarters of the way around the hillside.

"Bill," I said, "look at Edward. He is shivering like a leaf. We must call this off, go back to the hospital, warm up, take care of the patients, and come back when we can. My sister is arriving from California tomorrow morning early. But perhaps I can get away in the afternoon tomorrow."

"No," Cone said. "Give me the keys to your car. I'll take Eddie to it and start the heater. I'll leave him there. You and I can finish the hillside in an hour."

Edward objected. "I always shiver like this." Stubborn, he turned away and moved on ahead of us. He scraped out the snow from under a wrecked Ford car. It had rolled down the hill and lay there upside down.

Suddenly we heard him shout and saw him waving something and capering about. We ran to him. Sure enough he held aloft a little bottle. He was shivering and laughing all at once and using the strangest Cockney language in which the word "bloody" appeared and reappeared. The label was plain to read, the paraffin sealing unbroken, the formalin solution frozen and the block of tissue safe within the transparent ice.

We found a dozen more bottles, perhaps. No more than that. We tried to lift the Ford to look under it but it was too heavy for us. So we drove back at last, through the miles of small houses and stores that make up the vast French-speaking section of northeast Montreal. Yes, we were reassured but still very far short of our goal.

Next morning an emergency of another sort came to me and I could not return to the Rosemount Dump. But a few days later, the telephone rang. It was Dean Martin calling from the medical school across Pine Avenue. He had heard the story of the lost barrel. "Why didn't you let me know? Some of the men from the university Grounds Department are ready to help you right away." Bill Cone went with them in their truck out to the Rosemount Dump again. They turned the derelict Ford car over — the one that we had not been able to move. Underneath, they came upon our lost treasure!

In my correspondence file, I have found a letter written a few days later, December 14, 1928, a letter of thanksgiving, addressed to the dean:

"I cannot thank you enough for your kindness and energy, which are responsible for getting back our lost specimens. We do not know exactly how many were lost, but it seems to me that we must have the larger part of them, and these that have been returned are as good as ever. Even the labels are quite legible thanks to their coating of paraffin and the bottles can go into our files without any further work upon them.

"I know now what the prodigal son went through when he 'would fain have filled his belly with the husks that the swine did eat' and how his father felt when the son returned."

During the days of searching over the Rosemount Dump, Edward Dockrill came down with a cold. He had returned to the search alone after our first visit there. The cold developed into pneumonia and Dr. Cone had him admitted to the hospital. But there he did recover. There were so many threats of tragedy as well as times of rejoicing in those early days of arrival.

10

My Sister

Next morning early, my mother arrived at Windsor Station and my sister Ruth was with her. I had tried to get them to postpone this visit and had indeed telegraphed them on December 1 when I discovered that my wife was ill with a high fever. Helen had mumps — a disease that can be serious in an adult. But my brother-in-law, Jack Inglis, had wired back from Los Angeles, "Too late to cancel . . . Ruth's condition seems urgent."

A wise physician will never "doctor" himself or the members of his family if he can help it. And yet there are times when he must act even though he fears that his concern may hamper his judgment and make his hand unsteady.

I met their train and brought them home. Mother's hair had turned white. She was calm and determined. Ruth smiled, but she seemed a little dazed. Thus they came with me to 200 Côte Saint Antoine Road before breakfast. After they had been greeted with delight by our two elder children, they went upstairs to their rooms. I noticed again that Ruth was unsteady. She fumbled for the stair rail as if she could not see it. They stopped in the upstairs hallway to wave from the doorway at Helen, who lay in bed, her face painfully round and swollen.

My questions after we left the railroad station had told me the story. Ruth had had increasing headaches and vomiting. Recently, Mother told me quietly, there had been frequent convulsions, which Ruth herself did not remember. They had thought, on two occasions, that she was going to die and gave her artificial respiration. Jack Inglis had called my friend, the Los Angeles neurosurgeon, Carl Rand. He gave her something to restrain the attacks and advised her to go to Montreal without delay. So Mother had sent her telegram and had come. On the way, she had been terrified, in spite of herself, lest Ruth might have more attacks on the train.

When Ruth was ready for breakfast, I went to her room with my ophthalmoscope. I could not wait. There, standing close to this sister of mine, of whom I had so many precious boyhood memories, I brought my right eye close to hers, pupil to pupil with only the lens of the ophthalmoscope between them. Sure enough! There it was! The swelling of the head of the optic nerve — dreadful swelling, and there were little red hemorrhages, each bordered by a white margin, that extended out menacingly over the surface of the surrounding retina.

This was proof positive of a very high degree of pressure within the skull. It had gone too far. She might well go blind within a day or two. Her loss of sight, if it came, would not get better as it had in the case of the patient who had the pituitary tumor, the first patient I had operated upon in Montreal. This blindness would be irrevocable.

My knees grew suddenly weak and for a moment I thought I might fall. I put a hand on Ruth's shoulder to steady myself and waited until control returned to my knees, pretending to study her retina. Then we went out into the hall, laughing at old jokes as in the old days, and down the stairs to breakfast. At the breakfast table, Ruth seemed her old self — lovely blue eyes, slow speech, radiant smile, perfect teeth and rollicking laugh.

When I watched my mother unobserved, I saw how very tired she was. When she looked at me, I thought she seemed frightened and there was a question in her eyes. Something she could not, or would not, put into words.

A year or two earlier, Ruth had begun to have frequent small seizures, I learned. At that time, in a desperate effort to cure her daughter's strange fits, which were thought to be due to "nerves," Mother had become a Christian Scientist. Ruth had gone along with her and taken that treatment. Mother's letters had become rather noncommittal then in regard to Ruth. Perhaps she felt that she and I no longer spoke the same language.

And now, was it too late? I suspected that she herself was asking that question. And so was I. What was I to do? Mother and I did not discuss the question at once.

Colin Russel came to the house after breakfast in response to my telephone call. He examined Ruth and was as genial and reassuring as only he could be. The three of us drove to the Royal Victoria, where X rays were taken of her head. Bill Cone was waiting for us there.

The films showed a clearly defined shadow of calcium granules deep in the middle of the right frontal lobe of the brain, or possibly under it. Dr. Edward C. Brooks, the radiologist, looked at the wet X-ray films for us.

"The calcification that we see," he said, "must have been forming there slowly for a good many years. She has a brain tumor. It may be benignly encapsulated or it may be slowly malignant."

Cone and Russel came home with us. We gave Ruth something to relieve her headache and urged her to go to bed, which she did gratefully. Dr. Archibald had been operating. He came hurrying in now, having seen the X rays. I asked Mother to take him upstairs to see the patient. When he returned to us, the consultation was on and we entered the little front parlor. Sitting close to Dr. Archibald, so he could hear, I summed up the case for them. I could see the whole story in long perspective now.

My sister was forty-three, six years older than I. At the age of fourteen, she had begun to have occasional "splitting headaches." The tumor had probably started its growth then. When she was nineteen, she had what must have been a major epileptic seizure. As a gangling boy, I could remember listening in terror to the sounds of a convulsion, standing outside the room in which she slept. A doctor came, and as he entered the room, I was horrified to get a fleeting glimpse of Ruth lying unconscious on the bed. I heard it said, erroneously of course, that this was all due to "nerves." I wondered what that meant. That was 1904 and Ruth was up next day, as well as ever.

The following spring she was twenty and was married to Jack Inglis, who had been her teacher in high school. Between the ages of nineteen and forty, Ruth had four similar attacks at long intervals, all of them, no doubt, due to the irritation of the unsuspected tumor. But she bore Jack Inglis six lovely children and was a happy wife and mother in a successful family. Then, in the last three years, smaller attacks appeared more frequently. It was then that my mother and she turned to Christian Science, under the misconception that the cause was something that could be controlled by the mind.

I summed up the case as follows: "My sister has had a brain tumor for almost thirty years. I'd like to think it is benign and encapsulated. But the fact that it seems to have begun to grow rapidly in these last months suggests that it may have become malignant, even if it was benign at the start. Surgical removal, which might have been relatively easy once, is difficult and dangerous now. But if I were in her place, I would ask for a radical attempt to remove the whole growth, however dangerous it might be to my life. But I would not want to be paralyzed. I'd rather die. If it can't be removed completely, then I would ask the surgeon to be as radical as he can be, short of paralysis. I would hope then for a year or so of useful life before the beginning of the end.

"She has many things to do that are important as mother and wife. The two youngest children are boys, about six to eight years old. Carl Rand might have done the operation in Los Angeles. But it was my mother, I think, who insisted on bringing her here.

"Now," I concluded, "we could probably take her to Cushing or to someone else and get her there before she goes blind. But we will have to hurry. Please, make the decision as if this woman were not my sister. I must not influence your thinking in any way. When you want me, you will find me with Helen upstairs."

It seemed a very long time. But Bill Cone came to call me at last and I returned with him to the front parlor.

As I entered the room Archibald asked me this: "If you were to do this operation, could you do it as if she were not your sister?"

I hesitated. At last, I said yes.

He smiled. "I think then that you should go ahead. You'd better admit her to the Royal Victoria the first thing tomorrow morning."

I looked at Colin Russel. "Yes," he said, "Bill tells us you can do it. I think you should. And your sister told me that, if any operating is to be done, she wants her brother to do it."

"She doesn't know," I said, "what might lie ahead. I would want to do this operation under local anesthesia. It is safer that way. She would be awake, at least until the time of closing the incision. I may want to map out the motor gyrus with her help using the electrode to be sure of avoiding paralysis.

"If she can face it without being emotional, I'll be all right with Bill Cone's help."

Then he, Cone, spoke for the first time: "You can do it, Wide. I will help you. It is better for her this way."

I felt reassured. Then I turned to Archibald. "I'd like to get Miss Anne Penland, the anesthetist at the Presbyterian Hospital, to come and help me too. We work together well. She would sit with the patient as long as she is awake and tell me how she is and put her to sleep when necessary."

If this tumor, I reflected, is really growing within the right frontal lobe, this may prove to be the largest removal I have ever made. It might well be very like the operation I had carried out just before leaving New York, on the patient William Hamilton. That was done under local anesthesia, too. It was done to remove a very large scar of the right frontal lobe. But there was no pressure in his case. Miss Penland had helped me with that operation. She was Allen Whipple's chief of anesthesia.

"Would Dr. Howell, your chief anesthetist," I said to Archibald, "object if I were to ask Miss Penland to come to the Royal Victoria for this operation?"

He laughed. "Billy Howell would be delighted. As a matter of fact, Howell is feeling rather guilty since he is responsible for your wife's mumps. He was just coming down with mumps himself when you and Helen dined with the Howells not long ago."

The consultation was over. The die had been cast. Archibald stood up and put his hand on my shoulder. That was all. Then he said, "May I go up to see Helen?"

I followed him up the stairs. He knocked and, opening her door, he stood in the doorway. I watched over his shoulder. She was sitting up in bed, propped up on pillows. She had come to the height of the disease. The parotid glands were so swollen over the angle of each jaw that her face was as round and red as a harvest moon.

"Well, well!" Archibald exclaimed and stood there shaking his head.

"I know," she replied, "I know it. I look like a fool at a tragedy."

"No, not a tragedy," he replied. "It's not a tragedy for either of you. Russel and Bill Cone and I have decided that Mrs. Inglis should have her operation done here in Montreal. Wilder is the one to do it. His whole life's training has prepared him for this. And you will help him to face this challenge as you have on many an occasion before this. Mumps," he added, "doesn't last forever, you know. You will feel better soon and you'll laugh at the memory of what you looked like in the mirror."

I realized that Edward Archibald had taken his own way to help both of us. He waved and went quickly down the stairs. Helen looked at me and tried to smile. I shrugged and nodded and closed her door.

Mother was waiting at the other end of the hall. I went to her now. She had heard what Dr. Archibald said. For Ruth, this was the end of a very long, long road, and for my mother too.

"We would have come sooner," she said, "but you were sailing for Germany at the time of her first bad attack. I thought you would never return. Then, after you did arrive in Montreal, you were so busy, 'running circles' as you wrote me, 'in the two hospitals.'"

Now I understood what she had endured. She was silent. Then she added: "Life for me has been something of a blur of pain and anxiety. But now, my son, you are ready. You will have the strength, and your hand will be guided."

I called Allen Whipple on the telephone in New York, and he assured me Miss Penland was free and would be keen to help with my sister and could come up to Montreal that night. "Better to be there a day ahead," Whipple explained.

There were other details to be considered in advance. I rehearsed it all with the instrument nurse, Kathleen Zwicker. We tried out my modification of Foerster's protective screen. The screen was his own device to permit careful observation of the conscious patient during his long operations under local anesthesia.

Foerster's procedure involved suturing the sterile sheet, or drape, to the skin of the shaven scalp after it was sterilized. The drape was then carried straight upward and fastened to a metal frame that stood on the floor and straddled the table. Thus it formed a wall. The patient's head was on one side with the operator, his assistants and the nurse. The patient's face and body were on the other side with those who might be needed for companionship and control.

My modification of this arrangement was to attach an angulated metal frame to the operating table. When the patient's scalp had been sterilized and injected with novocaine, the protective sheet was sutured to the scalp and carried up about fourteen inches above the patient's head. It was then spread horizontally for twenty inches over the angulated frame, forming thus a shelf. From the shelf, the drape was carried on upward again two or three feet to be fastened finally to the bar at the top, which was attached firmly to the table below.

This would allow my instrument nurse to stand on a platform at the side and above — instead of being behind the surgeon's back, as she was in Breslau. She could place the most important instruments on the sterile shelf before me. We had resurrected a heavy German operating table and fastened these attachments to it securely. Meanwhile, the patient could look out under the shelf. A nurse or physician, sitting beside the operating table, could talk to the patient, face to face, and could deal with body, arms and legs as needed. When electrical stimulators were being used, the patient could be watched and asked to report each sensation and each thought that might come to her or him.

The next day, Miss Penland was there but I had little time to talk to her. An even more urgent emergency had presented itself, in which another life hung in the balance. A man had fallen down an open elevator shaft in the hospital. He had a bad head injury, with severe laceration of the brain. He had to be operated upon at once. So Miss Penland helped Miss Zwicker and Dr. Cone and me to do what proved to be an excellent dress rehearsal for the following day.

I knew what to do for that man. The experimental study in New York, as well as the object lesson of Foerster's patients in Breslau, had shown me how, in saving his life, to lessen the danger of post-traumatic epilepsy later on. This is the way a physician must proceed. You crystallize your conclusions and act accordingly. But, if you are open-minded, you will question your conclusions again and again and modify them as life unfolds and new experience brings you confirmations or doubts.

In preparation for my sister's operation, I talked to her, as I would to any other patient, trying to be honest and unpretentious, while keeping my own doubts and fears to myself. I looked at the situation through her eyes and explained what had to be done, without the use of needlessly technical terms.

I described what it would be like, if she had the courage to face it, and how much it would help me, if she would go through her operation under local anesthesia. She agreed and I rehearsed the day: "Breakfast will come to you in the form of a long drink of high-protein liquid. Your hair will then be shaved completely. But it will grow back very fast while you wear a very attractive turban and, who knows, the good Lord may make it come in curly!

"There will be no pain except for an initial needle prick or two. Once the scalp incision is made, you should feel nothing, since the skull and the brain have no capacity for sensation in themselves. You will hear sounds, of course. But you can talk to Miss Penland about them. She will be close to you. And Dr. Russel, whom you know and like, says he wants to sit beside you, too. I shall talk to you when I need your help. You may speak to me anytime. I will explain, and I'll tell you if there is anything for you to do."

The morning came and Ruth was wheeled into the operating room. How strange to see my sister there, her head so bald and white and shiny on the head holder. She looked at me with wondering blue eyes and smiled doubtfully. I sterilized the scalp myself and injected novocaine ever so gently. Then she disappeared from view as the drapes were placed, forming her protective wall. But she talked a great deal, much more than I expected, telling me stories of her children. They were her pride, of course, and her joy. At last, after the skull opening had been made, I begged her to postpone her talking, since I must begin to concentrate on something else.

The tumor was, as we had feared, within the right frontal lobe. We worked for hours, taking that tumor out and trying to leave the untouched brain so normal that there would be no more epileptic seizures. At last we had carried the removal of the frontal lobe back to the motor gyrus. To make sure, I touched the gyrus with an electrode. It caused the hand to move. We could go no farther on the surface. To remove this would cause permanent paralysis of voluntary movement.

This was already the largest brain removal I had ever made. But, to my dismay, the growth was not all out. It extended underneath — gray, firm, malignant-looking tissue on the floor of the skull. Enormous veins came up through the tissue. They must connect directly with the venous sinuses in the dura beneath. The sinuses were capable of a very rapid bleeding, which would be very difficult to control.

I stopped and looked at Bill Cone. He shook his head. "Don't chance it, Wide." I hesitated, arguing silently within myself with that other fellow, that daimon. There is a daimon that goes about with one and tries to keep him out of trouble. He was telling me now that Bill was right. "But," I argued within myself, "I undertook this operation because I was afraid another surgeon would turn back too soon, not knowing how much she had to live for."

Out loud, I said to Bill: "This may be all there is." I passed a heavy thread around the mass and pushed the thread down with one finger, forming a surgeon's knot. As I tightened it gently, the thread began to cut the growth from the base. There was no bleeding.

"Miss Penland," I said softly. She appeared from behind the wall of drapes and held up the chart, on which she had been recording the pulse and respiration and blood pressure. Everything was normal. "Mrs. Inglis," she said, in a low voice, "is doing well. She was a little tired and I think she is asleep now."

I knew that Miss Penland had inserted a needle in the vein of the patient's arm and was giving her a little saline solution to satisfy her need for liquid. She had a bottle of blood available that could be used, instead of the saline, at a moment's notice. The blood had been matched carefully to the blood of the patient, so there would be no delay and no reaction. Miss Penland was a wonderfully resourceful woman, never flustered, quick as a flash in action.

So I tightened the knot of my thread, little by little by little, cutting the mass of tumor gradually free from the dura at the base, and hoping that the grip of the thread would close off all of those enormous veins. But suddenly, just as I thought I had succeeded, there came a rush of blood swirling up from the base of the skull and hiding everything in a rapidly deepening pool of blood. I reached in with my gloved fingers and removed the remnant of the tumor mass, exerting strong pressure downward with the fingertips. Then I packed a great wad of hot, wet cotton wool down to the bottom of the pool — Miss Zwicker had it ready for me, taking it out of very hot saline solution. I pressed it down strongly while Cone used the automatic sucker to clear the blood away.

Ruth began to move, as if the pressure hurt her. But she did not speak and she may have fainted for a little while. We waited. The blood flow did stop in time. Thank God for that! She had, however, lost a great deal of blood.

To quote from my surgeon's note dictated after the operation: "The patient's condition now became quite critical, and the pulse weak. She was transfused three times in succession and saline solution kept running into the vein of the arm slowly between transfusions."

Little by little, I was able to take out the cotton packing and substitute a pad of coagulating muscle tissue (removed from adjacent temporal muscle) for it. We stopped the bleeding from other points and examined the field, washing it out carefully. Then we saw it! There was more of the growth present. It had passed across the midline, extending underneath the dura into the left cerebral hemisphere. I did not dare to follow it farther. When I admitted that, I felt the daimon within me heave a sigh of relief.

The high pressure within the head, that had made the operation so difficult at the start, had vanished. Her eyesight had been saved. But I had failed to free her from an eventual future threat.

We washed out the cavity for a second time and closed the dura mater carefully. Then, through a small opening in the dura, I filled the space where tumor and lobe had been with warm saline solution. The solution and the muscle would do no harm. We replaced the trapdoor that had been cut in the skull, and fastened it down securely with silver wire at several points. Then we sutured the scalp laboriously with a double layer of fine silk sutures. Only the outer layer of sutures was to be removed on the fifth day. The buried layer would remain in place and prevent fluid from leaking. Finally, the drapes that formed the protective wall were taken away and a firm white dressing applied to the patient's head.

Miss Penland had not found it necessary to give the patient any drugs to produce sleep during closure. Consequently, Ruth was still awake as I stood beside her for a moment with my finger on her pulse. She looked up and summoned a tired smile. Then she spoke quietly: "Well, little brother, have you finished? I knew you could do it." Then, after a pause, "I'm sorry I have been so much trouble to all of you."

I left the operating room and went alone to the surgeon's dressing room, wondering what sort of cells the microscope would show us in the tumor tissue we had removed. Would the cells prove to be fast-growing and rapidly malignant? Or slowly growing? One way, her reprieve would be short, the other way she might have years for happy living. But, either way, I had failed. What I had left behind would probably kill her in the end.

I sat in the dressing room lost in thought, one sock on and the other in my hand. I wanted to weep. I had known her so well and loved her as a boy. As I sat there, C. B. Keenan came in to change his clothes, a rather formidable general surgeon of long experience.

"Why," I burst out, "should anyone want to operate on brain tumors? I've worked all day long, using every facility, and still I have failed." (I don't know why I should remember this admission of weakness. But I do.) Keenan looked down at me and grunted, saying nothing. Presently, he left the room. He was a kindly man. But, after all, what was there for him to say? Except, perhaps, "Keep your chin up."

There was a great deal for me to consider and reconsider, soberly. I stayed on there alone in the dressing room, talking to myself. I knew that the surgery of intracranial neoplasms could be like that. Why shouldn't it come to my sister? But if we could get such patients early, we might cure them perhaps. These growths always produced epilepsy if they were present long enough. I thought I knew why now.

And there was something more to be considered in this case: What had I done to her mind and her personality when I made such a large removal of the right frontal lobe? Would she be different as a person, a wife, a mother? I had been concerned about that after the operation on William Hamilton. He did seem to be unchanged, but I had not been able to study his postoperative course carefully enough in New York. I must do better than that here in Montreal, and there were so many other things I wanted to do!

I had done the best I could to remove all of Ruth's tumor. I made a conscious effort to forget it. One must not look at failure. Her eyesight was saved, her headaches gone, her life saved. And this surgical setup, this way of using local anesthesia and the new instruments — all these had been put to the test in my sister's operation. They served their purposes well.

So, my mind drifted away to other matters. If I could open the door more widely to the surgical treatment of epilepsy, it would open the way to brain physiology and psychology. And then, sometime perhaps, we would make a more effective approach to the mind of man. How long I sat there, forgetting to dress, I've no idea.

My mind turned, at last, as it always did, to the future plan. An unfinished application for financial aid lay on my desk at home. I would finish up the details and send it off at once, addressing it first to the Rockefeller Foundation. If that failed, I would turn elsewhere — get help somewhere. Nothing would do, short of an institute where neurologists could work with neuro-surgeons and where basic scientists would join the common cause, bringing new approaches.

Next morning when I went to see my sister in her hospital room, she seemed herself. She smiled and said her headache was gone. Colin Russel, who, with Miss Penland, had sat beside her through the long operation, was there before me that morning. We left her room together and he accompanied me to the Laboratory of Neuropathology.

"Are you wondering," he asked, "what the loss of her right frontal lobe may have done to Mrs. Inglis?" I nodded. We discussed the possibilities. Then he said, "I will watch her and follow her, and someday I will write out my impressions for you." The following quotation comes from what Dr. Russel wrote, years later.

"I dropped in to see her in her room between 8 and 8:20 on that evening, after the removal of her frontal lobe and, although she was somewhat nauseated and had been vomiting, probably the result of the local anesthetic, she expressed her appreciation of what she considered my kindness in giving up my time, so perfectly."

Then, Russel added, "She said that she had felt so afraid of causing distress by making an exhibition of herself and that I had helped her. When I remarked that the only exhibition I had seen was one of the best exhibitions of courage that it had been my fortune to witness, she expressed her gratitude so nicely that one could not help wondering how much the frontal lobe had to do with the higher association processes."

Cone and I discussed the nature of this tumor at great length and had an opinion from Percival Bailey. We agreed the tumor was made up of oligodendroglia. It was my interest in these very cells that had taken me to Madrid. I had learned much about them, but not what causes them to grow or how to stop the growing. They had multiplied very slowly for years, forming a tumor within the brain. On the other hand, when I saw that some of the cells seen under the microscope were, I thought, giving birth to daughter cells too actively, I had doubts about the future. This was a fear, a misgiving, that I kept to myself. But, because of it, I arranged to have Ruth given X-ray treatment in Los Angeles, hoping to slow down the cell multiplication.

Outwardly I rejoiced with Ruth and all the others at her recovery. It did seem miraculous. The night before she and my mother were to leave for California, there was a winter carnival on the wooded slopes of Mount Royal. We bundled her and my mother in warm clothing, and took them to see it. Ruth was delighted with the snow, the tobogganing, skiing and skating and the French-Canadian costumes and songs and gaiety. After they left Montreal, the first letter sent back to us was from Ruth.

"On the first Monday after arriving," she wrote, "Jack took me to a dinner and dance for Rotary Ladies' Night. It was such fun. Everyone seemed so surprised that I could dance and seem as well as ever. Perhaps they felt I should be in a wheel chair. I wore a tight blue hat I had last summer with my blue dress.

"Of course," she continued, "no one can know what it means to be back in my own little corner and to feel I'm really needed . . . the meadow larks that abound here did their share to make me welcome and the mocking birds."

A year after the operation, she wrote on the anniversary date, December 11, 1929:

"This has been the happiest year of my life. . . . It has been a very wonderful year with new life, new strength, new hope. . . . I am thankful I can picture you as you will be when Christmas comes to Montreal — the sunshine in the dining room and study, the cheery open fire, and the children going out to skate and coast or ski, the cars slipping and sliding, the cold crunch of the snow."

There are many kinds of "follow-up" report that come to a surgeon after operation. This is the kind I like best. There are times when one has saved a life at operation and the patient goes out to spend it to no good purpose and for no one's happiness. The surgeon may score such an operation as a success in his follow-up calendar and yet he takes much less satisfaction from it.

To the patient, I suppose, life that is granted unexpectedly must seem a priceless gift. Life that comes as a reprieve after one has faced the menace of death must have new meaning and bring a particular joy to the heart of one who is thoughtful and courageous, as my sister was.

For eighteen months she seemed her old self. Then her symptoms returned one after the other. Eventually, at my own request, Dr. Harvey Cushing did his best to save her in a second operation in Boston. Thus she had a second reprieve and returned to her family a second time. But this rescue was of short duration. Death took her, at last, with merciful suddenness, and she died almost three years after coming to Montreal.*

During the visit of my mother to Montreal, there were, of course, no letters to her and so there was a gap in the record of my thoughts and the events in my life. Into this gap my mother inserted the following terse note:

"Ruth and I left home for Montreal, December 2, 1928, and a few days later, Wilder did what the doctors told him no one else could do as well . . . if he had the nerve. He removed a tumor from Ruth's brain. It was a trial few men could have undertaken but there are few men like my son Wilder. After a wonderful recovery, Ruth and I left for home February 6, 1929."

No man should blush to admit that his mother speaks well of

* See note 39.

him. He should blush if she does not, for he must then know that he has indeed fallen from grace.

The resentment I felt because of my inability to save my sister spurred me on to make my first bid for an endowed neurological institute. It was while Ruth was a patient in the hospital that I completed the details of an application to the Rockefeller Foundation. Dean Martin and Professor Archibald were, I think, taken by surprise. And I realized later that I myself was not yet ready to draw final plans. But I made the application nevertheless and, happily, it proved to be a fortunate decision.

II

A Plea for the Endowment of Science

The chief in any clinic or laboratory should have a special personal relationship with graduate students. They are lonely and highly impressionable and they have almost always some hidden strength that enables them to teach the chief some things before the year or years of work are over. Thus, the chief does well to start the newly arriving fellow on a problem he would be delighted to undertake himself if time permitted.

While my sister was still in hospital, the second research fellow arrived for graduate study, one of the ablest and certainly one of the most attractive of those who were to come to us through the years, bringing their varied talents, ambitions, desires and needs. This was Dr. Dorothy Russell, who was already well trained in general pathology by her service under Professor Turnbull at the London Hospital. Hugh Cairns, who was developing his own neurosurgical clinic at "the London," arranged for her to come to us on a Rockefeller Foundation Fellowship.

Like Ottiwell Jones, she wanted a year to study the application of the Spanish methods to the human brain and to brain tumors. I was glad to welcome her to the laboratory for I wanted to see someone with her ability undertake a critical study of the origin of microglia in the brain. She accepted the challenge eagerly. With her involved in this project, and Jones studying the origin of oligodendroglia, I looked forward to following each step in their researches with eager curiosity.

Many in Montreal welcomed us and our research fellows hospitably into the life of the community. My wife and I were initiated into the sport of skiing and soon we organized a skiing weekend for my Princeton classmates of the Johnson Club (Bill Chester, Francis Hall and Paul Myers and their wives) at the Chalet Cochand in Sainte Marguerite, Quebec.

Shortly before Christmas that first year in Montreal, we devoted one late afternoon and evening to the reading of Dickens's *Christmas Carol,* following the pleasant tradition in which we had been included as guests by Hugh Auchincloss during our years in New York. Thus began what was to become an annual occasion to which our closest friends, and the fellows working with me through the years, were invited.

But I had a serious project in mind. As I have said, it was difficult, and sometimes impossible, to capture Professor Archibald long enough for thoughtful discussion. Even though we passed in the hospital corridor or at the entrance to the operating rooms and exchanged a warm greeting, he was invariably in a desperate hurry, late for the next appointment and followed by a train of young assistants. This explains my letter to him of January 18, 1929:

"The enclosed plan for an Institute for Neurological Investigation may take you somewhat by surprise. The idea and the plans have been slowly taking form in my mind. It is not a small undertaking but a large one and, after the building is secured, it would require a large budget. It is my hope that the Rockefeller Foundation would be interested in such an undertaking."

I thought the projected building could be placed behind the hospital with a direct overhead entrance into our present laboratory and another into the hospital and the operating room.

Attached to the letter was a detailed estimate for an institute of neurological investigation. Accommodation for forty bed-patients and seventeen laboratory rooms would be provided in a building of seven floors attached to the Royal Victoria Hospital. The front elevation of the building was sketched in pencil on an odd piece of Biltmore Hotel letter paper. The initial cost of building and equipment was to be:

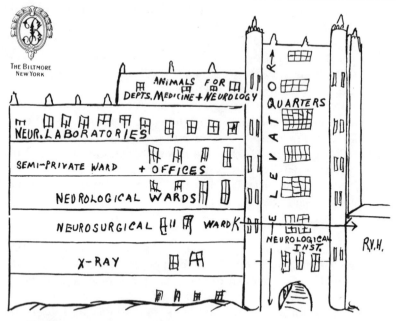

Sketch of proposed Institute for Neurological Investigation enclosed in the letter of January 18, 1929, from Penfield to Archibald. "The idea and the plans," the letter said, "have been slowly taking form in my mind and I believe this is the right way to meet the need." Note that the direct entrance from the third floor of the institute was at the back of the hospital adjacent to the University Medical Clinic on the left and the hospital operating room corridor on the right.

Clinical	$284,000
Scientific	168,000
Endowment to cover public patient deficit	200,000
	$652,000
Estimated yearly scientific expenditure	$ 34,000

Dr. Archibald did find time to see me, and we sat in his office. He held my letter in his hand and looked at me for a long time with his quizzical smile while his mind seemed to race over the proposition from the end back to the beginning.

"I didn't realize," he said softly, "that you would move so quickly, Wilder. I guessed it would come someday."

"I would have talked with you before," I said. "But I couldn't seem to catch you. I've done a lot of thinking since Ruth's operation."

He smiled again and nodded. "I'm so happy because of her wonderful recovery. . . . Well, talk with Charlie Martin. If the dean says yes and you want to go to the Rockefeller Foundation — you have my blessing. I understand your thinking."

I called on the dean. He laughed in surprise when I said I proposed to go alone. But he approved the plan. He had visited Dr. Pearce himself with very good results for McGill. He told me how to go about it, and so, twelve days later, on January 30, I wrote Dr. Richard M. Pearce, director of the Division of Medical Education, Rockefeller Foundation, New York:

"Would you be good enough to give me an interview if I came down to New York sometime in the near future? I should like to submit to you a plan for the development of an Institute for Neurological Investigation here in Montreal. . . . I have been here long enough now to work out the details of such an undertaking at McGill. . . .

"The institute as planned would continue to form an integral part of the Royal Victoria Hospital without losing contact with general medicine and surgery, but with concentration of all the methods of treatment and investigation of neurological cases. . . .

"This project meets with the entire approval of Dean Martin. I preferred, however, to present it to you entirely on its merits. . . ."

Dr. Pearce replied on February 2:

"I should be very glad to see you sometime at your convenience to discuss with you your plans for an institute for neurological investigation at McGill. . . . I should add however that in view of the recent gift to McGill for stimulating research in surgery, especially on the neurological side, I think it very doubtful if the Trustees of the Foundation would consider a comprehensive plan at this time. I should nevertheless be very much interested in knowing your views."

The interview took place at the Rockefeller Foundation on February 18, 1929. I submitted an application by word of mouth, and I have no record of it. As I reconsider the whole affair now, I think it may have been one of the most successful applications that was ever refused. The interview must have followed the outline of my letter to Archibald. Certainly it asked the foundation, through Pearce, to make it possible to build and run an institute. Failing that, I asked for ten thousand dollars for immediate research.

To judge from the preparatory notes that are preserved, I must have emphasized to Pearce that this was not intended as a purely local undertaking; that I believed we could provide a center for neurological thought that would serve the whole continent, and that we could work effectively upon the unsolved problems in neurology unhampered by the artificial division between medicine and surgery.*

It is a weakness of mine, and sometimes, I suppose, strength, to put a failure out of mind and to forget the accompanying disappointment by turning to some more hopeful endeavor. This may explain why I did not immediately report this interview in my weekly letter to Mother. A month later, I wrote in answer to her inquiry:

"Did I not tell you of my interview with Dr. Pearce at the Rockefeller Foundation? He told me this was not the time for McGill to ask again as they had just been given a grant which, he thought, would go to me at least in part. . . . I told him that I should have come to him for help to create an institute for neurological research regardless of what university I moved to, on leaving New York. I added that the place in which it was to be built did not matter. To which he agreed.

"I was right, as I told you [in an earlier letter], that he is particularly interested in assisting neurology just now. They [the foundation] are helping Vogt and Foerster (in Germany), and they have two other proposals similar to mine for this country [the United States] on hand now, one from Cushing and one from McCarty in Philadelphia.

"He said he had watched my work for a long time," the letter

---

* Not long before my visit to New York, Jonathan Meakins had drawn me aside one morning and said, "My policy as chief of the Department of Medicine is to unite our neurology with Archibald's neurosurgery and so create a new department of neurology and neurosurgery at McGill."

continued, "and would like to back it. He also told me he did not expect me to remain at McGill."

Then the letter concluded: "In the last analysis I believe no help will come from Pearce unless Montreal can build for, and care for, the patients to the extent of half a million dollars. Then they (the Rockefeller Foundation) might well build the lab. and contribute to the scientific budget."

Although my institute application was refused and no grant for research was made, I learned a great deal from our very frank conversation. Dr. Pearce was a blunt man and, fortunately for me, he had been a pathologist before 1921, at which time he was made Director of Medical Education at the Rockefeller Foundation. This probably explains the fact that he was quite familiar with what I had published on neuropathology after our return from Spain in 1924. Also, he must have seen the summary of my travel to European clinics with its rather presumptuous criticisms and recommendations for neurology and neurosurgery that I had sent to his Paris representative, Alan Gregg, just before leaving Germany for Montreal.

Pearce had made the public statement that "a transfusion" to neurology and psychiatry, as he had expressed it, would be a wise strategic move in his own approach to the betterment of medicine as a whole. This, no doubt, explained the assistance he had just given to Foerster and to Vogt, whom I knew so well. I think he was considering one further grant to North America, an even larger one than those in Germany. Consequently, I was dismayed when he told me that applications were already before him from Philadelphia and from Boston for help to build a neurological institute.[*]

When Dr. Pearce saw that my hopes had been dashed by his refusal, he told me to go ahead and "saw wood." This struck me as small consolation and it hurt my pride, perhaps mistakenly. I told him, a little defiantly, that I would do that regardless of any institute or foundation. Then I wondered if he meant there was still hope of a more favorable action by the foundation. As there was nothing more that I could do about that, for the moment, and no other foundation in existence, that I knew of, likely to consider such a large undertaking, I turned back to patients, to

[*] See note 40.

the evolution of our team and to the blind hope that the money
for expansion of our work would come from somewhere, as manna
came to Moses and his people when they journeyed blindly into
the wilderness long ago.

In his clinical career, no doctor can control, or even guess, what
patients will come, what problems they will bring to him. He can
only hope for cases that lie within the range of his prepared approach to medicine — or those that will challenge him in genuinely
creative ways.

My sister, coming to me with her headaches and convulsive
seizures two months after my arrival in Montreal, had presented
the immediate necessity of operating to remove an enormous brain
tumor. This extremely large removal of frontal lobe was to nudge
me on to studies of the frontal lobe for years to come. What was its
function? How was it that pressure within the right frontal lobe
produced seizures of the same type as those of Hamilton, who had
had a contracting and shriveling scar in the same position? Did
the two conditions produce a similar effect upon the blood vessels
and thus upon the nourishment of the remaining nerve cells?

Madeleine Ehret Ottmann, who had asked me to examine her
son in Breslau, and who had understood the reason when I refused, waited for me to become established at the Royal Victoria
Hospital only two months longer than my mother and sister had.
Then she submitted the boy's problem to me again. This time she
did it through her divorced husband.

He wrote while I was busy making my application to the Rockefeller Foundation. Thus, on January 28, 1929, Mr. William Ottmann, Sr., came to Montreal by appointment. Obviously the
divorced mother and father were united in action now by their love
for this, their only son. The father, I discovered, was an impetuous
extrovert who used his leisure hours, when away from business, to
command a United States Army Reserve infantry regiment. Otherwise he was a business executive from Brooklyn.

He had come, I have no doubt, to make his own appraisal of me,
and to make a judgment of the institutions to which I had come
from New York. We sat together in Archibald's office. The window
looked out pleasantly from the second floor at 900 Sherbrooke
Street West. Across the street was the snowy campus of McGill

University. An arching avenue of bare but lofty elms led from the entrance gate up to the small stone memorial that stood on the grave of James McGill. Beyond the memorial was the original academic building, Dawson Hall, looking out on the world with impressive but very conservative dignity. It reminded me of Nassau Hall at Princeton.

On each side, Victorian buildings of odd design were scattered over the campus. Above and beyond, on the rising shoulder of Mount Royal, were the medical school and the Royal Victoria Hospital. Nothing very modern or likely to impress the man opposite me. Nothing to compare with the new home of New York's Columbia-Presbyterian Medical Center and their Neurological Institute, towering above the Hudson River.

On the desk before me lay a summary of the case of William Ottmann, Jr., and a report from Otfrid Foerster. "I proposed ventriculography," Foerster wrote, "but Mrs. Ottmann was somewhat afraid to have the boy operated upon." Having placed all the evidence before me, Mr. Ottmann set out to interpret it for me, naïvely. I had to be firm and ask for silence, while I wrote in longhand my own summary of the problem. Finally, I questioned the father and made further notes on his own observations.

Medical treatment, in the hands of excellent physicians, had already failed to control the attacks of this sixteen-year-old boy. He could not attend school with other lads of his age but was being educated by a tutor. At the moment, he and his mother were living in a club at Lake Placid, New York. The parents had become desperate about the future.

But I promised nothing. There was a reasonable suspicion of an objective brain abnormality of some sort. I could only study the boy completely for a beginning. This meant discovering, if I could, the nature of the abnormality and determining the pattern of his attacks. The sequence of movements, sensations or thoughts in each attack was our only guide to the location of the cause within the brain. Finally, we would reconsider.

Surgery in such cases as this was unheard of, but I had reached the stage of wanting to look at every case of epilepsy and to demand, "What is the cause here? Can I do something, however difficult and daring, to remove that cause?" I would have to begin with the small operation his mother had feared to let Foerster undertake, ventriculography. When I proposed it, the father agreed eagerly, and, as he took his leave, I realized that, in spite of my cautious words, he expected a miracle. Such expectations are always embarrassing, based as they are on little more than hopeful thinking.

After his return to Brooklyn, he wrote, "I left your office with a deep sense of appreciation of your courtesy as well as your interest, and I expressed to Mrs. Ottmann my great confidence. . . ." It seemed that I had passed my oral examination at his hands!

So it was that mother and son came to Montreal on March 18 and William joined the small group of my private patients in rooms at one end of the fourth floor of the Ross Memorial Pavilion. There was among the remarkable Royal Victoria nurses who looked after them an atmosphere of gaiety and excited cooperation in the establishment of the new specialty.*

A ventriculogram was carried out in the case of William Ottmann according to the technique of Dandy (see page 67). X rays showed clearly that the left cerebral hemisphere was smaller than the right. A one-sided injury to the brain at the time of birth, before the infant's head had begun to grow, could have caused that. I asked Mrs. Ottmann and she said William had been born after a very long period of labor. Forceps had been used at last to bring the head through the birth canal.

But even supposing that this was the original cause, what was I to do about it now? The brain seemed to be working well enough except when it exploded in a discharge. Then the boy had one of his devastating attacks.

Seeking the hidden cause and catching the culprit in a medical mystery is just as intriguing as searching for the villain in a murder mystery. When young Dr. Arthur Conan Doyle opened his medical consulting rooms in London, patients were too slow to come to him with their problems. So he turned impatiently to the

---

* Patients had been coming to me in those early months, referred by doctors for the usual neurosurgical complaints. But they were also coming, to my surprise, because of the particular interests, mentioned in my first talks, outside the then accepted field of a neurosurgeon's practice: chronic headaches that may follow head injuries; hydrocephalus and the spinal deformities that occur in babies (called spina bifida); adults who complained of heart pain or leg pain and who could be helped by operation on the nerves that control blood vessels; and, of course, most often the unusual cases of epilepsy.

making of his own case histories. Casting himself in the role of Sherlock Holmes, he solved his own imagined mysteries. He closed his consulting rooms to find a continuing challenge and creative delight as a writer, not unlike the challenge and excitement that can come to us who remain behind in the practice of medicine. But the doctor must be a repairman, if he can, as well as a detective. Diagnosis is never enough.

The sequence of movements or sensations or even thoughts at the beginning of a patient's habitual attacks was the only certain clue one could depend upon at that time to tell *where* the discharge was originating within the brain. We decided we must get a clear and certain description of William's attacks. So I withdrew all the medicines he had been taking and asked special nurses to watch him day and night, expecting he would have attacks.*

But William's epilepsy seemed to have disappeared. No attacks came. We tried to produce them by having him overbreathe. Still he had no attacks. At last, we let him leave the hospital without his previous anticonvulsive medicine, concluding that our ventriculogram had had a temporarily beneficial effect on the tendency to attacks, as it sometimes does.

We had come to the beginning of the long summer vacation at the medical school. I looked for a medical student who wanted a lucrative job and found one, Gordon Petrie. He was an excellent student and just the one to be a friend and a fellow golfer for William as well as an observer for me. He agreed to devote the summer to it, and before he and William left, I schooled him in what he was to observe, what to report about the attacks when they should begin again.

Then Mrs. Ottmann made the first of her astonishing efforts to help us in our research endeavors. To Cone and me and our little band of workers, her gift was unexpected. Incredible. Suddenly, there were many hoped-for things that we could have and do. From New York, she sent a letter, May 21, 1929, enclosing a check for ten thousand dollars.

"This represents," she wrote, "my contribution toward your research work in epilepsy. I do so want to help a bit and I do hope

---

* See note 41.

you will be able to buy monkeys. . . . Hoping that you and your dear wife and little ones are well . . . you will understand . . . Madeleine Ottmann."

On July 12, I wrote a letter to Richard Pearce at the Rockefeller Foundation that was, I am sure, a surprise to him.

"You will remember, perhaps, my coming to New York to see you with regard to a grant for an institute for neurological investigation, or failing that, a grant of ten thousand dollars to help carry on our investigation of epilepsy.

"I have just received an unsolicited check for ten thousand dollars from the mother of one of my epileptic patients for research in epilepsy. . . . I am writing this to you partly because you seemed to be interested in our work, and partly in order to write you a letter *without* begging for money, which may be something of a novelty to you. . . ."

Dr. Pearce replied, sending me his congratulations and best wishes. One might well ask what impelled me to write that slightly defiant letter. It did not mean that I had given up all hope of Rockefeller help. On the contrary, I thought Pearce and I understood each other, and were somewhat alike, each being a pathologist at heart. He would, I felt sure, take this as a reminder, however oblique, that we in Montreal were capable of making enthusiastic use of the help he had refused; a reminder, too, that here there were men of a younger generation who might make good use of the major endowment that he had in mind to make to neurological science, even though they must compete for it against such distinguished applicants as Harvey Cushing.

I did not dream then that this first application I had taken to New York and this letter I had written would be answered someday without any further begging on our part, except by indirection.

12

Epilepsy — Can Science Find a Cure?

Twelve days after Mrs. Ottmann sent the letter with the check enclosed, she sent me a telegram from New York, announcing that she was, herself, to be operated upon in the Presbyterian Hospital for cancer of the breast. The surgeon was to be my friend and former surgical chief on the second division, Hugh Auchincloss. I expected this, for we had discovered the growth when she complained of vague symptoms while still in Montreal. I telegraphed in my reply: "My heart goes out to you now."

When she had recovered from her operation, she joined her son and Gordon Petrie at the Westchester Club. But William proceeded then to have the expected major attack (the first one in six months). Petrie saw it and described it for me satisfactorily in every detail and began again to give the boy the best medicine available to decrease the chance of further attacks.

On September 22, Mrs. Ottmann wrote me her version of the attack and added, "William is playing an excellent game of golf. . . . Mr. Petrie [who had just left to return to medical school] was an admirable chap and one of the finest young men I have ever met. We miss him very much." Then she inquired about rumors of new cures for epilepsy.

On September 26, I wrote to her: "I do not want William to come back to Montreal now. We are not ready for him yet. . . ." Then I added, to show her what we were busy about:

"I have in hospital at the present time a lad of fifteen who has attacks strikingly similar to William's. I am hoping that the results of this study may cast some further light on William's problems.

"You speak in your letter of various cures, and rumors of cures. It is often difficult for the lay person to decide what is true and what is false in the practice of medicine. I wonder if it would be a reassurance to you if I promise to let you know of any advance that may occur, at any time throughout the world, in regard to epilepsy. . . . I am giving my life to the study of this condition, and shall not be ignorant, very long, of any really valuable advance. . . ."

I knew, and I am sure she surmised, that she might not have long to live. (I had learned from Auchincloss that the cancer had proved to be a very malignant one.) So I continued: "I have a particular interest in helping William. It is not only because I am fond of him and of his mother, but also because she has helped us so generously in our studies."

A month later Mrs. Ottmann wrote from the Westchester Club. William was having attacks weekly in spite of the medicine. She described one that she had just seen from the beginning, giving all the details. It was, she said, "one of the most severe convulsions William has ever had." It had been preceded a few hours earlier by a jerking of the right hand that interrupted his golf game. "Is there anything," she asked, "you want me to do?"

Meantime, her physician, my friend Rawle Geyelin, had returned to New York and was practicing medicine again. I wrote to him on November 1. "The more I learn about his [William's] attacks, the more evident it becomes that each one arises in the cortex of the left hemisphere and somewhere in the region of representation of the right hand. He has, several times, had jerking of the eyes before the movement reached the hand. I conclude that excitation probably passes [across the cortex] through the frontal eye field."

I was pointing out that the irritation, which led to each fit, must arise in an area that is very close to the speech centers. Speech is localized in the left hemisphere of a right-handed man. No removal of gray matter of any size in this area would ever be justified. That would leave the boy aphasic, unable to speak perhaps for life.

Was there anything else to be considered? I wondered. Was any operation thinkable? Or, should I advise medical therapy, hoping that better and more effective drugs would be discovered at some future date?

William himself was game for anything but he knew nothing about his own attacks. He was, in any case, more interested in golf and he was in no hurry. But his mother was. She lay awake at night, thinking of the future. What would happen to him if she should die? Perhaps she had a premonition that the time was shorter than we medical men could know.

What I had written her was true enough. Although there were other things that demanded my attention in those early years at Montreal, I *was* "giving my life to the study of epilepsy." The appeals for help from a succession of epileptics distressed me. William was only one of them. The problem of the mechanism intrigued me and I sensed that we had valid new clues that might bring us to a new understanding.

The studies with the microscope in Breslau had led me to suspect that abnormal closure of the blood vessels and alterations in blood circulation of the brain might be an important element in causation. I thought I could deal with the nerves to the arteries of the brain, as I had already learned to do for the arteries of the heart and the lower extremities. Like René Leriche in Strasbourg, I had become less of a scientist. I was willing to be an opportunist, not waiting for complete understanding, urged on by the patient's need in this field, as he, Leriche, had been in the field of blood-vessel surgery in the arms and legs. His aim was to relieve pain and to increase the circulation.

The case of Henry Howland illustrates one of my tentative approaches to the problem of epilepsy in those first Montreal years. This young man suffered from unlocalized epileptic seizures. I proposed that we should remove all of the vascular nerves to one side of the brain, taking time to study him, and then probably remove the blood-vessel nerves on the other side.

Stanley Cobb had returned from Munich and was now professor of neuropathology at Harvard and chief of neurology at the Boston City Hospital. He had referred this patient to me, hoping I could do something by neurosurgery for this boy whose outlook, because of his seizures, was otherwise so hopeless. He agreed to my proposal.

So he and I explained the plan to the parents. Since they were desperate, they approved gratefully. I went ahead, removing all the nerves that enter the skull, on one side, on the carotid and vertebral arteries. Cobb and I were frankly astonished as well as delighted when the patient's generalized attacks changed into one-sided attacks. So I repeated the procedure, which is a difficult one, on the other side. While I was stripping the nerves from the carotid and the vertebral arteries on the second side, there were alarming complications. But, that is another story.*

I reconsidered the case of William Ottmann. He had something wrong with the cerebral cortex on the left side. It was producing epileptic seizures. Should I expose it in a frankly exploratory operation? I could do that alone, of course, without seeking further advice. If there was a simple, understandable lesion to be removed, I could remove it with the help of Bill Cone and the advice of our own neurologist, Colin Russel. But this focus of trouble was near the speech area. No brain removal, such as Foerster had carried out, should ever be considered there. I wondered whether there might not be an abnormality of the blood vessels that was interfering with brain circulation. Was there any way to correct such an abnormality?

If only we had had an institute for neurological investigation in Montreal, we might have had people like Cobb and Wilhelm Spielmeyer at hand to help me decide what action could be taken. They would help to bear the responsibility if something went wrong too. These two men were making epilepsy and the circulation of the blood through the human brain their lifelong subject of investigation, as I thought I was prepared to do.

I was not afraid to explore, laying bare the whole surface of the hemisphere, although it was a little like running swiftly along the edge of a precipice. A slip could mean loss of speech, or paralysis, or death. But if I exposed the brain and closed the skull again, and did nothing more, and, even supposing I left the patient no worse off, what a disappointment. Mrs. Ottmann, nearing the end of her own journey through life, could not wait. Why not use the power of her wealth to conjure up the advantages of a scientific institute for a day?

* See note 42.

I talked with the patient's New York physician, Geyelin, on the telephone. He had no suggestion except "exploratory operation." I went to Boston and talked with Cobb at the Boston City Hospital, showing him the evidence. He shook his head. "Our conservative neurological treatment doesn't offer young Ottmann very much. You had better operate and explore that left hemisphere. It is certainly small as compared with the right one."

I met Mrs. Ottmann by appointment that same afternoon in Boston and put the cards on the table, so to speak. I explained, as best I could, this very complicated situation. The pattern of her son's convulsive attacks pointed to an origin of irritation in the cortex of the left hemisphere near the control area for the right hand, or, perhaps, in the adjacent speech area. I thought I could expose the brain and close the skull again without accident. If there was no abnormality I could remove, I might at least discover why this hemisphere was small and what had caused the difference between the two sides.

"If you will permit me to spend your money," I said, "I might bring the advisers I may or may not need to my operating theater. There are two other neuropathologists who are working on a similar hypothesis to mine in their studies of epilepsy. If they would join me in Montreal, and if I do not find an objective abnormality that I can remove, then perhaps, before I give up the effort and close the incision, I might precipitate one of William's attacks and let them see the brain during a seizure as I have seen it often enough. If, then, we decide there is something more to do, I'll do it.

"But, it may well be," I added, "that, after all, I shall do nothing important. Only close and give you back your son, hopefully unharmed. Nevertheless, with Geyelin's help, we will in that case plan a conservative medical regime for his life."

"Oh, yes," she said, "I would be so grateful to you if you would do just that. Bring anyone who can help you from anywhere."

I named Stanley Cobb as the neuropathologist interested in brain circulation and as an expert in the medical treatment of epilepsy. I specified Wilhelm Spielmeyer of Munich as the specialist who knew most about the neuropathology of patients suffering from various types of epilepsy. And I wanted Geyelin present too.

On my return to Montreal, I telephoned or cabled each consultant, promising travel expenses and a thousand dollars as a fee or contribution to his research work. I selected and reserved the services of the most expert special nurses.

When the consultants arrived, Colin Russel and Cone and I welcomed them — Geyelin, Spielmeyer and Cobb — and briefed them. The operation took place January 7, 1930. We had, it seemed, our institute for neurological investigation, if only for a day. Would we hit upon a new approach to the surgical treatment of epilepsy? The chances were small indeed, and I knew it.

Nevertheless, this was the way I would have liked to approach every suitable critical case.

We began the operation early. Mrs. Ottmann saw her son lifted onto the heavy German operating table and strapped in place securely and trundled away. She understood it all, she was ready to see him risk his life. He had so much to gain, so little to lose.

William entered the operating room, his shaven head supported on a sandbag, jesting and laughing quietly with Nurse Mary Roach, who walked beside him. She had become my expert anesthetist and was to be his friend for the day. This boy, whom I had first seen at sixteen in Breslau, was now eighteen. He was about to prove himself a man — courageous, calm, cooperative, eager to help in any way he could.

I marked out the line of intended incision on the scalp with a fine swab dipped in iodine, and injected the novocaine to render the scalp insensitive. The drapes were sewn to the scalp and carried upward over the shelf to the frame above his head to make his tent and a wall that shut him away from the surgical team while his head projected back into the field of operation. Everything was sterile on our side of the drapes.

In the few days before operation, I had prepared William for this, explaining as much as he could understand. I have often wondered at the courage of my patients. It called for true heroism to lie there, looking out beneath the awning of cloth, hearing and sensing the grind and the thud of drill and Gigli saw as the trapdoor is cut, hearing the crack of the bone when the skull door is opened. After that, patients often doze, finding themselves suddenly drowsy, but they rouse at once, alert and keen to answer questions they know are important, when the time comes for that.

I never witness this heroism without fresh admiration for the stuff that makes a human being. It is the spirit that ennobles him or her for a lifetime. The combined mechanisms of brain and body, matchless though they be, are nothing without the spirit. "We are such stuff as dreams are made on, and our little life is rounded with a sleep. . . ."

"I hope you can produce one of my attacks," William said. "This is the first time I've ever wanted to have one. I'll warn you, if I can, when one is coming on, but I'm not sure I can talk then. How soon will I be able to play golf after the operation? Can you do something to improve my putting?"

"I can see now," I replied, "where the golfing skill hides its own machinery. But it would not be fair to your opponent if we put in a new part, would it? Even if I could?"

We laughed and I carried on. To be a great golfer! That was his most immediate dream. But he would have many other dreams. Could we help to make them come true?

The consultants had come into the room now and were watching. We examined the cerebral cortex carefully. An unusually large artery emerged from the Sylvian fissure and pulsated actively as it coursed over the pia mater. Otherwise the cerebral cortex was normal in appearance, except for moderate atrophy (wasting) of the convolutions. That degree of atrophy was not normal at eighteen although it might be at sixty years of age.

I called for the electrode and applied a gentle current to certain points on the motor gyrus. It produced movement in the right hand and arm, as expected. I asked him why he was moving his hand. "I'm not moving it," he replied. "You must be doing it."

Next, I decided to determine, if I could, the area of cortex from which the attacks were coming. I hoped to do this without producing a big attack. I hoped (in vain) that he would say, "I feel as if an attack is coming on." So I changed the electric current from galvanic to faradic, since the latter was more likely to produce a seizure. On the second stimulus, William did go into a seizure. Alas, he gave no warning of it and it proved to be a major seizure, quite a violent one. The nature of the movements was described to me by Miss Roach as the attack progressed. The sequence was the same as in his usual attacks. Of this we could now be certain. Those who watched below the protective awning held him on the table with strong arms. The rest of us watched the brain. Bill Cone and I stopped the venous bleeding that broke out, as usual, from many points. When the convulsion was over and the patient lay quiet but unconscious, the arteries began to beat as if they were hoses attached to a source of high, rhythmic pressure.

I had seen all this before. There was no clue here, no guide to action. My heart fell. Alas! All this preparation for nothing? I stood silent, staring at the brain, my back to the consultants, thinking how foolish I had been to hope to find a hidden cyst, or an aneurysm, or a birth scar. There was certainly no abnormality here that I could remove. The point on the cortex from which the electrode had launched the attack was in or near the speech area, where no removal was to be considered. Well, I thought, I would have to close up and hope I had not made him any worse. The consultants would give their advice in regard to conservative treatment for life. Then they would go their way and I would be left to cheer the patient on his way as well as possible, in spite of the vast sense of failure.

Then, to my surprise, I saw a change. Something was appearing that I had never seen before. On the crown of the curving surface of some of the convolutions, snowy white patches had appeared. This was in the area that was obviously nourished by the large "unusual" artery that we had noted when the brain was first uncovered.

I stepped aside and asked the consultants to come close and watch while I sent a message to Miss Harriet Blackstock to come to the operating room and make a drawing. She was a medical illustrator recently returned from a period of study under the great medical artist Max Broedel, at Johns Hopkins. I had warned her to be ready, just in case we discovered something unusual.

She came and I asked her to draw what she saw, exactly as she saw it. While we discussed the meaning of this phenomenon, the patient moaned and grunted, gradually returning to consciousness. I had a feeling of secret joy. I had summoned the men most likely to help me to understand this strange appearance. We must interpret and decide. But, after all, what action could one take?

One must act sometimes before all the evidence and all the proofs are in. There were now two courses of possible action before me.

First, I could attempt to remove the delicate sheath of nerve fibers on the large artery. This should free its branches from such spasms. No surgeon had done this on the surface of the brain. But, even if I could do it successfully and it did stop the attacks, the cure would be of too short duration. Such nerves would grow back in time and so the constrictions would return.

The second possibility was to block that artery, destroying it forever. There must be some sort of complementary and compensatory circulation from all the surrounding arteries on the surface of the brain and within it. Their smallest branches must join up with the smallest branches of the artery to be destroyed. If this compensatory circulation would take over the nourishment of the gray matter fast enough, all might be well. But if compensatory circulation failed or was too slow to develop, the whole area of gray matter would die, as it does in any permanently crippling "stroke." It was the control of the right hand and the use of speech that would be in jeopardy.

Perhaps my stimulating electrode had produced the patches of artery constriction? No, I reasoned in answer to that.

"There are only one or two snowy patches of anemia on the motor gyrus where my electrode was used to cause the right hand to move. But most of the patches are behind that and below it, where I did not stimulate. They are in the great temporal speech area (the area of Wernicke). If the attacks began here, one could understand why he always failed to speak at the onset of a seizure. The anemic spots," I pointed out to myself and to the consultants, "form a triangle whose apex is below, near the point at which this large unusual artery makes its entrance onto the surface of the cortex from the depth of the fissure of Sylvius. It curves upward, as you see, over one convolution. Then the artery plunges into the brain again. This triangular portion of the cortex must derive its major blood supply from that artery."

The artery was pounding now with the pressure of blood from each heartbeat and yet it was obvious that no blood could be reaching the brain tissue where these white patches had appeared. The conclusion was inescapable. Spasms had developed in some of the small branches of that artery. These spasms were shutting off the gray matter beneath each anemic white patch so it could receive little or no blood. Nerve cells could not long tolerate such anemia, we realized, without suffering some permanent damage.

These patches had appeared *after* the attack. Therefore, artery constriction was not the immediate cause of his fits, but it might be the background cause. The development of the patches suggested that this artery had too much vasomotor nerve control. It was like the arteries outside the brain that are capable of spasms, not like the arteries normally inside. If that artery had been that way from the time of birth one could understand why the left hemisphere grew to be smaller than the right.

In our previous studies of the cause of epilepsy, Spielmeyer and I had been in remarkable agreement. He had described scattered small areas of nerve-cell destruction around small arteries at autopsies in various types of epilepsy. This had suggested to him an interference in blood flow through these little arteries.

Similarly, I had, myself, found scattered islands of neuron destruction in the gray matter adjacent to each of the brain scars studied in Breslau, and before that in New York. The arteries that grew into the scar during the healing process came from outside. They would carry vasomotor nerves with them that were normal enough outside the dura mater, but quite abnormal inside. They would then be capable of much greater individual constriction, like the one we were watching.

"Perhaps," I suggested to Spielmeyer as we stood in this operating room consultation, "this artery, which is capable of such spasms, is causing scattered points of damage in gray matter between attacks and, at the same time, is producing the irritability that causes the fits.

"Are we seeing in these artery contractions the cause of this patient's attacks?"

Spielmeyer nodded emphatically and seemed very excited. There were other links in the chain of cause and effect of epilepsy still to be considered. But a surgeon cannot always wait. As I have said already, he must at times be an opportunist. He feels the patient's insistent need, and hopes with the patient's hope.

And then, coming to the end of consultation, I asked each consultant in turn whether, in his opinion, I should remove the large artery whose branches entered the area of brain in which the snowy patches of anemia had appeared. After discussion, each of them answered, "Yes, remove the artery."

But Cone, standing at my elbow, muttered, "Don't do it, Wide." He spoke for caution, as he had in my sister's operation. That contrary voice shook me. I respected Cone's judgment. But I knew very well he was thinking of what a disaster, if it should come, would do to me as well as what it would do to the patient.

I might well have recalled an incident from my graduate student days in London nine years earlier. The location of the origin of irritation that produced the fits was the same as that of the appealing Cockney woman whom Gordon Holmes had examined before the graduate students in the Outpatient Clinic at Queen Square. Her trouble, he had said, was "too close to the speech centers to make it safe to refer her to the surgeons." I had thought then that I hoped never to become such a bungling type of surgeon. I would learn all that anyone else knew.

Well, here I was. Would I bungle? Or could I steer a safe course? Would I do better to turn back and take no risks? In the end, the decision was mine to make. If the surrounding arteries did not take over and provide normal compensatory circulation, the patient would be aphasic and paralyzed and I would never forgive myself. More than that, who could be certain that this would free him of his attacks?

I waited for William to regain consciousness after the seizure. A young friend of his had come to Montreal to be with him. I asked that he put on a mask and gown and come into the operating room. I listened to the two friends talking.

Finally, I turned and said to the consultants: "I think, if I were in the patient's place and believed, as I do, that this is my only chance to be freed of these epileptic attacks, I would say: 'Go ahead, I'll risk it.' "

So — I went ahead. I tied off the artery at two points and removed the vessel in between those points for later study. His spontaneous talking stopped. With a feeling of foreboding, I closed the dura, replaced the bone flap, closed the scalp, applied the dressing, and watched him leave the operating room with Miss Roach.

I went to the dressing room, wondering when and if the lad would speak again. Before I had finished dressing, someone knocked. The operating-room orderly put his head around the door. "Good news," he said. "Miss Roach told me to tell you: 'The patient was able to speak to his mother and the nurse when he arrived in his room.' "

But, next morning, when I went to Bill Ottmann's room, he looked at me with a questioning expression and reached out his left hand to me. The right was paralyzed. He smiled a crooked smile, but he could not speak. I glanced at the special nurse who stood on the other side of the bed. The same question was in her eyes.

"Don't worry, Bill," I said. "This will clear up in a few days." He looked puzzled and I realized that he was completely aphasic. He could neither use words nor understand them. But he understood my gestures and my smile. The nurse laughed with relief and was reassuring, as only a good nurse can be.

To Mrs. Ottmann, who had taken a room for herself at the other end of the hall, I said: "William is aphasic. He is paralyzed too on the right, but he is quite alert and conscious. There is always an area of swelling of the brain after a procedure of this sort. It should clear up about the fifth day. And there is one thing more: Don't be alarmed if he has some attacks. They may come as evidence that the surrounding arteries have taken over the work of the one we removed. The attacks may come while the gray matter is passing through an irritable stage on its way back to normal. When you go into his room, show him by your manner that you are not worried."

She looked at me searchingly. She was trying to read the thinking at the back of my mind. I looked at her and guessed that she had slept very little through the night in spite of the sedative I had given her. I noticed, too, how thin she had become since her own operation for cancer. She knew I was telling her what I honestly believed. But she must have been well aware, also, that I could be wrong as well as honest.

To tell the truth now, I was also frightened, deep down inside, but I knew I must never show it. There followed, for me, four days of hidden anxiety and outward optimism. On the fifth day, William did have a right-sided epileptic attack followed by a series of one-sided seizures. And then, thank God, the prophesy came true.

In between the attacks, voluntary control of movement appeared in the right arm and leg. By the sixth day, words had come back to him and he understood speech. The aphasia had vanished! The laughter in William's room took on an altered ring and no one cared that the boy's speech was slurred and that the right hand was still clumsy. We knew all would be well. On the seventh day, I wrote to Geyelin in New York.

"William is clearing up amazingly after a series of seizures. No aphasia now, only anarthria [slurred speech]. Right hand still clumsy. It is obvious that it was the return toward a normal state of circulation in the brain that made the cells irritable and gave us a day of epileptic fireworks. He was conscious during these convulsions and remembers it all now."

William Ottmann, Sr., came to Montreal as soon as his son was out of bed and his head dressing removed. The last letter I had received from him before the operation contained the alarming news that he had been diluting his son's prescribed medicines secretly "for fear of drug addiction." When he arrived in Montreal, he added considerably to general gaiety since he was so sure the "miracle" he had predicted (on no good grounds) had come to pass.

Shortly after the father arrived, I was informed that the people on the sidewalk below the Ross Memorial Pavilion had been used as targets for a peashooter, and that they heard roars of laughter issuing from an open window on the fourth floor. It was William's room, of course. And the culprit was a well-known Brooklyn businessman and soldier who was, at heart, a naïve, uncontrollable and irrepressible boy.

He left us in a few days. Soon afterward, Mrs. Ottmann returned to New York to consult her own physician. William stayed on and I established a rehabilitation program for him since I discovered he had his own psychological problems. I hoped he would prepare to return to school for some of the education he had missed. He remained in Montreal three months, taking lessons on the typewriter, among other activities.

With each day and week and year that Bill Ottmann lived on without a seizure he and those who were close to him were more and more certain that he was cured. But doctors do not deal in miracles nor can they look into the future. A cure of epilepsy can be claimed only after the patient lives his life and sails at last into another harbor to come ashore and sail no more.

Physicians may wonder that I have reported these two cases here (of Henry Howland and William Ottmann), instead of describing them anonymously as usual in some medical journal. These two reports, as given here, are accurate in every detail as far as reports go. These cases proved to be most important in the story of the Montreal Neurological Institute, because of what the father of one and the mother of the other did for us.

In the case of Bill Ottmann, the clinical result was indeed gratifying. But I was never prepared to make a final analysis of the reasons for success. My action was that of a hopeful and somewhat daring opportunist.*

* See note 43.

13

Madeleine Ottmann

M eantime, the Montreal project in neurology was moving forward, in the laboratory, on the wards, at the Wednesday conferences and in the university classrooms. Colin Russel and the other neurologists were in and out of the Laboratory of Neuropathology with problems of their own. There was a growing sense of something wonderful and new.

Cone raised the morale of everyone in our team and set up a remarkable standard of excellence. He ran the laboratory with tireless enthusiasm, kept an eye on all my patients, as well as his own, for he was beginning to carry out his own operations and showed great skill. He devised better ways of providing detailed care for our patients, who presented the most difficult problems for our nursing staff — patients who were paralyzed or epileptic or unconscious. He took it on himself to help nurses and orderlies and interns to develop new procedures, from better ways of doing bed baths to the aseptic techniques of surgical dressings and needle punctures and the handling of catheters.

He seemed tireless. Each morning he returned, punctual and ready to drive ahead with a laugh, although he had worked with research fellows in the laboratory the night before and had made rounds to all the patients with a sleepy resident surgeon. He extended his help to the neurologists, too, and was quickly in demand for consultation by physicians and surgeons of other departments of the hospital.

But, he could not bring himself to write up his research. He was too much a perfectionist for that. By January of 1930, he had been trying for three years to write a chapter on the microscopic structure of the optic nerve for *Cytology and Cellular Pathology of the Nervous System,* the book I had undertaken to edit.

The book had grown to a great size. The manuscripts of thirty chapters were on my desk, ready for final editing. I felt a little desperate about it. Consequently, after the Ottmann operation, I asked Cone to take two weeks off to write up his chapter while I took care of the laboratory and the clinic. He agreed with alacrity. But he said, "Before I start writing, I want to make a few better 'preparations.' "

The authors who had turned in their own manuscripts early were writing me, asking why the book had not appeared. There was another major delinquent from whom I had heard nothing. That was del Rio-Hortega in Madrid. He, like Cone, but unlike Cajal, found it difficult to crystallize and to write. I realized that if Hortega did not send me his chapter on oligodendroglia, I would have to write it myself. So, I cabled him again, and sternly. This time he answered at once by cable, promising to send the completed chapter on a specified date.

Bill Cone spent his whole two weeks enthusiastically making more and more beautiful preparations and working far into the night. He showed me them with delight. But he did not rest and the chapter was not written.

But there was help in sight. John MacMillan, the excellent ophthalmologist at the Royal Victoria, was working with him now. He was so impressed by the new microscopic sections and all that they were learning about the structure of the optic nerve and the retina that he agreed to be coauthor of the chapter. He undertook to write the manuscript. With that promise, Cone came back on service and freed me for my own breathing spell.

There have been times in my life when I became desperate and wondered whether I could keep my head above the flood of work that must be done. This was one of those times. I realized that I must get the manuscript off to the publisher, complete or incomplete. Mrs. Ottmann's gift of extra money for research was running out and I thought I must make up my mind what to do about that.

"Work piles up," I wrote in the weekly letter, "and it seems insurmountable, however little one sleeps." I had grown tired and confused. So Helen, who was herself working every bit as hard as I on her part of our common career, arranged to take time off from the family. Making arrangements for a week away, we hid ourselves in the Hermitage Club on the eastern shore of Lake Memphremagog, eighty miles from Montreal. Here a newfound friend, Sydney Lyman, had given us a temporary membership.

Except at the week's end, we were the only guests. The snow was deep and it seemed a place of peace and vast silence. Cone, I knew, would look after Bill Ottmann and do my work in the clinic as well as I — better, in fact. So we slept, forgetting all our cares, as long as we could sleep. Awakening at last, we found that life had taken on a long perspective and the remainder of the week that lay before us seemed almost endless.

During the previous summer holiday on this lake, at the end of our first year in Canada, we had bought two deserted farms. They were side by side with a mile or more of frontage on the lake's shore. But the property was ten miles away from the Hermitage Club. We could see where it must be behind the rising shoulder of a mountain across the lake. We had even been able to establish an experienced farmer on the place. It was to become our summer home and I had reasoned (naïvely) that Erick Jackson, the farmer, could make the farm pay for its upkeep and for his salary, once he was established there.

Jackson came to see us when we telephoned him from the Hermitage, riding in a light sleigh to which he had harnessed Maud. Maud was a spirited plow horse, the better half of a team we had bought from Dan Jones, a neighboring farmer. Looking out of the windows of the club, we saw Jackson coming swiftly along on the winter road that crossed the frozen surface of the lake. Maud even pulled him up off the road and over the bank, to come calump, calump, calumping through the deep snow, right up to the front entrance of the club. There, we talked about the farm and the cows and the sheep he wanted to buy, and our breath was white in the frosty air.

When he started home, we put on our skis and skijored behind him far out on that magnificent lake, which extends thirty-two miles from Magog in Quebec southward to Newport in Vermont.

These are the lovely highlands of what is called the Eastern Townships of Quebec, les Cantons de l'Est.

The sun was setting as we dropped the skijor ropes and waved good-bye to Jackson. Warm color had come to the snowy plain. Our skis carried us smoothly back toward the Hermitage, shish, shish, shish, while a sense of peace and strength came to us, and satisfaction that we owned a place of our own here. Mount Orford to the north and the Owl Head to the south towered into the unbelievable blue of twilight.

Exhilarated, we vowed to each other that we would hold on to this beautiful bit of Memphremagog lakeshore, if we could, as our country home, even if the project in Montreal should collapse, and even though the idea of an institute for neurological investigation should take wings and draw us after it to some other city.

This was a strange time for us. We had discovered that, in Montreal, we were still considered Americans, and each time we returned to the States we were hailed as Canadians. We seemed, for the time being, to have no country of our own. But here, in the Townships, we felt at home. Sydney Lyman and Eric Fisher, who owned nearby farms that bordered on the lake, had welcomed us. Their wives had made us feel that we belonged. We were happy to join their company.

After dinner in the warmly lit dining room, we sat before a blazing fire and talked about the dream that had carried us north to Montreal. We had been here a little over a year. The idea of an institute now seemed to be no more than a daydream. It called for endowment. But the outlook for an endowment was not promising. The financial world was paralyzed by the Great Depression of the nineteen thirties. That explained why we had been able to buy two deserted farms so cheaply, using only a part of the indemnity that had come to us because of my being blown up by a German torpedo.

Who would have money enough to endow my project? I felt that Richard Pearce would have helped us in the end. But Pearce had died suddenly and unexpectedly. George Vincent, the distinguished president of the Rockefeller Foundation, had resigned and was being succeeded by a lesser leader, Max Mason. No successor to Pearce, in charge of medical research, had as yet been appointed.

I could think of no one at all to whom I could appeal for the gift of a million dollars — no one unless, perhaps, it was Mrs. Ottmann. Could she do it? Would she consider it? But she had become a friend. I could not carry an application to her, as I had to Pearce. I was reluctant to bring myself to write her a begging letter.

But, all the same, I might draw for her a bold picture. If she saw that picture as an opportunity, she would thank me. If not, she could ignore it and there would be no need for her to make an embarrassing refusal. I was like a chess player who sees before him only one possible move and decides at last to make it although there is little hope of winning the game.

Next day we turned to other things. I had brought a heavy suitcase filled with manuscripts. I laid out all the finished chapters for *Cytology and Cellular Pathology of the Nervous System* on a large table and saw that the work was good. Some of the chapters were very good. As editor and organizer, I would make a contribution greater, by far, than anything Cone and I could have achieved with the textbook we had thought we might write.

Bill Cone, it seemed, could not be made into an author, and I was beginning to realize that science is, in some ways, like football. Bill Cone was a tackle, a magnificent tackle. But, you could not make him into a quarterback, and he did not want to call the plays. Many of the authors of the *Cytology* had done far better than anything I could have done in a field that was their own. I was learning that in science, as in football, the captain should not carry the ball himself in any play if others on his team could do it as well, or better.

When we returned to Montreal at the end of this long and delightful week, the book was ready to be mailed. There had not been so much for me to do after all, and it was easy to see what to do when my head was clear. I was exuberant as I cleared it off the table. It could go to Paul Hoeber, the impatient publisher in New York, and the delinquent chapters could follow shortly. So the manuscript went off, and the Cone and Hortega chapters did follow shortly.

And now, I would go on with courage, using up the funds for research, pushing on the work that promised so much. I would do it as if I knew help would come. I would not retrench or retreat.

I could not appeal to Archibald or to his friends for help in research. His own need was too great. The dean was doing all he could. I would make my last move and write the letter Helen and I had planned at the Hermitage Club. I would send the hint of endowment to Mrs. Ottmann as soon as her son should leave Montreal.

But, strange to say, before I could make this move we had planned, Mrs. Ottmann made another unexpected move herself: On April 3, 1930, the following appears in my weekly letter to Mother:

"I received a check from Mrs. Ottmann yesterday for $10,000 for research in epilepsy. It will help very much." This seems now a ridiculous underdescription of our reaction. Like her first gift, a year earlier for the same amount, this second gift was unsolicited and it brought rejoicing to us who formed the inner circle of neurology in the Royal Victoria. I told her this and thanked her at once.

But, realizing that time was running out and that so much more than our immediate research was at stake, I went ahead with the writing of the hint nevertheless. On April 18, 1930, when William Ottmann, Jr., left Montreal, I wrote my letter as planned.

"William left hospital last night. The nurses told me, on the fourth floor this morning, that they miss him very much, as we all shall. . . .

"I am enclosing my account for the remaining professional charges. I fear you may think this has been a rather expensive undertaking, but the total must be well under the outside figure I quoted to you in Boston.

"There was one moment in the operation when the consultants all earned their fees. If you will recall the story of that first week after operation, you will realize what we had to weigh in the balance at the operating table. . . .

"William's own case has actually opened up a new horizon. It has carried us from the simple brain-injury cases to the much more complex blood vessel group to which he belonged, and, I believe, hundreds of thousands of other sufferers do belong.

"I shall never be able to cope with this problem, nor realize fully the opportunities presented already by the clues we have in hand, until I have a group of men with me in an Institute for Neurological Investigation attached to the Royal Victoria where we can concentrate patients, laboratories and young investigators.

"I know it is impossible of realization, as the whole undertaking would cost a million dollars. But, if I ever do get it before I'm senile, the problem William has presented us will become the central theme of investigation. . . ."

Eight days later, I was in the operating room when a nurse brought in an urgent telephone message from Mrs. Ottmann in New York. She was ill, but wished to see me as soon as possible. I sent word I would come to her apartment on Park Avenue next morning. On the train to New York that night, I did a great deal of thinking. Had she actually taken the letter I sent her as an opportunity to establish an institute? In that case, I would have to draw up specific plans. I would have to remain in Montreal. The die would have been cast.

When my train arrived in Grand Central Station, I took a taxi to her apartment on Park Avenue, stopping on the way to leave my bag at the University Club. I was prepared for a discussion of an institute for neurological investigation, but not for what happened.

In the apartment's lobby, a message was waiting for me. It was from her attorney, a Mr. Mooney. He wanted to see me at once. I ignored his message and went up to her apartment. A nurse was waiting for me there. I told her that the attorney could reach me at the University Club later in the morning. The nurse shook her head.

"Mrs. Ottmann," she said, "has been losing ground very rapidly. Her doctor says it is the cancer. She seems to know she is dying. She wants to see you alone."

I was appalled. I had no idea her condition could change so rapidly. I entered the darkened room. She was lying in bed. Her eyes were closed. I saw how she had changed. Her hand on the coverlet was very thin, her cheeks sunken.

Thinking she was asleep, I stood quietly waiting. I looked about the room. On the table was a small pile of unopened letters. I was startled to recognize my own scrawling handwriting there. I looked

again. It was the letter I had written. It was unopened, the letter
I had posted nine days before! As I turned back, she was looking
at me.

"Oh, I am so glad you have come," she said. "There are some
things I hope you will do for William."

"Of course," I said, "anything."

She told me what these things were. They were not difficult and
not very important. Then she added:

"Will you look after William?"

"Yes," I said, "I'll do anything I can."

She looked at me earnestly. "He will have so many problems,
here in New York, without me. William is only eighteen, you
know."

She paused. Then she looked up again and smiled. "I'm happy
he is well. So happy! Thank you. He is a good boy."

Her eyes closed. She seemed to have fallen peacefully asleep, as
if she were very, very tired. Death, I realized, was knocking at the
door, coming perhaps as a friend. Meanwhile, she was using all
the strength at her command "to plan for William." She was trying to do the impossible — to guide and protect her son after
death should carry her off.

How long I stood there I have no idea. I was content that she
should never read my letter. My mind went back over her gallant
struggle since she sent the Breslau police to call me to come to
see her.

So much had happened in the eighteen months that had followed! At last she opened her eyes again and smiled a little.

"I talked to Mr. Mooney this morning. He has some things to
say to you." She held out her hand and I kissed it. Then I hurried from the room and on down to the out-of-doors, struggling
to hold back my tears. I turned off Park Avenue and came to the
East River, where I sat alone on a wharf.

"It was a beautiful New York spring day." I quote from the
letter I wrote my mother that night. "In early spring, there is a
curious perfume in the air in New York."

Then there follows a paragraph that betrays the fact that the
writer still had mixed feelings about becoming a Canadian.

"Curiously enough, I was greatly relieved that there is to be no
institute — no immediate effort to organize, no plans for a build-

ing. . . . If she had read my letter and said yes, I would have been anchored outside the U.S.A. I discovered that I had a dread of that. . . . Sometimes I like English people better than Americans. But, all the same, there is something about the spirit of the U.S. that thrills me . . . I discover that I am still an American inside. But," I concluded, evidently not quite sure of myself, "if it comes to it, I shouldn't want to leave Montreal!"

I remember well that hour alone on the waterfront, while tugs and barges came and went so close at hand. Added to the sense of compassion for Madeleine Ottmann, I remember the feeling of relief that I need not now make the final choice of nationality. And I recall the sense of relief that I was not yet called upon to put down on paper the finished version of the idea for an institute for neurological investigation. I realized that I was not quite ready for that.

At the University Club, I found a letter waiting for me. It had come by hand from Mr. Mooney: "I wish to carry out a direction," he wrote, "that Mrs. Ottmann gave to me in your behalf this morning, before your train arrived."

When I went to lunch with Mr. Mooney at the Lotus Club, I met in him an attorney who was altogether perfect in manner and dress. His large round eyes seemed to bulge with pleased importance and he used long words that smacked of the writing of many wills for the well-to-do. In spite of myself, a tune and a song began to run through my mind from one of Gilbert and Sullivan's light operas: "I am the very model of a modern major general."

It was some time before he considered the appropriate moment had arrived. Then he asked in a low voice, as if I were an accomplice, if I could give him a statement of the charges for my professional services to William, including operation, study and care. I had enclosed this statement in my handwritten letter that now lay unopened on Mrs. Ottmann's bedside table. When I told him the sum, he said: "She wants me to pay it at once and she instructed me to add this check for two thousand dollars as your fee for coming to New York today." *

Then, after a pause, Mr. Mooney added: "Mrs. Ottmann has given me permission to disclose the fact that in her will she has

* See note 44.

bequeathed to you fifty thousand dollars which she described as a 'modest foundation of money' to be used by you in research wherever you may decide to go.''

I returned to Montreal. Eight days later, word came to me there that Madeleine Ottmann had died. The message was from her brother. Alas that she should leave her son and that he should lose so wonderful a mother! But, considered in another light, she had slipped away in triumph.

Our moment of good-bye came back to me. I stood again at her bedside:

"William is only eighteen, you know. But I'm happy he is well. So happy! Thank you. He is a good boy.''

I recalled our first meeting only nineteen months before in the Breslau nursing home — a well-dressed woman, delightfully quick in her perceptions. When I said it would be better if I did not examine William, she understood. How amazing that she should plan to come to us and should force me to face the problem of her son's epilepsy as the first of a long Montreal series of such problems!

The Ottmann drama, which I have described in this and the preceding chapters, was acted out against the background of our struggle to establish the Montreal neurological project. Ordinarily it is the doctor's business to penetrate quickly and deeply through the social defenses of a patient or a parent. He comes thus to the secret places of the soul and understands the hopes and fears and sorrows that may lie there hidden away from others. He grieves or rejoices with the patient briefly. But the relationship is ordinarily a one-way affair. He studies and tries to help. Then he leaves that patient and passes on to another, and another.

The doctor keeps his own hopes and fears and aspirations to himself, ordinarily. My relationship with Mrs. Ottmann was different. She insisted that I should do something for her son. But, at the same time, she explored the secret places of my own hopes. She understood me. She perceived my problems and helped me as if she could see into the future more clearly than I myself could.

I had reasoned blindly (if reasoning it was) that added help would come to our project like manna from somewhere, provided the research to be supported was worthy of it. I had asked the Rockefeller Foundation for the minimum needed. Mrs. Ottmann gave, at first, exactly what they refused. That check for ten thousand dollars was what she hoped we would use to study the problems that patients brought us, one of whom was her son.

Only later, I came to realize that Richard Pearce's refusal of my first application to the Rockefeller Foundation was fortunate. My idea of an institute in 1928 was ill-formed and in some ways unwise. During our first eighteen months in Montreal, which were the last eighteen months of her life, Mrs. Ottmann gave us, without being asked to do so, exactly the extra help we needed, when we needed it, to carry us through three years. During those three years, the idea of an institute for neurological investigation that I had presented to Pearce was to evolve and change little by little, approaching maturity.

From a practical clinical point of view, her gifts made it possible for me to elaborate two approaches to the problem of epilepsy. One was a study of cerebral circulation with an attempt to control blood flow. The other was the approach begun with Foerster. It consisted of treatment by means of surgical excision of abnormal areas in the brain under local anesthesia. This second approach was already opening the doors wide to a strategic study of the anatomy and physiology of the cerebral cortex of man.

These were projects on which teams of workers could begin their studies at once. They called for modern and ever-changing equipment and new skills that could be made available in an institute. That larger project was not properly her affair. And so, in the end, I was glad my letter to Mrs. Ottmann came too late to be read and lay unopened on her bedside table. That was my problem, not hers.

She and I had been involved in a desperate effort to save her son for an active life if possible, knowing that her time to live was so short. She gave me the help I needed when I needed it, without being asked. William was hardly aware of the issues involved. He faced the risks.

The reader might well ask, "Was the operation on her son really a success? Was the patient cured of his epilepsy?" The answer is yes and no. He lived a normal life, considering himself cured. William was married at twenty, two years after operation, and was as happy as most people. He died of a coronary attack, at thirty-five, eighteen years after the Montreal operation. He did have one major convulsive seizure, the first, six years after the operation, a second in the thirteenth year, and a third in the seventeenth year.

The operation on William Ottmann was the only one of its kind. I did not repeat it. In all my experience, I was never faced by that phenomenon again.

Perhaps only a woman could have had the intuition to let me see how urgent her problem was and yet let me come to my own conclusion about her son in my own time. Only a gentle woman would have rewarded me as graciously as she did. Only a clever one could have been so timely about it.

In retrospect, I marveled that I had been so presumptuous as to plan in haste that far-flung consultation, and so daring as to take the risk I took when I tied off the large artery that had behaved so strangely on the surface of the brain after William's seizure. Now that Mrs. Ottmann was gone, it was too late to thank her. One could only remember. I purchased a morning coat and took the train to New York to attend her funeral in the vast Saint Patrick's Cathedral. There I joined her son and brother and her many sorrowing friends.

The help that Madeleine Ottmann gave to our Montreal project was given, as if by stealth, without discussion. She knew I would have worked just as hard, if not as effectively, without it. I believe that, from the start, she saw clearly my hidden hope of serving society, and certainly she understood all too well the anguish of those who suffer in that society. Compassion and understanding prompted her to put the tools I needed into my hands when she saw that I needed them. And so she became a *fellow builder* with the others who had joined us, and who were yet to join us, in our common undertaking.

14

Faith of a Scientist

"We know that our work is rightly both an
instrument and an end. A great discovery is a
thing of beauty; and our faith — our binding
quiet faith — is that knowledge is good. . . .
"So it is with us as scientists, so it is with
us as men. We are at once instrument and
end, discoverers and teachers, actors and observers."
— Robert Oppenheimer in his
Reith Lecture *

In December 1930, nine months after Mrs. Ottmann's death, I began to examine our situation in Montreal realistically. At the
present rate of activity, her bequests would not carry us very far
beyond the end of the year of 1931. What then? The financial
world was passing through what came to be called the Great Depression. Our laboratory in the Royal Victoria Hospital was being
supported for routine purposes by the anonymous friends of the
professor of surgery, Edward Archibald, and by a small added
stipend from the university budget of the professor of medicine,
Jonathan Meakins. But these two major departments had less income than they needed for their own purposes. I could not expect
great increases from them. McGill University had no academic
salaries for us or our associates. The Royal Victoria Hospital governors had withdrawn their promise of a grant to our laboratory
before the death of President Meredith, and the superintendent,

* J. R. Oppenheimer, "Science and the Common Understanding." B.B.C. Reith
Lecture, Oxford, 1953.

W. R. Chenoweth, had not suggested any alteration in their policy.

Obviously, continued support of growth, if it was to come to neurology and neurosurgery, was likely to come only from outside sources, and through our own efforts. Bill Cone had lived quietly on his promised full-time salary as director of the laboratory. During the first year I had accepted the guaranteed monthly sum volunteered by the surgeons at the Royal Victoria. At the end of the first year I had just been able to pay back from my private practice what they had advanced.

Now, the Royal Victoria was preparing to provide space within the hospital for a small private consulting suite that I would use on a modified full-time basis. This was similar to my previous arrangement in New York. It was something new in Montreal, a concession that enabled me to support myself entirely from private patients without having to leave the hospital. I was able to give other patients, who did not pay, equal care in the wards and the outpatient clinic. Thus, I had established my own full-time scheme, and could spend that full time working within the Royal Victoria and going outside only when needed on a consultation.

The excellent level of the practice carried out by the neurologists in the Montreal General Hospital and those in the French-speaking Hôtel-Dieu and Hôpital Notre-Dame made quick transfer of selected patients for neurosurgery possible. Meanwhile, we laid plans to train neurosurgeons for the staffs of these other large teaching hospitals.*

The five o'clock neurological conference each Wednesday served many purposes for the promotion of neurology and the well-being of patients. Because Cone and I were the only neurosurgeons, we had been able to do what would have been more difficult for neurologists to do alone. Thus, we had drawn together those who were interested in the problems of the nervous system in the larger hospitals of Montreal and Quebec.

The language barrier had been crossed. Brilliant French-Canadian neurologists were working with us in conference and laboratory and cooperating with us in the handling of neurosurgical problems to the benefit of many patients. I had improved my ability to talk French and could communicate with French-Canadian

---

* See note 45.

patients using their own tongue effectively, if sometimes painfully.

But all this was no more than marking time. I grew impatient. On December 7, 1930, I wrote in the weekly letter:

"The Devil of Discontent has driven me to begin drawing up another appeal to the Rockefeller Foundation for help to found a research center in Montreal." And a little later I wrote, "I have been reading Abraham Flexner's new book on universities. It is very interesting and helps me to plan my approach to the Rockefeller Foundation and to outline the possible ideal institute."

So, at the start of our third year in Montreal, I reviewed the situation as a preparation for a second application. Let me describe that review realistically, filling in the background of life in Montreal, personal as well as professional. Life's decisions are made, and its inspirations come to one, in the balanced living of life. And who is to say what is most important? My most useful ideas have occurred to me in times of talk and laughter, coming from other people. They have come, too, in sudden moments of silence when beauty placed a finger on her lip, or during that other sort of stillness, while one is writing down his thoughts on paper. At such times a scientist may hope to formulate his own personal faith.

Let me attempt to sketch what life for us was like in our vacation land in the Eastern Townships. During a short winter vacation, Helen and I took the four children, with their German governess and the cook, to our farm on the slopes of Lake Memphremagog. Jackson, the farm manager, met us at the tiny railroad station in South Bolton, driving the ponderous plow team. He had hitched them to a hayrack he had taken off its wheels and mounted on snow runners.

Onto this roomy bobsled we vaulted with a sense of great adventure, and found ourselves snug and warm in the hay beneath the buffalo robes. The children shouted and sang as we were pulled so smoothly up the shoulder of Mount Peevee. The road had been rolled, not cleared of snow. It was smooth and the runners made no sound.

As we came over the mountain's shoulder, the sleigh bells rang out merrily and we trotted along the level way. The breath of horse and man made clouds of white that hung in the clear, cold air. The spruce trees and the firs, all loaded down with freshly fallen snow, seemed to bow a welcome as we passed them on the way to Sussex House, our old, remodeled farmhouse.

This home in the wilderness was roomy and warm when fires were built. Its windows looked out on open fields that swept smoothly down to the great white blanket of snow that hid Lake Memphemagog. The slopes called for toboggan, sled and skis. The children, now thirteen and twelve, four and three, tumbled out of doors at every opportunity.

My stay during that holiday had to be brief. But the change and the beauty helped me to look at life in long perspective, as it often does. "I have never seen the lake more beautiful," I wrote my mother, "snow storms, mists over the mountains, startling blue sky. . . . Sparkling snowflakes glint down in the morning air while the sun shines through this frosty falling of what, in June, would be the morning dew."

But the questions that went about with me, at the back of my mind, could no longer be ignored here in this silence. What had we in Montreal to show an agent of the Rockefeller Foundation or any other possible benefactor? The embryo of a many-chambered institute of neurology? How pretentious! Any visitor to our modest arrangements at the Royal Victoria Hospital might laugh at such a claim. But — that is what it was — *an embryo*.

The idea that had been mine at first was mine no longer. It had entered the minds of many others and was alive. The idea was growing larger all the time. It was shared by nurses and doctors and technicians and orderlies and patients and their relatives and indeed the medical students.

But what had we to show to a critical visitor? A consulting room in the hospital, efficient operating rooms and a few patients in and out of their beds here and there. And, of course, the Laboratory of Neuropathology. Even this was not impressive in outward appearance. A visitor could see the same sort of thing in other hospitals. Would he realize that our laboratory was different? It was here that the heart of the embryo was beating.

But the laboratory, as I have said, did not look like much: three rooms at the end of the hall in the University Clinic. One room had been partitioned to make an office for Bill Cone, the laboratory chief, and a room for the technician, Edward Dockrill. After seven years he had taught others his skill as a technician and was about to return to England.*

The second room had likewise been divided into two, an inner, closet-sized office for me with desk, microscope, shelves and a big window, and an outer room in which the secretary, Miss Hope Lewis, kept her files and typewriter. She made the reports and coordinated everything. She presided over the telephone, welcomed visitors, and kept away intruders. In fact, she was my personal secretary as well as the clerical and executive staff. And all of this she managed with dignity, kindness and humor.

Then there was the third room. It was luxuriously *un*divided. In it, graduate fellows worked at benches shoulder to shoulder for longer or shorter periods. I never heard it said that it was crowded, but it must have seemed so to strangers. Here, visitors were welcomed and neurologists came and went.

Most important, this was our neuropathology conference room. We were proud of the work we had done in neuropathology and neurocytology. This was what had brought graduate students to us. The precious specimens we had brought from the Laboratory of Neurocytology in New York, then lost and retrieved, were central jewels among the laboratory treasures. Some had been opened for further use. The others were still in formalin in the same little paraffin-sealed bottles that had been hauled away so carelessly to the city dump.

Pathologists and clinicians, young and old, came to this room, speaking French and English; also the hospital's first specializing psychiatrist, David Slight, and occasionally foreign visitors of all nationalities. From the cloistered seclusion of the Hôtel-Dieu, the French-speaking nun who was chief technician in that hospital's laboratory came to learn the Spanish silver methods by special permission of her Mother Superior.

And the professor of pathology, Horst Oertel, who had greeted my ambitions for neuropathology with Teutonic contempt when Archibald and Meakins asked him to take me into his institute, had changed in his attitude. He showed us every courtesy now, although it was always from the proud distance of the Patho-

* See note 46.

Workers in the Laboratory of Neuropathology within Professor Meakins's University Clinic of the Royal Victoria Hospital, spring of 1929. From left to right: Ottiwell Jones, research fellow from the University of California, San Francisco; Maurice Brodie, resident in neurology and neurosurgery; Dorothy Russell, research fellow from the London General Hospital, London, England; Hope Lewis, secretary; Colin Russel, neurologist; Wilder Penfield, neurosurgeon; William Cone, neuropathologist; Edward Dockrill, technician.

logical Institute. Indeed he had even invited me to lecture to the undergraduates in his university course.

For our Friday Afternoon Neuropathology Conference, many crowded into our little conference room, bringing microscopes from near or far for the occasion. Cases were reviewed and diagnoses made or checked by study of the sections. Cone and I took opposite sides on some point or other in almost every case, and our heated disagreements became famous. I suppose most of those present realized that, after hearing other points of view, we staged these arguments for teaching purposes. Few, perhaps, perceived how much Bill and I enjoyed them and how close we were in understanding and affection. We used to laugh and carry on the business of the day with recurring reconciliations, knowing that it is far better to be wrong than without an opinion.

Neuropathology was a basic science for neurosurgeons, as well as for neurologists and psychiatrists. It would always have to be a subject for further investigation and for teaching in any neurological institute, generation after generation. So I had set out to cover the whole field as best I could on my return from Spain, using the new metallic methods for many clinical purposes. Eventually our findings were made available in a variety of publications.* This was a part of my preparation that was over now.

These studies were supplemented by further publication of brain-tumor classifications, a subject to which Percival Bailey and Harvey Cushing were making important contributions in Boston.†

My university and postgraduate training was a thing of the past now, twelve years of it, followed by nine years of learning and exploring with the microscope, while acquiring the skills of neurology and neurosurgery. All this was, in a sense, preparation for the planning of our institute project. But my allegiance was to something beyond all this. That is true of good investigators in general, I suppose. They summarize accurately and publish so that others may make use of their findings. Thus they serve a cause that is above their own research. That was why I had summarized and put our findings on record.

Now, having done that, I was ready to play my part in an ap-

* Some of these papers are cited in note 47.
† My own turning from neuropathological research to human neurophysiology at this time is discussed in very general terms in note 48.

proach to the mystery of the mind and brain. But how was anyone else to know that? How could I call for the help we needed?

I could at least boast to anyone interested that we had been fortunate in the quality of the graduate students who had come to us to be trained, and to do research. It was they who gave to our clinic its true distinction, and yet when I examined my university report of them, it seemed a commonplace.*

Coming to Montreal I had been reassured by the fact that William Cone was coming with me. Now Cone had blossomed into a fully qualified operating neurosurgeon, as well as an able neuropathologist capable of taking over what would be his part of the work. Now I needed more such able men to join the team, many more. But where would we find other men like Cone, and why should they choose to come to Montreal — unless, perhaps, we could build and equip and endow a shining institute for teamwork? I had clues and leads and plans waiting for them.

Thanks to our present way of operating on conscious patients under local anesthesia, and thanks to the use of many techniques for helping patients, many new projects were beckoning and promising new knowledge and greater understanding. Beyond epilepsy and brain circulation, there was the call to map out the cortex and to listen to the patient giving us clues that might lead to unsuspected mechanisms within the brain.

During his early years of life, a scientist may be, indeed he must be to some extent, an end in himself. But as he passes through the initial stage of experience, he becomes more and more an instrument that may be used in a cause. It could be, of course, a cause that would lead to human betterment, and such a cause might well have a legitimate appeal to a philanthropic foundation, like the Rockefeller.

My problem then was to make someone see that the study of

---

* The department report, which describes their work, was made to the university for 1931. It is quoted at length in note 49. The graduate fellows who had followed Dorothy Russell and Ottiwell Jones were Earl Brewer, Maurice Brodie, Jerzy Chorobski, Arthur Elvidge, Joseph Evans, E. Lyle Gage, T. I. Hoen, Norman Petersen, George Stavraky, I. M. Tarlov, Arne Torkildsen, Arthur Young.

the physiology of the human brain will bring, someday, an understanding of the mind of man — if not in my time, sometime.

And so I dreamed, in 1931, daydreams of what the embryo within the Royal Victoria Hospital might become. I had an inner faith that the way would open before us and that I would be able to organize a new research and to focus my attention at last on the nerve circuits of the brain and the blood-vessel control of circulation within the brain.

Thus I would come back to the neurophysiology that I had left in Oxford and could study in man at last: the localization of brain function, the physical basis of the mind, the nature of epilepsy, and cerebral blood vessels. No one shared these daydreams with me, not yet, not even Bill Cone or Colin Russel. No one shared this faith with me, that doors would open, a faith I could not explain.

Outwardly, we went on using up the Ottmann bequest and I was restless and fearful of the future, and felt the urge to do something about it. Then something quite unexpected happened.

On February 5, 1931, I received a letter. It came from one of the trustees of the Rockefeller Foundation itself, Charles P. Howland, the father of my young patient, Henry.

"Gregg is back," he wrote. "We had a word about you. He would rather have you wait until his schedule gives him a breathing spell. He means to go over the ground with you. I suggest you make a note on your calendar to bring it up about May first, if you have not heard from him by then."

This was news. It was Alan Gregg, then, who was to come onstage. After Pearce's unexpected death in 1930, there had been a long interval, and one had heard rumors of a radical change in the policy and purposes of the Rockefeller Foundation. It was at that time the largest and best-organized charitable institution in history. Through it, John D. Rockefeller, said to be the world's richest man, had been setting an example that governments were soon to follow.

I sent a copy of Howland's letter to Charles Martin, dean of medicine at McGill, and added: "Mr. Howland seems to be a friend in court. Evidently, under these circumstances, the thing for us to do is to wait."

I put away the nearly finished draft of my second application to the foundation, and turned to other matters with a wonderful sense of relief. A word had been spoken in our behalf in the corridors of the Great Foundation.

But the "Devil of Discontent" was not silent long. Time was passing and money was running out. What sort of man was Gregg? Was he a politician in philanthropy, trying to please a trustee and the parent of a patient? Trying to keep me, an unwelcome applicant, still? In any case, I could not now complete my application until May. I wondered what else I might do.

Then I hit upon a way of beating the Devil about the bush. It came about so naturally as follows: I had been invited to discuss the tumors of the brain that could not be cured by surgery, at the Academy of Medicine in New York. Helen and I had planned to make this the occasion of a second short winter holiday. We took the day train to New York on Saturday, March 7.

Sometimes the birth of an idea may make the commonplace strangely memorable. We had a long, peaceful day's journey. While having lunch in the dining car, we passed along the very margin of Lake Champlain, and saw, scattered over its snowy expanse, small, black, portable huts. Some of the doors stood open and one could see men fishing through holes they had cut in the ice. But my mind strayed away from the scene.

"I wish I knew what Alan Gregg is thinking," I remarked, betraying what had been lurking at the back of my mind, "and I wish I knew what sort of a man he is."

"Why don't you go to see him?" my wife asked. She reminded me that I had had a fellowship from his Paris office in 1928, and that it was to him I sent that long, long report on the neurological clinics of Europe. "You divided the men you had seen into two groups."

I laughed. For I had divided "the sheep from the goats" — those with open minds on the one hand, and those with closed minds on the other — all of them — the neurologists, neurosurgeons and laboratory men of Europe. It was a most presumptuous report, to say the least. I wondered what Gregg, this man I had never met, thought of it.

Then I sat up. "But of course! How right you are! Why shouldn't I call on him? I'll do it as any grateful former traveling fellow might, without referring to applications or institutes or future financial assistance. What he wants to avoid, I suppose, is the necessity of saying yes or no until he has come to terms with his new job."

We went to the theater that evening and saw *The Barretts of Wimpole Street,* featuring Katherine Cornell as Elizabeth Barrett Browning. That night we slept, content, in a hotel bedroom many floors above the world. Next day was Sunday and we returned to suburban Riverdale of happy memories and visited many good friends there. On Monday I talked to Gregg on the telephone, and on Tuesday I called on him in his office at 61 Broadway. It was on the southern tip of Manhattan Island. Here was another scene I remember as if in the flashback of a moving picture.

We looked down from the twenty-seventh floor. The harbor was spread out below with the Hudson River on the right and the East River on the left and Long Island Sound hazy in the distance. Ships moved swiftly over the water and whistled from time to time.

We had a long and, to me certainly, a fascinating conversation about neurology and the neurologists and neurosurgeons and the investigators of Europe. Gregg seemed to know them all and I soon realized that he did remember the report I had sent to him of my six months in Europe, two and a half years before. He could contribute much from his own experience and observation since then. He was keen to have the added information about Vogt and Foerster that I could give him, as well as about my contacts with Gustav Roussy, the neuropathologist who had become dean and academic leader in the University of Paris.

He was much interested, too, in the neurosurgeons of Great Britain, whom he had helped, and the neurologists of Queen Square, London, whom he hoped to help by a coordinated plan for neurology and neurosurgery.

Gregg loved to tell stories, some of which I could match. So, from time to time, we roared with laughter during what was a noncommittal, if enjoyable, two-hour interview. Recalling Howland's warning, however, I told him little of our present hopes. For Gregg's part, he told me nothing of his plans as director. He gave no hint as to whether he was even familiar with my application for help to build an institute that Pearce had refused in 1929.

I learned a good deal about his general point of view and the professional challenges that he must face. I learned a great deal about the whole field of foundation philanthropy from the philanthropist's point of view.

I began to realize, with some surprise, that the resources of the Rockefeller Foundation were not as unlimited as I had assumed. (I am beginning to draw on information about Gregg and the Rockefeller Foundation that was only partially available to me in 1931.) Nearly thirty years later, at the time of my retirement from active practice, I embarked on a biography of Alan Gregg.* During the study that preceded that writing, I learned to admire the vision and the altruism of John D. Rockefeller, and was intrigued by the approach that he and his distinguished associates, one of whom was his son, made to humanitarian philanthropy.

While Alan Gregg and I talked at this first meeting in New York I realized that we, in Montreal, had no hope for help in our large undertaking unless Gregg himself should prove to be an eloquent advocate of investigation of the brain and the mind as a way to human betterment. And so, I decided to take this as my cue in the remaining minutes of our talk, and in the months that lay ahead. Saying nothing about the Montreal needs, I dilated on all that might be achieved by neurology for the advancement of medicine and indeed for the future of all mankind. This was, after all, the subject on which I could most easily wax eloquent. It is possible, I suppose, that Alan Gregg saw through me, as easily as Mrs. Ottmann evidently had done, and Mr. Howland as well. Gregg may also have surmised our needs, our hidden plans and even my dreams.

I concluded after the interview that one splendid, new neurological institute might possibly be created now with their support, but only one. As far as they were concerned, it would have to serve as an example.

I could plan and create such an institute. I knew exactly what was needed. I was sure the time had come because I was ready for it. If it was not to be the Rockefeller Foundation, then the means would come to me from other sources. This was what my inward self was saying. I told myself that this was a preposterous expec-

---

* See W. Penfield, *The Difficult Art of Giving: The Epic of Alan Gregg* (Boston: Little, Brown, 1967).

tation. But all the same, deep down inside I knew the time must be at hand. This was a matter of faith. Faith is something that you know. Belief is something else. Belief is open to reason. Not so with faith. All this was what one might call inner thinking.

Outwardly I was reasonable and practical. I had an almost irresistible urge to reach out and fight for the chance to do it. I could not bear to wait any longer now that the period of preparation in Montreal was over.

I cannot rationalize my own thinking at this time. But I can strive to report it honestly. It is as if there were two persons within me then, as indeed now. One is the man who concentrates on any task given him, becoming unconscious of all about him. The other is the extrovert who turns to the environment and is humane and practical and reasonable as other men are.

During that interview at 61 Broadway, I had learned that Gregg's attitudes to life, to science and to the practice of medicine were surprisingly like my own. And I knew, after this first meeting, that we would always be friends. He had gone into medicine and into professional philanthropy to do what he could to make the world saner and happier. I had gone into medicine and science for the same reason and purpose. I knew now that he would make his own decisions, and be frank about them, in his own good time.

After Helen and I returned to Montreal, I reviewed the situation in the light of what I had learned: Dr. Alan Gregg of Harvard, after medical service in the First World War, had spent almost three years reporting health conditions in the wildest regions of Brazil for the Rockefeller Foundation. Richard Pearce brought him back to New York in 1922, and two years later sent him to Europe as his own assistant in charge of the Paris office of the foundation and of medical philanthropy in Europe. Now after seven years Gregg had returned to the New York office as Pearce's successor in a foundation whose orientation had altered and whose horizons had enlarged to embrace political science, the arts and agriculture, in addition to public health and medical education. Returning to New York in 1931, Dr. Gregg, as director of medical sciences, was taking over the work of Pearce abroad and Abraham Flexner (who had resigned) in the United States.

The overall challenge that Alan Gregg faced in 1931 was not a simple one.*

What Gregg told me at our interview that was relevant to my immediate concern was that he would make no new decisions and launch no new projects until he should return from his next summer vacation. I decided my best strategy therefore was to continue the dialogue with him on behalf of the brain and the mind as the most promising field of effective philanthropy, even if it did nothing to improve our prospects in Montreal and resulted only in promoting some financial bid from Otfrid Foerster in Germany, perhaps, or Gustav Roussy in Paris, or from one of the many excellent neurologists in the United States, such as Stanley Cobb. So I pursued the subject of neurology, and on my return to Montreal wrote to Gregg:

"If you decide to come up and visit us, we shall be delighted. . . .

"Because of our discussion of the situation in England, I am enclosing a copy of some of the letters that passed between F.M.R. Walshe and myself this winter, thinking you will find them amusing. . . ." †

So I completed my oblique approach to Alan Gregg in the spring of 1931. I had learned a great deal about the Rockefeller Foundation of New York, and even more about the man, Alan Gregg. The unfinished application that I had put away was like an unpublished play in which I had cast Gregg to act in the major role. He had only to speak his lines. But, how blind I was! The curtain had already gone up on a play that involved us both and other actors. I myself could only wait for my cue, to come onstage and to act out my part in a larger plot. And other actors, unknown to me, were waiting in the wings. Who was the playwright?

Robert Oppenheimer was to express the faith of a scientist, in his Reith Lecture a few years later. I quoted him at the opening of this chapter:

"So it is with us as scientists, so it is with us as men. We are at once instrument and end, discoverers and teachers, actors and observers."

---

* See note 50.
† Extracts from this correspondence with Walshe appear in note 51.

15

The Philadelphia Challenge

We put all thought of help from the Rockefeller Foundation out of our minds. It was preposterous to expect that Alan Gregg, on assuming the role of director of medical sciences, would choose Montreal in a world of medical beggars and, from the whole broad field of medicine, select neurology for his first large undertaking. But, in any case, I had made my approach to him, oblique though it was, and he had said he would visit McGill in the autumn. After that, neither he nor the foundation is mentioned again in my correspondence during the spring of 1931.

Prior to all this, in October 1930, a university department, neurology and neurosurgery, had been created at McGill with a seat on the faculty of medicine. Following the proposal of Meakins, the professor of medicine, I was appointed professor of this new department that crossed the boundary between medicine and surgery. I suppose this was inevitable, since it placed me in a strong position to seek financial help. And yet I was embarrassed. Before accepting this appointment, I had a long talk with Colin Russel. I could understand that it might be something of a heartbreak for him, after thirty years as neurologist to the Royal Victoria. In my weekly letter to Mother I described this talk:

"I told him I didn't want it [the professorship] if it bothered him. He suggested that my title be changed to Chairman of the Executive Committee. . . . We had a long talk, and parted firmer friends than ever. . . . We recognized that this will always be a double-headed unit and the chief could, in the future, be a practicing neurosurgeon or a neurologist with equal propriety."

Colin Russel was a wise, blunt, lovable man, married happily to Evelyn Molson, daughter of an old and respected Montreal family. He had joined Bill Cone and me wholeheartedly from the beginning, after his initial hesitation.

It was a happy company that we had at the heart of the new department, considering the fact that there was so little security for the future. In 1931, we decided to push ahead, striking out after every promising prize that seemed to present itself in the field of research. We decided we would spend the fifty thousand dollars that Mrs. Ottmann had left to me, for fellowships and investigation in our growing group with no thought of what would happen when the money ran out. Together, we preferred to sail on an *excellent ship* and, if no help should come, run on the rocks and sink, rather than drift safely toward nowhere on a raft.

Russel's sardonic laugh and unfailing enthusiasm gave tone to our whole company. He was much more than an experienced clinical neurologist and well-trained neuroanatomist. He took delight in argument and teaching. He brought out uncounted pictures and lantern slides of cases for the teaching of students. The instruction of medical undergraduates became a common project.

"Damn it!" he would repeat with a chuckle. "This is just what I meant to do when I left Queen Square. But I had to wait in line before I was allowed at last to take over neurology in the Royal Victoria. Then I had no help. Gad! I'm glad to have you neurosurgeons come along and set up the game. But I warn you fellows not to get it into your heads that you are neurologists and so take over our practice."

Bill Cone, who had been my first pupil, was that no longer. He was a host in himself, for he was fast becoming a brilliant operator and technician. Through his rapid current reading, he had acquired an encyclopedic knowledge. He was a tireless teacher of nurses and interns and research fellows. To patients he was the Good Samaritan who never slept. To his colleagues he was the unselfish friend. He and Russel were delighted companions in the clinic, but Bill found no time for play and for social life, and I was concerned for fear that someday he would break under the strain of unremitting struggle.

A neuropathology conference in the Montreal Neurological Institute, 1952–1953. From left to right, standing: Joseph Stratford, Lamar Roberts, Gilles Bertrand, Gordon Dugger, Donald Baxter, Shaffica Karagula, Fred McConnell, Armando Ortiz. Foreground: Wilder Penfield, William Cone, John Hunter, John Roth. Photograph © Karsh, Ottawa.

But no. Not in the early years. He was exuberant in his work as long as I would handle budgets and administrative details for him, and write out the conclusions of our work together from time to time. He was the technical genius and the warmhearted medical humanist who made the ship that we three had launched something unique.

So it was that by 1931, many had been drawn into the project, and teamwork was making it possible for each of us to do what no man could do alone. We had a common goal and a common loyalty. And yet how different we were in outlook. Russel and I found relief in rugged sport outside the team environment. Cone was happiest when, like a shepherd, he could account for every

sheep and could nurse the young and injured. I made a report to
the dean of the medical school that described the research of all
in the department early in 1931.*

But my own efforts are more easily revealed by what I did and
hoped to do for certain patients. The stories of one or two have
already been woven into the tapestry of this tale. These patients
led to another project, a piece of research partly in Boston and
partly in Montreal.

When Stanley Cobb had opened his neurology clinic in the
Boston City Hospital, he had begun with his associates an investigation of the action of the arteries that nourish the animal brain.
On the other hand, I had begun my study of brain scars in 1921.
This had been followed by surgical removals of selected brain
convolutions as treatment for epilepsy and that had led to a suspicion that epilepsy might be treated also by a *second method:*
some form of operation on patients to alter the blood supply of
the brain. Thus, I too had begun a collateral study of the nerve
control of the brain's arteries.

Any doctor who is deeply involved with his patients is inevitably pushed and pulled through life by their hopes and their
despairs. But the practitioner, and particularly the specializing
practitioner, does control the direction of his evolution when he
meets medical problems for which there is no routine solution.
What he does depends on the questions he has been asking himself
about the condition.

In my own case, for example — following my study of the pathology of the scars of traumatic epilepsy in Germany, I had begun
to ask myself this question: If you can often cure the patient who
has a scar by removing the injured area of brain in which the
arterial circulation differs so much from that of the normal brain-
circulation, could you not help others who have seizures (not
caused by a scar) by altering the circulation of the whole brain?

When I operated on William Ottmann and, seeing no way of
stopping his seizures, I produced an attack with the brain exposed,
the strange constriction that took place in an artery, before our
eyes, forced the consultants and me to face the question: Can we
perhaps prevent his seizures now by altering the control of blood

* See note 52.

flow through this part of his brain that we have proven is causing his fits? When I tied off the artery, I took a chance of paralysis. He did well, but I did not publish his case. By publishing it here in this book, I am not necessarily recommending that others should take the same chance by repeating the same operation. I am, however, pointing out that there is much work still to be done in this field of investigation, work I could not find time to follow through to its logical conclusions.

Stanley Cobb, whom I called to help me in the case of Ottmann, had opened his own neurological clinic in the Boston City Hospital. He had asked himself similar questions in regard to epilepsy and launched a study of brain circulation in animals. I did the same with the help of our research fellows, studying the nature of the nerve control of arteries in the monkey brain, as soon as Mrs. Ottmann's gifts made it possible for us to buy monkeys.

Cobb as professor of neuropathology at Harvard had obtained a laboratory grant from the Rockefeller Foundation to study epilepsy and had been able to gather about him a group of able young men who were helping him in various ways to make the study. Among them were men who were to distinguish themselves in the clinical field during the years to come — William Lennox, Houston Merritt, Tracy Putnam, Frederick Gibbs *et al.**

I suppose it was while serving as a trustee of the Rockefeller Foundation that Mr. Charles P. Howland learned of Cobb's interest in epilepsy. He and Mrs. Howland had been desperately searching for someone to solve the unsolved problem presented by their son Henry. They took him to Cobb. Cobb brought him to Montreal and I studied him, but found no obvious abnormality in his brain. Cobb and I discussed the boy's problem. No standard treatment seemed to offer hope.

Finally, the Howland parents, who understood the situation completely, agreed when we proposed to do to Henry what, I had discovered, did no harm, at all events, to monkeys, and what we thought might benefit Henry. I removed all the vascular nerves on the arteries that entered his skull. This would, we argued, do to him, more completely, what we had done to Ottmann, and do it more safely. At that time, in 1931, he, too, was having no at-

---

* See note 53.

tacks. Was this only a temporary cure? Or did we really have an exciting clue that was leading us to more effective therapy?

In any case, this was how it came about that Mr. Howland, meeting Gregg, as he returned from Paris to New York to become director of medical sciences, took it upon himself to talk to the new director about Montreal. This caused him to write to me advising me to leave Gregg in peace for the time being. It explains why I put away my second application, which would have asked for help to build an institute.

A critical observer might have smiled and called it foolhardy to see two heads of clinics, Cobb and Penfield, who had so much to gain from the Rockefeller Foundation, choose the son of a trustee for a first, frankly experimental operation. But Henry himself made his own appeal. Like Bill Ottmann, he was an intriguing youngster in his own right, albeit interested in writing poetry rather than playing golf.

In the meantime Cobb and I had decided to combine our separate research studies of the circulation of the brain. In Montreal, one of our research fellows, Lyle Gage, a midwestern American, had been busy producing laboratory epilepsy in macaque monkeys. We were about to carry out on them what we called the Howland operation to see if it would cure them.

Jerzy Chorobski, a graduate worker from Poland, and I had already done the Howland operation on a preliminary series of monkeys a year previously, removing the tiny nerves that run on all the arteries that enter the skull. We wanted now to discover how removal of those artery nerves had altered the reactions of the monkey brain. For that purpose, we needed the methods available only in Cobb's laboratory.

A brilliant research fellow of his, Dr. Harry Forbes, had devised a tiny window that could be set into a monkey's skull quite painlessly. The window made it possible to study the arteries on the surface of the brain. The microscope, set in place, magnified them so that they looked like enormous hoses pulsating with each heartbeat.

So we took ourselves to Boston to the laboratory of Stanley Cobb — Gage, Chorobski, six monkeys and I. We must have seemed a motley crew, entering the Boston City Hospital! One of the monkeys eventually escaped and was lost in the ventilating system of that vast hospital for two days. Rumor had it at one time that he had been found in bed under treatment as an unusual Boston patient.

The results of a week of experimentation were illuminating as far as anatomy and physiology were concerned, and we returned to Montreal, hopeful of applying the newfound knowledge to the cure of epilepsy. But, as I have pointed out, the epilepsy mystery is as old as the history of man, and the story of our varied attempts to cure it is too long a tale to tell here.*

During the following few years I carried out a series of operations upon the arteries to the brain in human cases of so-called idiopathic epilepsy, and finally abandoned the procedure, not as a failure but as of inconclusive benefit. In the case of Henry, the operation did really seem to help him greatly. It could not be called a cure.

Through the years that followed this combined Montreal-Boston interurban research, our friendship was to lead Cobb and me to a continuing correspondence, and to many vacation adventures together, which Helen and I were to enjoy with him and his delightful wife, Elizabeth Almy Cobb. Eventually, in 1968, it fell to me to pay tribute to the man in a memorial address in the Harvard chapel, "Hail and Farewell to Stanley Cobb." It was published in the *Archives of Neurology* of that year.

Early in 1931 Helen and I received sudden notice that the house in which we lived in Côte Saint Antoine Road was no longer for rent. The owner must sell. We received a telegram to this effect from the agent while we were attending a medical meeting in Quebec. I remember that we discussed the matter in our bedroom in the Château Frontenac. With our future so insecure, we hesitated to buy, even if we had the money. It would be like casting out another anchor to hold us in Montreal.

Helen asked me then if I had received any serious suggestions of a return to an American city. I said no, and then qualified that statement. Since I had been in Montreal, there had been no written suggestion of a place for me elsewhere. There had been talk, and there had been idle rumors. And a year earlier, I called to

* See note 54.

mind, in the spring of 1930, a very distinguished professor of pharmacology from the University of Pennsylvania, Dr. A. Newton Richards, did seem to be considering the possibility of an invitation to move to Philadelphia. He was in Montreal then to attend a medical congress.

We met quite by chance. I was walking across the campus of McGill University to get to Dr. Archibald's office in the Maxwelton Apartments, where I was still seeing my patients. As I reached Sherbrooke Street, Richards hailed me. I knew him well by reputation and I had visited him in his Philadelphia laboratory, before we left New York, to ask him some questions about the work that he and his assistant, Francis Schmitt, were carrying out on blood pressure. That work was of importance to certain of my New York patients since I was beginning, then, to carry out operations for the reduction of high blood pressure.

Professor Richards was a unique character, always blunt, unexpected, and definitely awe-inspiring to a younger man.

"Penfield," he called.

We shook hands. Then he looked at me for an embarrassing moment.

"Penfield," he said, "how old are you?"

"Thirty-nine," I replied.

"God!" he exclaimed. "How wonderful!"

It was a startling greeting to say the least. I suppose that is why I remember it so distinctly. Then he talked at some length about Charles Frazier, the neurosurgeon and head of the Department of Surgery at Pennsylvania, who was about to retire. He dilated, too, on the career of William G. Spiller, the much-respected neuropathologist and professor of neurology, who was also on the eve of his retirement. But, if Richards was thinking that I might be of some use to them in Philadelphia, I presumed he must have discarded the idea, for I heard nothing more from him.

Consequently, on our return from Quebec to Montreal, Helen looked for a possible house to rent. For a few days she had no success. Then she received a spontaneous telephone call from a friend of ours whose husband, the manager of the Royal Trust Company, had died very recently. It was Mrs. H. B. MacKenzie.

"I want you and Dr. Penfield to have our house," she said. "It would be exactly right for you and your family." We went to see her house. She was charming. All that she had said was true, and more. We fell in love with the house.

But she wanted to sell. We wanted to rent. Our answer was no. But we would think it over. That evening at Côte Saint Antoine Road, we talked about the MacKenzie house and told the children about it. It was not far away, at 4302 Montrose Avenue. So, after dinner we walked along Montrose past the house, taking Wilder and Ruth Mary with us. It was a brick colonial-style house with a pleasant garden on a lower level. The garden fell away toward the Saint Lawrence River. One could see Nuns' Island and the blue expanse of the Saint Lawrence and mountains rising on the horizon in the Eastern Townships in the light of the setting sun.

When we got home I told Helen that the house was everything for which I had always hoped. She agreed, and the children, standing round-eyed with excitement, nodded eagerly. "Let's get it then," I said, "if she will drop the price. We may have to leave Montreal, it is true. But we can't see into the future. Why worry about it? No one seems to want us anywhere else."

We scraped together all the money that was left from my *Sussex* torpedoing indemnity after we'd bought our farm and added to that a sizable mortgage. Kind woman that Mrs. MacKenzie was, she did lower the price and we bought the house and the garden and moved to 4302 Montrose Avenue on April 15, 1931.

Then came Professor Richards. A week or so before our move into the new home, I had received a letter from him. He would like to see me in Montreal. He did not say why, and despite my suspicions, I knew that it was too late to change my mind about buying the house. But I asked him to come the day after our move.

Dr. Richards arrived and we sat in my diminutive new consulting room in the Royal Victoria Hospital. "There are changes in the wind at the University of Pennsylvania," he said, plunging into the middle of matters. "We have a new president, Gates, who is planning for a period of reorganization. In the medical school a new hospital is to be built. It will house two reorganized departments, orthopedics and neurology."

Then his quiet words, which I am quoting now from my weekly letter, made a wave of something like fright sweep over me, as if I had stumbled to the brink of an unexpected chasm. "The Department of Neurology," he said, "will include neurosurgery. That department will have a large endowment to provide a permanent budget for scientific work. We want you to accept the professorship of the new department. You will be given a free hand to organize it as you think best."

He paused. When I did not speak, he added, "Formal invitations from the university and the hospital will be coming to you in due course." And he continued: "The fact that Charles Frazier the neurosurgeon is retiring now from the professorship of surgery and the fact that William Spiller is to retire from the chair of neurology in a little over a year makes it possible to amalgamate neurosurgery and neurology. There are strong men about Spiller and the same is true of Frazier — Isador Ravdin will succeed him as head of the Department of Surgery. He is a close friend of yours, I know, and so is Francis Grant, the neurosurgeon. They want you to come, and so does Cuthbert Bazett, the head of physiology. I'm told you two were friends at Oxford and that he asked you to come along with him as his assistant when he came to Philadelphia ten years ago.

"We need someone now who can draw neurology and neurosurgery together and can start some basic research in the field. We hope you will say yes."

I had caught my breath at last. "Your plan is almost exactly the plan that I have outlined in an application that I had thought to send to the Rockefeller Foundation. For a moment I wondered if you had seen it. It has never been sent. It lies hidden in my desk at home."

Richards laughed. "No," he said. "I did not see it, but I might have guessed what would be in it after you and I talked a year ago. I have thought about this matter a good deal since then. It is logical to combine neurology and neurosurgery but the adjustments will not be easy."

I broke in on him, having gathered my thoughts at last. I realized, I said, what a wonderful honor Dr. Richards did me. Weir Mitchell was the first outstanding neurologist in American medical history and Spiller, following him, had taken the lead in clinical and pathological neurology. I'd always admired him from a distance. He and Frazier had given us the best example of co-operation and friendship and leadership, even without joining the two departments. Their work together on the treatment of intractable pain was a classic in the field.

"But, quite frankly," I said, "we like living in Montreal. We like the schools and the environment for the bringing up of children. On the other hand, unless I am given a permanent university and hospital budget here and an adequate place for our group to carry out the work, I must be ready to move away. Since I talked with you on your chance visit here last year, McGill University has combined neurology and neurosurgery in one department and the adjustments have been made."

Then I added, "Please let us keep your proposal a secret until we can make a decision. Alan Gregg has promised to visit us in September. There is very little chance, I know, that he will be interested enough to recommend support from the Rockefeller Foundation for neurology in Montreal. If he does say no then almost certainly I shall accept your invitation, although Dean Martin talks as if he could raise the funds for an institute from wealthy Canadians.

"If it should prove to be possible to build a neurological institute in Montreal," I continued, "then I shall face a decision that is difficult indeed. But whether I go or whether I stay, I hope my associate William Cone will continue with me. Let us keep this a secret from everyone, except Bill Cone and his wife Avis. Working with him makes me twice as effective, and I hope he would say the same in a reverse sense. Only with him, could I hope to continue Spiller's contribution to neuropathology."

After Newton Richards left, I did what I had to do at the hospital in a daze and returned home early to talk to Helen. It was a day to remember. The horizon had changed. The sky, it seemed, was a deeper blue and ships of the mind were sailing swiftly out to sea from another harbor. The lurking fear of failure that I suppose had always been with me was gone now. The Devil of Discontent had been silenced. I was satisfied to await developments.

The months that had followed Mr. Howland's letter, advising me not to make a formal approach to the Rockefeller Foundation, had turned into a time of waiting for developments. "Decisions," I wrote in a later letter to my mother, "have a way of making themselves if one can give time to them." The Cones and the Penfields guarded the Philadelphia proposal as a deep secret, not wanting to disturb the life and lower the morale of those in our Montreal team.

In 1884, five years before I was born, William Osler received an invitation to go to Philadelphia when he was professor of the Institutes of Medicine at McGill University. When I was a Rhodes scholar, we asked Osler to speak to our "American Club." He came to us then on February 12, 1916, and told us the story of his life, sitting on the table informally. Here is a part of it:

"I was resting in a German town," Sir William said, "when I received a cable from friends in Philadelphia, stating that if I would accept a professorship there I should communicate with Dr. S. Weir Mitchell, who was in Europe and who had been empowered to arrange the details. I sat up late into the night balancing the pros and cons of Montreal and Philadelphia. In the former I had many friends, I loved the work and the opportunity was great. In the latter the field appeared very attractive, but it meant leaving many dear friends. I finally gave it up as unsolvable and decided to leave it to chance. I flipped a four-mark silver piece into the air. 'Heads I go to Philadelphia; tails I remain in Montreal.' It fell 'heads.' I went to the telegraph office and wrote the telegram to Dr. Mitchell offering to go to Philadelphia. I reached in my pockets to pay for the wire. They were empty. My only change had been the four-mark piece, which I had left as it had fallen on my table. It seemed like an act of providence directing me to remain in Montreal. I half decided to follow the cue. Finally I concluded that inasmuch as I had placed the decision to chance I ought to abide by the turn of the coin, and returned to my hotel for it and sent the telegram." *

Perhaps, if my situation in Montreal had been the same as that of Osler, I might have followed in his footsteps, at least as far as quick decision in regard to the Philadelphia challenge was concerned. But although Osler had been on the faculty of McGill ten years when his invitation came, he was only thirty-four years old, still unmarried and relatively unattached. He too was a clinician

---

* The text of this Oxford address is also reported in Harvey Cushing's biography, *The Life of Sir William Osler* (Oxford: Clarendon Press, 1925), vol. I, p. 220.

and a pathologist, but he had yet to write his magnum opus: the textbook of medicine. I had summarized my basic work before coming to Montreal.

My situation was different too in other ways. I had a wife and children, a farm and a house and an undivorceable colleague, William Cone. I had too, as Osler certainly had, a growing company of friends and colleagues to be considered. Archibald and Meakins had, each one of them, changed the pattern of his professional evolution to fit and to promote my project.

I visited Philadelphia accompanied by Bill Cone. We saw the plans. They seemed to have the funds that were necessary without further begging. There was what seemed to us to be an embarrassment of riches as far as resources and staff and tradition and culture were concerned.

Later I went there with Helen, and after we had looked at the city and its suburbs, she returned to Montreal and I stayed on to talk with various distinguished members of the faculty of medicine of the University of Pennsylvania, such as Richards and Spiller, and also my friends Detlev Bronk, Cuthbert Bazett, Isador Ravdin, Francis Grant and others. Perhaps the letter that I wrote from the Hotel Sylvania in Philadelphia to my wife on June 11, 1931, sums up my immediate reaction to the invitation.

"Don't you hope we aren't forced to leave Montreal," the letter read, "our home and the farm there, and come here? As I write, it's hot. There is noise, and the sound of trip-hammers.

"Let's stop going at such a frightful speed. I care nothing for fame. I only want to fulfill — what is it? — to find the secrets that God meant me to find. I can do it better perhaps in lower gear. Let's gear down. I want to seize and understand the children too before they slip through my fingers with the sands of time. I want to be near you as the years roll around."

These personal and family considerations might seem to be of little importance at a time like this. But they weigh themselves into the balance, and who can say how great the pull of gravity may be upon them in the pan?

We continued our life routine without decision. I was host, that spring, to the Halsted Club, later to be called Halsted Society. This brought fifteen alert young surgeons to Montreal. In the Halsted Club program I prepared for them was a symposium by

Dr. Archibald and his assistant, Norman Bethune, on the surgical treatment of tuberculosis of the lung. It was new then and exciting.*

The First International Neurological Congress took place in Berne, Switzerland, early in the following September. This was a welcome opportunity for me to discover what was happening in neurology and neurosurgery and allied science around the world. It was a chance, also, to look back at Philadelphia, and at Montreal, through the unprejudiced eyes of others, and to talk to former friends and teachers. If I was to go to Philadelphia it was clear I should have to use Francis Grant, as well as Cone, on my neurosurgical staff. Grant was going to the congress, and so we arranged to cross the ocean together, second class, on the S.S. *Bremen,* which made the journey in the record time of four days.†

The thought of taking the chair of William Spiller sobered me. I would be at home in his laboratory, but I could not compete with the best neurologists in the clinical practice of neurology. I did not want to, and it would be absurd as well as impolitic to try. And yet someone must preside over unification as well as expansion in our field of medicine. I must plan the work for basic scientists and I must speak their language. Grant was prepared to carry on neurosurgery for Frazier but he was not prepared for this. Was I?

The team captain's problem is always the same, wherever and whoever he is: to choose a team and to work with each individual toward a differing, well-chosen objective. He must be master of one skill and a "Jack" of all the others.

To use again the metaphor of the sunrise, the problem is to have a clue in each area of darkness, as to where dawn will break and the gold appear. Newton Richards would understand, as Edward Archibald had understood. Each of them had seen "dawn break" in his own area of exploration.

From Berne on September 1, 1931, I wrote: "Here I am at the First International Neurological Congress — six hundred representatives from forty-one countries. Many have spoken of my

* See note 55.
† See note 56.

'Philadelphia offer.' I don't know how the leak of information occurred. Not through me.

"Schüller [professor of neurology in Vienna and an expert in the X-ray diagnosis of brain conditions] rushed up to me with this excited exclamation: 'When you go to Philadelphia, I will go with you. As assistant, of course. You must not think of anything else.' "

Schüller was a likable Austrian and one of the surprisingly few Viennese professors whom I had placed in the first category of a teacher "with an open mind" when I had visited European clinics.

"There was a bookstall," the letter continued, "in which books were advertised for sale, at congress headquarters. There, I was startled to see my own name as editor of *Cytology and Cellular Pathology of the Nervous System*. The publishers had sent a special set in three volumes and I saw it for the first time. I picked up a volume to examine it. But when the bookseller praised it, I flushed and did not confess to him that I had ever heard of it before. It seemed so strange to see this child of mine, mature and able to speak for itself!

"Most of the people who wanted to talk to me were interested in microscopical work. I suppose that shows that my clinical work is not important yet. The paper that I read before the congress on encapsulated tumors of the brain was not important."

Cushing and Sherrington were given honorary degrees by the University of Berne, during that congress. In retrospect one can only wonder that Ivan Pavlov, who was also present, was not given a similar accolade. Like Sherrington, Pavlov was an animal neurophysiologist and a Nobel Prize laureate for medicine and physiology.

Harvey Cushing, as a neurosurgeon, was to be the featured speaker at the great congress banquet. But before that, on the second night of the meetings, he gave his own private dinner for pupils who had worked with him at the Peter Bent Brigham Hospital in Boston, adding to the guest list certain notables. In the afternoon before his dinner, as I passed through the hotel lobby, I caught a glimpse of him in the dining room. He was moving back and forth about a very long table, all set for the dinner, putting the name cards of his guests at their places. When he caught sight of me, he called me to him.

"Wilder," he said, "I want you to sit at the end of the table opposite me. You are my senior pupil here in Berne. I have put Sherrington on your left and Foerster, with Geoffrey Jefferson of Manchester, on your right."

"Cushing," my letter continued, "is the most unexpected man I know. He either snubs me, or envelops me, but what a dynamic force he is! His report to the congress was the most outstanding paper of all, describing his results with two thousand verified brain tumors. He closed with the statement that this was *his last complete report*. He retires from neurosurgery this year, at the age of sixty-two." *

I remember his dinner as an impressive event. John Fulton, always the quick-minded member of any company, proposed a toast to Cushing that, quite properly, expressed the gratitude of the guests. When he did so I realized that this was what might have been expected of me, at the other end of the table where he had placed me. But I am slow at such things unless I have done my homework in advance, which in this case I had not.

I was so delighted to talk again to Sir Charles Sherrington. In fact, I was almost oblivious of all else. Foerster, on the other side, was involved in discussions with Jefferson. They were my friends and comrades. Sherrington was my master. I realized it now. He was seventy-four years old at this time and was not to retire from the chair of physiology at Oxford for another five years. His mind was as lively as ever and his chuckle just as intriguing.

Sherrington had pointed the way toward the unexplored place of understanding when I entered medicine. I had done many things since then. I had learned the methods of his friend Ramón y Cajal and applied them to human anatomy and pathology. Now I was ready to begin a new approach in which I hoped to become a physiologist studying the brain of man. Could I, at forty, gather together a group that would make a worthwhile physiological approach to the working of the brain while carrying on routine neurosurgery for the relief of pain and the removal of tumors and treating focal epilepsy by radical excision? Could I make adequate use of the new facilities that would be available to me in Philadelphia? (Or was there a chance of its being Mon-

* See note 57.

treal?) Would I, when the time came, have the wit to ask important questions of the human brain? Would I understand the answers, as the man sitting at my left had done in the experimental laboratory?

The next evening, Theodore Weisenberg asked me to dine with him alone. He was the editor of the *Archives,* the leading American journal of neurology. He was, after William Spiller, to quote from my letter again, "the leading neurologist in Philadelphia." (Osler had called it the Hippocratic City, *Civitas Hippocratica.*) "Weisenburg," the letter continued, "outlined the personalities of the most important men, not forgetting himself. It is quite a help to me. What a job Philadelphia would be! But what a field!"

The unexpected coming of Ivan Pavlov from the U.S.S.R. created a stir at this first international congress of neurology. It was to be my only personal contact with this great physiologist.

Pavlov was eighty-two, but it was rumored that he was now making an absolutely new approach from physiology to the field of psychiatry. He did just that, showing us that progress toward the understanding of man and his behavior can sometimes be made by elucidation of mechanisms in the animal brain that are related to the mind.*

So the First International Neurological Congress came to an end. While there I had seen neurology through many eyes. But I had the urge to be aloof and alone for a little time, to think things out. And I wanted wise counsel. I knew I could get this from the Queen Square teachers of neurology who were practicing in London, and particularly from Gordon Holmes. A proud tribe of consultants, they were. I had been a hardworking pupil in that school and I was sure of their sympathy and understanding. So I arranged to spend ten days in London after the close of the congress. I would catch the *Bremen* back to New York when it made its call at Southampton.

In London I stayed with Dr. and Mrs. Gordon Holmes, and they made me free to come and go as if I were a returning son. I had danced with Mrs. Holmes at the congress ball and I took her to the theater in London — pastimes for which I had a great liking, but for which Holmes found no time in his busy life.

* See note 58 on Pavlov's lecture on neurosis.

Each day I read current neurological literature quietly in the library of the Royal Society of Medicine, and accompanied a different neurologist as he went about his hospital rounds: Holmes, Francis Walshe, George Riddoch, Charles Symonds, Russell Brain. Most evenings I dined and talked with one or another of them.

The weekly letter records my reactions, for example:

"Charles Symonds is one of the most popular of the younger consultants. He is neurologist in chief at Guy's Hospital and had me to dinner. We talked long about mutually interesting things in neurology. Many of these English physicians have an unconscious reserve and dignity. They are conservative and put the care of the patient and the maintenance of a Harley Street exterior before everything else. And yet, they are anxious for new ideas, and a little wistful about the opportunities for institutional and laboratory study that we have managed to establish. They do good work but they are too much insulated from the world."

It became more and more apparent as we talked together that an institute and a university department of neurology could give such men what they wanted most — facilities for diagnosis, equipment for treatment and a university establishment for research. They felt the need for teamwork in which hospital, university, and medical practice would play balanced roles. It was clear that this would serve the needs of the patient and the purposes of science.

It began to be clear to me that this could be established in Montreal if we could carry on as we were going. It would be more difficult to do it in Philadelphia. It would be most difficult to achieve it in London unless there were changes in the patterns of medical practice there.

I realized something else. I had come to feel more at home in London with English neurologists and in Montreal with the doctors and nurses there than I could ever feel now in Philadelphia, or so I thought. I liked the English way of life. I knew now I could be naturalized and take on all the loyalties of a Canadian quite happily.

I knew also that the institute plan as we had worked it out in Montreal was good enough. But, since only the University of Pennsylvania was offering to make such an establishment possible, I would have to accept that challenge and go to Philadelphia. We must plan to make the move. But I would wait before making a final statement to see what Alan Gregg would say.

On leaving London, I wrote in the weekly letter, "I am crossing with John Fulton, a remarkable fellow. His mind is so much quicker and more retentive than mine that he makes me a little despondent. I had thought of asking him if he would give up physiology at Yale and come into neurology at Pennsylvania. But I am not sure Arnold Carmichael [neurologist and laboratory investigator at Queen Square], whom I saw in London, wouldn't be better. John, of course, would probably not be willing in any case."

On September 22, 1931, the *Bremen* docked in New York and I sent off a letter as a cautious reminder to Alan Gregg. "There is something of a movement on foot at McGill," I wrote, "to expand the work in neurology. I hope you will be able to come up and tell us what you think of the situation and whether the foundation is likely to care to help with it."

Gregg had himself only just arrived back in the foundation offices after his summer holiday on that same date, the twenty-second.

In Montreal, I found a letter waiting for me from Professor Richards to say that official invitations to come to Philadelphia with "the fullest freedom for the development of an institute and the material resources with which to do it" were on the way. Closing with a typical flash of humor, he expressed the lively hope that "events in Montreal will not move too rapidly."

There had been a good deal of action at McGill as well as in the University of Pennsylvania during the weeks I had spent abroad. But there was no time to consider these things now. My mother, in California, was critically ill. A few hours after my arrival in Montreal, a telegram was delivered to me from my brother, Herbert, saying Mother might live two months or three days. I left for California by the first train. There was much to think over during the three-day journey, wondering whether she would be alive on my arrival. It was about two months since my sister, Ruth, had died from the pitiless regrowth of the tumor that I had tried so desperately to remove, and Dr. Cushing after me.

Mother had stood by Ruth to the end. Then she had seemed to

collapse suddenly. When it was apparent that she was losing ground because of a kidney ailment, she had asked to be taken to the shore to be near the sea where she could hear the sound of the surf.

So, I found her in a cottage at Hermosa Beach. She was in bed in the home of a kindly woman, who gave her practical nursing care. Rather suddenly, I was told, she had grown worse, perhaps due to a heart attack. For several days, Death knocked at the door, but Mother, at seventy-three, was not ready to go. She had work she wanted to do. And so it seemed that Death, the ancient friend of the aged, stopped his knocking and passed her by. He was to postpone his call for four more years.

Mother was already getting better when I arrived. She knew me and smiled as I entered the room. There was little I could do for her at first except to get her a hospital-type bed and to devise ways of elevating her swollen legs. But soon she showed improvement that seemed miraculous. Remembering everything she had read in my letters in the years past, she asked searching questions. Indeed, she seemed almost her old self again.

"After Ruth was taken from us," she said, "I passed through 'the valley of the shadow.' But now, I seem to see the past and present clearly. Leaving Spokane with you three children, I had many heartaches that you may never have understood. But I did not leave it all behind. Something of your father as he was before that year in the wilderness lives on in you."

Finally, one morning when I came to the house beside the sea, I found that Mother's bed had been rolled out onto the sunny porch where we could hear the slow recurring sound of the surf and smell a salty something in the wind. She pointed to letters lying on the counterpane and I saw they were the recent handwritten letters I had sent her from Montreal and Berne and from London and from the returning ship.

"Mrs. Mills kept these," she said, "while I was in dreamland and I have read or reread them all this morning. Tell me now all that you and Helen are deciding and what Dr. Cone and Dr. Archibald are thinking."

So I described the situation simply. Since my return from abroad I had received the full details of the Philadelphia proposal. To my astonishment, I discovered that Richards himself had made an appointment with Alan Gregg to ask for added help from the Rockefeller Foundation.

"What is still more surprising," I continued, "is that McGill University, on its own, has done the same thing. Dean Martin and the principal, Sir Arthur Currie, have made an application by telephone. They called Max Mason, the president of the foundation, directly while I was still abroad."

"What is going to happen?" Mother asked.

"I don't know. Gregg sent word that he is coming to Montreal next week on October 10. I must leave you, alas, before that time, so I can meet his train."

She smiled and nodded. "Your years of preparation are over," she said, "and you can determine your future. Don't try to make a decision too soon. The way will be clear and the decision will make itself. So wait, son. I always knew there was important work in the world for you to do and now, at last, you are ready to do it."

She looked off into the distance and seemed to be listening to the roll and pound of the surf. We were never very demonstrative, she and I. We understood each other. She laid her hand on mine now and smiled again.

"It has been such a joy to me to go along with you and your wonderful wife, Helen, thanks to your Sunday letters — even though I have been far away so much of the time. Take me with you still until I do come to the end of the road.

"But now I'm going to be well again." Her eyes lit up with the old enthusiasm. "I'm going back to the *Story of Sarai*." *

Mother did regain her health and worked again on this manuscript with great enthusiasm. But, when I saw her four years later on a visit to California, she was again confined to bed. At the age of seventy-seven, she was still working on the *Story of Sarai,* and a completed manuscript lay on her bedside table. Not long after this, on May 5, 1935, news came to us in far-off Quebec that my mother had died. So, she came to the end of the road, and there were no more Sunday letters.

It was her interest in the life of Sarai and her hope that I would finish her project for her that led me, eventually, to try my own hand at historical fiction.

* See note 59.

16

1931: Incredible Interview

On October 10, 1931, I arrived early at Westmount Station to meet Alan Gregg, who was on the overnight train from New York, as Archibald had met me in January of 1928 when I came to visit on that earlier day of decision. No one could know what Gregg had in mind. He was stopping off in Montreal on his way to Chicago. It could well be that he meant to explain to us why the Rockefeller Foundation was not prepared to give money to neurology.

I reviewed our contacts with the foundation as I walked up and down the arrival platform: I had applied to his predecessor at the Rockefeller Foundation, Richard Pearce, asking for help to build an institute for neurological investigation in Montreal in January 1929. That was three months after our arrival in Montreal and I received, as might have been expected, a refusal. But a kindly one. "Keep on sawing wood," Pearce had said.

When Gregg came from Paris to New York in January 1931 as successor to Pearce, I had begun the preparation of a much larger and more elaborate application. But then on February 5, 1931, following the first meeting of the Rockefeller Board of Trustees, Mr. Howland had written that he and Gregg had talked about me and he (Howland) advised me to hold off, not to send my application. But how did Howland know I was writing one?

In any case, I had put the application away. Instead, in the following March, I called on Gregg at his office in New York. I discovered then that he was familiar with the report I had made to his Paris office in 1928 while still in Germany. That was on the subject of teachers and teaching in the broad field of neurology in Europe. During my call on him in New York, no reference was made to the hopeful application hidden away in my desk. Then in April, Richards came unexpectedly onto my little stage, inviting us to come to Philadelphia with no mention of the Rockefeller Foundation.

Following that, I had left Montreal to go to the International Neurological Congress. When I returned I learned that the two universities, Pennsylvania and McGill, were making applications very much like the one I had never sent.

I had a feeling that I knew what was going to happen, and yet I told myself it couldn't happen. I was a little like a woman considering marriage, who feels sure that someone is going to say what she has been hoping to hear. She has made her own indirect approaches. Now she can only wait and wonder.

The train came roaring in and stopped. No one appeared for what seemed a very long time. Then I saw Alan Gregg swinging down from one of the Pullman cars. The porter handed him his bag, and Gregg came striding along the platform — a tall, gangling, broad-shouldered man with sandy hair, beetling eyebrows, and ruddy face. He looked at me smiling for a moment and I discovered how blue his eyes were.

I drove him home to breakfast. Helen welcomed him, followed by all four children. They joined us at the breakfast table and Fräulein Bergmann with them. That was our invariable rule for breakfast, since I might not see them all day otherwise. There was much laughter and talk, partly in English, partly in German, which Gregg seemed to speak easily.

After breakfast Gregg and I went to my study. Suddenly my legs felt weak and I sat down abruptly. I was prepared for an explanation of just why the foundation could not help us. It was for this, I thought, he must have come. He would do it in a nice way. He opened his briefcase, which he had placed on my big desk. It was the desk I had bought with Mrs. Ottmann's unexpected fee for visiting her in New York. He drew out a folder full of papers and slapped the lot down on the coffee table.

"This," Gregg said, turning to me, "is exactly the sort of thing for which we are always searching at the Rockefeller Foundation. I have the application you made to Pearce. I think I understand what you want to do. You have a plan that gives real promise in a field that is calling desperately for exploration. We can do no more than provide you with the optimum environment. You will have to direct the work. We want to see it go on and on, following the leads that come to you. Don't ever thank us. We thank you. You will be helping us when you do your job." *

Gregg's face had flushed as he made this astonishing statement. But he had spoken slowly and with great precision. Then he sat down. I remember that I made some sort of incredulous exclamation, and was tongue-tied. I realized he was referring to that first application, the one I had made to Pearce. But that was two and a half years ago. It never was detailed. I tried to remember what was in it. Everything had grown larger in my mind since then — the plan, the opportunities, the estimates, the building idea. I didn't know what to say. But this blunt, perceptive, kindly man in the chair over there was watching me and waiting.

"We have united neurology and neurosurgery here," I said cautiously, "into one academic and hospital department now."

"Yes, I know," he replied.

I wondered who had told him. Was his information accurate? Anyway, he was waiting for me to go on. So I blurted out a sort of spontaneous paraphrase of my credo, pointing out that this was the most complicated and most promising unexplored body of knowledge in the whole field of medicine; that there were approaches to mental disease and to the physiological mechanisms of the mind that we might make when we had the setup and equipment and the team; that I believed that psychiatry should be separate from neurology and neurosurgery in hospital practice for some years to come, but that all three should be joined together somehow in thought and plan, in the laboratory for scientific study, and in teaching — recalling my conversation with Adolf Meyer at Johns Hopkins ten years back.

Only a separate neurological institute to house patients and

* I described this interview when I wrote the biography of Alan Gregg, *The Difficult Art of Giving: The Epic of Alan Gregg* (Boston: Little, Brown, 1967). I spoke then in the third person, calling myself A.P., for Associate Professor. It had not crossed my mind at that time that I would one day write the story more from my own point of view.

laboratories side by side would serve the purpose, I continued. But for the good of the patients and to make sure that each specialist preserves a broad perspective and continues to be a member of one overall general medical team, the institute must be built very close to a general teaching hospital. Thus each man can keep close contact with all departments of medicine. There must be an active exchange of service and consultation between them.

Gregg got up and stood with his back to the glowing fireplace. "The plan is sound," he said, "to work quietly at problems of the human brain, bringing together different kinds of scientists. It will draw to one focus men with fine minds and widely differing gifts for years to come. There will be urgent need for such work as long as there are universities."

He talked on and I wondered. After all, who was making this proposal? He could do it as well as I. He seemed ready to take it out of my hands. I really had not made an application. McGill University had and Pennsylvania had. But neither one knew the details of my hopes and plans. Neither did Gregg, for that matter, unless — yes, of course. He may have guessed my hopes and plans during our talk in his office the previous March. I remembered his telling me how disappointed he was when the Rockefeller scheme to give millions to the University of Paris fell through because there was no agreement on how to spend it. He had been disappointed not to be able to help neurology and neurosurgery at Queen Square. I realized suddenly that what he was doing now was what he had wanted to do. He realized how great were the research opportunities in neurology, and how much an advance here would achieve for medicine and for mankind. I realized suddenly that I could *help him*. How strange! And what an incredible interview this was. They wanted me to do — they, meaning Pennsylvania and McGill and this man who seemed to stand at the very center of financial power — wanted me to do just what I had been hoping to do.

"A neurological institute," I interjected, "should also serve as a clearinghouse for all the hospitals of a city and other cities. On the academic side, the members of the staff must be in touch with the science and the medicine of all the world."

Gregg nodded. Then he made a statement that stunned me. "It

does not matter to us where you want to launch it — Montreal or Philadelphia or some other city — provided there is evidence of local interest and enough local support to make the work go forward into the future with gathering momentum."

"Do you mean that?" I asked.

"Yes, it is what we would like to see you carry out somewhere."

He waited, and so I told him what I had been thinking. Montreal is a quieter place for study, I explained, quieter than New York or Philadelphia or even Baltimore. Tradition and awareness link Montreal with Europe, especially Great Britain and France, as well as with the United States. Our location here, above the American border and just off the main highroad to the great American university centers — might well prove to be the best place in which to be influenced by the work in other centers. It might be the ideal place in which to do constructive scientific work on the brain and the mind of man, work that might in time influence thinking in other centers.

"This is not a dream," I added, wondering if he would agree. "It is a plan that will work."

I hesitated, although there was so much more I wanted to say. Gregg nodded again and took up the story. "Whatever a man's business or profession may be," he said, "sometime in his career, early or late, he should draw up a plan, complete down to the last detail. I like to quote from something the German poet Goethe said: 'It is very important to know exactly what you want in life because you are so very apt to get it.' Tell me what the plan is. What will it cost?"

"First and foremost," I replied, wanting to dodge his blunt question for the moment, "the form in which assistance comes is most important. We need a capital endowment for science. It should be placed in the hands of the university. The income from it should be restricted from the very start, so it can be used only for scientific and academic purposes. That will protect it from encroachment upon it by hospital costs. The income from the endowment should create a scientific budget adequate to cover the costs of the first few years, and so make it possible to take on young career men. In time, if the work is good, it will attract whatever further financial support may be required."

I hesitated, wondering whether he might not be thinking in

terms of expenditures far below the amounts I had in mind. But Gregg smiled. "Go ahead. Tell me. What is your budget estimate?"

"I have calculated," I replied, "that the annual scientific budget will amount to sixty-one thousand, four hundred fifty dollars annually." I half expected a protest.

But he replied quietly, "Well, the trustees might listen to the idea of an endowment of a million dollars, but that would bring in less than fifty thousand yearly at present rates of interest. What next?"

"The construction of an adequate neurological institute would cost, I am told, a little less than half a million dollars. Half of the space would be devoted to rooms for science and teaching, half to the care of patients. We want less than fifty special beds."

"The foundation," Gregg observed, "would expect a considerable initial financial contribution from local sources. I might persuade the trustees to contribute fifty percent of the cost of such a building. They are not at all interested in meeting hospitalization expenses or clinical deficits."

Alan Gregg turned and examined the shelf of reference books beside my desk. "Words interest me," he said. "I enjoy books like these. This is a good selection."

Then, turning back, he looked at me from under his shaggy eyebrows. "All right — now I need to know what financial support can be expected from citizens and government here in Montreal."

I shook my head. I couldn't answer that question. He would, I told him, have to put the question to the dean. I thought the dean was very hopeful a few days ago. He said that when a large sum of money is really in sight, neither the Scottish and English citizens of Montreal nor the French-Canadian mayor and premier will let it go, even if it does cost them a good deal to keep it here! I asked whether Gregg had an appointment with the dean and the other important people.

"Yes." He nodded and grinned at me. "I know I must get to work. Have you ever heard what the New Hampshire farmer said? 'It ain't the work that takes the time; it's gettin' to it.'" He laughed. "Well, our talk has been a long one, but 'twarnt work. I understand a good many things at which I had only guessed before. The foundation trustees will make the final decision. But,

as I told you, this is the sort of proposition for which we are looking. I will help you to formulate the application, whether the
work is to be carried out here in Montreal or in some other city.
You can let me have your decision about that later."

I have recorded Alan Gregg's words on this fateful morning,
and mine, as accurately and realistically as I can, and within the
limits of my memory and records. Curiously enough, it is easier
to recall his stories, word for word, than it is the other more important things that he or I said. This interview and the one that
was to take place between us on the following day were most
important and yet they were completely off his record. He left
me and went to keep his on-the-record appointments with the dean
and others at the Royal Victoria Hospital and the university and
I was left to my own devices.

As I have already mentioned, Gregg had arrived back in his
New York office after a summer vacation, on September 22, 1931.
During the holiday he had brought his family from Europe and
established them in a house that he had purchased in Scarsdale,
a pleasant suburban village of New York. At the age of forty-one,
he was ready now to begin his active work as director of the Division of Medical Sciences, a post he was to hold for the next
twenty-one years. Although the winds of change were blowing
through the corridors of the Rockefeller Foundation, Alan Gregg
knew what he wanted to do in the broad field of medical science
and he had clear-cut ideas of how best to accomplish it. On that
first day in his office, he had made a note on his office calendar:

"Currie and Martin of Montreal — long distance telephone
through Max Mason's office. They want to come down on the
30th of September to see Mason about Neurosurgery. I told them
I could leave New York on the night of Oct. 9 for Montreal on
the way to Chicago and that nothing would be indicated in Philadelphia or Montreal as regards neurosurgery or neurology until
all the facts were in. . . . Both preferred my suggestion of a visit."

There was one other pertinent note on Gregg's office calendar
before he came to Montreal. It states that he spent a day in
Philadelphia and had discussions with Newton Richards, who had
asked for major help in Pennsylvania's project — to create a neurological institute and support a department of neurology and

neurosurgery. There is no statement on the calendar or elsewhere as to what Gregg had in mind to do about these applications.

It must have been late at night, in his hotel room on October 10, after his meetings with Dean Martin and others, that he made the following note:

"Martin quotes Taschereau, the Prime Minister [of Quebec], as saying that, though it would be difficult to give an outright gift now, the province could give $25,000 annually as long as the Institute was functioning. Martin says the city would give $10,000 and thus the cost of patient care could be guaranteed. Building calculated to cost $492,000." (In the end, the province did give twenty thousand and the city fifteen thousand dollars a year.)

It was Gregg's custom, when traveling for his foundation, to make notes at the end of the day for his office diary and sometimes notes in his personal diary. For the two days he spent in Montreal he listed in his office diary the people he met at the official luncheon and dinner, as well as his visits and other contacts. He did not mention his first talk with me on Saturday morning, or the one that took place next day.

Looking back at our morning interview, I had a strange feeling that Gregg and I had each written a play for unfolding events and speeches, plays that were much the same. But as soon as the play was on and each was acting out his part of the plot, it was clear that this was a larger play and neither of us was the playwright. Archibald and Martin at McGill, and Richards too, at Pennsylvania, had thought to be playwrights. But they were merely actors, like us, offstage for the moment, but actors nonetheless.

I had worked and prepared and waited all these months and years for a door to open that would show me where I was destined to do my work in the world. But now, strangely, I found myself still onstage. Dramatic action had stopped. I must pick up my pen and write out my own lines and plan the plot for many others.

17

The Germinal Idea

The second day of Alan Gregg's visit to Montreal was Sunday and he came to lunch with us at 4302 Montrose Avenue. He seemed to take delight in talking German with our two youngest children and they were charmed by him. After dinner we went to the living room for coffee. He looked at Jeff, our freckle-faced three-year-old. Turning to Helen and me, he said, "Jeff reminds me very much of our son Peter. Not long ago, Peter and I went for a walk on a Sunday afternoon in Scarsdale. I caught some water spiders for him. At first, he was fascinated. But presently, he looked up at me and said, 'When you take out stickly bugs to show me, Daddy, I think, "What can I *do* to give that man?'" Gregg turned and looked out the window. The maples were changing to red in the garden below. I looked too, and then I realized that he was trying to hide the tears that came easily to this man of quick emotion.

After coffee, Gregg and I withdrew to my study for a leisurely talk. "Let me remind you," he said, "that I have made no promises to you except to help you prepare the application to the Rockefeller Board of Trustees in regard to Montreal, Philadelphia or some still more favorable city."

I said I understood that. The talks between him and me were personal, whereas his talks with the dean and other important persons were formal and on the record. With them, he spoke less for himself and more for the Rockefeller Foundation. I added then that I supposed he had spoken for the foundation when he went to Philadelphia the previous week and Newton Richards told him that Pennsylvania would like to help to build an institute.

Gregg nodded. "Then," I said, "surely, since you and I are talking on a personal level I can tell you how grateful —" At the sound of the word "grateful," he held up his hand and exclaimed, "No." Then he changed the subject completely.

"Since leaving medical school," he said, "I have met many medical men in many parts of the world. Among them there were two who stand out as great men. Both were physiologists and both were working on the nervous system. One was Sir Charles Sherrington at Oxford. The other was Ivan Pavlov in Leningrad. I suppose you feel it is quite natural that genius should be drawn to the problems of the nervous system?"

I laughed and reflected. Here was a man with whom I felt at ease. Was it because his ultimate purpose in life was like my own? He was beginning on his major career now, and was ready for it after long years of thorough preparation, very different years of preparation from my own.

To my mind, we had settled our affairs, he and I, as far as we could for the moment. The next move could be made only after I had let him know whether the plan was to involve Montreal or Philadelphia or another friendly city. He would then place the plan before the trustees of the Rockefeller Foundation and he would proceed to argue our case. Since our interview of the day before, I had felt as if I stood on a high place where I could look out across the world and I wanted to discuss university cities with him.

But Gregg had no idea of terminating his own plan for the discussion. He settled back into the cushions of the big red chair in my study and looked at me as if he were, in fact, examining a horse. So I waited and thought to myself that Gregg was going to speak his lines now as he had planned to speak them in the play that he had prepared for these two meetings.

"Tell me," he said, "how did this idea come to you? When was the plan born? Tell me the story."

I looked at him vaguely. All at once he had made me realize that this was the end of the story of my search for help. I had hoped for this and at the same time had told myself it could not come to pass. But it *had* come to pass, and I must begin to plan what lay beyond. We could build an institute, of course, but that would be no more than a beginning.

"When you left New York," he prompted, "the Presbyterian Hospital was about to move uptown. You could have carried on there, and eventually, no doubt, at the New York Neurological Institute when they moved uptown. Was there something new and different that you had in mind?"

Then, when I still hesitated, he explained: "In foundation philanthropy, you know, we gamble on men as if they were horses. Wallace Buttrick was always talking about this. Buttrick, you may not have known. But he was one of the early architects of policy in regard to Rockefeller giving. He was always looking for the man with what he called 'a germinal idea.' In practice, we do back the man. But we do not always discover the story of the idea from its start to its maturity."

I saw he was serious and I knew his train would not be leaving Montreal for several hours. So I made the effort to tell my inner story, looking back across the first forty years of my life. Not an easy thing for anyone to do on demand. The "germinal idea" that Gregg expected me to discuss was of course the neurological institute. But the institute was only a practical means to an end. The purpose that called for it and the purpose that could be fulfilled through it were important.

Early in life, I explained to him, I was certain that there was work for me to do in the world. Some might think it strange that I was so certain then. But it was not until I went to Oxford for a second time, as a graduate student, that my purpose took on its specific plan — to become a brain surgeon and to apply basic science to the needs and problems of patients in the neurological field of medicine. I learned how to carry out critical research and discovered how thrilling it was to make little discoveries of truth about the nervous system.

What Gregg had referred to as a "germinal idea" did not come to me until after I had discovered, to my disappointment, that I simply could not carry out an effective approach to knowledge of the human brain and could not make use of that knowledge all by myself. That realization came after we had built up our own laboratory in the Presbyterian Hospital and after I had undertaken to write a complete textbook of neuropathology. I realized that someone else, somewhere in the world, was ready to do a better job on almost every chapter, one after the other. So I became an editor and organizer. I wrote one or two chapters, but the other thirty-odd chapters of a complete cytology and cellular pathology of the nervous system were written by men who thus became my colleagues.

Then, of course, came the idea of an institute through which my own life's purpose could be carried out. It was a simple commonsense plan. I could see how to organize it for each specialist, just as I had the editing of the *Cytology*. Some of the men who would come on staff, I hoped, would give me the specialized help I needed in my own exploration and treatment. The call for an institute was self-centered at the beginning, but it broadened rapidly into an altruistic establishment to serve the patients better and promote neurological research as never before. Nevertheless I still expected, in the end, to carry out my purposeful approach to brain and mind after the institute should be built. If I were not to do so I would have to acknowledge personal failure.

"In answer to your question," I said to Gregg, "as to whether this institute, which you propose to support, will be different from other neurological institutes, the answer is, 'Yes, I hope so.' There will be many members of staff who know the meaning of a personal purpose in the field of science. It will be built close to the departments of medicine and surgery of some large university hospital. Thus, neurology will be in close and constant contact with general medicine and surgery and all the facilities of a great modern hospital.

"You asked me," I continued, "what was wrong, to my mind, in New York. In retrospect, the disadvantage of the eventual arrangement at the New York medical center was this: The new Neurological Institute would still be at the distance of a ten-minute walk from the new Presbyterian Hospital. That might have been one good reason for my not remaining. But I suppose I would have stayed on, welcome or not, and separated from general medicine or not, had not chance — call it destiny if you like — intervened.

"Edward Archibald, professor of surgery at McGill University, came to New York in June of 1927 to invite me to take over his neurosurgical practice in Montreal, and in January of 1928, he offered support for a laboratory of our own. He came at exactly the right moment. I wanted independence and I had just reached my own conclusion as to how to solve great problems in the neurological field. I knew, by then, that no man alone could do what had to be done.

"In the three years that followed our coming to Montreal, the idea developed and a team appeared. I learned many things from Colin Russel and Bill Cone and the French-speaking neurologists and particularly from the patients I treated. The great need for teamwork became so evident.

"In a sense," I added, "I have been through this sort of organizing before in my football career, as a coach, and playing the game as an individual and calling the signals as a quarterback, and doing it all, not as an individual, but in the hope that the team would score as many goals as possible."

Gregg nodded and rose from the depths of the red chair to walk about the room. He stopped in front of me. "Perhaps Buttrick's phrase 'germinal idea' should have purpose added to it. Purpose should be germinal and the idea should be practical."

Then he added, "I've been thinking practical thoughts. Whether you decide to remain here or go to another medical center, there will be years between now and the final establishment of an institute. The plans we discussed yesterday may take quite a long time to mature, even if you do remain here."

Again, there was a twinkle in his eyes. "You might not like to see the research of your little group here run out of funds in the meantime. Had you thought of making an immediate application for an interim grant for research, say fifty thousand dollars a year, and possibly a grant to restore and preserve that last bequest from Mrs. Ottmann? If you could do that, the annual income from her fifty thousand dollars might have some special uses here or elsewhere."

I felt my face and neck grow hot. At last I must have spoken. I don't remember now just what I said. But it must have been this: How wonderful to be able to go on doing the research and the academic work we want to do right up to the opening of an institute somewhere — without my having to worry about it, or to beg for it.

Gregg had thought about the years of building. It had not occurred to me that these years would prove to be the most difficult of all. But I was soon to discover it. There was, however, something I felt I must say to this man before he should leave for Chicago.

"Please sit down," I said. "You must allow me to speak. I feel the way your son Peter must have felt when you took out 'stickly bugs' for him. 'What can I *do* to give that man?' Thank you, Alan Gregg, for doing what you do and for the way in which you are doing it. My hope for the future is like your own. Be assured that we will do the best job we can and will not forget to bring to the patients comfort and kindly care as well as understanding and sometimes scientific cure."

18

Difficult Years of Building

Following Gregg's incredible interviews, the Penfields and the Cones had decisions to make. The situation presenting itself in Philadelphia had been clearly outlined during the late summer of 1931.

Action in Montreal now went forward rapidly under the enthusiastic leadership of Charles Martin, dean of medicine, who was acting as vice-chancellor of the university in the absence of Sir Arthur Currie. At the end of three weeks, I was able to write in my weekly letter:

"October 30 . . . The Province of Quebec has promised $20,-000.00 and the city of Montreal $15,000.00 yearly for support of [patient deficits in] a neurological institute. . . . It is an awkward position for me just now," I added. "Philadelphia also is in a position to build and set up an establishment on an even larger scale. . . . These decisions have their implications for a sort of eternity, and the responsibility is great. . . ."

From the start of that present indecision, it had been a foregone conclusion that the Cones and the Penfields would return to the United States or remain in Canada, together. Bill had not been with me during my revealing interview with Gregg. This is, I think, significant. He was loyal to my projects in a more personal way, always the Good Samaritan, the tireless, selfless physician, taking a keen delight in serving the sick. But in spite of this and his brilliant retentive mind and his loyalty to the ideas of scientific perfection, I suppose Bill Cone never quite understood the hopes and the thinking at the back of my mind.

As far as my own personal philosophy of life was concerned, I had adopted a scale of ultimate priorities: first to be considered was a responsibility to wife and family; second, allegiance to my work in the world and to the teamwork that developed; and third, the friendship and happiness to be found in normal living. What the order of priorities was that would determine his way of life was not for me to judge.*

Bill Cone and I found at first that decision between Montreal and Philadelphia was difficult to make. Each of us wanted, if it were feasible, to remain in Montreal with the friends and the many enthusiastic recruits who had joined our team. We wanted to continue in the relative quiet and the freedom that had been ours in Montreal, to elaborate professional relations and associations with English and French neurologists. At the same time we were intrigued by the glamour and the drama of Philadelphia.

Helen and I had mixed feelings. We were enchanted by the Canadian wilderness and we liked the Montreal way of life. We were challenged by the bilingual society of this cosmopolitan city, and, I suppose, a little frightened by the highly respectable history and the formal social undertakings of Pennsylvania.

The Philadelphia challenge tempted me professionally. But could I handle the job? And could I draw the varied characters together, such as William Cone, who would come with me, with Francis Grant, the able neurosurgeon already there, and with the able group of neurologists headed by William Spiller and Theodore Weisenberg?

"The affairs of the Montreal Penfields will very soon be decided definitely," I wrote on November 19. "Bill Cone and I have just spent two days in Philadelphia, ending with an afternoon in New York when I talked again alone with Gregg. . . .

"The University of Pennsylvania is so much bigger than McGill, and there are many people there like [Cuthbert] Bazett and [Newton] Richards who would be a great help if alongside." This

---

* In the years that were ahead, the time would come when he would be surprised that I should put loyalty to our work in the world, and to the achievement of the team that he and I had created together, above the claims of our own personal friendship.

was to me the great advantage. There were so many stimulating people. "*But,* on the other hand," I confessed to my mother, "I feel smothered when I am there; I should (in time, I fear) be forced to give my life to administration and committees and honors, and stop my own constructive work. Is it not too much of a good thing?" There I seem to have left the decision for a while. No other city beckoned to us.

My mother's words came back to me: "Don't try to make a decision too soon. The way will be clear and the decision will make itself. So wait, son." That is what we did, all four of us. In the end, the decision to remain in Montreal was made without question. It was as much a matter of the heart as it was of the head. Cone and I would carry on with Colin Russel and Archibald and Meakins and Dean Martin and our other Montreal friends.

On Monday, November 23, 1931, I sent a telegram to Alan Gregg at the Rockefeller Foundation: "Have thrown in my lot with McGill. We expect to have application in your hands by Saturday. Wilder Penfield."

In Montreal's bid of the past month or two, it had been Martin, dean of medicine, who had taken the financial initiative. He had explained it to those who controlled the action of the hospital, the university, and the governments, as well as to certain public-spirited citizens whose help must be secured. They had to be convinced. He had met objections with optimism. He did it so willingly and with such boundless enthusiasm that I could hardly believe him or even recognize myself and my achievements in his descriptions. It was Martin, so to speak, who had made himself attorney for the case before the university and hospital boards as well as the governments and public in Canada. In New York, Gregg alone could argue for our cause.

On November 28, 1931, my weekly letter was written from New York's Biltmore Hotel. "You never quite know," I wrote to my mother, "where the next letter from your kaleidoscopic son will be postmarked, do you? I feel a good deal like a kaleidoscope that has at last come to rest for a moment. The bits of glass that fall into changing patterns in my head have assumed a final pattern, but a disturbing jangle still echoes through the vacant portions of that cavity.

"Dr. Martin and I," the letter continued, "are here to set the

McGill undertaking before Dr. Gregg. . . . In the past week, while preparing for this moment, I have renounced practice. At first I drew plans, to scale, steadily for three days; meanwhile Martin was working, against some opposition, for backing and cooperation — in hospital and university. At the end of these days he had the scheme through the boards of university governors and the hospital. The institute was to be built with money raised by McGill and, as planned at first, it was to be owned and operated by the hospital.

"We spent all Saturday afternoon with Gregg," I continued, "and then he told us that the *whole scheme would have to wait* six months, until the May meeting of the trustees, because of the large number of urgent appeals. (It seemed clear that our project was approved. But the money allowance would go to schemes that could not wait.) Well!" I added. "We are set for Montreal anyway. But unless an institute really does come in the end, I shall be footloose."

For several months, there was no further mention of an institute in my letters. Our minds turned to matters that were trivial or routine.

In April of 1932 the trustees of the Rockefeller Foundation did finally reconsider Gregg's proposal of an institute for Montreal. They passed it. Their grant was made to McGill University.

On the day of the public announcement I left Montreal for Chicago, ostensibly, as I wrote to my mother, "to attend a meeting of the Society of Clinical Surgery. But in reality, to avoid the fuss (in Montreal) and to discuss clinic organization with a number of men whose opinion I value.

"Helen," I continued, "will have sent you a clipping about the grant of $1,232,000. It is what we have been working for, of course, and what Gregg almost promised as long as six months ago. We asked for $150,000 more than that.

"Well," my letter concluded, "it is a friendly quiet city. We like it. Dr. Martin is ecstatic over this development. It is a triumph for him as dean, of course." He, more than any other man in Montreal, made it possible.

Here is the first paragraph of the clipping that appeared as an editorial in the *New York Times,* April 21, 1932, under the heading "Illocality":

"It has been prophesied by an eminent authority that we shall come to glory in 'illocality' — that instead of looking for our sanctions to the past, we shall increasingly look around the globe and take or encourage the best wherever it rises to view. That the Rockefeller Foundation should have crossed the border which divides Canada from the United States to give munificent support to a neurological institute in connection with McGill University is an apt illustration of this tendency." *

Late in March 1932, when it was clear that the Rockefeller Foundation was about to award the proposed grant to McGill, I began to plan the cooperation that was essential between hospital and institute, if there was to be an institute in Montreal at all. But I met only a strange unwillingness on the part of the Royal Victoria's superintendent. Was he, I wondered, fearful of exposing the business organization of the Royal Victoria to the university? Or was it possible that he was still loyal in some strange way to the man who had brought him from the Bank of Montreal to the hospital? Could he possibly preserve the antipathies of Sir Vincent Meredith toward Archibald's plans? No hospital governor asked me about plans or ideas. These men of wealth listened to Chenoweth behind closed doors. Members of the medical staff were different except for one or two who were friends of Pathologist Oertel.

"March 27, 1932 . . . I have been struggling with hospital and institute coordination this week. We cannot seem to plan to be in close enough touch with the other hospital activities. We had a phone call from [Isador] Ravdin in Philadelphia. [He had followed Charles Frazier as general surgeon and as professor of surgery there.] Would I come to Pennsylvania, he asked, if our institute plans fell through? Well, I replied, I might."

But my hand was on the plow. It would be so difficult to turn back now. I had survived the displeasure of Vincent Meredith until the end of his career. Surely I could induce an obstinate hospital superintendent, who could not or would not bring himself to cooperate in this hospital-university project.

In April 1932 the principal and vice-chancellor of McGill Uni-

* See note 60.

versity, Sir Arthur Currie, returned from a prolonged trip abroad. He would, I was told, relieve the dean of medicine, Charles Martin, of his responsibility for the neurological institute. Together with the chancellor, Edward Beatty (later Sir Edward), he chose the architects for the building at once, a Montreal firm, Ross and MacDonald.

Now that financial backing was available, it fell to me to take the initiative and to translate an idea into a perfect building that would serve the purposes of the future. I must also create a perfectly running establishment that would be a part of a modern hospital and that might, in time, become "a cause" to which succeeding generations would be loyal. For it to succeed, the establishment must, in time, take on the qualities of immortality, which can be discovered only within a university in modern society. Those of us who are optimists believe that it is within the university that institutions may hope to establish a sort of immortality of what is good for man.

I had made a rough sketch of my first idea of an institute. It was to be attached to the back of the Royal Victoria Hospital by a bridge for direct internal traffic across the alleyway. But this was soon discarded because there was too little room at the back of the hospital.

By midsummer we were working on plans for a building on University Street and a bridge attached to the third floor of the Royal Victoria crossing the street. When the architects were appointed, I discovered that we were most fortunate to have the enthusiastic cooperation of a clever architect, R. H. MacDonald, who understood the need of accurate detail. He also had other talents that architects should have, such as general knowledge, culture, independent resourcefulness and a sense of humor.*

I knew by now exactly what was needed and Mr. MacDonald allowed me to draw the original rough outlines.

On July 28, 1932, I wrote: "My chief concern is the blueprints for the institute. Floor by floor we have gradually developed the thing. I have drawn up the original for each floor and the architect takes each plan and molds it. Then I work it all over and get criticisms and outside ideas. Finally, I give them an altered

* See note 61.

scheme. Then we blueprint it and we repeat again. We must have done six or eight complete sets of blueprints. I worked until four this morning and they have the results to work on tomorrow."

With the architect and contracting engineer, we surveyed laboratories in selected cities. On July 17, 1932, I made a flying trip with Professor Colin Russel to New York and Cleveland. The visit was described in the weekly letter:

"We saw many medical schools and buildings and drew ideas from them. Our scheme is different from anything that has been done. . . . We shall have few beds, not over fifty, and shall focus all our attention on the patients in them from every angle, sending away chronic patients to be cared for elsewhere. I would like to think that the whole place will be perfect for the study and the treatment of neurological ailments.

"I have been recalling something," I continued, "from my visits to Paris. There is a statue that I remember. It stands at the foot of the stairway leading up to the medical library in the University of Paris. It was a copy in white marble from a statue done by a man named Barrias in colored marbles in one of the Paris museums. It is the figure of a young woman, heavily cloaked. Only her face and part of her breasts can be seen. The gown seems to be held up to the breasts by a scarab. At the base of the pedestal are the words 'La Nature se Dévoilant Devant la Science' — 'Nature Unveiling before Science.' I have treasured a photograph of it ever since those days (I even carried it in my pocket for a time) and always longed to have a copy of that statue.

"The other day in Cleveland it occurred to me while I was walking along the street that, at last, I might have a copy made, and place it in such a position at the entrance that it would suggest, to one entering, the ideal I have in mind for the whole institute. There should be something more of course. The other thing has to do with pity for the suffering of our brothers. I don't know what to do about expressing that. Perhaps that feeling could be added in a further legend, an inscription."

More than a year later, the following note appeared in one of my letters.

"I have spent several evenings working on an inscription to go on a stone slab that occupies an important position on the outside

The Montreal Neurological Insti-tute, 1934

Dedication tablet facing University Street, Montreal Neurological Insti-tute

of the institute.* At last, after much thought and consultation, I have boiled it down to the following legend:

DEDICATED

TO

RELIEF OF

SICKNESS

AND PAIN

AND

TO THE STUDY OF

NEUROLOGY

"It seems as if one might have written it instantly on the back of an envelope. I also sketched the background on which to place it, a shield with a rising sun at the top and on either side a human brain with its curving spinal cord below it to outline the side of the shield. I don't know whether the architects will find it satisfactory. It has been a little difficult to get them to accept my crude and unexpected anatomical suggestions as they do not fit in with the usual suggestions of architectural design. I could not bring them to put a brain into stone anywhere until I brought them a drawing of one done by Christopher Wren, and now they have sketched it for just over the door, and it is I who now hesitates!"

MacDonald and I had plenty of time to consider and reconsider the architecture of the institute. Currie and his university advisers could not make up their minds to build the perfect little building we had planned. During the year, he had tried to make sure that promises of money from the governments already obtained by Martin would be forthcoming. But Currie was neither financier nor politician. He tried to raise new money. But in 1932, at the bottom of the Depression, there was no new money, so it seemed. He took me with him and we went to New York and begged for a further grant from the Rockefeller Foundation. It was to no avail. For me it was a time of maddening frustration.

Nevertheless, one can only sympathize with Sir Arthur Currie, who was entering what was to be the last year of his life. He was

---

* This stone slab was "transplanted" May 6, 1976, and words added: "Inauguration Pavillon Wilder Penfield Pavilion 6/V/76," to dedicate the start of new construction.

still an enormous figure of a man. He had been commander in chief of the Canadian combat forces overseas during the First World War, and was, no doubt, a great leader of men in such surroundings. Now he was dictatorial, but unsure of himself, immature and boyish at heart. He must protect McGill, he thought, against financial loss.

At last, when it seemed that costs for equipment were rising sharply, Sir Arthur called a meeting in his large office that looked out across the campus of McGill with its lofty elms. I came hurrying to it on the run from the bedside of a patient, critically ill in the Royal Victoria. I arrived a minute or two late, and Sir Arthur's very loyal secretary, Mrs. Dorothy McMurray, shook her head at me in obvious disapproval. But she showed me in, and I found the members of the building committee, who were also members each of a different faculty, sitting about Sir Arthur at a large table. My friend, architect MacDonald, was also present, I saw with relief.

To my horror I discovered that the vice-chancellor had in his hands a set of plans omitting two of the eight and a half floors of the Montreal Neurological Institute. "We must cut the coat," he said firmly, "to fit the cloth."

One could only have a feeling of affection for Sir Arthur, but we had come to the end of persuasion and waiting. So I said what I should have said six months earlier perhaps:

"You will have to go ahead with this project without me. The grant of money was made to the university. No one will want this coat as you have cut it. If you should change your mind and want my help to put the project through, you must undertake to build a neurological institute that is perfect in every functional detail even if we should not be able to quite complete it."

Then I added one thing more. "You are worried, Sir Arthur, because McGill is accepting ownership of an institution that is part hospital, something she has never done before. Don't worry. If our work is any good at all, the university will never be called upon for funds. This institute will pay its way with money that comes to it for that purpose."

Currie, who had been smoking a pipe to console himself, now knocked out his pipe deliberately, and brought his enormous closed fist crashing down on the table.

"Damn it! They told me you would say just that. Well, I've made up my mind what I would say in case you did." He laughed and then added, "We can't go on without you whether we like it or not. The university will have to take a chance that you know what you are talking about, and that you and Cone and Russel and the others can run your own show and keep us out of debt after the building is built. But have we enough money in hand to build it, the way you want it, now?"

Fortunately I had the added fund of fifty thousand dollars that Mrs. Ottmann had given me and Gregg had replaced when nearly used up. I pledged it if it should prove to be really needed to meet the construction costs. But, still more important, our architect, Mr. R. H. MacDonald, who was present, knew ways of unexpected saving in this time of Depression building. We had only cooperation from the university from that time onward.

So the builder was chosen, and in June of 1933, final building plans were accepted. In the autumn came the laying of the cornerstone. This became Currie's gesture and he made it in dramatic military style. On October 6, 1933, the day forever set aside to honor our founder, James McGill, Sir Arthur Currie invited the Governor-General, Lord Bessborough, to Montreal to lay the cornerstone.

That procession marching up University Street reminded me of the ones we had grown accustomed to in Oxford. Some of the professors wore crimson or scarlet doctorate gowns with swank soft hats such as those the Scottish universities award. The Governor-General's bodyguard was led by a youngster six feet five in height with all the splendor of Scottish kilts. But I was embarrassed and did not want to play in this game.

"At the laying of the stone," I wrote my mother, "Currie talked and the Bishop blessed, and I had a desire to weep and to run away. . . . Such occasions are flourish and empty vainglory. . . . The cornerstone-laying is for the builders. The opening will be for us who know its meaning and who will enter its walls as a monastery to disappear, I hope, from **public** attention."

So the Montreal Neurological Institute finally began to grow on its chosen site, an eight-and-a-half-story building of gray Montreal stone, on university property running along the east side of

University Street, beside the Pathological Institute. Thus, it was placed directly opposite and rose above the Outpatient Department of the Royal Victoria Hospital.

There was another threatened confrontation, much less important to us than Currie's year-long timidity had been. When the skeleton of the building structure had gone up, it came to the attention of some of the members of the hospital's board of governors that a bridge across University Street for a corridor into the hospital was proposed. A message came to me by word of mouth, forbidding it in somewhat colorful language.

One can only conclude that Superintendent Chenoweth had failed to show them the blueprints that were submitted and had long since been approved by hospital and university. Sir Herbert Holt, who had become president of the hospital in succession to Vincent Meredith, was also a governor of the university and had instantly agreed to match personally J. W. McConnell's offer of a hundred thousand dollars when told by Martin that the Rockefeller money might come to Montreal if citizens would meet the cost of half the building of an institute.

Consequently, I was not a little surprised to receive this message from Chenoweth: "If they build a Goddamn bridge across University Street into our hospital, I won't give a cent to construction." The message was said to come from Holt, although one may wonder.

I asked Bill Cone to come with me, and we climbed the scaffolding to the third floor where there was a cooling breeze. We looked down to the city along University Street and across the street into the corridor thoroughfares of this hospital that we hoped to serve and work with. I could approach that board only through the superintendent. So I sent him word that we must carry on with the previously agreed project according to plan and that this would be done at once.

So, a graceful bridge was built across the street to connect directly with the main corridor of the third floor of the hospital. Holt paid over his generous gift to the building project quite happily at the proper time. And he seemed to be pleased when we named the third-floor ward after him. The university assumed ownership of the institute and it was proposed that the hospital would undertake the hospitalization care of patients in the institute.

The bridge over University Street. The entrance to the Montreal Neu-rological Institute may be seen on the left under the arch. Beyond, hid-den by the bridge, is the Pathological Institute. On the right are towers in the façade of the Royal Victoria Hospital.

At last the building was under way, and we could watch it grow in stature and in accordance with its purposes, like a vigorous child. We discovered what seemed to us beauty in the outward form. Inside the building, much attention was given to the needs of nursing supervision.

Only a few short weeks after the laying of the cornerstone, Sir Arthur Currie died unfortunately and unexpectedly. We were not able to tell him that, thanks to the splendid work of the architect R. H. MacDonald, the institute was built, without too far exceed-ing the original financial estimates, although one of the two ele-vators had to be omitted temporarily and some furnishings were incomplete. In the end, I had used a considerable portion of my treasured Ottmann Memorial money but we managed to replace that again.

Now I must turn away to more important matters that might well have upset all our plans. In the year 1933 to 1934 antibiotic drugs were yet to be discovered. Lobar pneumonia was a dreaded disease. In these attacks it often happened that, as infection spread through one or both lungs, the fever rose relentlessly until the crisis came on the fifth or perhaps even the seventh day. Then, if the patient was not to die, the temperature was expected to fall suddenly and the lungs to clear up.

Helen and I had loved the Canadian wilderness, somewhat as my father had the wilderness of the West. But during that last winter before the Montreal Neurological Institute was opened, we faced tragedy there and the wilderness seemed cruel. After Christmas, Helen took the children and the red setter by the train that ran twice a week to South Bolton. Erick Jackson, our farmer, met them and drove them the three miles over the mountain to Sussex House, safe and warm, it seemed, in the bottom of the bobsled, drawn by our mighty plow team, Maud and Mike.

I had planned to come down a few days later over the subsequent New Year's Day. But the next day, a telephone call came back to me. My thirteen-year-old son, Wilder, said, "Mother is in bed. She has a pain in her side and she talks funny."

"What about her breathing," I asked. "Is it fast?"

"Yes."

He had told me all I needed to know. It was pneumonia and the weather was very cold. That night it had been thirty-five degrees below zero Fahrenheit in Montreal and forty-two degrees below zero in South Bolton, the coldest weather since we had come to Canada. The roads were all blocked to automobiles. I gathered medical supplies and caught a fast train next morning to the town of Magog, where a driver with an excellent horse and cutter met me and took me swiftly over the snow the fourteen miles to the farm, where I arrived with one cheek frozen.

I sent no letters to my mother during the next three weeks that I stayed on at Sussex House, excepting one brief one, on December 31, 1933, in which I told my mother what was happening, and that a nurse, Miss Constance Winter, had arrived, and I was giving Helen serum injections.

"We are so far away, and I am unfamiliar with this sort of treatment. But all goes well," I remarked hopefully, "except for very high temperature and severe pain; and she is confused. It is terrible to stand aside and watch her fight alone. She will come through all right I know. Once in a while I am afraid." Then I added, "Long before you receive this letter she will have passed her crisis and be convalescing. And if you have received no telegram you will be sure all is well with her."

One other letter later came to light. It was written to Mr. Chenoweth, the superintendent of the Royal Victoria Hospital.*

The pneumonic crisis did not come on schedule. Day after day the fever continued without a drop, and during all this time Helen was delirious. I kept communication by telephone with those most skilled in internal medicine in Montreal. Cone came down and landed on Lake Memphremagog below us in an aircraft shod with skis. He floundered up the hill through the deep snow, took samples of blood for culture, shook his head, and returned to Montreal, where the blood samples were studied while he continued to care for my patients and his own.

The visiting physicians would not leave us. When, at length, Professor A. H. Gordon had to return to his own patients in the Montreal General Hospital (hobbling on a cane because of a toboggan mishap) and Raymond Brow returned to the Royal Victoria, Jonathan Meakins and Sclater Lewis came from the Victoria to replace them for a second week.

In time it seemed best for the German governess and the other children to return to Montreal, while Wilder stayed on with me. We alternated in the care of the wood-burning furnace. Every two hours around the clock, four-foot sticks of maple wood had to be thrown with a resounding echo into the firebox in the cellar. This kept the hot air flowing through the registers upstairs and down.

Wonderful special nurses came to us and attended to every detail that might make a difference and even save Helen's life, as only good nurses can.

At last, on the nineteenth day, while I was visiting Helen a few hours before dawn she looked at me as she lay in bed and I thought I saw the beginning of understanding in her eyes, the eyes that had turned to me as to a stranger for so long.

"Are you," she asked, "my father? Or, or my, or my husband?"

---

* See note 62.

Her brow felt cool again for the first time in so long. I hurried off to awaken Professor Meakins.

"I think the time has come."

He rushed to her in his pajamas, thermometer in hand, and I followed. We waited two long minutes for the thermometer to register.

"Sure enough!" he whispered to me. "The crisis has come. She is going to get by."

Never was the struggle against death more closely contested. Never, during it, did a woman and her husband receive more kindly help from medical colleagues and nurses, and from local farmers, and from friends of all descriptions and places. Helen's had become a celebrated case. In a few days we brought her by stretcher, on the bobsled that Jackson had converted into a covered ambulance, to South Bolton and back home by train.

Returning to Montreal, I took up the life again that would have been broken and changed had she been taken from me. The weekly letters began again from 4302 Montrose Avenue:

"Jan. 21, 1934 . . . Helen is safely back in the Ross Pavilion and is doing well. . . . Her room is a bower of flowers. She has such a legion of friends! Mostly people she has been nice to, because they needed it. . . . Ruth Mary kept count of the telephone calls that came to the house to inquire about her, during the first day or two after our return — sixty-four calls from forty-two people!"

Then I added the following: "I just came across the enclosed beginning of a letter to you that was never sent: '*Helen is getting well.* What words those are! Sometimes during the past eighteen days as I watched her lying in bed burning with fever, I have faced the meaning of other words. Once while I had been nursing her at night, I looked out over the moonlit snow to the little burying ground beyond the Glen Brook fence to the south of us. I could see the headstones black against the snow, and I faced what it meant. I should have sold the farm of course and what would the children do without her? After that, for days and nights I did not dare to look in that direction. I didn't even look out the windows to the south.' "

Helen recovered her strength but she did so slowly. The long continued toxic delirium had left partial loss of hearing and of vision that did not clear up for weeks, and the long continued consolidation of the lung left easy cardiovascular fatigue. All of this was slow to clear up. But, clear up it did.

A feeling of thankfulness and security seemed to have come to my family. On our return to Montreal, I went before a judge and became a Canadian citizen, a British subject. I became an elder too, as I had planned to do, in the Presbyterian Church of Saint Andrew and Saint Paul.

In March we worked out a satisfactory plan for decoration of the institute entrance with the architects' guidance. And I found an excellent motto for the ceiling (thanks to Dr. William Francis). It was from Galen's objection to the teaching of Hippocrates that brain wounds were invariably fatal — four Greek words that may be interpreted: "But, I have seen a brain-wound heal."

The first group of young neurosurgeons that we had trained was ready to leave us. With Arthur Elvidge, a newly trained neurosurgeon on our staff, they called themselves the "Old Guard" and asked to be photographed with Bill Cone and me (see page 325). Lyle Gage was going to Peru, Joseph Evans was going to Cambridge to work with Professor Edgar Adrian (later Lord Adrian), Jerzy Chorobski back to Warsaw and Arne Torkildsen back to Oslo.

The Sunday letter of May 21, 1934, showed how my wife had regained her strength:

"Helen has been down in the country since Monday cleaning up the whole place, both Sussex House and also the lakeside cottage, which is going to be rented by Douglas Abbott, a young lawyer with an attractive wife and nice children.* This is very fortunate as the income will help to 'make both ends meet,' on the farm.

"Canadian weather," the letter continued, "resembles a slightly spoiled beautiful girl with a good heart but a bad disposition. After being horrid for much too long a time, she suddenly turns right about and makes up for everything with so much charm that you vow again you always loved her! . . ."

I, too, had come down for that weekend and I listened from the

---

* Douglas Abbott had a distinguished career and became a justice of the Supreme Court of Canada.

Staff of the Department of Neurology and Neurosurgery, the Royal Victoria Hospital and McGill University in the spring of 1934 before the opening of the M.N.I. From left to right, standing: Olan Hyndman, Jerzy Chorobski, Robert Hardwood, Theodore Erickson, Arne Torkildsen, John Kershman, William T. Grant, Ralph Stuck, George Stavraky. Seated: Lyle Gage, Arthur Elvidge, Norman Petersen, Arthur Young, Colin Russel, Wilder Penfield, William Cone, Joseph Evans, Wilbur Sprong.

porch of Sussex House three hundred feet above the shore of the lake. "The birds were singing beautifully, and as one listened . . . one could hear, down over the meadow, an extraordinary concert of delicate songs — the bobolinks in the air and thrushes farther away along the lakeshore."

Moving into later spring, we set the opening of the institute for September. But still I could not bring about an agreement between the university and Mr. Chenoweth. He would not listen. My weekly letters tell an advancing story of exasperation on my part.

Summer came, and then, for the second time in 1934, my whole career was threatened. The first threat of tragedy had been Helen's illness in January, and now five months later, I was dismayed to learn that I was likely to lose my associate, William Cone, after all. He had received such invitations to return to the University of Iowa that I thought he would have to accept them.

On June 29, 1934, my letter began with a question: "What will Bill do? He has not told me yet. But Professor Bye was here from Iowa yesterday to see him. Their offer is to give him complete charge of neurosurgery at Iowa and a double professorship — one in neurosurgery and one in neurology. They offer him a larger income than I shall probably ever have. I have only been able to offer, eventually, to split the fees from the surgical clinic with him evenly. (That is my income, present and future.) . . . How can he refuse their offer? . . .

"My only hope," the letter continued, "is that he may believe that someday our group that is gathering in the new institute, by some stroke of legerdemain, may create the greatest of all centers of neurological thought, while he and I do something that neither of us alone could do. What is that fancy, that extravagant dream, against the complete control and easy living they offer him in the place that was once his hometown?

"The trouble is," I wrote, "Bill has left a facet on me that will be hard to hide. I have let laboratory detail go since he came to me in 1924. If he leaves me now, the best thing for me to do will be to get along without building up much of an operative clinic and to work quietly on at epilepsy. There is much to do on it, and life is so short!"

I was evidently thinking of us two as if we had been two round stones side by side serving their purposes, and after years — no longer quite round and independent.

So, Bill Cone took a trip out west during his summer month of vacation. When he returned, I was sitting in my tiny office in the Royal Victoria Hospital, my real headquarters within the Laboratory of Neuropathology, which was, in turn, within Professor Meakins's laboratory of medicine at the heart of the hospital. There Cone and I had been guests now for the almost six years that neurology and neurosurgery had been growing as an ever-lustier subdepartment within the hospital.

I was dealing with the day's correspondence that had inevitably to do with the business of the clinic as well as personal affairs. It is the letters and reports that flow through a clinic, a ward, a laboratory and a research project that form the bloodstream of the active life in any healthy medical unit. And every member of the unit, from top to bottom, must make his daily contribution to that stream. There is no substitute for discipline and efficiency.

In the midst of this routine business, I became aware that the typewriter of our efficient and much-loved laboratory secretary, Hope Lewis, had stopped its tapping in the adjacent room. I heard her cry out in her pleasant English accent, and then the rumbling bass voice and laughter of Bill Cone. Almost at once there was a knock on my door and the door swung open before I could reply. Miss Lewis had come in before him.

"Here is Dr. Cone, and he is bringing you the wonderful news for which we have all been hoping."

There he was, and, in a flash, I called back to mind how, ten years before, he had come down the stairs to the pathology laboratory at the Presbyterian Hospital, exactly the right man to help in my projects, a big thickset man with heavy features, strong and always kind and reassuring. His dark eyes had lit up now as they always did when he had good news. His brilliant smile made one forget all else. We had never been demonstrative, he and I. We were not now.

"I've made up my mind, Wide," he said, "to stay with you. We've come along together. You've been a straight-shooter. I need your help to do what I want to do in life, and you can't get on very well without me here. It's going to be great fun from now on. There will be no place like this in all the world, with the help of

Colin Russel and Norman Petersen and Fred MacKay and Don McEachern and the others."

All I could say in reply was, "Thank heavens, Bill." Then I added: "Yes, together it will be great fun."

In the early years, our relationship had soon changed from that of teacher and pupil to that of companions in a common effort. Ten years of this had marked each of us for life, leaving an articulating facet that strengthened us for work together and weakened us for work alone. He was stronger and abler than I in some ways. With that strength and with the Rockefeller endowment, I felt confident now that I could captain the teamwork that Alan Gregg had seemed to expect of us when he slapped his folder down on my coffee table in October 1931 and said, "This is the sort of thing we are always looking for in the Rockefeller Foundation."

We two, who began as physician and apprentice, had become remarkably interdependent. Bill became a skilled neuropathologist capable of being chief of the laboratory. He also became a very skillful neurosurgeon. He seemed to be almost tireless in both capacities.

Bill Cone made it possible for me to lead a double life and to be, at times, another person. I could run away for a weekend, not to rest in the passive sense of that word, but to use my muscles with good companions, to go on a dozen excursions of the mind, to laugh and to rejoice and to come back to my primary career, fresh and fit to cope with major projects and new endeavors. Only such a man as William Cone who was skillful and conscientious enough to care for my patients and my problems could have given me peace of mind during such an escape. Beyond that he could point to better purposes when I returned to our common tasks in the primary career.

I wanted to do the same for him and I tried to do so. But he was not willing, or perhaps able, to be that other person too. We balanced each other at work but not at play, or in our second careers. He worked incessantly for the common cause that was soon to have a home of its own in the Montreal Neurological Institute. I might almost say, he turned away from all his youthful enthusiasms and so had no second career.

Thus, I suppose Cone suffered from my weakness. The weakness was that I depended on others dangerously. If I had been deprived of his help it would have taken me years to build strength in others or in myself. But with him the team, though small, was ready for excellent performance. This applied to neurology as well as neurosurgery. Colin Russel and Fred MacKay depended on him almost as much as I.

Knowing now that all would be well, I could plan to mount a great expedition of exploration, the hope of which had led to the building of this institute. I could look out into the dark and wonder where dawn would break and gold would touch the palisades of understanding — understanding of the brain and the mind of man.

1934: The Opening

"Lord . . . establish thou the work of our hands"

— from Psalm 90

In the spring of 1934, as I have said, Canadian weather smiled on us as if she could never have been unkind. I returned to our summer place for a short weekend. We had decided to give up the attempt to convert this farm into a profit-making operation after five years of serious trial.

"We have not lost much money during the last two years," I wrote my mother, "but we have not gained anything, and I need my time and attention for other tasks." I had come, at last, to a general conclusion about this part of the Province of Quebec. I liked sport with the others of my family and begrudged the time demanded of me in the barns. The conclusion was this: Such rocky highland countryside can serve our country to better purpose by giving rugged strength to generations of hardy sailors and sporting young Canadians, than it can by growing grass for cows. Our English farmer, Erick Jackson, wanted more money than I could ever pay. So he undertook to sell off the livestock not too unwillingly, and laid his plans to move to a more productive farming area in Ontario.

"On June 29 bad news came to me unexpectedly. The university bursar found that no money had been paid over by the Rockefeller Foundation to the university to cover the academic budget for the past year. Thus, we had expended $50,000 that was not there! When I wrote to the Rockefeller comptroller he answered that none was due, as the building of the institute had not been completed as expected." During Currie's many postponements, I had not thought to warn the Rockefeller Foundation.

"Imagine our horror," I wrote, "when we found that the terms of the gift showed the comptroller right. I phoned New York and Dr. R. K. Lambert, Gregg's assistant, came to Montreal at once. I spent a day sweating over figures and talking with him. He has returned to New York now and will circularize the trustees of the foundation to gain their decision as soon as possible.

"It is a stupid, silly performance on my part," I concluded. "But if they do not 'come across,' I shall be in a difficult position. Just resigning would not help much. I offered to throw in such research funds as still remained in my possession."

Dr. Lambert, to my great relief, acted quickly, circularizing the members of the foundation's board of trustees. After an anxious period, he wrote me on July 19 that they had authorized a generous grant of fifty-four thousand dollars.

We were now in midsummer, 1934. I was vastly reassured to have our research expenditures covered. I had always thought Chenoweth would draw up an agreement that could be signed by hospital and university to cover costs and organization of hospital management of our patients. This he did, finally. But I had declared repeatedly that I would never recommend signature by the university until the hospital established communication across the bridge.

So it was that I seem to have been in despair on July 28, 1934, when I wrote in the weekly letter: "Institute things are in a hopeless snarl. I had looked for a signed agreement by August 1, but Chenoweth has now told me the *hospital refuses direct passage from the bridge* to their main corridor."

This, which could have been planned so easily, had now become awkward because of a few feet of space to be lost by the Children's Ward. Our patients on stretchers and our food trucks returning to the Royal Victoria kitchens would cross on our third-floor bridge only to meet a maze within the hospital, consisting of an elevator down and another up to the hospital's main corridor on the third floor.

"I was all for smashing things at first," the letter continued, "but I have gradually simmered down now."

By August 6, it was clear that I had lost the battle of the bridge.

I spoke in the weekly letter to my mother of "the first block and the first failure on my part to put through what was necessary for proper development of the institute. . . . I refer to direct passage from institute through to the main corridor of the hospital. It was promised before the building began and is refused now that the bridge is built for that purpose."

Then I added, "I wrote a letter of protest to Sir Herbert Holt, president of the Royal Victoria Hospital, and saw [Edward] Beatty, who is chancellor of the University. Beatty would not back me, and the hospital governors set my protests aside in a special meeting, and I am informed that certain governors expressed themselves as feeling they had been 'most generous' with me. I could make no personal presentation but I must stay on the job and see what can be done. . . . I told Beatty the university was letting me down, and he said I was an obstinate devil."

Perhaps I was. Perhaps I am. But I simmered down again (even the devil must do that since he does not seem to win every encounter). But soon I had forgotten the issue (almost) as did everyone else. The members of the medical and nursing staff of the Royal Victoria cooperated with us so enthusiastically and the whole project of the Neurological Institute was such a thrilling adventure with its modern functional equipment that I, like all the others, turned to the future with excited anticipation.*

But the opening ceremony was close upon us by the time the operative agreements were signed. Knowing that official invitations would soon go from the university to Alan Gregg, I wrote him as follows: "I have appealed," my message began, "to a number of friends among the neurologists throughout the country to come [to the opening] as a gesture of friendship and understand-

---

* The Royal Victoria Hospital did not make a direct connection between the institute's bridge and the hospital's third floor corridor until 1940, six years after the opening ceremony of the institute. It was then that Dr. George Stephens established a new regime as superintendent, succeeding Mr. Chenoweth.

For six years members of the staffs of both institutions walked across University Street and through the R.V.H. Outpatient Department. Or they followed the food trucks and stretchers from the institute across the bridge to an elevator down in the R.V.H. and a rather remote elevator up. That elevator was also used to serve a one-way purpose to carry corpses from the hospital to the subterranean passage across University Street and into the Pathological Institute.

ing, and, so far, have received only acceptances. I wish you could come on that basis even though you feel you cannot come as an ambassador."

It may seem strange to the reader that in this letter I used the word "country" when referring to "friends among the neurologists" on this continent. In matters of academic and professional life and thought, one is apt to think of *American* and *Canadian* as describing undivided parts of one society. I was thinking spontaneously of this North American Country in which I felt myself one of many fellow workers, without political or cultural separateness. Indeed, there is a world of neurology in which there are no subdivisions. To those who work in that world, man is the common problem. In that world there is so much to understand, and there are many to help.

It was now six years since we had come as strangers to this city and this land. And what a warm and helpful welcome we received from those without and those within the medical profession. From the very beginning the physicians and surgeons and the nurses of the Royal Victoria cooperated with the plans of Archibald and Meakins and Cone and me.

What a remarkable group of doctors we discovered here, marked as they were by the McGill stamp of conservative excellence! They helped us to develop neurology and neurosurgery, as friends and colleagues in an ever-enlarging medical team. There was no exception to this assistance from the clinicians of this hospital, and also from the other hospitals of both languages in Montreal and Quebec City.

And now before this ship is thought to be launched and sailing out to sea, let me add one further observation about the nurses who came aboard. The nursing of neurological patients is particularly difficult and particularly important. Doctor and nurse must work together with the patient in close understanding. Fortunately for us, the wonderful Royal Victoria School of Nursing undertook our patients as a challenge from the very beginning. Miss Mabel Hersey was superintendent of nurses (1908–1938) in the Royal Victoria, a tall, impressive, quiet woman of whom Florence Nightingale herself would have been proud.

With the opening of the Neurological Institute, she selected, to be our director of nursing, Eileen Flanagan, R.N., whose leadership in this field was to make us all proud in the years that followed.*

So at last the day came. On September 27, 1934, McGill University opened the Montreal Neurological Institute "with that observance of ceremony," to quote the words of Dr. Archibald, "and with that dignity which are proper to such a great enterprise."

At three o'clock in the afternoon, three hundred guests were gathered in the two larger wards of the institute, one of which was provided with loudspeakers for the overflow attendance.

At ten minutes before three o'clock, the principals who were prepared to enact the symbolic ceremony had gathered in the medical school two hundred yards away. They were ready to march up University Street to the institute, gowned in robes as splendid as anything the Middle Ages could have produced, a splendor that, nowadays, only a university can bring forth to astonish the beholder: His Worship Camilien Houde, mayor of Montreal, who was to unveil the Barrias statue in the entrance hall; Dean Charles F. Martin, who was to be chairman; Professor Edward Archibald, who would read the Foreword; Athanase David, minister of public health in the Province of Quebec, who would speak on neurology and public health; Professor Harvey Cushing of Harvard, who was to give the first Foundation Lecture; William Cone, neurosurgeon and neuropathologist, who would express our appreciation to Cushing, acknowledged leader of the modern school of neurosurgery; Gordon Holmes, the senior neurologist from the National Hospital in London, who was to give the second Foundation Lecture; Colin K. Russel, senior neurologist of the Royal Victoria, and Fred H. MacKay, senior neurologist of the Montreal General Hospital, who were to express appreciation to Holmes, much-loved neuroanatomist and teacher of us all; and finally the director-to-be, who was in a daze, wondering that so much had come to pass.

It had grown dark as this procession was in the making. An effort was made to speed up the preparations, but to no avail. At exactly the appointed moment the procession emerged from the

---

* Miss Flanagan has looked back to that beginning recently, and I have quoted from what she wrote in note 63.

medical school and descended the steps and turned to march up University Street. But at that moment the heavens opened and rain fell with great suddenness. The institute and the bridge alike had vanished from view. The marchers turned and fled back up the steps and into the medical school, bedraggled. The wind blew, lightning flashed and thunder roared as if to forbid this vain-glorious ceremony!

I had an uneasy feeling, and called to mind the fact that the late president of the Royal Victoria Hospital, strongly supported by the learned director of the Pathological Institute that was now next door to our institute, had been opposed to Archibald's whole plan of bringing neurosurgeons to the hospital. Perhaps the gods on Mount Olympus might have been on their side after all! Perhaps they were still displeased. Perhaps Sir Vincent Mere-dith was standing now in the presence of Zeus!

McGill University was, at the time of this opening ceremony, accepting an institute that was also a hospital. It was the univer-sity's first venture in hospital ownership. If it had not been for this fatherly action, the newborn institution would have seemed an unwanted orphan after the hospital decided not to own it.

We waited, but there was no end to that storm. Finally a fleet of taxis had to be summoned and, carrying us across the water that was rushing down Pine Avenue and into University Street, delivered us in wet gowns into the shelter of the institute. Once we were inside the building, the storm and the apparent dis-pleasure of the gods were quite forgotten.

Five or six patients had already been admitted and wheels had begun to turn that will never be stopped as long as we, and our successors, dedicate ourselves to the "relief of sickness and pain and to the study of neurology."

Two days before the opening, I had used the new operating room and was enchanted by its quiet convenient efficiency, the "black rubber" floor, the arrangements for routine photography of the brain and for easy, safe communication and consultation with basic scientists and surgeons and fellows in the viewing stand. At last, here was proper equipment for a surgeon to use who wanted to add the science of physiology to the art of surgery. Here was a place where a new school of neurological nursing could de-velop along with neurosurgery and neurology.

All that happened at the opening has been recorded for posterity in a book published for the staff of the institute.*

I shall not repeat what can be read there, excepting only to recall the words of Edward Archibald and to place them where the reader may find them. I remember them now, rather than the words of other famous speakers.†

On September 30, 1934, alone with my wife, I wrote to my mother from the silence of the hills. This was my only serious description of the opening ceremony, since the foregoing description was obviously slightly flippant:

"The Montreal Neurological Institute is now an accomplished fact. Gordon Holmes arrived to attend the opening exercises on the 18th of September and stayed with us until the 29th, when he went on to New York. You remember he was my principal teacher in London. He is so congenial now and I liked him as I never did before, on this trip, because I had come to know him better. . . .

"Friday, the 27th, was the formal opening and I felt sort of dazed. Twenty-five of the invited out-of-town guests had accepted. That filled me with very great pleasure for many of them came out of friendship, pure and simple: Stanley Cobb (Boston), Allen Whipple (New York), Percival Bailey (Chicago), Byron Stookey and Henry Riley (New York), Max Peet (Ann Arbor), Cuthbert Bazett and Francis Grant (Philadelphia) and so many others. Cushing came and was accompanied by John Fulton [already his prospective biographer]. Cushing and Holmes gave the Foundation Lectures.

"At one o'clock, before the opening, I gave a luncheon for the Foundation Lecturers and for Beatty, Holt, McConnell, Hodgson, Martin and a few special guests for the lecturers. Everyone was cordial and appreciative. That evening I gave a dinner for forty-six, the out-of-town guests and the institute staff, at the Mount Royal Club. There was such a feeling of friendship and congratulation that I went home very happy and sort of surprised to be so.

"Next day the out-of-town guests stayed over and we gave them dinner in the evening at Montrose Avenue before their trains left.

---

* *Neurological Biographies and Addresses* (London: Oxford University Press, 1936).
† See note 64.

"Now that they are all gone, Helen and I have run away. I am closing the farm operation here, and having some work done, and sleeping. Helen too is planning and sleeping. She made a wonderful hostess. It made all the difference."

We have come to the end of an adventure in medicine and science. The autobiography that is part of it is, at least, accurate thanks to my mother, who kept and copied my letters to her.

I claim no particular credit for the "germinal idea." It had to do with the institute, of course. But the idea was so obvious and inevitable if one were ever to carry out the purpose that had come to me — to understand the brain and the mind of man, or even to approach this task.

I believe with Robert Oppenheimer that there is something mysterious about the evolution of human opportunity for one who is playing a valid role in science. I would, myself, extend what he says beyond the limits of pure science and apply it to all those who prepare sincerely and well, and who work to make this world a better place in which to live.

"Our faith [as Oppenheimer phrased it] — our binding quiet faith — is that knowledge is good. . . . So it is with us as scientists, so it is with us as men. We are at once instrument and end, discoverers and teachers, actors and observers." *

When I suggest that all who sincerely seek the truth and labor, after adequate preparation, to make the world a better place in which to live might easily discover that they share the "binding quiet faith" of thoughtful physicists, I speak from experience.

I am sure that it must have been with others as it was with me: When one finds his work in the world and begins to carry it out, he may make a thrilling discovery — that he is in some sort of partnership with the Creator of the Universe.

Good-bye to you readers who may have come with me on this conducted tour through boyhood and manhood that ends with the opening of the Montreal Neurological Institute. I tried to write understandably and to think simply, hoping that many might find it intriguing to follow a true adventure on through real life to the end of the telling.

---

* See note 65.

Alan Gregg

Epilogue

S omeone else may choose to tell the story of the institute after its doors opened in 1934. It is not my purpose to attempt that, although I have made a brief reference to events that led to the second foundation of the Montreal Neurological Institute, nineteen years after the opening.*

Rather, in this epilogue, I want to speak once more of my friend Alan Gregg and to recall one last time those people and events that shaped my life.

When Alan Gregg came to us at the time of the second foundation, his personality seemed unchanged. He was quickly responsive, warmhearted and even more prone to tell stories. The shaggy brows, beneath which his eyes twinkled, were white now, as was his hair. A mellower understanding seemed to have come to his mind. He pointed out, with a chuckle, that "the greatest and deepest need of any medical institute is to be needed."

In his formal address, he stated his conclusion as to the art of effective giving in two brief paragraphs.

"As one," he said, "who has had thirty years' experience, both direct and vicarious, with widely different forms of financial sup-

---

* See note 66.

port to institutes and departments of medicine and surgery and various special fields, I believe that endowment — whether from government or private sources — is the soundest way to secure optimum results when it is certain the work to be done is needed.

"The steady confidence that is conferred by endowment calls out from scientists honesty and steadfastness of purpose; the hesitant uncertainty of short-term grants all but insults the intelligence, if not the sincerity of the recipient, and certainly makes a mockery of long-term planning. Experience is our teacher in this matter."

We who received the Rockefeller help might have made reply here from our experience. If Gregg had recommended that the Rockefeller Foundation should give us a corresponding sum of money over the years, in successive short-term grants, this institute would never have been born. (Or its birth would have been another undertaking.) And how much less enduring would have been the reasons for our gratitude.

Finally, Alan Gregg in his formal address turned to the Montreal institute itself:

". . . If I were asked," he said, "to name a single grant that the Medical Sciences Division of the foundation has made since 1931 that I consider ideal in purpose, in performance, in local response and in national and international influence, and in the character of our relationships maintained from the very beginning, I would say without a moment's hesitation the grant to the Neurological Institute of McGill University." *

Does this come to the eye of the reader as an unseemly boast? The members of a team rejoice if a goal is scored. They are proud when the team goes through a reasonably successful season. But there is no cause for any one person to blush because of the wonderful tribute Gregg paid us at the end of nineteen years. We place his tribute on the record with pleasure and take this opportunity to return our thanks.

We will always be grateful to the founder of the Rockefeller Foundation, of course, for the initial creative gift of money that came across the border from the United States to Canada in 1934. But most enduring will be our sense of gratitude because of the

* See note 67.

way in which the money was handled, creating an institute, endowing it, and leaving it to put down its own regional roots and thus to grow into a human institution that will live on into the foreseeable future.

Gregg seemed to believe that history would repeat itself for the good of mankind. He gave an address at the Johns Hopkins Hospital, in 1950, in which he described a "heritage of excellence ready at any time to burst into bloom again." Indeed, one who was recently dean of that medical school borrowed that phrase for his outstanding book, *Heritage of Excellence.**

But excellence is a word that only historians may use. What can we, as workers, hand on here in Montreal? Only this — a heritage of effort and achievement and a heritage of hope. This we can bequeath.

Those who have explored together and who have heard the "everlasting whisper" as they toiled along, side by side at bench or at bedside, have already shared a common excitement. Such a man is changed by this contagious experience. He becomes an explorer. And thus, one worker passes on, inevitably, a heritage of achievement, whether discoveries loom large or small in the years as they pass.

Each member of the team knows full well that he has a further responsibility of his own. He should, from time to time, write out for others to read his own reply to the "everlasting whisper." That explains why, in 1973, I dropped my work on this present manuscript, *No Man Alone,* for a whole year and wrote an account of my own exploration of brain and mind. It was the account of a pilgrim's progress that had begun when the institute was opened in 1934 and continued up to the time of the writing.†

I have seen myself succeeded by able men in what we have come to call the M.N.I. (Montreal Neurological Institute), and I remember how Gregg laughed at himself when he was about to retire. "Nothing succeeds," he said and chuckled, "nothing succeeds like

---

* Thomas B. Turner, *Heritage of Excellence* (Baltimore and London: Johns Hopkins University Press, 1974).
† This interim book was entitled *The Mystery of the Mind: A Critical Study of Consciousness and the Human Brain,* with discussions by Dr. William Feindel, Professor Charles Hendel and Sir Charles Symonds (Princeton and London: Princeton University Press, 1975).

successors." The joke may not have applied in his case, but I have found it apt enough in my own.

Theodore Rasmussen succeeded me as the director and playing captain on an ever-stronger team. He returned to Montreal from Chicago University in 1954 and began the takeover six years later in 1960, when I did finally drop the reins of directorship.

It was Ted Rasmussen, later on, who insisted I should tell the story I have finished at last in this book. It was his idea that the story should come to its end at the time of the opening in 1934, which it does. Neither Rasmussen nor William Feindel, who has now succeeded him, had anyone to help him quite like Bill Cone. Cone died, alas, in 1959, the year before my final retirement, and I realize that he took something of me with him.*

There is a gay, generous, helpful spirit that has come to dwell in the Montreal Neurological Institute. Many have contributed to it, as Bill Cone did. Many have delighted in it, but none can take it away. When I study the photograph on page 343, taken some forty years after the founding of the Neurological Institute, I seem to see three men who are proud to be, or to have been, a part of this continuing fabulous enterprise. In any case, I can discover little evidence that either hard work or success has weighed very heavily upon any one of the three directors.

Things changed as soon as the institute opened. The building had no sooner been completed in 1934 than new clinical approaches to neuroscience made it necessary to provide for certain work we had not visualized. So a temporary addition was built, with prompt Rockefeller and J. W. McConnell aid, at the back of our stone building to house a new Department of Electroencephalography. That made it possible to bring Herbert Jasper on the staff to develop this specialty and to collaborate with us, and with me in particular, in my own approach to neurophysiology. Not long afterward, the coming of K.A.C. Elliott to the M.N.I. meant the birth of neurochemistry here as a clinical and basic discipline.†

After William Feindel, on whose well-ordered desk the institute's present plans for building and for future achievement lie, had read the manuscript of this book, he quoted from Shakespeare's *Tempest:* "What is past," he said, "is prologue."

* See note 68.
† See note 69.

Left to right: Theodore Rasmussen, director, M.N.I., 1960 to 1972; William Feindel, director, M.N.I., 1972 onward; Wilder Penfield, director, M.N.I., 1934 to 1960. Photograph by Judy Little, 1974, on the occasion of the fortieth anniversary of the birth of the Montreal Neurological Institute in 1934.

I am content to leave it at that. Biography and history can do nothing better than to formulate, from time to time, prophetic prologues for the next generation.

The steady flow of recruits who come to the Montreal Neurological Institute brings a sense of happy security for the future. Thus, many able workers are doing, and many more will do, what no man alone could do.

The objectives of these men are clear and greatly varied. The scientists among us seek full knowledge of the brain of man. Some seek an understanding of his mind. The clinicians seek wisdom in the field of human behavior, even though it must be based upon the half-truth that is ours today. The clinicians, too, seek wise ways of cure for their patients and enlightenment that will help them meet the most crying needs of man and his vast family.

No man alone — these words have been repeated so often in the pages of this book! But one discovers that they have taken on a deeper meaning. Workers have need of the genius and the criticism of other workers, of course. But beyond that, they should come in time to read the design and the purposes of the Creator of our Universe, and seek to know his will.

Notes

1 (reference from page 9). The career plans of my most intimate friends were varied. My roommate, William Chester from Milwaukee, was planning to go into law. Francis Hall, from Boston, was going to Harvard Medical School. Paul Myers, his roommate, was going into law and politics. He, like me, would have to earn the money to put himself through the graduate years. Max Chaplin, from a New York suburb, was going to be a minister and perhaps a missionary.

These were close friends. We formed a club for the discussion of literature and life that met occasionally of an evening. Because its avowed purpose was conversation, like that of Dr. Samuel Johnson's famous Literary Club, we often referred to it as the Johnson Club. The role of Johnsonian leadership was played by Chaplin, although the ablest conversationalist was Myers. After graduation from Princeton, the members of the Johnson Club continued to gather almost annually (with their wives who, *mirabile dictu*, proved to be congenial) in various pleasant places in the United States or Canada for meetings that might last for a weekend or even a fortnight.

2 (reference from page 31). Beyond medicine, how curious that Dr. Green and I should have read Xenophon's *Anabasis*. Xenophon was a Greek soldier, but also a scholar. His *Anabasis* was his journal account of the retreat of a mercenary army of ten thousand Greeks after its defeat in far-off Persia. They marched up the Tigris River, through the mountains, and back to the Mediterranean and Greece. Xenophon described Greek thought and life against a Persian background. Xenophon was himself a pupil of Socrates and a contempo-

345

rary of Hippocrates in the early fourth century before Christ. I little suspected then that I would myself one day write the story of Hippocrates, the Father of Scientific Medicine, in the form of historical fiction,* and that I would be so thankful for this early familiarity with Greek life and language.

It was not until I returned to Harvard to give the Dunham Lectures in 1949 that I met Robert Green again. He was quite celebrated among Harvard graduates by that time, as an outstanding teacher of anatomy. He had carried on in the high tradition of Oliver Wendell Holmes, who was an obstetrician, author and poet, as well as the professor of anatomy and physiology at Harvard for thirty-five years (1847–1882).

3 (reference from page 36). William Osler (1849–1919) was born in Ontario, educated at Trinity College School, Toronto University, and McGill University. Beginning at the age of twenty-six, he occupied the chair of medicine at McGill, and then, in succession, at Pennsylvania, Johns Hopkins and Oxford. At Johns Hopkins (1889–1905), he wrote his famous textbook of medicine and was one of the founders of that new hospital and medical school, along with William Halsted and William Welch. Osler may be said to have introduced the technique of bedside teaching there, following the tradition of Edinburgh that had come to him at the Montreal General Hospital. (He had also seen the technique used during his graduate study years in Germany.) While in Baltimore, he led in the movement to abolish what I may call hearsay or traditional therapy. He depended only on accurate diagnosis and specific therapy when it existed. He showed how to use wise psychology always.

At Oxford his interest turned to literature and medical history and the gathering of a medical library, which he was eventually to leave to McGill University. In these thirteen years of relative retirement, he rounded out his remarkable career, and taught English-speaking physicians around the world through his essays and addresses.

In those days, the medical school at Oxford covered only the first half of each medical student's teaching course. This they did extremely well, devoting three years to it. But the students were forced to go on to the clinical years in one of the hospitals of London, or elsewhere, as I did in the Johns Hopkins Hospital. The same was true in Cambridge University at that time.

4 (reference from page 59). Abraham Flexner had been a schoolteacher, headmaster of a successful private school in Louisville, Kentucky. He

---

* *The Torch* (Boston: Little, Brown, 1960).

left this to take his doctorate at Harvard University, following which he carried out a survey of medical teaching in the United States and Canada. His famous report, in 1909, to the Carnegie Foundation resulted in the closure of the poorer schools of medicine in the United States and Canada. It initiated healthy introspection and reorganization in the better ones. In 1910, Flexner became a member of the General Education Board. Medical philanthropy in the United States at that time came under the board. In all, seventy-eight million dollars was spent in this excellent campaign, beginning with Johns Hopkins. But not even in the vast Rockefeller reservoir was there enough money to make Flexner's scheme work without some modifications.

5 (reference from page 60). Recently, while busy with this chapter, I wrote to Harry Murray. He had become a psychologist and was, until recently, a professor at Harvard, but in 1920 to 1921, he was planning to become a surgeon. His reply, which came from Cambridge, Massachusetts, December 1971, is amusing:

"Dear Pen," he wrote. "We met (you and I) in 1920, at the International Congress of Physiology at which some researches . . . that I had conducted at Harvard were reported by L. J. Henderson (who originated the hypotheses). I was about to return to the U.S.A. to start my surgical internship at the Presbyterian Hospital. My high estimation of you — at first sight — was largely determined by your presence at the Congress, and thus your exemplification of the principle which I had adopted for my own life: that a surgeon should undertake fundamental researches related to his elected field of technical operations. You, I would guess, were the *only* surgeon at the Congress; and I was the only would-be surgeon (possibly). It was easy to spot *you,* since you were already doing to some extent what I was dreaming of doing. 'It takes a thief to catch a thief.' . . ."

6 (reference from page 65). The applied research that William Clarke had proposed to me is not difficult for the uninitiated to understand. The brain and spinal cord constitute the central nervous system. They are vastly complicated, it is true, being made up of nerve cells and fibers all individually insulated and carrying electrical impulses in circuits that control the body and serve the purposes of the mind.

But the enveloping membranes that cover the brain, the arteries and veins that enter and leave it and the "third circulation" within and about it are easily understood.

The central nervous system is separated from the rest of the body by a double layer of connective tissue called the meninges. The outer layer, named, by anatomists of old time, the "hard mother," or *dura mater,* is a tough sheath. The inner layer is more delicate. It was called the "soft mother," or *pia mater*. The cerebrospinal fluid is water in which certain salts are dissolved. It is formed within the cavities of the brain, the ventricles, and flows out to surround the brain and spinal cord beneath the pia mater, where the fluid is constantly being absorbed.

Thus, the brain and the spinal cord float, one might say, in a circulating watery bed (the "third circulation" of Cushing). The meninges, and the fluid, form a remarkable protecting and insulating barrier that delimits and surrounds man's central nervous system.

When a bullet or a fragment of bone or the surgeon's knife penetrates the pia mater, the spinal fluid leaks out for a while. Then it stops and the break in the insulation heals if there is no infection. (Infection might mean death from meningitis.) But when the meninges heal a mixed scar results. This meningeal scar is an abnormal mixture of nervous and body elements. Our problem was to identify the cells involved in this healing and scarring of the brain. The hope was to discover, if possible, why some scars produce epilepsy.

7 (reference from page 86). Frank Meleney, a remarkable young surgeon and bacteriologist, who had just returned from the Peking Union Medical College in China; John Hanford, a quiet, skilled member of what has since come to be called the Whipple school of surgery; and Fred Van Buren, no less skilled.

8 (reference from page 86). A small group of young surgeons, of whom I was one, gathered in New York in 1923 to found the Halsted Club, later called the Halsted Society. Years afterward (1969), I found the opportunity to pay tribute to Halsted in a published paper: "Halsted of Johns Hopkins: The Man and His Problem as Described in the Secret Records of William Osler," *Journal of the American Medical Association,* 210:2214–2218, 1969.

9 (reference from page 94). The metallic methods, used for selective demonstration of cell groups in the nervous system, attracted attention when Camillo Golgi used silver to demonstrate neurons. As already described in the text, Golgi and Cajal were awarded the Nobel Prize in 1906 for their demonstration of the finer structure of nerve cells, using these techniques.

The demonstration of the vastly numerous non-nervous cells within the central nervous system is another story, however: W. Robertson used platinum impregnation to demonstrate what he called "mesoglia" in 1900. Cajal described the gold chloride-sublimate method for neuroglia in 1913 and 1920. Finally, Pio del Rio-Hortega described a silver method that would demonstrate what he called the microglia and the oligodendroglia in 1918 and 1920. All of the glia cells (*glia* is the Greek word for "glue"), taken together with the blood vessel cells, constitute the non-nervous, or interstitial, tissue of the brain. These are quite different from neurons, or nerve cells. The non-nervous cells react vigorously to infection or injury.

10 (reference from page 107). At this period, Percival Bailey and G. Hiller (1924), working in Cushing's laboratory in Boston, A. Ganz (1923) in Holland, and A. Metz and H. Spatz (1924) in Munich, had begun to use Hortega's published method to study microglia. The Germans and Dutchmen called them "Hortega cells."

11 (reference from page 110). "Al illustre neurólogo . . . homenaje de consideración y de cordial simpátia de S. Ramón Cajal, Madrid 9 de Julio del 1924." The autograph may be translated: "To the distinguished neurologist Dr. Wilder Penfield, a tribute of respect and cordial sympathy from S. Ramón Cajal, Madrid, July 9, 1924."

12 (reference from page 112). After I returned from Spain I wrote several biographical essays: "The Career of Ramón y Cajal," *Archives of Neurology and Psychiatry*, 15:213–220, 1926; "Santiago Ramón y Cajal, 1852–1934," *Archives of Neurology and Psychiatry*, 33:172–173, 1935; an obituary of Hortega, "Pio del Rio-Hortega, 1882–1945," *Archives of Neurology and Psychiatry*, 54:413–416, 1945.

13 (reference from page 117). Frederick Tilney, professor of neurology at Columbia, was a man of great drive, a leader in neurology and the real architect of the modern Neurological Institute of New York.

As a young man, Tilney had been a neuroanatomist at Columbia University, a prolific writer and a vigorous leader of neurologists. But in later years, his mind had come to be occupied with ambitious administration and the cares of a lucrative practice. Tilney's predicament was a good example of how difficult it would be to create, in the midst of this great metropolis, the quiet thoughtful atmosphere for any field of clinical medicine. Albert Lamb, in his excellent story of the Columbia-Presbyterian Medical Center, referred to the "hurlyburly of New York" as compared to the relative quiet to be found for medicine in Baltimore at that period.*

New York had its threats as well as its advantages. Unless a successful physician was protected by some modification of the full-time system of practice, as we were in the Presbyterian Hospital, New York might well prove to be too much for even the most idealistic and energetic of academic clinicians. Tilney was all of these things. He was ambitious, idealistic, hardworking, creative, but he was also a successful practitioner. Some of his wealthy patients contributed money to

---

* Albert R. Lamb, *The Presbyterian Hospital and the Columbia-Presbyterian Medical Center* (New York: Columbia University Press, 1955), p. 167.

promote his plans for the institute. His able young assistant, Henry A. Riley, carried on their authorship of the Tilney and Riley textbook of neuroanatomy.*

But in time, Tilney the builder became too busy to teach or to do research. So it was that William Cone came to work with me in 1924.

14 (reference from page 119). The Laboratory of Neurocytology was formally a part of the laboratory of surgical pathology of which Arthur Purdy Stout was chief. He was an able pupil of William Clarke, who was still teaching students how wounds heal in the medical school across Central Park. Stout was to succeed to Clarke's title as professor of surgical pathology at the Columbia Medical Center in a few years.

15 (reference from page 120). This letter that I wrote in 1926 shows how much I had in common with these two young neurosurgeons. Something beyond the practical aspect of neurosurgery was then the true objective of each of these two young men, both of whom were to become leaders in our profession. Subsequently Percival Bailey went to the University of Chicago as neurosurgeon. Years later, he was professor of psychiatry at the University of Illinois in Chicago. His initial basic approach to the nervous system was by way of anatomy and the microscopic pathology of brain tumors.

In addition to neurosurgery, Dr. Loyal Davis carried out basic research, at Chicago's Northwestern University, on the physiology of decerebrate rigidity in animals, the problem I had proposed to study on my visit to Detroit in 1921. Davis operated on a long series of experimental animals with his associate, the neurologist Lewis Pollock. Instead of cutting through the brain stem by the Sherrington method, as we had done, they produced a transverse lesion by what they called "the anemic method," tying off the nutrient arteries to the midbrain.

16 (reference from page 121). Throughout the field of neurology, the microscopic structure of the nervous system had rather suddenly become a subject of great interest. There were numerous reasons for this. Physiologists wanted to know which cell types might be identified with this or that function in the brain. Pathologists wanted to know what cellular elements gave rise to the tumors that grew so frequently within the skull. Neurologists and psychiatrists hoped to see clearly the cell changes that might accompany all the diseases that attacked the nervous system.

17 (reference from page 130). Paul Hoeber was at that time publishing Cowdrey's *Special Cytology* (New York: Hoeber, 1928) and I had my-

---

* Frederick Tilney and H. A. Riley, *The Form and Function of the Central Nervous System* (New York: Hoeber, 1938).

self contributed one chapter to it entitled "Neuroglia and Microglia: The Interstitial Tissues of the Central Nervous System."

18 (reference from page 130). *Cytology and Cellular Pathology of the Nervous System* was long in the editing and the publishing. But it appeared in print at last from the house of Hoeber, New York, 1932, in three beautiful volumes. When, eventually, the first edition of this reference book went out of print, I received letters of inquiry from laboratories all over the world. But I was too busy making clinical use of what I had learned to undertake a second edition. At long last, in 1965, Hafner, New York, reprinted it without change.

19 (reference from page 137). When Professor Oertel returned, empty-handed, in the spring of 1923, from his search for likely candidates for the post of chief surgeon in the Royal Victoria, he reported to the president of the board of hospital governors, Sir Vincent Meredith. One can only conclude that Meredith then undertook to scout for himself.

He and Lady Meredith were to be in Great Britain that spring, 1923, in any case. Sir Vincent seems to have interviewed at least one possible candidate. There is no official record of this, but the Meredith chauffeur, Donald McLean, who was himself born in Aberdeen, tells me this: "When Sir Vincent and his lady returned from abroad, I drove to the dock to meet them. On getting into the car, Sir Vincent remarked: 'McLean, we have found a famous doctor for the Royal Victoria Hospital. He comes from Aberdeen like you.'"

Not long after this, a "famous doctor" arrived in Montreal. He was Sir Henry Gray, a Scottish surgeon. It was said that Gray had been assured that the chair of surgery at McGill would come to him, in due course, after he assumed his duties as chief surgeon. He inspected the hospital. Shortly after this, he was appointed to the post of surgeon in chief by Meredith, acting for the governors' House Committee. The appointment was announced, as Sclater Lewis points out, in the Scottish press in April 1923. But official notification of it did not reach the hospital's medical board until two months later.*

Meanwhile, the combined hospital and university Selection Committee, the existence of which had been ignored by Meredith, had proceeded to recommend Edward Archibald, aged fifty-one. He was duly appointed professor of surgery by the university. Thus, there were two surgical chiefs at the Royal Victoria, one in charge of teaching, the other in charge of the surgical patients.

---

* D. Sclater Lewis, *The Royal Victoria Hospital, 1887–1947* (Montreal: McGill University Press, 1969).

Henry Gray, aged fifty-three, was a forceful, rugged Scot, born and educated in Aberdeen, an energetic surgeon of very long experience, being a veteran of the Boer War as well as of the 1914–1918 war. In Aberdeen, Gray had not been made professor. He had the reputation of being peculiarly independent.

In Montreal, Sir Henry proved to be a good-hearted man, kind to his patients, rough and ready, blunt and tactless. If he had been told that he would be made professor, it must have been difficult for him to adjust. He tried, unsuccessfully, to reorganize the academic Department of Surgery. He tried to take over the teaching of medical students. He was blocked, of course, in both these attempts, by Charles Martin, the dean, and by Archibald, the professor. Meanwhile, relations between the hospital president and the dean of medicine were less than cordial.

Gray declared that he could operate just as well without wearing rubber gloves. The wearing of sterilized gloves was a habit that had been introduced to surgeons by William Halsted, at the Johns Hopkins, in 1890. As the years passed, it had come to be an almost universal precaution to prevent infection.

At the end of two years, in 1925, tragedy struck in the wards of the Royal Victoria Hospital. There was a sudden outbreak of what every surgeon fears, gloves or no gloves — postoperative infection. It had come to Gray's patients. Whether this was due to the bare hands or to something else cannot be decided now. There was, however, a storm of amazed criticism and Sir Henry resigned from the Royal Victoria to set up his own small private clinic elsewhere in the city. Thus, catastrophe brought an end to two years of unhappy friction at the R.V.H.

20 (reference from page 138). The donors were Sir George Stephen and Sir Donald Smith. These two merchant princes were first cousins, both of them born in Scotland. Because of their services to Canadian society, both were later elevated to the peerage — the one as Lord Mount Stephen, the other as Lord Strathcona and Mount Royal.

21 (reference from page 141). Edward Archibald was born in Montreal and reared there, the son of Judge John Spratt Archibald. He and his two brothers had the intellectual head start that comes to any early bilingual individual. Each boy took a part of his schooling in Grenoble, France. Subsequently, each had a distinguished professional career. The eldest, Sam, became professor of law at Cairo University and was later a highly successful practitioner of law in Paris. John was for a time a fellow of All Souls', Oxford, and later a barrister and solicitor in London.

Edward was twenty-one when the Royal Victoria was opened in

1893, an undergraduate at McGill, majoring in modern languages. He graduated in medicine there in 1896, having taken one year of his medical course in Europe, where he divided his time between the French University of Montpellier and the German University of Freiburg. He took his surgical training at the Royal Victoria and did a year of postgraduate medical study in Germany.

Returning to the Royal Victoria, he fell victim to tuberculosis but after a year, having taken the cure at Lake Saranac, he returned to surgery. Enforced inactivity inevitably mellows the mind and sensitizes the perceptions of a well-balanced man already endowed with intellect and culture. Certainly it was so with Archibald. But he derived other advantages from what seemed to be his great misfortune. He gained knowledge of the dread disease, pulmonary tuberculosis, and from the teaching received from Edward Livingston Trudeau, his physician at Saranac. Subsequently, in 1912, Archibald was to be the first surgeon in America to treat the disease by surgery (thoracoplasty).

But, after the tuberculosis and before he turned his attention to the surgery of the thorax, he had seen the need of developing neurosurgery. This was the period in which Harvey Cushing was doing the same in Baltimore. In 1906, Archibald spent three months of graduate study under Sir Victor Horsley at the National Hospital, Queen Square, London. In 1908, Archibald wrote the chapter "Surgical Affections and Wounds of the Head" for Bryant and Buck's *American Practice of Surgery*. In the same year, Harvey Cushing wrote a similar monograph, "Surgery of the Head," for another handbook, Keen's *System of Surgery*. These two men might well have advanced neurosurgery concurrently had not Archibald's attention been deflected (fortunately for me) to thoracic surgery.

W. E. Gallie, Toronto's leading teacher of surgery in a somewhat later period, wrote of Archibald that he "changed the character of surgical education in this country from the purely clinical to the scientific." Archibald's fame was bringing an excellent reputation to the Royal Victoria Hospital, a fact that seems to have escaped Meredith's attention. What Horst Oertel thought, who can say?

In any case, Gray came to the Royal Victoria as chief surgeon in 1923. Sir Henry Gray was a "character" and the two years during which he was chief surgeon had been a difficult time indeed for Archibald, the professor of surgery. Archibald, however, had carried on, with forbearance, as best he could. He, too, was a "character," a gentle and forgiving one, a dreamer and an idealist and a scholar.

It is surprising to discover that Archibald's publications on the surgical treatment of pulmonary tuberculosis, which absorbed his attention at the time, continued right through the period of the Meredith-Gray affair. He published six papers on the surgery of the thorax in 1922, one in 1923, three in 1924 and five in 1925. Within the hospital, a group of excellent young surgeons had already gathered about Archibald: F.A.C. Scrimger, Gavin Miller, John Armour, Archibald Wilkie, C. A. McIntosh, Howard Dawson, Donald Webster. In 1928, Norman Bethune was added to the group.

As Meakins was to express it in his eventual tribute to Archibald, the latter began in Montreal with "thirty years of academic sterility behind him." R. A. Macbeth wrote recently in a Glasgow University publication, "Archibald emerges as the first true surgical scientist of note on the Canadian scene."

Archibald was an eloquent speaker in either English or French. He delighted in prolonged discussions at the Mount Royal Club. But most of his discussions and much of his thinking were carried out in hospital corridors or on the street, where he might stand oblivious of the flight of time. On one occasion, he was discovered reading a medical journal, sitting on the back seat of his car before the hospital. It had slipped his mind that his chauffeur was away on holiday!

Of course, his tardiness was very trying, at times, to his associates as well as to his patients. Dr. William Howell, who was anesthetist in chief at the Royal Victoria, and a medical historian in his spare time, probably waited longer hours for Archibald than anyone else, excepting only Mrs. Archibald (the former Agnes Barron). Nevertheless, with the exception of her, I suppose, no one loved him more than Howell.

In preparation for a small congratulatory ovation tendered Archibald when news came that he was to receive an honorary doctorate from the University of Paris, Howell wrote some doggerel verse. I quote from it now, not because of its poetic beauty (?), but because what the doggerel said was true. Here is part of Howell's tribute to Archibald: *

> *You've only brains and industry,*
> *Good breeding, kindness, modesty,*
> *The faculty of making friends*
> *With ne'er a thought to serve your ends;*
> *Sound judgement, sympathy and skill*
> *To comfort and to heal the ill.*

---

* See also "Edward Archibald" by W. Penfield, *Canadian Journal of Surgery,* 1:167–174, 1958.

> *O Edward, you would be sublime,*
> *If only you could be on time.*

Sir Vincent Meredith was born in 1850 in London, Ontario, and was educated there briefly, for he began to work for the Bank of Montreal as a boy of seventeen. Eventually he was transferred to Montreal and, at the age of thirty-eight (1888), he married Isabel Brenda Allan, the daughter of Andrew Allan, vice-president of the Allan Shipping Line. In 1913, Meredith was elected president of the Bank of Montreal and, in the same year, president of the Royal Victoria Hospital. In 1914 he was created a baronet in recognition of the significant assistance he was giving to the Canadian war effort during the First World War.

Thus, the president of the Royal Victoria Hospital during the nineteen twenties was a forceful, self-made man. In 1923, he seems to have agreed with George Armstrong, the retiring chief surgeon and professor, accepting his opinion that a practical surgeon would be better for his hospital (and more likely to fill the private wards) than would a so-called research surgeon like Archibald. So in 1923 he invited Sir Henry Gray from Aberdeen to become chief surgeon.

22 (reference from page 141). Malloch was a former Montrealer who had given up internal medicine to follow his interest in medical history. He had been called to New York to be director of the famous medical library of the Academy of Medicine there. I had known him when I was an undergraduate at Oxford and he was a Beit Memorial fellow studying in England. His life, like mine, had been deeply influenced by William Osler.

23 (reference from page 147). Horst Oertel had been born in Leipzig in 1873. He graduated in medicine at Yale University in the United States. He then returned to Germany to study music and philosophy at Würzburg. Following that, he took his graduate training in the laboratory of the great German pathologist Rudolf Virchow, who died in 1902 at the age of eighty-one and who was justly considered the founder of cellular pathology. Oertel then returned to the United States, where he taught pathology for a time. Later, he joined the staff of Guy's Hospital, London. From there he was called to McGill University as professor of pathology in the spring of 1914.

He wrote a textbook of pathology and followed it step by step in his class lectures. In spite of this, or perhaps because of it, he was immensely popular with the undergraduates.

Professor Oertel was a bachelor who lived at the Ritz Carlton and enjoyed good conversation and music. He became the staunch sup-

porter of Sir Vincent Meredith, the hospital's president, and he, with
certain of his medical cronies, was a popular dinner companion of
another prominent Montreal bachelor, Sir Edward Beatty, longtime
president of the Canadian Pacific Railway and also chancellor of Mc-
Gill University. Beatty's mansion, like that of Meredith, looked down
on the city of Montreal from the south side of Pine Avenue as it ran
over the shoulder of Mount Royal. The Royal Victoria and the Pathological Institute were farther along to the east on the north side.

Dr. Rocke Robertson, principal and vice-chancellor of McGill University from 1963 to 1970, who was a medical student in 1928, has
written, at my request, a very different portrait of Oertel from my
own. "I have been," Robertson says, "as you know, a great admirer of
him. I can well imagine how stubborn, domineering and difficult he
was and I am quite sure he would have blocked your way if he could
have, and this would have done a great disservice to the university.

"At the same time, some of the qualities that made him so unpopu-
lar with those who might compete or work against him were the very
features that impressed his students, both undergraduate and graduate. He was domineering to students in the most extreme way, and
frightening, but precise and intelligent and with a touch of grim
humor that saved many a tense situation.

"You have said, in the biographical note which you sent me, that he
followed the text of his book on pathology step by step in his lectures,
and this is largely true, but I think what made him popular and certainly impressed the students most, in my experience, was the way in
which he conducted his Saturday morning clinics in the Pathological
Institute. These clinics were supposed to be given to fourth year students, but any third year or fifth year students who could possibly
get away on Saturday morning would flock to these clinics, and the
amphitheater was always filled to the brim and vibrating with excitement."

24 (reference from page 147). Professor Meakins's son, Dr. Jonathan F.
Meakins, told me recently that his father had described this discussion
to him more than once before his death. Until that morning, the idea
that he could or should squeeze this lusty infant laboratory into his
own, already crowded, rooms had never crossed his mind. But, suddenly, he saw the whole proposal about to collapse, and he made
what he called a split-second decision.

25 (reference from page 149). Dr. Lewis Reford and Mr. A. A. Hodgson,
a Montreal businessman, had married the daughters of Mr. Duncan
McIntyre. Dr. Reford's words did much to make up for the hurt I
had carried away from the meeting with Oertel. Reassurance from

them, I surmised, may well have explained Archibald's sudden telegram after seven months of silence. Mr. McIntyre did so much for medical education that the McIntyre Medical Sciences Building was eventually to be built on his property and named gratefully for him.

I discovered, too, inadvertently, that various individual surgeons on the Royal Victoria Hospital Medical Board had volunteered to help Archibald make up his deficit, if my own income from private practice should fall below a certain level during the inauguration of the plan.

26 (reference from page 157). It is a curious coincidence that, while the manuscript of this chapter was still on my desk, Edgar Kahn, a neurosurgeon who was then engaged in writing his own autobiography, sent me pages from his manuscript in which he described Hamilton's operation. He had used his daily diary to recall the details. He stated that he and Dr. Max Peet of Ann Arbor, Michigan, were in my operating room that morning, a fact that I had forgotten.*

Kahn was Peet's surgical assistant at that time. He stated, further, that when the scar and brain had been widely exposed, I turned to Dr. Peet (whom I knew well and admired greatly) and asked him what he would do. Peet replied: "I'd remove the whole damn thing!" He meant, of course, all that was abnormal. Kahn suggested that the radical removal that followed was the first large brain removal, or lobectomy, of its kind to his knowledge.

27 (reference from page 161). When the New York Neurological Institute finally followed the Presbyterian Hospital and the College of Physicians and Surgeons of Columbia University uptown to 168th Street on March 6, 1929, the hospital services of neurology and neurosurgery for the whole new medical center were transferred to the institute. Thus the ambition of Tilney was fulfilled. He was not the founder but he organized and established this great center for neurological study and treatment. Neurology and neurosurgery were not combined in one academic department. Charles Elsberg had developed neurosurgery in the Neurological Institute of New York from its very foundation in 1909 onward. In 1944, Elsberg wrote an interesting history of the institution from 1909 to 1938, *The Story of a Hospital* (New York: Hoeber, 1944).

28 (reference from page 162). This sum of twenty-two hundred dollars had been arranged by agreement between the hospital's medical board and the superintendent to cover services in the way of reports that our Laboratory of Neuropathology would have been expected to

---

* E. A. Kahn, *Journal of a Neurosurgeon* (Springfield, Ill.: Charles C. Thomas, 1972).

make to the rest of the hospital. It was in addition to the support promised by Archibald's anonymous friends in the Reford-Hodgson families, which was to be paid as promised. The "money available" that I expected to use to replace the hospital's contribution was in a small fund, the residue of money given me by grateful New York patients, to be used as I liked for my research projects, and unexpended at the time of my departure from New York.

29 (reference from page 163). The major study periods spent abroad were important in my wife's career as well as in mine. Helen and I had been engaged to be married in August 1914. Subsequently she taught school for a year, then returned to Milwaukee Downer College to complete her university training, and prepare for her subsequent career by taking German and French as well as history and literature, while I went off to carry out my first two years as medical student.

After our marriage in June 1917, we left immediately for five months of wartime hospital service in France in which both of us served and learned in different ways. The two years 1919 to 1921, Helen spent with me at Oxford and London as mother and wife while I carried out my postgraduate medical studies. In 1924 came the romantic and illuminating six months of study in Madrid with the Spanish histologists and finally, in 1928, these six months of living in Germany.

There, I could now prepare to launch the many-sided work of a neurological institute. And there our children could have the advantage of a bilingual conditioning of the brain that inevitably promotes ability and the career of any well-educated man or woman.

My wife made of our family and of my professional career a life project of managing and teaching. Thanks to that, many things came to us. Happiness was one of them. Perhaps one might say that such success as came to me professionally is another.

30 (reference from page 170). Vladimir Ilich Lenin had a first stroke in 1922 and a second, more crippling stroke, in 1923. During the latter episode, he lost control of speech. Foerster told me that, during his visits to Moscow, he was questioned anxiously by many members of the inner political coterie. Lenin's death, in 1924, opened the contest for succession, and was followed by a free-for-all struggle among the Communist giants.

31 (reference from page 171). There are many intriguing sidelights that one could throw on the surgeons and neurologists in the days when modern neurosurgery first stood on its feet as a specialty. Harvey Cushing had talents outside the field of technical surgery. He was a compulsive and artistic intellectual by the time he moved from Baltimore to Boston in 1913. He had been inspired by the great physician,

who was also a great humanist and scholar, William Osler, as well as by William Halsted, that rare Johns Hopkins surgeon who gave to the world local anesthesia and who conquered his own cocaine addiction while creating a new school of surgery in America.

Sir Geoffrey Jefferson of Manchester was a man of intriguing whimsical philosophies. He was a surgeon who schooled himself in neurology by direct observation of the patient after the manner of Hughlings Jackson. Sir Hugh Cairns was a rugged, likable Australian who brought the Cushing technique to London and later to Oxford, as Herbert Olivecrona did to Sweden and Norman Dott, a cultured Scottish technical genius, did to Scotland.

In France, Clovis Vincent eventually accomplished, in a sense, what Foerster had done in Germany. Vincent was a neurologist who assisted Thierry de Martel, a proud and brilliant technician in surgery. Vincent was vain as well as brilliant. But he combined neurology and surgery successfully after the death of Martel.

In Philadelphia, the excellent anatomist and neurologist William Spiller established effective teamwork with a surgical perfectionist, Charles Frazier. Together, they did much to advance the treatment of intractable pain. In Ann Arbor, one of Frazier's pupils, Max Peet, a homespun, likable man, became an excellent neurosurgeon and also a distinguished ornithologist. James C. White at the Massachusetts General Hospital in Boston, like his teacher in that hospital, Jason Mixter, was a cultured, sports-minded Bostonian who brought perspective and practical conclusions to the treatment of intractable pain.

But this is not the place to attempt to do justice to the story of the establishment of modern neurosurgery. In this process, surgery was introduced into neurology, or perhaps it was vice versa. Perhaps the surgeons had to become neurologists before deserving the title "neurosurgeon."

In the foregoing paragraphs, I have mentioned the names of some men I knew personally and came to admire. In doing so, I may well be unfair to others, more distant in place and interests, like Ernest Sachs in Saint Louis and Howard Naffziger in San Francisco.

The contribution of Walter Dandy to the establishment of neurosurgery was most important. Dandy was Halsted-trained, as Cushing was, but he lacked the things that Cushing acquired when he sought out the friendship of Osler. Generalization is dangerous and yet I would say that the best specialists are those who, in later life, keep the windows of the mind and the heart open to the world beyond their specialty.

32 (reference from page 171). They had two daughters, Margaret and

Marthe. Since the time of this description, both daughters have become biological scientists, the one in Scotland and the other in the United States. Like their mother before them, they have come to fame for their own research, quite independently.

33 (reference from page 176). This report, when finished, was sent to the Paris office of the foundation, where Dr. Alan Gregg was in charge of European affairs. He forwarded it, as I discovered later, to Dr. Richard Pearce in New York.

34 (reference from page 193). Colin K. Russel graduated in arts at McGill University in 1897 and in medicine in 1901. In his long vacations from medical school, he had taken part in historic explorations of the Canadian subarctic wilderness. In undergraduate life, he became a stalwart football player among other things. He spent three years in postgraduate neurological study after graduation. Neuroanatomy was his major interest and he had worked in the Neuroanatomical Institute of Constantin von Monakow in Zurich. Finally, during his training period, he had been appointed resident physician in the National Hospital, Queen Square, London, where he was a colleague of S. A. Kinnier Wilson and the immediate junior to Gordon Holmes, then pathologist to the hospital. Returning to Montreal, he became assistant to Dr. James Stewart, neurologist at the Royal Victoria Hospital.

35 (reference from page 195). Arthur W. Young and J. N. Petersen were assistants to Dr. Colin Russel, chief neurologist at the Royal Victoria. A. W. Morphy and Norman Viner were assistants to Fred MacKay, chief neurologist at the Montreal General. Other staff doctors soon began to join the conferences actively or passively, since the discussions were sometimes lively and made an excellent show.

36 (reference from page 196). Perhaps a brief reference should be made here to French-Canadian culture as it was in 1928 in the Province of Quebec. The system of education, as well as the language difference, had served to set the French Canadians apart, outnumbered and surrounded as they were (and are) by the English-speaking culture of the North American continent. The young professionals and artists of French Canada turned to France for graduate training and inspiration. But here, too, they discovered, on reaching Paris, that the culture in which they had grown up was different from the culture of France.

In French Canada, education had been supported and directed for four centuries by dedicated priests and nuns rather than by the ecclesiastical orders that sent them out from France or the Catholic Church in Rome. Education was religious in form but it was strongly classical in substance. French-Canadian culture, as I came to know it, was delightful and life in French Canada had certain greater satisfactions and virtues than were to be found in the English-speaking cultures of Canada and the United States.

I believe, with Gilbert Murray, that Greek thought and literature have in them, still, a strength and simplicity, an originality and beauty far too often missing in so-called modern thought and literature.*

The rapid change that has taken place since the "quiet revolution" in French-Canadian education during the nineteen fifties and sixties has accompanied the postwar economic retirement of church and private citizen in favor of the provincial government. Educators in this new regime should take care, then, that something quite unique and precious is not lost from the culture of a people. It was something that came to them through their familiarity with the classics in school and college. It was something, to use the words of an ancient decree by the Delphic oracle, that "made gentle the life of the world."

37 (reference from page 197). Pierre Masson was, at the time I came to Montreal, writing a chapter for my book, the *Cytology and Cellular Pathology of the Nervous System*. No one in the world had had more brilliant success in staining the cells of the nervous system by methods other than the silver impregnations. His special stains were in use everywhere.

38 (reference from page 198). Jean Saucier, from the Hôtel-Dieu, was a clinical neurologist whose graduate training had been carried out in France and also in the United States. In his spare time, he was an accomplished violinist. Two others should be mentioned. Emile Legrand, like Saucier, was on the clinical staff of the Hôtel-Dieu. He was a neuropsychiatrist, a delightful extrovert and a sportsman. Antonio Barbeau was an enthusiastic neurophysiologist from l'Université de Montréal. He had literary talent and he was a clinical neurologist too, with an interesting appointment on the staff of the Hospital for the Insane in the great Bordeaux Jail.

39 (reference from page 220). The contribution of Ruth Inglis to an understanding of the function of the right frontal lobe was a considerable one. My instinctive reaction was to withhold this case from publication. But, in 1935, more than six years later, I did what I believed she would have had me do. I published the case and two somewhat similar cases with the help of my associate, Dr. Joseph Evans, in *Brain*, March 1935. It had the title "The Frontal Lobe in Man: A Clinical Study of Maximum Removals."

* Gilbert Murray, *The Rise of the Greek Epic* (Oxford: Oxford University Press, 1907).

The end of Ruth's life came suddenly in September 1931, almost three years after my operation. Carl Rand, a distinguished neurosurgeon in Los Angeles and my friend, went to her home in Van Nuys then, bringing with him an assistant of Cyril B. Courville, pathologist at the College of Medical Evangelists, whose name I do not know. They carried out an autopsy at my request, and sent the brain to Montreal, where it was studied exhaustively.

Dr. Russel's thoughtful letter was published then in full. We concluded, from the three cases reported at that time, that Ruth, like the others, had lost some of her capacity for initiative and planned action. But there was no loss of capacity for insight and introspection, no change in what had been her normal behavior. My own assessment of her loss of brain function is as follows.

Fifteen months after the operation in Montreal, I was able to spend an evening in the Inglis home in Van Nuys. Ruth's husband, Jack Inglis, had become a widely respected educator. At home he was a high-spirited, devoted husband, who was also a patient and understanding one. Her children reflected the unselfish personality of their mother. This normal happy home provided a better background for study than the consulting room of any psychologist.

On the day of my arrival, Ruth had planned to get a simple supper for me and four members of her own family. She had looked forward to it with pleasure and had the whole day for preparation. This was a task she could have completed with ease ten years before. When the appointed hour arrived, she was in the kitchen, the food was all there, one or two things were on the stove, but the salad was not ready, the meat had not been started, and she was distressed and confused by her long continued effort alone. It seemed evident that she would never be able to get everything ready at once. With her husband's help, the task of preparation was quickly completed and the occasion went off successfully with the patient talking and laughing in an altogether normal way.

The right frontal lobe had been partly taken from her by the infiltration of the tumor, and I made the removal complete. She expressed the remaining functional deficit simply: "I can't think well enough."

I concluded that "the loss of the frontal lobe has, for its most important detectable sequel, impairment of those mental processes which are prerequisite to planned initiative."

40 (reference from page 227). Nevertheless, I was convinced that the plan I presented to him was the right one — to unite the neurological physicians and the neurological surgeons in one cooperative team; to iso-

late them with their patients in an independent university department together with selected basic scientists, and yet to keep the whole unit in close functional contact with all the other disciplines of medicine and surgery; and to develop neuropathology and neuroanatomy and, in time, neurophysiology, as an intellectual meeting ground with psychiatry and psychology. These things were not being done in the New York Neurological Institute, or in any other institution in the world.

41 (reference from page 231). For this new specialty, nurses were learning new techniques. They watched and recorded the signs and symptoms that were important, day and night. They saw and recorded for me the movements of each epileptic fit and asked the patient what he felt at the moment. At last I was beginning to learn the minute details of every fit and I felt a new excitement. And the patients themselves had begun to tell me what no patient would tell Professor Foerster because of his mantle of German discipline and awe that shut him off.

42 (reference from page 236). In the end, the boy was greatly improved by the operation, if not cured. It is an amusing commentary on our lack of caution that the father of this patient, on whom we decided to carry out this frankly experimental procedure, was Charles P. Howland of New Haven, Connecticut, a member of the board of trustees of the Rockefeller Foundation. Cobb was receiving a grant for neurological research from the foundation at that time and I had, to say the least, much to gain from the goodwill of this foundation, one of whose avowed purposes was to promote medical science.

43 (reference from page 246). The cases of Henry Howland and William Ottmann were never reported in a medical journal because they are part of a considerable series of operative cases in which I tried, subsequently, with varying success, to relieve patients of attacks by removal of vasomotor nerves on the arteries of the brain. The results were encouraging. But I never did report the series. I was not yet willing to recommend an operative procedure for general use by surgeons.

I continued my own effort to develop the operation of excising pathological areas of brain. Gradually, this took up more and more of my time as an operating surgeon and I abandoned the attempt to cure other types of epilepsy by altering the circulation of the brain. Perhaps some neurosurgeon will carry on, someday, where I left off.

44 (reference from page 255). Professional men sometimes have their hidden longings. With this check, I was to buy a better workbench for my study at home than I had ever hoped to own — a beautiful, big, rolltop desk — and I had two companion bookcases made to match.

They have stood by me now for forty-five years in times of work and reflection.

45 (reference from page 260). We had been forced to give up operating in the Montreal General Hospital since we concluded that the lives of patients might be in danger during the hours and days that followed each operation while Dr. Cone and I were busy in the laboratory. Since our laboratory was at the Royal Victoria, we were forced reluctantly to transfer patients for operation to the R.V.H. as a temporary measure until a neurosurgeon could be trained for the General's staff.

46 (reference from page 263). Edward was my first technician. Indeed, except for surgical interns who came and went in the Presbyterian Hospital in New York, he had been my first assistant. The story of our relationship is unusual.

It almost began when I was aboard the S.S. *Sussex* in the English Channel in 1916, waiting for the ship to sink. The bow of the ship had been blown off by a German torpedo. Our lifeboats had taken all the passengers and crew that could crowd into them and were rowing toward France or England, leaving a hundred or so souls on board the ship, which, we supposed, was sinking. We were out of sight of land. The sea was calm on a sunny March afternoon. Smoke appeared on the horizon and then a ship. It came directly toward us. The remaining passengers and crew about me shouted and crowded the rail, ecstatic with newfound hope. The boat grew larger. Then suddenly we saw it alter its course and steam away over the horizon.

Edward was a cabin boy aboard that ship, which, he told me years later, was a Norwegian trawler under strict instructions from the owners to stay away from sinking vessels for fear of further attack from a waiting submarine.

Eight years later, in 1924, when I was junior attending surgeon in the Presbyterian Hospital, Dockrill appeared as one of the orderlies on the surgical ward. When I was given a room where I could work in the hospital laboratory of pathology, Edward heard of it and applied promptly for the post of technician, saying he had worked in the laboratory at Queen Square, London. I took him on. Unfortunately he seemed to have learned little or nothing as a technician in London. But we gave him the glasses and the medical treatments he needed. He gave me a startlingly fierce loyalty as if he were a member of a crew and I the captain, bound on a far journey together.

During the six months that I was away in Madrid, he worked steadily preparing microscopical sections to show me on my return and trying out the Spanish methods for himself with great enthusiasm and some success. He and I always seemed to be in sympathy whenever I found time to be with him. I liked him, and admired his pluck and hoped he would learn to live a happy life with his fellows while we were in New York. But when Cone and I moved to Montreal, we left him behind there. Friction had developed far too often between him and others in the laboratory.

Nevertheless, he followed us without an invitation, and asked to sign on in Montreal. When Cone accepted him he did help with our technical task for a time. He and I worked out a new silver method. He did the work and I made the suggestions of what modifications to try. We succeeded in demonstrating the nerves on the arteries within the brain in areas where they had never been demonstrated before. The nerves and their endings could be seen selectively stained. They were beautiful.

I published the results (*Archives of Neurology and Psychiatry*, 27:30–44, 1932) and stated that "I have now been able to demonstrate nerve fibers on the intra-cerebral blood vessels throughout the central nervous system by means of certain modifications of histological method devised by our technician, E. Dockrill."

But during the first three years in Montreal, Edward became discontented and moody. Finally the time came when Dr. Cone decided to replace him. Dockrill agreed quite readily. In his spare time, he had written a novel and sent it to a publisher. The amazing thing was that, considering his rather brief education, he was able to complete it. The publisher refused the manuscript and returned it to me, saying it was a caricature of me. It was easy to see that I was the villain who had risen to fame on the shoulders of the poor technician. He himself was cast in the role of rebellious hero, like Ernest in Samuel Butler's *Way of All Flesh*. He had often quoted from that book. It was the first book I gave him to read during the lonely life he led in New York.

Dockrill made a real contribution, for a period, to the launching of our neurological project, and I shall never forget his pluck on the day when he and Dr. Cone and I searched for the lost bottles at Rosemount Dump, and the defiant dance he did across the garbage cursing and laughing in triumph when he, first of all, found one of the little bottles.

So Edward Dockrill, the initial member of my crew, returned to England in 1931. Perhaps he was happier there. I hope so. He was keen, tenacious, and as far as I was aware (except for the novel's caricature) always loyal to me. His revolt went beyond our little ship to the inequalities of opportunity in society and its injustices.

The captain of any crew or team has many problems. He must give credit always to whom it is due, and he must give promotion to those who are prepared to serve the common good. But he hopes that those on the team will be loyal to the ideal that he, the leader, has set up, not to the leader himself. So, teamwork and companionship and high morale develop and the figure of the leader fades from view, as it should.

47 (reference from page 265).

    1. "Principles of the Pathology of Neurosurgery," chapter six in *Nelson's Loose Leaf Surgery* (New York: Nelson and Sons, 1927).

    2. "Neuroglia and Microglia," chapter in *Special Cytology,* edited by E. V. Cowdry (New York: Hoeber, 1928).

    3. "Neuroglia and Microglia — the Metallic Methods," a chapter by Penfield and Cone, in McClung's *Handbook of Microscopical Technique* (New York: Hoeber, 1929).

    4. *Cytology and Cellular Pathology of the Nervous System,* 3 vols., edited by W. Penfield (New York: Hoeber, 1932).

48 (reference from page 265). In the early years I had struggled to comprehend the microscopic structure of the brain and to increase knowledge as opportunity presented. I tried to cover the whole field. But in the end I came to a more reasonable attitude, and settled for what I could learn and still move on to other purposes.

My attention was directed at the outset to the microscopic appearance of the cells within the brain, as they appeared on surgical removal or after death — first, when they were normal, and second, when they were reacting to abnormal conditions. I studied them, too, when they were multiplying to form growing tumors. Some of the tumors were benign, some malignant, but all might kill the patient unless he was sent to a neurosurgeon for removal of the growth.

I had studied the cells of the brain, too, when they were forming scars and when blood supply was shut off. I had noted their appearance, especially when patients had become epileptic, hoping for clues to treatment and understanding.

And this was useful knowledge, but I was a surgeon and my interest turned more and more to alterations as I saw them taking place in the nervous system during life. What happened each time a patient had a fit? Were these changes occurring primarily in brain cells or in the blood vessels that nourished them? What about the mechanism that must explain the mysterious action of the brain? This was normal brain action, neurophysiology.

How completely my interest had passed, by 1931, from neuropathology to neurophysiology and epilepsy, was shown when, early in the spring of 1931, the organizers of the First International Neurological Congress (to be held in September at Berne, Switzerland) scheduled me to discuss the pathology of brain tumors, allowing forty minutes for my presentation. I was flattered but neither pleased nor challenged. I had already sent off a paper on gliomas to the *Archives of Neurology and Psychiatry* and another on the classification of brain tumors to the *British Medical Journal*. Neither study had as yet appeared in print. But why do it over again in another form? Writing never came quickly or easily to me.

Perhaps the fact that my sister was dying of her own glioma recurrence made this task the more distasteful. It should have made me the more willing to undertake it. But I had no further clues to follow. I chose instead to prepare a paper on the benign tumors that arise from the meninges covering the brain and the sheaths of the nerves. That was yet to be summarized.

But my heart was not in that either. When I learned that Professor Gustav Roussy had not been placed on the program, I begged the organizers to give half my time to him. I knew Roussy, for he had long been a student of neuroglia and was a sincere enthusiast, although of recent years he was turning to university politics. He was pleased and I was even more pleased. At the close of the congress he sent me a beautiful histological atlas that occupies an honored place on the shelves in our laboratory.

49 (reference from page 266). From the report of the subdepartment of neurosurgery, 1931:

"During the year of 1931, work has continued in the Hospital and in the Laboratory of Neuropathology. Dr. Elvidge was succeeded as resident in neurosurgery by Dr. T. I. Hoen, who comes here from the resident service in neurosurgery at the Peter Bent Brigham Hospital, Boston. [Hoen was neurosurgical resident to Dr. Harvey Cushing in the closing year of Cushing's brilliant career.]

"Dr. Earl Brewer was succeeded as neurosurgical intern by Dr. E. L. Gage, who had finished his work for the degree of Master of Science in the Laboratory of Neuropathology. The subject of Dr. Gage's thesis was "The Effect of Vasomotor Nerve Section on Experimental Epilepsy." Dr. A. R. Elvidge became neurosurgical research fellow in pathology in charge of routine pathology in the laboratory. Dr. J. Chorobski has continued his second year working in the laboratory as Neurosurgical Research Fellow.

"Dr. Maurice Brodie is continuing his studies of the sequelae of encephalography. Dr. I. M. Tarlov is continuing his second year in the laboratory also on a neurosurgical research fellowship. Dr. A.

Torkildsen has given up his resident's service and is continuing with research in the laboratory and on a clinical clerkship in the wards. Dr. G. Stavraky has joined in the neurophysiological research work in the laboratory on a Rockefeller Fellowship. Dr. Joseph Evans has returned to the laboratory after a year of work at the University of Chicago and several months at the University of Minnesota. He will continue his research on epilepsy toward the degree of Doctor of Philosophy.

"The clinical and research work has continued as in former years with the exception that a combined piece of investigation of the intracerebral vascular nerves has been undertaken by Dr. J. Chorobski and Dr. Penfield with Dr. Stanley Cobb and Dr. Jacob Finesinger of Harvard University. Some of this work has been carried out by the same men in Boston.

"Dr. Petersen has continued to work on certain aspects of epilepsy under the Madeleine Ottmann Research Fellowship.

"Under the leadership of Dr. Colin Russel and Dr. F. H. MacKay, clinical neurology at McGill has of recent years reached a high level of excellence. The advent of Dr. Wilder Penfield and Dr. William Cone had filled out the work in this field from the surgical and scientific points of view.

"There has developed since the arrival of Drs. Penfield and Cone a close association with the French-speaking neurologists and for the past three years combined neurological conferences for discussion of mutual problems have been held at regular intervals. In addition to the neurological staffs of the Montreal General and Royal Victoria hospitals these conferences are attended by such outstanding specialists in neurology from the Hôtel-Dieu, Notre-Dame and other hospitals, as Drs. E. Legrand, R. Amyot, A. Barbeau, J. Saucier and, from the city of Quebec, A. Brousseau."

50 (reference from page 272). The great foundation that Alan Gregg served was dedicated to the "well-being of mankind." This really meant the people of all the world. The initial strategy that had been urged upon Mr. Rockefeller Senior by Frederick T. Gates, between 1909 and 1913, was to improve and to stimulate medical education and to help eradicate the endemic plagues of the world.

It is interesting that Gates, although a layman, had read the new textbook of medicine written by Dr. William Osler. Gates realized from that reading that a fresh, critical, scientific approach could now be made in medicine. Gates had remarkable insight and it is clear, in retrospect, that this was, in truth, the time in the history of medicine when the aid given could be most effective.

When Rockefeller agreed to his proposed strategy, the attack was begun with a contribution of unparalleled magnitude, through medicine, to the people of China. With it, the Peking Union Medical College was built and supported in Peking. The great campaign to control the endemic plagues of the world followed, and vast assistance was given to medical education. In the United States, this was carried out by Abraham Flexner, and eventually in the rest of the world by Richard Pearce.

The Peking Union Medical College, which was to house the finest medical library in Asia and which trained a small band of highly expert Chinese physicians, made it possible, in time, for the Mao Tse-tung government to bring health and well-being to that vast nation. The academic excellence of P.U.M.C., as it was called, together with the teaching of medical missionaries, made it possible to establish Western medicine in the university hospitals of an otherwise isolated people, even after 1949 when Mao came to power and communication with the West was cut off for a considerable period. This great Rockefeller project to which, by 1947, forty-five million dollars had been contributed, did achieve its altruistic objective.*

After that, the foundation turned to public health. Under Wycliffe Rose, they made a worldwide attack on the great endemic diseases, including hookworm in the United States and malaria in the tropical countries. At home, American medical education was purged and improved under the leadership of Abraham Flexner. Medical education elsewhere in the world was stimulated selectively by Pearce, seconded by Gregg, during the critical period of social and financial reconstruction that followed the First World War.

From the time of his entrance, as a general educator, into the field, Abraham Flexner did great things for medicine in the United States, beginning with his own investigation and report, and continuing through the vast expenditure of Rockefeller money that he made available from the General Education Board. It was Flexner who introduced "full-time medicine" in the United States. But he became, in time, a difficult autocrat. He tried to force the men he assisted and there was a growing revolt among physicians in the United States at the time of his resignation from the General Education Board in 1928.

The policy of medical aid adopted by Pearce, as director of medical sciences within the Rockefeller Foundation, differed from that of Flexner, who operated under another Rockefeller endowment, the Gen-

* See W. Penfield, "Oriental Renaissance," *Science*, 1941:1158–1161, 1963; and W. Penfield, "China Mission Accomplished," *Canadian Medical Association Journal*, 97:468–470, 1967.

eral Education Board. Pearce picked men who were going in the right direction according to his judgment, and helped them. But he did not force them.

When Alan Gregg took over responsibility for philanthropy in the field of medical science in 1931, he was replacing Pearce and Flexner in a foundation whose orientation had been altered. Frederick Gates was gone, Wycliffe Rose and Richard Pearce were dead. Flexner was out, but not down! (After retirement, Abraham Flexner had written his book, during a year's lectureship in Oxford, on the universities. He had done this with remarkable wit and speed. Following this, with the financial backing of Louis Bamberger and Mrs. Felix Field, brother and sister, Flexner was very busy creating, by himself, a new educational institution, an American version of Oxford's All Souls' College. He named it the Institute for Advanced Study and established it at Princeton.)

Between 1928 and 1931 the foundation changed its structure and its immediate objectives. This was done under the leadership of three men: the chairman of the board, John D. Rockefeller, Jr.; the retiring president, George E. Vincent; and the young friend of John D., Jr., and John D., Sr., Raymond B. Fosdick. Their decision was to turn away from assistance to medicine as the exclusive objective of benefaction.

By 1931 the name of the division of which Gregg was to be director had been changed from Medical Education to Medical Sciences, and there were other directors intent on giving away the foundation's income in other good causes. Thus there was the first division, Public Health, and the second, newly named the Medical Sciences. Added to these, there were the three recently created divisions: Social Sciences, Natural Sciences, and Humanities. Consequently, in 1931, the directors of all five divisions would have to compete for funds before the board of trustees, and it was evident that the days of really large grants in the field of medicine had passed and were not likely to return.

How Gregg and the president of the foundation, Max Mason, felt about the need for financial help in the field of psychiatry may be surmised, however, from the following notes in Gregg's personal journal. On April 9, 1931, he quoted Mason as opening a discussion with a gesture of loyalty to the new orientation of the foundation, using these words: "We ought to stick to the decisions made in 1929 to avoid aid to medical schools as such."

Let me add here parenthetically that Mason himself had watched while his first wife was taken from him by a progressive psychosis that no one could cure. She had been his high-school sweetheart, a lovely, brilliant girl. In addition to this, he had seen her sister succumb to a similar mental illness. It was, perhaps, because of this sad experience that Mason followed the above statement with a question.

He asked Gregg, wistfully, if he thought "there were anything more important than a study of mentality, personality, etc., in a concerted attack."

Gregg replied: "The only policy that, in my mind, competes closely with that would be picking off the best men and aiding them in whatever field, if they were getting good results."

51 (reference from page 272). I had written a paper by request on the scope of neurology. It had been contributed to a general symposium on medical education and published with other contributions in the *Archives of Surgery* (18:1335–1338, 1929).

It was not a brilliant piece of writing, but it summarized my conviction that, ideally, all the various approaches to knowledge and treatment, in the field of neurology, should be carried out by members of a coordinated team, who should also retain close relationships with the other disciplines of general medicine. In the course of the discussion I had added: "The outstanding neurosurgeons have come to have interests and insights in common with neurologists. In fact they have become neurologists if they were not at the start. . . ."

F.M.R. Walshe was a neurologist whom I had known in London (1920–1921). After I sent this reprint to him he wrote in reply, making an eloquent and slightly vitriolic protest, and urging that neurosurgeons should have a training beyond that available in a neurosurgical clinic.

Fundamentally, Walshe and I were in agreement, although the difference in our points of view made this amusing argument possible. He was a loyal friend and a follower of London's teacher of neurology, Gordon Holmes. I was the same. And, to the extent that I could be called a neurologist at all, I was a pupil of Gordon Holmes. The letters do throw light on the state of neurology at that time, although each of us may have overstated his case as one is apt to do while making a point in an argument. The truth, as Walshe observed, was somewhere in between. He had had some experience in the United States, a few years before these letters were written, when he spent an academic term at Johns Hopkins as visiting lecturer in neurology.

Here are a few excerpts from the letters, which were sent to Alan Gregg complete, beginning with the first letter from Walshe:

56 Portland Place
London
Jan. 6th 1931

Dear Penfield:

Very many thanks for your letter and reprints, which I am always delighted to have. . . .

Would you think it impertinent of me to break a lance with you over the views on the neurosurgeon expressed in your paper 'The Scope of Neurology.' Of course, I do not raise the question as a personal one, but as a matter of general interest and principle.

No reasonable man will dispute that it is a counsel of perfection that the neurologist might profitably be his own surgeon, but this proposition carries with it the proviso that the man who attempts to do this must be both a trained neurologist and a trained surgeon. Yet whatever you may say in public about it, can you honestly tell me that any but the exceptional neurosurgeon in America has had a genuine neurological training?

It seems to me that neurosurgeons in America evolve along either of two lines: either they abandon the attempt to learn and use clinical observation and then announce that by ventriculography alone can a localizing diagnosis be made (cf. Dandy in 'The Intracranial Pressure in Health and Disease,' p. 385) or, in due course they announce that they are neurologists who chance to have the advantage of being able to carry out surgical treatment. This is the popular method. . . .

In fact, their equipment for general neurological practice is little more than a superiority complex, a surgical technique, some knowledge of one corner of neurology and a whole heap of ignorance.

I had an opportunity of seeing a few years ago in America (not in Boston, let it be said) the way this admirable notion of the surgeon-neurologist actually works out. . . . If the unhappy patient happened to have paralysis agitans or epilepsy, that was his misfortune. If he had a vast glioma filling one hemisphere, then the hemisphere came out. I must admit that it was so skillfully removed that the wretched victim of this surgical ecstasy survived — a bedridden, demented hemiplegic with a head like three-quarters of a water-melon, draped with a sagging scalp. Nevertheless, he continued to breathe, eat, make noises, and wet his bed for many months longer than life would have been possible had he not been mutilated, and he was therefore a neurological success. . . .

Let it be said that some useful lives were saved, but many were needlessly sacrificed or made intolerable. It is my belief that a sound preliminary training in clinical neurology — organic and psychological — would eliminate all this. . . .

In the circumstances, I feel that the young neurosurgeon is trying to 'get in on the top floor,' or to mix my metaphors, he expects with no preliminary training to spring Minerva-like from the head of Cushing, full-armed and with nothing to learn, after a single year's gestation.

If you want us to take the surgeon-neurologist seriously — as anything better than an impostor — you must do something better than this. The time and pains you yourself have taken to acquire a most comprehensive experience in clinical and laboratory neurology shows that this is what you yourself really think, but it is not what you say in your paper.

I hope that you will not take umbrage at this violent attack on your views, but I feel so strongly that 'diagnosis by operation' is the only goal that you will arrive at in America if you train neurosurgeons to think that they can dispense with clinical experience over the whole field of neurology.

So you must excuse the garrulity of an Irishman (though Heaven knows, this can be trying enough!) who states his case rather more strongly than he really holds it. I shall not mind if you reply that I am a fox without a tail, or a reactionary dotard.

With best wishes for the New Year — and when you chance to meet him, the same to McNally [Dr. William McNally, distinguished otolaryngologist of Montreal].

Yours sincerely,
F. M. Walshe

Department of Neurosurgery *
Royal Victoria Hospital
Montreal
January 20, 1931

Dear Walshe,

I shall have to admit that your 'lance' has gone through a weak link in the neurosurgical coat of mail; but the blood that it spills is not all mine. You are quite right that the greatest weakness of most American neurosurgeons is deficient knowledge of neurology. Unfortunately that includes me as well. But you make the mistake that in my little paper I am defending the American neurosurgeon and holding him up as the model combination of neurology and neurosurgery.

On the contrary, I intended that my thesis should be interpreted as an attack upon the tendency in the United States for neurosurgeons to ignore neurology and the tendency elsewhere to *reverse the process*. I intended to point out that the neurosurgeon should no longer spring from the ranks of simple surgeons, but I was entirely incapable of that lovely phrase, 'he expects with no preliminary training to spring Minerva-like from the head of Cushing.'

You are a good deal like the novelist Sinclair Lewis, who makes Americans seem a little more unlovely than they are, by overdrawing certain ugly truths and ignoring certain other flattering characteristics with which we like to feel ourselves endowed. Most of us consider the

---

* Shortly to be changed to Neurology and Neurosurgery.

whole man and shudder at hemispherectomy as a treatment for brain tumor.*

The second generation neurosurgeons here are taking neurology and pathology as the essential part of their training. I refer to Bailey, Cone, Davis *et al.* In the third generation, there are six young men working in our clinic here now. They will spend years in pathology and neurology before taking on the protective armor of neurosurgery. They may come to you for some of their training. But in fairness to Dandy the larger part of his work results in benefit to his patients however heretical his approach to neurological problems may seem. . . .

Now let me have a go with my lance. Last week I was talking with a distinguished English pathologist. I shall not tell you from what large city in England he came; it was not from London. He made the following naïve observation. He said: 'Brain surgery always seems to me so very difficult. One can never tell what is wrong inside the head until he has a look and then the operation is always followed by a rather awkward fungation!' . . . †

The farther neurology divorces itself from therapy, the more certain will be the disappearance of this specialty. Neither the philosophy of Hughlings Jackson nor the outmoded methods of Horsley are sufficient to meet the situation today.

The time has come to give Dandy's ventriculography and encephalography a proper place in a neurological clinic without prejudice against it. . . .

It is absolutely necessary for me to cooperate with neurologists who do not have to stand long hours on their feet in the operating room. If nine-tenths of neurology is nonsurgical as you state, then there must be in a neurological clinic more neurologists than neurosurgeons. Your complaint and mine are almost identical but you direct your attack against neurosurgery, while I feel that the key to the situation is for neurologists to change their attitude as well.

But while I am at it, I should like to criticize neurosurgery as practiced in Boston, Baltimore, and at Queen Square. I refer to the attitude that neurosurgery means tumor-surgery. Brain tumor-surgery is hardly half of what neurosurgery should cover and it is the least encouraging and least stimulating half.

But I must stop. This letter is already out of hand and I have not

---

* Hemispherectomy is the term used here to describe the surgical removal of a whole hemisphere producing complete paralysis of one arm and leg in the hope of removing a malignant tumor completely. Only a few such operations were carried out.

† As used here, the word "fungation" means a bulging of brain outward through an opening in the skull, due to an unsuccessful attempt to remove an expanding tumor. This was a complication that most operators in the modern school of American neurosurgery had learned to avoid.

the excuse of speaking editorially as you have — at least not anymore. I was an editor of the *Archives of Neurology and Psychiatry* for one week! At the end of that time the authorities of the American Medical Association discovered that I was a resident of Canada and therefore cast me overboard. You may consider this then the voice of one crying in the wilderness. It would be more appropriate to call it the defensive honking of a Canada goose.

Yours very sincerely,
W. G. Penfield

56 Portland Place
February 3rd 1931

Dear Penfield,

You have taken my lamentations very kindly, and your letter so wholly expresses my own views that it is not hard for me to agree with you. Possibly you are rather severe in referring to Horsley's work. At his best he was wonderful, and although his worst was dreadful, I still feel that on one of his good days he could do as well as any modern neurosurgeon. . . .

It is true that some unfair things are said at Queen Square about American neurosurgery. I don't defend them, nor can I deny that our resources in this country are wretched and that many suffer and die unnecessarily from lack of surgeons competent to deal with them.

It would be equally silly to pretend that all is well with clinical neurology here. . . . We are none of us doing what we should. As you say, a pious lip-worship of Hughlings Jackson will take us nowhere.

The French have been following Charcot's hearse so long that they have forgotten to have a new idea since he died. We are not quite so bad as they are, but the tendency is there. . . . Bad initial training and sloppy habits of thought are at the bottom of most of our faults, though it is always too late, alas! when we realize this ourselves. You have had far more than this, and I should be the last to throw my lance at you when I am far worse armed myself.

The war took four years out of my novitiate, and I have had to scratch hard for a living ever since — at least this is the unction I lay to my soul in explanation of my barrenness —, but what opportunities the young American generation has, if it will only consent to be disciplined and trained.

Lord! how I run on.

Yours sincerely,
F.M.R. Walshe

52 (reference from page 276). To Dean Martin, concerning research in the Department of Neurology and Neurosurgery, February 1931:

"In answer to your letter of January 30 regarding the research that has been carried on in our department, I can point out that there have been several different types of work going on. Dr. Colin

Russel has been doing some interesting work upon the relationship of congenital defects, in the blood vessels of the brain, to subarachnoid hemorrhage. He has also been making moving-picture studies of clinical cases, which were utilized in a presentation of a case at the American Neurological Association meeting in Atlantic City in May 1930.

"Dr. William Cone presented a study of the relationship of aseptic embolism to histological changes in the brain and the cellular changes in the spinal fluid. This piece of work is at present being published.

"Work has been continued upon the classification of cerebral tumors and a paper was read by me at the meeting of the British Medical Association at Winnipeg in the summer of 1930 on the classification of brain tumors and its practical applications.

"The major portion of the work that has been going on in the laboratory has had to do with various aspects of the problem of epilepsy and its relationship to the cerebrospinal blood vessels. Dr. Joseph P. Evans has completed a study upon the effects of different types of wounds upon the susceptibility of animals to experimental epilepsy. Dr. E. L. Gage is at present studying the effects upon experimental epilepsy in animals of the removal of various portions of the sympathetic nervous system. Dr. Jerzy Chorobski is at present studying the origin of the perivascular nerves of the brain. I have myself been chiefly interested in the pathology of traumatic epilepsy and have published several papers upon that subject.

"Most important perhaps is the fact that we have demonstrated that the blood vessels within the substance of the brain are equipped with perivascular nerve fibers like the blood vessels elsewhere in the body, a fact that up to the present has been denied.

"We have also found incontrovertible evidence that, at least in the case of epileptic patients, vascular spasms of the arteries on the surface of the brain are associated with epileptic seizures induced at the operating table. This opens up the possibility of obtaining further knowledge of the nature of epilepsy by a more careful study of the vascular mechanism of the brain.

"Dr. Cone and I have been working upon the method of treatment for spina bifida and the new treatment has met with gratifying results.

"The other things that are going on in the laboratory are of a miscellaneous nature. Dr. I. M. Tarlov is studying the finer structure of the cranial nerves. Dr. A. R. Elvidge is making a pathological study of a large collection of cases of hydrocephalus. Dr. M. Brodie is continuing his studies of the sequelae of encephalography. Dr.

J. N. Petersen is studying the vasomotor system of epileptics by special methods."

53 (reference from page 277). After the death of the principal founder of the New York Neurological Institute, Dr. Fred Tilney, Putnam became professor of neurology and neurosurgery there (1939). Following him, Merritt took over the leadership in the New York Neurological Institute and at the Presbyterian Hospital. Lennox became a leader in the study and treatment of epilepsy in Boston and Gibbs had a somewhat similar career in Chicago.

54 (reference from page 279). In the end, the Boston-Montreal collaboration did throw some light on the control of intracerebral arteries by branches from intracranial nerves that join these arteries within the skull. Two publications resulted: (1) "Vagal Pathway of the Vasodilator Impulses." Stanley Cobb and Jacob Finesinger, *Archives of Neurology and Psychiatry,* 28:1243–1256, 1932; (2) "Cerebral Vasodilator Nerves and Their Pathway from the Medulla Oblongata," Jerzy Chorobski and Wilder Penfield, in the same *Journal,* pp. 1257–1289, 1932.

55 (reference from page 286). Norman Bethune had come to Montreal as a graduate student to specialize in thoracic surgery with Archibald about the time that we arrived there. He was to come to fame in China when he organized a mobile surgical unit for the armies of Mao Tse-tung and eighteen months later died, a Communist martyr and hero.

Professor and Mrs. Archibald entertained us at luncheon with characteristic charm in their home on Westmount Boulevard. Among the members of this society who had become my good friends during the eight years since we had founded the club was Francis Grant.

56 (reference from page 286). "Chubby" Grant was a delightful companion. He had been distinguished, when an undergraduate at Harvard, as a boxer, and he was still an excellent sailor and outdoorsman. He had been born, by his own admission, with a silver spoon in his mouth in one of Philadelphia's highly respectable homes on the Main Line outside the city. But he was a unique character. We sat, of an evening, in a corner of the ship's lounge talking and laughing on into the night. That is my time for smoking a pipe. Grant smoked also, a country-style corncob pipe, the stem of which he had gradually chewed off until the bowl approached his prominent chin and nose in a way that caused other passengers to stop and stare and sometimes laugh. It was all the same to him.

Since he was a neurosurgeon, well trained by Frazier in Philadelphia and by Cushing in Boston, and since, like most neurosurgeons of the day, he had little experience in the basic sciences or neurology, we talked about his world of neurosurgery. Beyond that, he drew a vivid picture of the formidable social background into which my wife and I would have to introduce our family while I was busy living up, as well as I could, to the high tradition of Pennsylvania's academic past.

Here on the high seas, I saw many things with a greater clarity, including myself. I, who thought himself the neurosurgical pupil of no one in particular, was, in reality, the pupil of everyone. I was a jack-of-all-trades and I had plans that would make me a jack-of-further-skills that I would need in the years ahead.

57 (reference from page 288). In John Fulton's excellent *Harvey Cushing — A Biography* (Springfield, Ill.: Thomas, 1946) an actual diagram of the seating arrangement of this memorable dinner is shown, page 608. Cushing himself is flanked by Thierry de Martel of Paris on one side with Paul Martin of Brussels, and Dimitri Bagdazar of Bucharest with Percival Bailey on the other. William Welch was in the middle of the long table with John Fulton. Welch, who was at that time eighty-one years of age, had been professor of pathology in the Johns Hopkins Medical School and was recognized as the dominant force and the organizer of that school in its early days.

When Dr. Cushing said I was his senior pupil at the meeting in Berne, I looked at him in astonishment. He probably said this only because it suited his immediate plan for seating his guests. But in a way, what he said was true. I was his pupil in neurosurgery, and I did antedate Percival Bailey by a few months. In a certain sense, it might have been said that all young neurosurgeons my age were his pupils. But I had been an intern at the Peter Bent Brigham Hospital when Cushing returned from war service to become the hospital's chief surgeon again. I did make notes and drawings of every instrument and every maneuver in his surgical routines. I have them still.

But I did not step up from intern to be his resident and first assistant. I had no personal relationship with him such as that which bound me to Gordon Holmes a few years later.

Percival Bailey arrived at the Brigham Hospital in Boston a few months after me, a better man than I in many ways. He was invited by Cushing to become the resident, not I. It had not occurred to me that I might have been considered a candidate. My ambition had turned to Sherrington and to physiology, even from early student days onward. So Helen and I had sailed away happily for England, and I grew to be a neurosurgeon, without ever having known the tedious repetitions of most surgical residencies. But yes, I was one of Cushing's neurosurgical pupils.

When Harvey Cushing was a young man, he went abroad for his own graduate study. He spent a few weeks first as an observer in Sherrington's laboratory. He never worked under him. He also passed Sir Victor Horsley by, and moved on to Berne, where he worked with Theodor Kocher, the great Swiss surgeon, and with Hugo Kronecker on the physiology and pathology of intracranial pressure.

Thierry de Martel was, at the time of this dinner, the leading neurosurgeon of France. He had not been given academic standing at the Sorbonne, but he and his neurological associate, Clovis Vincent, had worked together in Paris and had spent some months together observing the work of Cushing in Boston. When the Germans entered Paris during the Second World War, Martel took his own life for fear he would have to serve them. Subsequently, Vincent, like Foerster in the First World War, being a neurologist and having assisted Martel, took up neurosurgery. He was appointed then to fill the first academic chair of neurosurgery in France after the war. Nonetheless, Martel had for a long time been first among the excellent technicians in the French school of neurosurgery.

John Fulton, although professionally a physiologist, was also in a real sense a pupil of Cushing. He went to Oxford as a Rhodes scholar and was trained in physiology by Sherrington. In 1931, at the time of this international congress, he had just been appointed to Yale's chair of physiology (at the age of thirty-one). Just before going to New Haven, he had done research with Cushing, to whom he was devoted. They shared a passion for medical literature and book collecting that had been handed down to both of them from William Osler. Cushing retired to Yale and died there in 1939. Fulton promptly wrote Cushing's biography, which closed with this apt description of Harvey Cushing: "Scientist, pathfinder, artist, writer and bibliophile — yes, but above all 'a good doctor.' "

58 (reference from page 289). As a young man in Saint Petersburg, now Leningrad, Ivan Pavlov had concerned himself first with the mechanism of digestion, and was recognized for the work by the award of a Nobel Prize. Later, when he turned to the brain, he had shown that, in dogs, the recognition of food or recognition of the kindly giver-of-food produced an outpouring of saliva in the mouth of the dog. This outpouring, he proved, depended upon a "conditioned reflex." The mechanism of the reflex was found to be located in nerve circuits within the dog's cerebral cortex and adjacent

brain. His evidence had been accepted, with acclaim, throughout the world as the physiological basis of all learning. Man, too, it was argued, must learn by newly acquired conditioned reflexes within the cerebral cortex.

Along with everyone else who could gain entrance to the crowded hall, I went to hear the great Pavlov, and discovered an alert, wiry old man, with fiercely bristling mustache and beard. He told us the following story with delightful enthusiasm.

In a sudden Leningrad flood, water entered the animal quarters during the night. The dogs had been forced to swim and cling to the upper parts of their cages as the water rose. When the plight of the poor beasts was discovered and they were rescued, it was soon realized that the harrowing experience had changed them. They had actually forgotten much of what Pavlov had taught them, no longer recognizing the signs of approaching food. The conditioned reflexes were gone. They behaved as men and women do sometimes when they have been subjected to conditions that are too difficult and too prolonged for them to tolerate. There was improvement when bromides were administered, as in the case of neurotic patients.

So Pavlov closed his lecture by talking about the physical basis of neuroses and of functional disturbances of the mind. At least I think so. Suddenly I could no longer understand anything. He had lapsed, without warning, from halting German into the speedy use of his native Russian tongue.

59 (reference from page 293). Mother had begun this story of the lives of Sarai and Abram in 1920, when she returned home from the year she spent with Helen and me in Oxford.

60 (reference from page 312). The editorial of April 21, 1932, in the *New York Times,* continued as follows:

"Three factors united to recommend a choice that ignored the latitude and longitude of the giver. The first was the man whose work in brain surgery attracted the special attention of those making search for the best place. Dr. Wilder G. Penfield, the head of the institute, was born in the State of Washington and had his education and special training largely in the United States, but he has been for several years at McGill University. Its reputation and administrative efficiency were also an element in the decision. Besides, the people of the province of Quebec and especially the citizens of Montreal showed interest and enterprise in welcoming such a foundation."

Then this editor concluded hopefully:

"Though this institute for research, clinical treatment and teaching in neurology, neuro-surgery and the whole realm of the nervous system stands on the further side of the St. Lawrence, its benefits will have no geographical boundaries. The world will find its way to the laboratories and clinics and lecture rooms of McGill, if the best that anywhere comes to be in this field of science is offered there. Fortunately for Canada, there was no tariff against such talents as Dr. Penfield carried over the border, and fortunately no duties can be laid against the results of the researches of the institute. They will become illocal under a law which happily prevails in the higher ranges of man's relationships."

61 (reference from page 313). R. H. MacDonald of the architectural firm of Ross and MacDonald was a creative genius. Without his help, construction could never have been finished without increased cost and with such grace and dignity as it was possible to add in the main building and in the bridge, attached as they were to the somewhat gloomy Scottish baronial towers of the Royal Victoria.

62 (reference from page 322). The letter had been preserved by Mr. Chenoweth and was discovered while Dr. Sclater Lewis was writing the history of the hospital, *The Royal Victoria Hospital, 1887–1947* (Montreal: McGill University Press, 1969):

"Your generous aid and the cooperation of so many of the hospital and clinical staff has meant more to Mrs. Penfield and to me than I can tell you. The equipment we have out here in the wilderness is quite complete. It has been 'touch-and-go' with her and, if she comes through all right as it looks probable now, we will have you to thank for helping to turn the tide. Dr. Cone has told me that he was overwhelmed with offers of assistance and evidently you considered putting skis on the ambulance!

"Mrs. Penfield is holding her own although there seems to be widespread involvement of both lungs. The oxygen is helping a good deal and the whole house is converted into a hospital with a full staff of nurses and doctors.

"Many, many thanks in which Mrs. Penfield will soon be able to join me, I hope."

63 (reference from page 334). "It was with great trepidation that I began my duties at the 'Neuro' [the institute was also given the nickname "M.N.I."] as I had had very little experience in that field of nursing. However, when Helen Eberle (later Mrs. Philip Cranstone), who had been working with the neurosurgical patients in the R.V.H., was appointed as my assistant, and Bertha Cameron as night supervisor, I was greatly relieved. They were both highly

competent, and they set the pattern for the nursing service on the
wards.

"The staff then consisted of Kathleen Zwicker (Mrs. D. Grier) in
the operating room along with Cora McLeod (Mrs. A. W. Gray)
and Eileen Kelly. Margaret Goldie (Mrs. Herbert Jasper), Lorraine
MacNichol (Mrs. E. Kemble) and Marian Currie were the head
nurses, and Margaret Casselman, Constance Lambertus, Evelyn
Scott (Mrs. J. Lorimer) and Kathleen Kidd were the staff nurses.

"This was the nucleus of what became a dedicated, expert and
harmonious group of nurses who contributed greatly to the reputation of the M.N.I."*

Miss Flanagan might have been justified had she listed Dr. Cone
here in the Department of Nursing, for he had begun to teach
nurses, learn from them, and devise new nursing maneuvers at all
hours of day and night. She might have added, too, that Miss
Zwicker, most expert of operating room nurses, helped me from
the very beginning; and Miss Mary Roach became our very skilled
anesthetist.

64 (reference from page 336). Archibald, and his friends within and
without the Royal Victoria Hospital, had set our stage for the
building of the Montreal Neurological Institute. It was fitting that
he should pronounce the Foreword then, and it is fitting that I pay
tribute to him now. I wish that my readers could see the man as I
do in my mind's eye, standing before us in that September gathering
— handsome, courtly, the product of classical schooling in English and in French and equally eloquent in both languages. Archibald was the English version of a Montreal Canadian endowed
with the grace and the strength of both cultures.

Dr. Archibald had his own occasions and his own ambitions to
consider. But his smile and his thought, that day, were for us whose
good fortune it was to work in Canada's newly built Institute of
Neurology. He spoke to us from the viewpoint of science and of
humanity. He spoke to our future, unmindful of his own. Here is
Edward Archibald's Foreword:

"Dr. Martin, Ladies and Gentlemen:

"We are met here today to open, with that observance of ceremony
and with that dignity which are proper to such a great enterprise,
the Montreal Neurological Institute.

"What does this building essentially signify? Surely it signifies a
lofty conception and a generous purpose. It is the outward and

---

* Quoted from Eileen Flanagan, *Memorabilia: The Montreal Neurological
Institute, 1934–1974* (unpublished).

visible sign of an inward and, in a pragmatic sense, a spiritual grace — grace of the givers, grace of the advisers and, not least, grace of those who have been chosen to work in it. Others will tell you of the givers. Let me speak for a moment of the workers and of their work.

"The nervous system is one of the most difficult parts of man's frame to understand. Few subjects in medicine have demanded of investigators as great an intellectual capacity or as arduous a labor. And in that very fact lies the reason and the justification for neurological specialism. The earnest man *knows* that neurology demands his whole life. But his guerdon is great. In no field of labor, perhaps, have intellect and hard work achieved a greater or happier reward, whether in the advancement of medical science or in the relief of physical pain and mental distress.

"To gather knowledge, and to find out new knowledge, is the noblest occupation of the physician. To apply that knowledge with understanding, and with sympathy born of understanding, to the relief of human suffering is his loveliest occupation; and to do both with an unassuming faithfulness sets the seal on the whole. This is the part of those who will work here.

"Progress nowadays is dependent not alone upon intellectual ability, but also upon excellence of tools; and this institute, with its equipment and its staff, represents those tools. Great discoveries, it is true, have been made in the past with simple or rudimentary appliances. But are we to ask Scott to discover the Pole in the barque of Christopher Columbus? Must we explore the Heavens still with Galileo's telescope? Shall we hope to find the cause of cancer with the help of a magnifying glass? No, ladies and gentlemen, we need perfection of tools, if we are to wrest from Nature her more hidden secrets. Therefore we rejoice to see here today this spacious and well-equipped building. It will, I am confident, be a center, not merely local or provincial, but international, to which will come students from many lands seeking a deeper knowledge of neurology.

"As the old Latin tag has it, the end crowns the work. But *finis* is not written here. It marks truly the end of one stage, but it marks also the beginning of another, a new stage, one full of promise and hope. Now will those whose joy it will be to work here step forth happily, with quickened pace, upon a new high road! And we, going upon our own occasions, wish them God speed."

65 (reference from page 337). Robert Oppenheimer was director of the Institute for Advanced Study in Princeton when Helen and I

spent the spring terms of 1958 and 1959 there. On each occasion, I became for the moment a member of the faculty of the Department of History of that institute by virtue of the fact that I was writing a historical novel concerned with Hippocrates — *The Torch* (1960). Thus my association was with Oppenheimer the scholar, rather than the atomic physicist.

66 (reference from page 339). There was no particular problem in regard to the support of the Neurological Institute until after the Second World War (1939–1945). During the conflict, the federal government built for us a Military Annex. This allowed us to care for Canadians returning from military service overseas with injuries of the nervous system. The neurosurgeon Kenneth McKenzie, trained by Cushing, was doing something similar in the center he had helped to build in Toronto.* By then, neurosurgeons were just beginning to appear in the large hospitals of other cities in Canada.

After the war, civilians came crowding into our temporary Military Annex and, because of this demand, it was impossible to close it, and tear it down, until a permanent wing had been added to the institute. The need for our expanding research, which had been interrupted by practical military projects of investigation, was equally great. And further, we found that after the war, the rapidly changing economy in Canada soon brought us to a financial impasse. In desperation, we even warned our well-wishers in Montreal that the institute would be closed unless local help came, and quickly. "This institute," we said, repeating what we had said at the start, "must always continue to pay its way with funds that were meant for it." Thus we shall never call upon the general funds of the university.

Our appeal for public assistance was made for hospital and research institute as a unit because the institute had achieved international fame in science circles during the war. But we always kept clinical costs separate from academic and research costs. It was the clinical costs that soared and threatened to close the doors of the whole institution. Thus the much enlarged support of public beds by the Province of Quebec under Mr. Maurice Duplessis made possible our reestablishment. Mr. J. W. McConnell then built the wing largely, and at the same time, doubled our scientific endowment.

And so, in 1953, we rejoiced at the coming of a second foundation. These were its objectives: greater scientific support, the opening of the J. W. McConnell Wing with more beds, and opportunity for renewed planning of research that was oriented again to the problems

* See E. H. Botterell, "Kenneth George McKenzie," *Canadian Medical Association Journal*, 91:880, 1964.

of the brain and the mind of man and to the purposes of human compassion.

Like the opening in 1934, which was described by the staff of the institute in a special volume (*Neurological Biographies and Addresses,* Oxford University Press, 1936) the second foundation was described (*Prospect and Retrospect,* Little, Brown, 1955).

When Alan Gregg arrived in Montreal in 1953 to take part in the second foundation, he had just been advanced to the post of vice-president in the Rockefeller Foundation. He was thus being given the opportunity to write out his personal conclusions. But ill health was about to take away from him the ability that was his, in younger years, to carry out creative work. He would shortly retire to live out an all-too-brief lease of life with his wife Eleanor in California. Thus the address that he made in Montreal came near the end of his active career, and was perhaps his clearest statement of the "art of creative giving."

67 (reference from page 340). Cushing wrote to Gregg unexpectedly during the summer holiday before the opening ceremonies of the M.N.I. when he, Cushing, may well have been considering the preparation of his own address on that occasion. It is recorded in *Harvey Cushing: A Biography* by John Fulton (Springfield, Ill.: Thomas, 1946), page 443. Gregg's reply follows.

"Your letter of August 2 came last night. Your account of the project to start a National Institute of Neurology was new to me, and so far as I know, did not have a traceable connection with the development at Montreal. . . . Perhaps you'll let me add a bit to this answer to your question? The more I see of men and things, the more I think causes are but rarely single and simple. Thus it was not merely a request from Penfield and Martin coinciding with a special desire on our part to help neurology which decided the matter; there was a conviction that it is *men* that matter, especially in a new undertaking. . . ."

68 (reference from page 342). Rasmussen, who had been trained for neuropathology and neurosurgery in the early years by Cone and me, left Montreal to become professor of neurosurgery at Chicago University. Thus he returned in 1954 very well qualified for new leadership.

Cone was only six years my junior. He had stood at my shoulder whenever I needed him for twenty-five years. He had his own outstanding career as a brilliant neurosurgeon. But he looked after me as if he were the senior partner in a delightful friendship.

I must confess that whatever I may have contributed to neurosurgery or to research, I have Cone to thank for making it possible to concentrate on the problem. He helped me with my patients as if he were my consultant and houseman. He and Rasmussen even made it possible for me to be absent from Montreal, when I was making my own approach to authorship, for months at a time.

Because of the help I had from him and indeed from all the others on the staff, especially the research fellows and the secretaries — Hope Lewis and her successor, Anne Dawson — the directorship at the M.N.I. never did weigh very heavily on my shoulders.

69 (reference from page 342). I have watched the process of inevitable loss by death and retirement. Colin Russel, admirable leader of Montreal neurology, was first to go. He retired in 1946 (died 1956), and was succeeded by a neurological scientist of great promise, Donald McEachern, who, alas, did not wait to retire but died in 1951. His regime was followed by the wise and effective neurological leadership of Francis McNaughton until his retirement as neurologist in chief in 1968.

There were a few who came and built constructively and moved along — Arthur Childe was our first specializing radiologist. He was followed by Donald McRae, as pupil follows master and goes beyond; George Olzewski, a brilliant Polish neuroanatomist trained by Oskar Vogt in Germany; André Pasquet in neuroanesthesia, followed by Richard Gilbert . . . but I must stop.

Index

Abbott, Douglas, 324, 324n
Aberdeen, Earl of, 138
Adler, Alfred, 43
Adrian, Edgar, 324
Alfonso XIII, 101
Alice (maid), 78–79, 109, 113
Allan, Andrew, 355 n. 21
Allan, Isabel Brenda. *See* Meredith, Isabel
Allen O. Whipple Surgical Society, 58
American Neurological Association, 121
American Practice of Surgery (Bryant and Buck), 353 n. 21
Amyot, Roma, 197–198, 368 n. 49
Anabasis (Xenophon), 30–31, 345–346 n. 2
Angus, R. B., 138, 144
Archibald, Agnes Barron, 201 354 n. 21, 377 n. 55
Archibald, Edward, 141, 156, 160, 176, 187, 191n, 192, 285, 305–306; observes WP operate, 122–123; invites WP to Montreal, 123–124, 133; WP visits at R.V.H., 125, 141, 143, 145–150; Meredith opposes, 135, 137, 151, 352 n. 19; career of, 140, 201, 351 n. 19, 352–355 n. 21; not able to raise money for WP's research, 193, 252; and French com-

munity in Montreal, 196; consults on case of Ruth Inglis, 209, 210–212; and first plan for M.N.I., 221, 223–225; work with Bethune, 286, 377 n. 55; gives address at M.N.I. opening ceremonies, 334, 336, 382–383 n. 64
Archibald, John, 352 n. 21
Archibald, John Spratt, 352 n. 21
Archibald, Sam, 352 n. 21
Archives of Neurology and Psychiatry, 279, 289, 367 n. 48, 375 n. 51
Archives of Surgery, 371 n. 51
Ariens Kappers, C. U., 174
Armour, John, 354 n. 21
Armstrong, George E., 135, 136, 355 n. 21
Asua, J. Jimenez, 98, 101–102, 110
Atchley, D. W., 114
Auchincloss, Hugh, 62, 72, 114, 223; treats Mrs. Ottmann, 233, 234

Bagdazar, Dimitri, 378 n. 57
Bailey, Percival, 108, 120, 161, 336, 350 n. 15, 378 n. 57; his work with brain tumors, 84, 94, 219, 265, 349 n. 10
Bamberger, Louis, 370 n. 50
Barbeau, Antonio, 361 n. 38, 368 n. 49
Barker, Lewellys, 27